名师名校名校长

凝聚名师共识
团结名师关怀
打造名师品牌
培育名师群体

顾明远题

沉浸酿郁 含英咀华

奉婷名师工作室悦读叙事撷英

奉 婷 / 著

图书在版编目（CIP）数据

沉浸酞郁　含英咀华：奉婷名师工作室悦读叙事撷英/奉婷著. —沈阳：辽宁大学出版社，2022.11
（名师名校名校长书系）
ISBN 978-7-5698-0891-9

Ⅰ.①沉…　Ⅱ.①奉…　Ⅲ.①英语文学—文学欣赏—师资培养—研究②英语—阅读教学—教学研究—中小学
Ⅳ.①I106②G633.412

中国版本图书馆 CIP 数据核字（2022）第 147341 号

沉浸酞郁　含英咀华：奉婷名师工作室悦读叙事撷英
CHENJIN NONGYU　HANYING JUHUA：FENGTING MINGSHI GONGZUOSHI YUEDU XUSHI XIEYING

出 版 者：辽宁大学出版社有限责任公司
（地址：沈阳市皇姑区崇山中路 66 号　　邮政编码：110036）
印 刷 者：沈阳海世达印务有限公司
发 行 者：辽宁大学出版社有限责任公司
幅面尺寸：170mm×240mm
印　　张：18.25
字　　数：390 千字
出版时间：2022 年 11 月第 1 版
印刷时间：2022 年 11 月第 1 次印刷
责任编辑：李珊珊
封面设计：高梦琦
责任校对：李天泽

书　　号：ISBN 978-7-5698-0891-9
定　　价：58.00 元

联系电话：024-86864613
邮购热线：024-86830665
网　　址：http://press.lnu.edu.cn
电子邮件：lnupress@vip.163.com

序言

PREFACE

“腹有诗书气自华”，是中国人公认很有道理的一句话。要在中国做一名有“华气”的英语教师，除了须在中华优秀传统文化中浸润熏陶，还须具备一定的英语文学素养，因为文学作品是体现语言艺术的重要形式。腹中的诗书，首先是读进去的。英语教师是双语教育工作者，须比别人读更多的书、看更多的文学作品。

然而，对今天的中小学英语教师来说，阅读英语文学作品，却并不容易做到。第一个障碍自然是时间：中小学教师的工作，是行外人士想象不到的繁重和繁忙。第二个障碍是功利的考量：在这个快速发展的时代，人们很难看到“腹有诗书”与自己事业发展的直接关联，因为文学作品对人的滋养，是一个“润物细无声”的渐进过程。由此产生了第三个障碍：评价体制的制约。今天对教师的评价，除了师德师风，注重的是教师对学科教学知识的掌握与运用，还有教师的教学实绩。对于英语教师，在学科知识的要求上，也鲜有提及英语文学素养的。那么，为什么还要读英语文学作品呢？于是，不知不觉中，英语经典阅读与英语教师、英语教学，渐行渐远了。而因与经典疏离，不免造成某些特质的欠缺；因某些特质的欠缺带来的一些问题，总会时隐时现地妨碍着我们幸福地生活和工作。看似无用的文学阅读，其实正是孕育傅雷先生所说的敏感之心灵、热烈之同情、适当之鉴赏能力、相当之社会经验、充分之常识的重要途径。

东莞市奉婷名师工作室，在主持人的引领下，聚集了一批脚踏实地而又追求“无用之用”的初中英语教师。她们在教研和教学上取得优秀成绩的同时，坚持一起阅读英语文学原著。她们同读一本书，并且以一人（轮流）导读、人人发表感想的形式，每周在云端一聚。她们读完了充满童趣的文学经典*The Secret Garden*、《圣诞颂歌》后，再向高难度挑战，开始阅读500多页的当代优秀作品《偷书贼》。只要肯坚持，挑战自然是成功的。意想不到的成果，就是这本《沉浸酡郁　含英咀华：奉婷名师工作室悦读叙事撷英》。

这本书记录了她们品读三本好书的历程，汇集了她们从不同角度对作品的感悟，也体现了她们阅读欣赏能力的逐步提升。她们从评析作品内容、分析人物性格、欣赏语言表达的精妙，到自然而然地进行英汉对比，如由英语的表达联想到汉语的成语；继而把作品与自身的生活经历关联，畅谈人生感悟。她们感受到了拓展文学背景知识的成就感，体验到了从日常琐事中抽身出来，沉浸在文学世界里的美妙。每周一聚的思想碰撞，让她们享受着共同成长的幸福。

这本悦读叙事给我们的显性启示有三个：

第一，名师工作室是构建教师发展共同体的优质载体。一群教师在名师的引领下，有了共同的发展目标，就能激发出自己原来都没有发现的潜能。一个人觉得做不到的事情，在一群人的互相推动下，大家一起做到了，阅读便成为悦读。

第二，时间真的像海绵里的水，是可以挤出来的。一旦一件事情成为你生命状态的一部分，那么，尽管你再忙再累，这件事情都会不可避免地发生，比如阅读，比如欣赏英语文学名著。

第三，优秀文学作品往往是现实生活的艺术化再现，与每个人都会有某种程度的关联，因此每个人都可以成为文学欣赏者，并从欣赏中陶冶自身情感，提升审美情趣，滋养品格与精神。只是很多事情的发生，确实需要一个契机。

至于这样的阅读活动会带来怎样的隐性成果，还需要时间的验证。可以预期的是，文学素养会随着文学阅读的开展而提高。文学素养的提高，将有助于我们更好地洞察、感悟、理解人类的生活本质，有助于我们从现实生活中获取超越功利的审美情感体验，做更幸福的人。教师们文化性知识的增长和拓展，将促进她们灵活延展、有效整合课堂教学内容，在教研上取得新突破。教师们的阅读活动将超越趣味性和工具性，在与文学作品的深层对话中发展自身的逻辑思维和批判思维能力，从而又能在教学上引导学生拓展知识视野、思维世界和精神境界。

这也是我对奉婷名师工作室本期全体成员的衷心祝福！愿以此与诸位共勉！

广东第二师范学院　吴慧坚
2021年11月

目 录

CONTENTS

上 篇 The Secret Garden

中 篇 A Christmas Carol

下 篇 The Book Thief

上 篇

The Secret Garden

◎ 内容简介：

故事主要讲述一个任性而孤僻的富家小女孩Mary，因为一场不可避免的瘟疫变成了孤儿，不得不寄居到叔叔家。叔叔拥有一个古老的庄园，庄园里隐藏着无数的秘密，有可以与许多动物进行沟通交流的小男孩，还有一座被封闭了整整十年的秘密花园。一次神奇的经历，使Mary闯入久已禁闭且荒芜的花园。Mary、农家小子Dickon和常年被关在阴暗房间里的病态少爷Colin，找到了开启快乐的钥匙，让花园经历了一次诗意的复活，许许多多的秘密最终被完全解开。

本书是20世纪著名的女作家弗朗西斯·霍奇森·伯内特的代表作。她在纽约长岛布置自己家的花园时得到了灵感。本书一经出版，很快就成为当时最受关注和最畅销的儿童文学作品，整个20世纪，人们一直在再版这本书，全世界的小孩都喜爱*The Secret Garden*。它曾经先后十几次被改编成电影、电视剧、卡通片、话剧、舞台剧。1993年，*The Secret Garden*被波兰电影大师霍兰德再次改编为电影，而这部经典影片再次使霍兰德获得巨大声誉。在英语的儿童文学作品里，本书被公认为一部无年龄界限的佳作。它作为严肃的文学作品被收入牛津《世界经典丛书》，并影响了两位诺贝尔文学奖得主T. S. 艾略特和D. H. 劳伦斯的写作。

Chapter 1-3 of The Secret Garden

导 读

本期我们分享*The Secret Garden*的第1章至第3章，“There is No One Left”“Mistress Mary Quite Contrary”“Across The Moor”。这部分给人的总体感觉就是dark，Mary的样子和性格，她身边的人和moor这个地方的环境给人的感觉都是dark。

当Mary被送到米塞斯韦特庄园，和她叔叔住在一起时，大家都说她是有史以来最难看的孩子。那也是真的。她有一张瘦小的脸和一个瘦小的身体，稀疏的头发和酸溜溜的表情。她的头发是黄色的，她的脸是黄色的。她性格也很不讨人喜欢，“By the time she was six years old，she was as tyrannical and selfish a little pig as ever lived...”。后来Mary去到另一个家庭里，那里的孩子都取笑她：“Mistress Mary，quite contrary.”。

她的原生家庭也不温馨。她的父亲在英国政府任职，一直很忙而且生着病。她的母亲是个大美人，但她只喜欢参加聚会，和快乐的人一起娱乐，她一点也不想要一个小女孩，Mary出生后，她把她交给了当地的一个奴隶阿亚（Ayah）照顾。阿亚被告知，如果她想取悦主人，就必须尽可能地让孩子远离人们的视线，这样就不会烦扰到大人。可想而知，Mary小时候就是缺乏爱和陪伴的。

离开印度后，Mary开启了去英国投靠叔叔的旅途，而这段旅途给人的感觉也是不明快的，略显阴森。“The carriage lamps shed a yellow light on a rough-looking road which seemed to be cut through bushes and low-growing things which ended in the great expanse of dark apparently spread out before and around them.”

来到英国时刚好是夜晚，文中对房子的描述也是带有神秘和恐怖色彩的，连同她的叔叔也是个自闭驼背的老头。“A house with a hundred rooms，nearly all shut up and with their doors locked—a house on the edge of a moor—whatsoever a moor was—sounded dreary. A man with a crooked back who shut himself up also！”

面对这样的情况，书里也暗示了Mary的迷茫和无助感。“The entrance door was a huge one made of massive，curiously shaped panels of oak studded with big iron nails and bound with great iron bars. It opened into an enormous hall，which was so dimly lighted that the faces in the portraits on the walls and the figures in the suits of armor made Mary feel that she did not want to look at them. As she stood on the stone floor she looked a very small，odd little black figure，and she felt as small and lost and odd as she looked."

但在这么多不良的情况和因素下，Mary还是有很强的适应性的，她还是坚强地活下来了。"But if everyone had got well again，surely someone would remember and come to look for her."

Mrs. Medlock怜悯地说："She is such a plain child，" ... "And her mother was such a pretty creature. She had a very pretty manner，too，and Mary has the most unattractive ways I ever saw in a child. The children call her Mistress Mary Quite Contrary..." "Perhaps if her mother had carried her pretty face and her pretty manners oftener into the nursery Mary might have learned some pretty ways too. It is very sad，now the poor beautiful thing is gone，to remember that many people never even knew that she had a child at all."。

从这些言语中我们也再次感受到：我们最好通过做孩子们的榜样来教育他们，而不是告诉他们该怎么做。她的话也再次深刻提醒了我们：在孩子成长的过程中，陪伴是非常重要的。

工作室人员分享

在开始阅读这本书之前，我先了解了作者及其写作时所生活的年代背景，希望自己能更深入地了解故事的背景。*The Secret Garden*是美国女作家Frances Hodgson Burnett在1909年创作的儿童文学作品，是她在纽约长岛布置自家花园时突发灵感而创作的。同时，*The Secret Garden*也是在受到浪漫主义运动的影响下创作的。浪漫主义思潮产生于18世纪末并在19世纪上半叶达到高峰，浪漫主义作家以自然为审美对象，借助想象、夸张、比喻等写作手法描绘人与自然相融一体、互相感应的和谐场景，表现天人合一的自然观和生态观，通过大胆的夸张、虚构、想象来呼吁人类回归自然。对自然的赞美、亲近是浪漫主义文学最常见的主题。我很期待通过阅读*The Secret Garden*这本书来学习作者是如何表达对自然的赞美的。

——陈雪芬

故事的开始，我们认识了女主人公Mary，一个性情古怪、孤僻、脾气差的小女孩。因为霍乱，Mary的父母都去世了，她在一夜之间变成了孤儿，不得不从印度被送往英国叔叔的庄园。寄人篱下的感觉让人不是滋味，这个陌生的生活环境更使她倍感孤独落寞。她讨厌所有的人，当然也知道自己不被人喜欢。书中提到的霍乱让我联想到了当下的疫情。霍乱在以前是致死率非常高的传染病，它发病快、传染性强。由于环境卫生问题，以前的非洲和印度的人们极易感染霍乱。文中是这样说的："People are dying like flies. It' s dangerous to stay in this town.You should go to the hills，where there' s no disease."。而现在经历的新冠肺炎疫情，对我们来说也是从来没有过的体验。居家隔离期间，我们每一个人都在默默地祈祷着疫情能够早点过去，让我们能够重新回到正常生活中去。

——董筱妍

在悲惨的遭遇面前，Mary没有选择哭泣，而是选择微笑面对，并且以自己的乐观感染身边的人，甚至让一个整天疑神疑鬼、卧床不起的Colin神奇地站起来了。如果她选择了哭泣，秘密花园也许就不会开启，Colin也许就不会战胜"心魔"。

作者用清新的笔触生动地描写了一个骄纵任性的小女孩Mary在遭遇家庭变故、失去双亲后，寄居于叔叔家的故事。然而，种种的不幸并没有击倒她，她坚强地生活着，并结识了热爱大自然的小伙伴Dickon。他们善良、纯真、健康、向上的精神，感染了庄园中的另一个人——性格怪异的Colin，他们在一天天地改变着，正如尘封的秘密花园在慢慢地发生着变化……

只有在宽松的环境中，我们才能健康地成长。爱心，会让我们更愉快、更健康。爱心加团结，具有无穷的力量。乐观、积极、微笑，我们才有精神，才会健康。病痛，往往只在我们心里。心里有病，才是最折磨人的病。

遇到挫折，我们应该像Mary那样，微笑面对。譬如桌子上只有半杯牛奶了，悲观的人可能会唉声叹气地说："太倒霉了，只剩下半杯牛奶了！"乐观的人则可能微笑着说："太好了，我还有半杯牛奶呢！"同样的境遇，心态不同，人生的轨道恐怕也会不同。愿我们每个人都拥有积极向上的心态，微笑着迎接幸福快乐的明天！

——郑剑湘

故事一开始便是压抑的。给我印象最深刻的是描述Mary的词语：一副不讨人喜欢的样子，一副酸溜溜的表情，病恹恹的，烦躁的，僵硬的，冷酷的，顽固的。由于长期被忽视，Mary的世界完全是灰色的。作为一个母亲，我真的无法理解她的母亲。她怎么能这样对待自己的女儿？文中有这样一句话："Other children seemed to belong to their fathers and mothers，but she had never seemed to really be anyone' s little girl."。其他的孩子都有自己的父母，但她从来没有真正成为任何人的小女孩。这句话交代了主人公从小生活在无爱的家庭环境里。由于缺爱，才慢慢形成了孤僻古怪的性格。后来随着故事的发展，女孩变得活跃、勇敢，热爱生活和身边的人。这中间发生了什么？孩子为什么会有这么大的变化？

我非常好奇，想迫不及待地读下去。

——关少娟

读到故事一开始对Mary背景的介绍时，我不禁心疼这个孩子，遇上了这么不靠谱的父母，失去父母后还要离开自己熟悉的环境去适应一个全新的环境，这对于一个孩子来说，无疑是个极大的挑战。而由于早期接受的教育不得当，导致Mary变成了一个非常不友好并且缺乏教养的小女孩，看到这种情况，我也不禁为她的未来感到担忧。但是看到第二章时，发现Martha原来有招治她！Martha教养孩子的方式，让作为读者的我学会了放手。只要大人肯放手，孩子就能做到。当孩子没有依赖的后路时，他是会学着去独立、学着自己成长的。在这个篇章里，Martha很多次跟Mary说："No，you have to go by yourself. I have too much to do."。"不行，你得自己去。我有太多的事情要做了。"是啊，大人要学着放手和示弱啊，这样孩子才会有更大的发展空间！

——莫洁文

在前三章里，我看到了一个爹不亲、娘不爱的面黄肌瘦的刁蛮野丫头。她是不幸的，因为从小就缺失了父母的爱、陪伴与管教，她变成了一个自私、任性、毫无教养的野丫头。但她也是幸运的，正是因为从小就没有被任何人管教，也就意味着她的思想没有受到任何的禁锢和影响，还是一张白纸，未来还有着无限的可能。而这样一个如同白纸的小女孩，因为霍乱，父母双亡，成为一名孤儿，如果她是在父母关爱下长大的话，可能已经痛哭流涕、悲伤不已了。可是因为从小就没有受到父母的关爱，当他们突然离开时她也并没有觉得悲伤或者想念他们。所以我想很多时候所谓的"血浓于水"可能是个假命题，并不是血脉本身带来情感的羁绊，而是相互的关心照顾和爱护创造出彼此的羁绊。虽然Mary和她的父母没有产生这样的羁绊，但我相信未来她一定会遇到能和她产生羁绊的人的。

——莫 然

通过阅读一至三章，我了解了主人公Mary。人人都说她是世界上最不讨人喜欢的女孩子，这话说得一点也不假。她小脸细长，身材单薄，一头稀稀拉拉的头发，还板着一张郁郁寡欢的臭脸。由于小时候缺乏父母的爱，她成为世界上最随心所欲、蛮横霸道的小霸王。文中对Mary外貌和性格的描写可算是细致入微、惟妙惟肖。

——宋 蕾

关于*The Secret Garden*这本书，我最早读过它的中文版本，记忆已有一些模糊，或许因为年少，我不曾有太多感触，只觉得文字优美，主人公的蜕变叫人欣喜，感叹生活还是美好的。在工作室的倡议下，我们开始了英文原著的阅读，却让我有了更多新的发现。英文的修辞手法，尤其是那些运用比喻修辞手法的词句，所描绘的画面栩栩如生。文中对人物的刻画所用的语言更是精妙。“She had a little thin face and a little thin body，thin light hair and a sour expression. Her hair was yellow，and her face was yellow because she had been born in India and had always been ill in one way or another.”

主人公长得并不讨喜，这病恹恹的状态，与她任性的性格形成强烈的对比，但这也很好地铺垫了主人公的成长历程，让人在品味故事的同时，也能认识到作者的写作手法。我相信通过慢慢地品读，会有更多不一样的新发现。

The writer Frances Hodgson Burnett led the readers into *The Secret Garden* in a stifling way.

——Ting Feng

A Spoiled Little Girl

“Mary Lennox was spoiled，rude and had a bad temper. Because she was often ill. She was thin，with a sad face. She complained a lot. No one liked her at all.” Children seemed to belong to their fathers and mothers，but she had never seemed to really be anyone’s little girl.

A terrible disease

“‘Poor little kid，’ said one of the men.‘There is nobody here.’” That is how Mary discovered that her mother and father were dead and the servants were dead too，because of a terrible disease. That was why the house was so silent. Mary Lennox was completely alone.

There was no one in India to look after Mary，so she went to England to live with her uncle，Mr. Craven.

An unpleasant trip

“The carriage lamps shed a yellow light on a rough-looking road which seemed to be cut through bushes and low-growing things which ended in the great expanse of dark apparently spread out before and around them. A wind was rising and making a singular，wild，low，rushing sound...it isn’ t fields nor mountains，it’ s just miles and miles and miles of wild land that nothing grows on but heather and gorse and broom，and nothing lives on but wild ponies and sheep.”

A cold reception

Mrs Medlock，her uncle’ s housekeeper，met Mary. Mrs. Medlock did not like Mary. She thought that the little girl as bad-tempered，rude and plain—and she was right.

“ ‘There’ s nothing for you to do there，and your uncle is not interested in you，’ said Mrs Medlock. ‘He’ s got a crooked back. He was a sour young man until he married.’ ”

All these are like a secret garden attracting the readers.

——徐 燕

Chapter 4-6 of The Secret Garden

导 读

本周分享的内容是*The Secret Garden*的第4章至第6章——“Martha” “The Cry in the Corridor” “There was Some One Crying—There was！”。

这三个章节与前面三个章节的明显对比就是女主人公Mary的变化。在印度的时候，Mary是病恹恹的、被宠坏的、尖酸刻薄的、坏脾气的、粗鲁的和固执的。当Mary被送到庄园后，她变得健康、富有好奇心、随和，并且开始会为别人感到难过。对于一个女孩子来说，她的身心都发生了巨大的改变。那么，导致她转变如此大的原因是什么？也许我们可以从下面的一些片段中找到答案。

片段一：

在花园里，Mary看到了老园丁Ben和那只可爱的小鸟——知更鸟。她以前不知道这是使她感到不快和生气的事情之一。当知更鸟看着她的时候，她似乎发现了这一点。

片段二：

Ben又狠狠地笑了一声：“我自己也很孤独，除了他和我在一起的时候。”他朝知更鸟竖起大拇指，“他是我唯一的朋友。”

“我一个朋友也没有，”Mary说，“我从来没有，我的奶妈不喜欢我，我从来没有和任何人玩过。”

“你和我很像，”他说，“我们是由同一块布织成的。我们俩长得都不好看，而且我们俩都像我们的脸色一样酸。我敢保证，我们俩的脾气都一样坏。”

其实Ben和Mary的性格很相似，说话都一样的尖酸刻薄，让人难以亲近，似乎Mary和Ben都意识到了这一点，而他们能够敞开心扉地聊天，让人觉得很温暖。她终于开始改变，竟然和跟自己一样臭脾气的人也能聊天。这些都证明了Mary已经被周围的人和事物所改变，并且看得出来她也愿意或者说乐于做出改变。

片段三：

这话说得很明白，Mary一辈子也没听过关于她自己的真实情况。无论你做什么，仆人们总是向你致敬，顺从你。她从来没有多想过自己的容貌，但她不知道自己是否像Ben一样没有吸引力，也不知道自己是否像知更鸟飞来之前他的样子一样酸。实际上，她也开始怀疑自己是不是“脾气不好”。她对此感到不舒服。

“你愿意和我交朋友吗？”她像对人说话一样对知更鸟说。

“你会吗？”她说这话的时候，既没有用她那刺耳的小声音，也没有用她那专横的印度腔调，而是用一种温柔、急切、哄哄的腔调，使Ben像她听到他吹口哨时一样吃惊。

而知更鸟更是一边引领着Mary走出原来的孤傲的自我走向富有温度的善良的新我的同时，一边也带领着Mary探索这座神秘的花园，去揭开它神秘的面纱。

片段四：

在庄园里，几天后花儿几乎完全盛开。一天早晨，她醒来觉得饿了，当她坐下来吃早餐时，没有轻蔑地瞥一眼她的粥或将它推开，而是拿起她的勺子，开始吃起来，一直吃到她的碗空了……

片段五：

她开始感兴趣了，觉得来到米塞斯韦特庄园并不感到遗憾。在印度，她总觉得热，又太疲倦，什么也不关心。事实上，从草地里吹来的清新的风已经开始把她幼小的脑子里的蜘蛛网吹走，使她稍稍清醒了一点……

片段六：

“呼啸”声似乎比以前更响了。就在这时，一件非常好的事情发生在她身上。事实上，自从她来到米塞斯韦特庄园，一共发生了四件好事：她觉得她好像理解了一只知更鸟，而知更鸟也理解了她；她在风中奔跑，直到她的血液变得温暖；她有生以来第一次能健康地感觉到什么叫饿肚子；她已经明白为一个人难过是什么滋味了。

也许在片段四到片段六，我们只看到了Mary自己的感受和变化，其实在庄园中一直陪伴在Mary左右的是Martha，可以看出Martha是Mary的第一个人生导师。在好心肠又独立的Martha的影响下，Mary逐渐对这个世界心生好奇，有了老园丁、知更鸟、Dickon、Colin等多个好朋友。这个自私的小女孩也开始渐渐学会爱别人、爱世界。所以，我最深的感悟是：

（1）如果你想变得更好，什么时候开始改变都不晚。

（2）自然界拥有神奇的力量。无论在身体上还是精神上，人们总是能被大自然治愈。

工作室人员分享

读完这三章，我对第4章的印象非常深刻。秘密花园里一片萧瑟。孤独的Mary在女仆Martha的鼓励下，开始尝试在庄园里寻找自己的乐趣。她认识了性格乖戾但善良的老花匠Ben。

两个同样刻薄、坏脾气的人，性格是如此的相似。年龄相差很大的两个人，一个是孤单、性格乖戾的小女孩，另一个是对孩子的闯入都会破口大骂的老人。这两个人能够自然、坦诚地对话，敞开心扉地聊天，让人感觉温暖、有治愈感。我想是Ben带领着Mary走进了大自然，使得Mary天真无邪的天性得到了充分的展示，并走出了令人窒息的深宅大院，来到充满生机、阳光灿烂、鸟语花香的大自然，这正如给幼苗一样茁壮成长的孩子的生活带来了一缕阳光和希望。

——王之光

Mary与女仆Martha的相处，是她心灵发生改变的开始，可以说Martha是Mary的第一个人生导师。例如，一开始接触，她们之间就发生了一次撕心裂肺的争吵。这时，Mary的孤苦、无助得以在一场大哭（burst into passionate sobbing）中发泄。而好心肠又独立的Martha因这样的哭泣不知所措，继而请求她原谅，这让Mary 第一次感受到安慰和友好。在Martha的影响下，Mary逐渐对这个世界心生好奇，有了老园丁、知更鸟、Dickon、Colin等多个好朋友，这个自私的小女孩也开始渐渐学会爱别人、爱世界。书中也有一个很美的意象：一只通人性的知更鸟。当Mary得知知更鸟喜欢她，并且把她当朋友时，她快乐得难以置信，从而迎来了她性格改变的转折点。西方传说认为，知更鸟的胸脯是因为沾染了十字架上耶稣的鲜血才变红的，因此，知更鸟被赋予了神圣的色彩，能够让人重获新生。

——郑剑湘

第四章到第六章向女主人公展开了一个全新的世界。文章以Mary的视角，对这个新世界的人和物进行了详细的描写。给我印象最深的是对Mary和Martha最初几天见面时两人性格冲突的描写。“Mary had always slapped her Ayah in the face when she was angry. She wondered a little what this girl would do if one slapped her face. She was a round，rosy，good-natured looking creature，but she had a sturdy way which made Mistress Mary wonder is she might not even slap back—if the person who slapped her was only a little girl.” Mary 对Martha处于观察试探阶段，如果Martha如印度仆人一样，估计Mary 生气的时候也会一巴掌打过去。幸运的是，Martha是以a round，rosy，good-natured looking creature的第一印象征服Mary的。

然而，Mary给Martha的最初印象就不怎么好了。“Martha had buttoned up her little sisters and brothers but she had never seen a child who stood still and waited for another person to do things for her as if she had neither hands nor feet of her own.” Martha从来没有见过一个孩子站着不动，等着别人为她做事，好像她没有自己的手脚一样。

两人都给彼此留下了深刻的印象。仆人没有见过如此懒惰、如此依赖人的孩子；孩子没有见过外形如此可爱、性情如此温和，目光又如此坚定的仆人。这里为后面的故事发展做好了铺垫，是Martha的独立、乐观、温暖改变了霸道、自私、坏脾气的Mary。

——关少娟

在阅读这几章内容时，总会有心灵受到很大震撼的时候，总会不由自主地投入到小女孩Mary的情感世界中。读完前三章产生更多的是同情、惋惜的感情，对于一些语言中所流露出的孤独而产生共鸣、难以忘却，如“It sounds as if there were no one in the bungalow but me and the snake.”。读完第4、5、6章后，心里有了暖意，为小女孩的逐渐变好而感到欣慰。她知道什么是饿，会拿勺子自己吃饭；由冷漠地听仆人Martha说话到留意Martha在说什么；对知更鸟说话的语气不是硬邦邦的而是轻柔殷勤、充满童趣的，“Would you make friends with me? Would you？I like you！I like you！...”；对十年从不让人进去的花园、深夜不时传来的嚎哭声产生好奇，并决定要弄明白。这三章的内容让我进一步感受到了“心若向阳花自开，人若向暖清风徐来”，心胸开朗、阳光的人才会受到他人的喜爱，生活才会变得丰富多彩。

——李 丹

Ben·韦瑟斯塔夫，那个园丁，表面好像冷酷无情，却是个爱鸟的人。Dickon，Martha的哥哥，是个可爱的男孩，擅长和动物打交道。他们都给Mary的生活带来了火花。而且Mary自己也在不断地改变，尝试着自己动手做事而不依赖他人。她也会做更多的运动来帮助自己改善胃口。书上也说她有时候看起来漂亮了，她也几乎可以微笑。

顺便说一句，我很欣赏Mary亲近大自然的部分。在第37页，“‘Nothing to play with，’ exclaimed Martha. ‘Our children play with sticks and stones. They just run about and shouts and looks at things.’”。虽然这里的语言显示出Martha并没得到很好的教育，但这在她的人格魅力下已经显得不值一提了。这部分让我想起了我的童年。那时候我们没有太多的学习压力，我们可以去很多地方。那时也没有那么多高楼大厦，只有很多原生态的地方。我10岁的时候常和朋友们一起在原野上疯跑，骑自行车和大笑，毫无拘束地乐在其中。当然，现在回想起来还是有一定危险性的。不过曾经有人说过：“More dangers，more adventures and more fun.”。危险有时恰恰意味着奇趣的旅行和乐趣！

——李秀文

在印度的时候，Mary是被照顾得很好的，连穿衣服都是仆人帮她穿的，宛然一个大小姐，但现在完全不同了。没人伺候她，没有人关心询问她做了什么或者告诉她要做什么。她现在不得不自己穿衣服，也学会了自己穿衣服，因为她知道自己在Martha的眼里是那么的无能和愚蠢。在这种情况下，Mary需要更加独立，去证明自己可以成为更好的人。这个章节告诉我们，一个人受了什么样的教育就会成为什么样的人。比如你从小都是衣来伸手、饭来张口，那么长大后就会指望着别人去帮你做事情，无法培养独立性。这一点让我自己反思在教育孩子的时候，也需要注意这个方面，不用把他们照顾得那么周到，他们是需要自己成长的。另外，环境是可以改变一个人的。我想这也是Mary性格的转折点之一。

——麦佩莹

一向享受着仆人伺候的Mary，一下子变得无人可依赖，事事都要靠自己。但我们可以看到，当Mary无人可依赖时她完全可以独立。周到的照顾使Mary变得娇气脆弱，狠心的放手使Mary变得独立自强，这两个现象形成了强烈的对比，也给读者以很好的教育启示。我们教育孩子时也一样，我们需要大胆地放手，让孩子锻炼，让孩子在实践中成长，要相信孩子一定会给我们惊喜的！在这个环节中，受教育水平不高的Martha却展现出很有智慧的引导方式，她没有训斥Mary让她感到不被尊重，也没有纵容她，而是比较理性客观地指出了她的问题，以身作则地给Mary做了个好榜样，教会她反思，以及要懂礼貌。看到这儿我不禁感慨："效果最好的教育就是'以身作则'，最难做到的教育也是'以身作则'，让我们向Martha学习吧。"

——莫洁文

在这几章中，Mary已经进入了新的家庭，并且感叹这里的装修如此奢华，可她依然是那个愤愤不平的小女孩。当Martha问她"Do you like the moor? "时，Mary回答道："No，I hate it."。这时候的Mary还是一个心中充满怒火，看什么都不爽的孩子。可是和Martha相处了一段时间之后，Mary慢慢有了改变，虽然她们一开始也是有着各种误会和小矛盾的，可是Mary也第一次遇到了一个愿意真心去了解她的人。Martha的那句"I don' t know anything"看起来好像是在说自己什么都不知道，但反过来理解就是我很愿意去了解你，虽然我暂时什么都不知道。在Martha的关心和照顾下，Mary的内心终于开始变得柔软起来，还知道安慰别人了。我很期待Mary后面还会发生什么样的变化。

——莫 然

通过这几章的阅读，了解到Mary从小在印度长大，缺乏父母的关爱，由土著阿妈全权看管，他们对Mary总是百依百顺、唯命是从，使得Mary成为一个自私、冷漠又任性的小孩。但自从来到了米塞斯韦特庄园，她对一切事物感到好奇，被有一百多个门锁锁着房间的一幢宅子，对那个秘密花园，尤其对那个哭声更是感到好奇，这也与这两章的标题相呼应。

——宋 蕾

这三个章节主要描述了Mary来到新的环境后从不适应到适应的过程，其间的各种任性。从她和仆人Martha的对话中我们可以感受到她对身边的人或事充满敌意和敏感。

“‘You thought I was a native！You dared！You don’t know anything about natives！They are not people—they’re servants who must salaam7 to you. You know nothing about India.

‘You know nothing about anything！’ She was in such a rage and felt so helpless before the girl’s simple stare，and somehow she suddenly felt so horribly lonely and far away from everything she understood and which understood her，that she threw herself face downward on the pillows and burst into passionate sobbing.”

在这两段文字里，从 horribly lonely到passionate sobbing，小女孩的动作让人感受到她的孤独与无助。而女仆Martha的一席话，让我们感受到她们之间的相处一定是一个温暖与融化的开始。

“‘You mustn’t for sure. I didn’t know you’d be vexed.

‘I don’t know anything about anything—just like you said.

‘I beg your pardon，Miss. Do stop crying.’ There was something comforting and really friendly in her queer Yorkshire speech and sturdy way which had a good effect on Mary. She gradually ceased crying and became quiet.

Martha looked relieved.”

但是作为孩子，Mary对这个陌生的环境也是好奇的，她发现了这个神秘的花园，想探究它的故事，同时也激发了读者跟着一起阅读和探索的欲望。

——徐 燕

这个章节让我想起我们之前谈到的父母教育是非常重要的，尤其是在儿童时期。如果父母教育是合适的、恰当的，它将对孩子的一生都产生积极的影响，从而去治愈他们的一生。如果Mary从小被教育要当一个得体的、懂礼貌的小孩，她肯定会做得比现在更好。幸运的是，她遇见了Martha、Ben和Robin，他们教会她要学会反思，要懂礼貌，要注重言行，当她言行不妥当时她居然还会感到不舒服。她也学着积极面对晨起这件事，也会开始感到饥饿，身体开始健康起来了。她甚至还知道要对别人感到抱歉。同时，让我惊讶的是孩子的学习能力和灵活变通能力。当面对变数时，他们是非常灵活多变的。所以我们不应轻易去否定他们，而是更应该通过树立好榜样去帮助他们建立信心，同时也不要低估大自然和人类本身的力量。

——袁泳施

Different people，Different sights

The same moor，different people find different sights. In Mrs. Medlock' s eyes，nor it isn' t fields nor mountains，it' s just miles and miles of wild land that nothing grows on but heather and gorse and broom，and nothing lives on but wild ponies and sheep.

But to Martha，it is such a great place.

"'I just love it. It's none bare. It's covered wi' growin' things as smells sweet. It's fair lovely in spring an'summer when th' gorse an' broom an' heather's in flower. It smells o' honey an' there's such a lot o' fresh air—an' th' sky looks so high an' th' bees an' skylarks makes such a nice noise hummin' an' singin'. Eh! I wouldn't live away from th' moor for anythin.'"

Only if we live in a positive attitude，everything around us will be nice. Can we enjoy life，can we live a happy life.

——Ting Feng

Chapter 7-10 of The Secret Garden

导读

本期分享内容为*The Secret Garden*的第7章至第10章——“The Key to the Garden”“The Robin Who Showed The Way”“The Strangest House Any One Ever Lived In”“Dickon”。在“The Key To The Garden”一章，我们看到了Mary刚睡醒就忍不住跟Martha分享：“‘Look at the moor! Look at the moor!’ The rainstorm had ended and the graymist and clouds had been swept away in the night by the wind. The wind itself had ceased and a brilliant，deep blue sky arched high over the moorland. Never，never had Mary dreamed of a sky so blue.”。这里作者用了多个动词表现暴风雨之后，风儿好像有生命一般，轻轻地来把迷雾和乌云拨开，而天空中是一片从未见过的干净又梦幻的蓝色。不得不说，作者真的有一双发现美的眼睛，我们经常见到的雨过天晴竟然被她描述得那么清新脱俗，心情不由得跟着晴朗了起来。

而Mary在看到美美的天空开启了元气满满的一天之后，又开始探究玫瑰花园的秘密，可惜身边的人们都不知道，也无法回答她，此时她看到了之前见过的那只知更鸟，而且她发现它好像认识她。“‘You do remember me!’ She cried out.‘You do! You are prettier than anything else in the world!’ She chirped，and talked，and coaxed and he hopped，and flirted his tail and twittered. It was as if he were talking.”这里作者用了一系列动词的排比，生动地描述了知更鸟听到Mary说话之后的各种叽叽喳喳的叫和跳跃，好像一个人在说话似的。这让Mary惊奇不已，于是她一边盯着知更鸟，一边跟着它，它飞到哪儿，她就跟到哪儿。没想到这一路走着走着，就来到了一个不久前被挖出来的、泥土还没干的洞旁。更神奇的是，她在那里竟然捡到了一把钥匙。这时Mary突发奇想：这该不会是秘密花园的钥匙吧？

第8章The Robin Who Showed The Way一开始就是Mary拿着手上的钥匙左看看右看看，一边看一边各种胡思乱想，幻想着自己拿着钥匙可以在秘密花园里做各种各样的事情。这时作者是这样描述Mary的心理的：“Living as it were，all by herself in a house with a hundred mysteriously closed rooms and having nothing whatever to do to amuse herself，had set her inactive brain to working and was actually awakening her imagination."。住在这样一个有着很多神神秘秘打不开门的房间的大房子里，她真的没有什么机会去做点什么让自己开心的事，而无所事事的日子反过来激发了她无限的想象力。后面还有一个有趣的细节就是Mary和Martha一起跳绳，而Martha说没有比跳绳更适合女孩子的运动了。从这里就可以看到两个女孩子的鲜明对比，Mary是充满想象力的，而Martha却思想禁锢。

到了第九章"The Strangest House Any One Ever Lived In"，Mary终于带着钥匙来到了秘密花园。这时，她发现那里真的是一个无人之境。一切都是那么静谧！她忍不住深吸一口气，然后才缓缓打开大门。而在那之后作者写道："Then she slipped through it，and shut it behind her，and stood with her back against it，looking about her and breathing quite fast with excitement，and wonder，and delight."这里的几个动词用得太生动了，先在门那儿迅速滑过去，一下子把门关上，背对着门，还伴随着兴奋又好奇的呼吸。简直就像做小偷一样。

当她终于走进了秘密花园，她突然感觉到这里实在太安静了，而她可能是近十年来第一个在这里说话的人。她想到"she was inside the wonderful garden and she could come through the door under the ivy any time and she felt as if she had found a world all her own."。她可以随时来这个地方——这个只有她知道的地方，这里就是她的秘密基地，她自己的小世界。

还记得刚开始Mary还是个面黄肌瘦的小丫头，可是当她在她的秘密花园里忙前忙后、挖土松地时，她甚至开始出汗了，而这些劳动让这个几乎没有笑过的小女孩脸上不知不觉地挂上了笑容。

这几章让我感受最深的就是以下几点：

（1）Beauty is everywhere，we just need to discover it.

（2）Sometimes owning a secret is like owning a whole new world.

（3）Giving is happier than receiving.

工作室人员分享

在这三个章节中，很多对环境的描写栩栩如生，很有画面感。比如：

"The rainstorm had ended and the gray mist and clouds had been swept away in the night by the wind. The wind itself had ceased and a brilliant，deep blue sky arched high over the moorland. Never，never had Mary dreamed of a sky so blue. In India skies were hot and blazing；this was of a deep cool blue which almost seemed to sparkle like the waters of some lovely bottomless lake，and here and there，high，high in the arched blueness floated small clouds of snow-white fleece. The far-reaching world of the moor itself looked softly blue instead of gloomy purple-black or awful dreary gray."

如火焰般灼热的天空，一面无底的湖水，雪白如羊毛般的云彩，真的是非常美。

主人公Mary也日渐成为阳光的女孩儿。“She walked away，slowly thinking. She had begun to like the garden just as she had begun to like the robin and Dickon and Martha’ s mother. She was beginning to like Martha，too. That seemed a good many people to like—when you were not used to liking. She thought of the robin as one of the people. She went to her walk outside the long，ivy-covered wall over which she could see the tree-tops；and the second time she walked up and down the most interesting and exciting thing happened to her，and it was all through Ben Weatherstaff's robin.”这是一个神奇的花园，它将开启许多故事与美好。期待接下来故事的发展。

——徐 燕

到目前为止，第8章是我在书中读到的最令人印象深刻的章节。在这一章里，我看到Mary变得越来越开朗。在第6章里，当她第一次到达沼泽地的时候，她是如此的孤独，以至于她想在家里养老鼠作为她的朋友。但是在第8章，事情发生了戏剧性的变化。她跑，她聊，她跳，她数，她挖，她除草，最迷人的是她开始高兴地笑。她和其他人更亲密了。她和Martha聊天，还和她握手。她想让Ben看到她跳绳。她开始喜欢周围的人。

Martha在Mary的改变过程中扮演了重要的角色。Martha是如此的可爱，她就像一个可以融化所有寒冷的壁炉。她满脑子都是外出时的快乐故事。Martha送了一件礼物和一根跳绳给Mary，让她高兴起来。事实也的确如此。她甚至教Mary如何通过亲吻来表达感激之情。Martha从她母亲那里得到了好消息。看起来她妈妈是个超级英雄。她是一个有12个孩子的聪明勤奋的母亲。不管他们有多穷，她总是很乐观。书里说：“Her mother had been glad to see her and they had got the baking and washing all out of the way. She had even made each of the children a dough-cake with a bit of brown sugar in it.” “Dickon said our cottage was good enough for a king.” “In the evening they had all sat round the fire，and Martha and her mother had sewed patches on torn clothes and mended stockings ...”是的，他们很穷，但他们还是很开心地聊天。Martha的妈妈喜欢做点小事，来让她的孩子们开心。她是个成功的母亲。

孩子们渴望得到关注，欣赏和参与我们成年人的世界。只要他们能够得到，他们就会向我们展示他们甜蜜的微笑，就像温暖的春天里盛开的美丽的花朵一样，向我们敞开他们温柔的心扉。所以我们要让他们更轻松、更快乐。Martha的妈妈提醒我，做点小事，给生活带来快乐和甜蜜，正是生活应有的样子。

——李秀文

读完这三章后，我发现这本书越来越有趣了。从这三章里，我意识到Mary和Martha之间的友谊已经慢慢形成了。她们过去不喜欢对方。Martha曾经很看不起Mary，觉得她只是个娇生惯养的公主。Mary也不喜欢Martha，觉得自己没有必要去在意这个不重要的人。然而，她们现在莫名地关心着对方，习惯了彼此的陪伴。Martha不在时，Mary甚至会感到孤独。在这些章节当中，我还挺喜欢描述周围环境和天气的文字，我想这些文字都能同时反映出Mary当下的感受。值得一提的是，给我印象最深的是Martha的妈妈。她真是个体贴的女人，很会关心别人，也懂得关心Mary的感受。我想这就是Martha那么善良的原因了，作为母亲的她，言传身教，所以她的孩子也是很善良的。这再次向我们展示了家庭教育的重要性。

——麦佩莹

在这三章里，Mary对周围的环境感到好奇。她勇敢地去探索。她学会了跳绳，这是她以前从未做过的；她遇到了一只知更鸟，想和它说话；她找到了一个花园。她用眼睛和心观察花园里的一切。我能感觉到她的兴奋。“When she had found ever so many more sharp，pale green point among the dead plants.”当我读到这句话的时候，我禁不住想，也许作者是把Mary比作了绿点。绿点代表希望和生命。Mary的变化很明显。“In this place she was beginning to care and to want to do new things. Already she felt less contrary，though she did not know why.”在这个地方，她已经开始关心和想要做一些新奇的事情了，尽管她不知道为什么。当Martha教她跳绳时，她学会了说“谢谢”。她在花园里冒险了三个小时，然后吃了顿丰盛的晚餐。她的心情发生了很大的变化，正如文中所说的：“She had been actually happy all the time.”“Everything was strange and silent and she seemed to be hundreds of miles away from anyone，but somehow she did not feel lonely at all.”。是秘密花园的新奇慢慢改变了Mary，是Mary的努力让这个死气沉沉的花园重新变得五彩缤纷。这充分说明了人与自然的关系——和谐、共生。

——关少娟

通过阅读这几章，我认为Mary在学习跳绳后，对Martha的态度和看法有所变化了。以前的她不习惯感谢别人，也不关注别人对她做的事，但这次Mary主动伸出手，想借此感谢Martha，这是一个很大的变化。Martha也有点不习惯，但却调侃说Mary应该亲她，由此看出，Martha还是挺幽默的。Martha的活泼俏皮，对Mary性格的变化有着很大的影响。

——陈雪芬

故事越来越吸引人，也越发暖心。一切都在往好的方向发展。在第7章中，我被雨后旷野的美丽而吸引。书中是这样描写的："The sky is of a deep cool blue which almost seemed to sparkle like the waters of some lovely bottomless lake, and here and there, high, high in the arched blueness floated small clouds of snow-white fleece. Hundreds of butterflies fluttering and bees humming and skylarks soaring up and singing."。

在这三章中，我也被一些充满爱的场景深深感动。比如Martha耐心教Mary跳绳，Mary仔细看并尝试的场景；Martha和Mary二人设法让Dickon去买些花种和工具的场景。至于这几章中的人物，我对Martha的母亲印象很深刻，她敏感、勤劳、体贴、和蔼可亲。她在乎Mary，叫Martha竭尽全力哄Mary开心，让她买根跳绳作为礼物送给Mary。这样的关爱让我感动。可以说，读者会情不自禁地喜欢Martha的母亲。

——李 丹

周围的人对Mary的影响是巨大的，Martha纯真、善良、开朗和爽快的性格深深地触动了Mary。Mary竟会说我喜欢你的妈妈，我喜欢Dickon。这是她性格的一个转变。Mary竟然会说没有人喜欢我，连我自己都不喜欢我自己，而且她说她从前从来没有意识到。这是她性格的另一个转变。Mary之前不知道自己不被人喜欢，甚至自己都不知道自己是一个什么样的人。但是来到庄园，和淳朴善良的Martha接触之后，她渐渐变得善解人意，懂得关心别人。

——宋 蕾

我们知道Mary的妈妈想给她找一个女老师，这是因为妈妈希望能有一个老师在她身旁照顾她并且陪她看书。但是Mary的心中却一直认为Martha是她的一个朋友，因为Martha能够清楚地知道Mary内心的惆怅和孤独。Martha能够读懂她心中所想，所以Mary给了她一个意味深长的坚定眼神。后来通过跳绳一步一步地拉近了她们之间的感情。因此，Mary也慢慢变得越来越开朗。

通过对Mary不想要女老师的细节描写，我们可以从中感受到她和Martha之间的感情和这份感情对她的某些影响。

——董筱妍

在这三章里面，Martha和Mary的相处模式发生了改变。原来她们彼此不喜欢对方，Martha看不惯Mary的娇生惯养，从"Martha had buttoned up her little sisters and brothers but she had never seen a child who stood still and waited for another person to do things for her as if she had neither hands nor feet of her own."可以体现出来。Mary也因为Martha是仆人而看不起她。但是渐渐地，她们之间发展出了友谊并习

惯了对方的陪伴。这么可喜的变化到底是什么促使的呢？细读这几章内容，我们可以发现，当Mary表现得不讨人喜欢时，Martha并没有跟她硬碰硬地发生冲突，而是用自己的温和、可爱和善良感动了Mary，从而促使她们的关系发生变化。这使我想起我所学的《正面管教》，Martha给我们做了个很好的示范，当孩子表现不好时，成人首先要做的就是冷静，接纳孩子的情绪再引导孩子的行为，当我们接纳孩子的情绪时，往往很快状况就得到改善了。

——莫洁文

Chapter 11-14 of The Secret Garden

导 读

今天分享的内容是*The Secret Garden* 的第11章至第14章——“The Nest of the Missel Thrush” “Might I Have a Bit of Earth? ” “I Am Colin” “A Young Rajah”。这几个章节的关键字是change。过去的Mary是瘦小的、阴沉的，她不想向外界打开心扉。但是遇到了更弱小的Colin以后，她开始想变得强壮和去学习如何关心他人。“When she saw poor Colin，she showed her love for him.She wanted to tap him to sleep. They talked and laughed.She wanted to bring Colin back to life.” Colin激发了她的保护欲。

后来Mary遇到了Dickon。“‘I'm growing fatter，’ said Mary，‘and I'm growing stronger. I used always to be tired.When I dig，I'm not tired at all.I like to smell the earth when it's turned up.’” 她以前看起来弱不禁风，但是现在她要努力多吃点儿长力气，她再也不会感到疲惫，她对生活中的每一天都充满着希望。

“‘Will you come again and help me to do it? ’ Mary begged. ‘I'm sure I can help，too. I can dig and pull up weeds，and do whatever you tell me.Oh! Do come，Dickon! ’” 面对强壮的Dickon，她会主动寻求帮助，也乐于帮忙做一些力所能及的事情，她不怕苦不怕累，这样的Mary就像是完全变了一个人似的。“‘To plant seeds in—to make things grow—to see them come alive，’ Mary faltered.” 当她和Dickon一起在地里埋下种子的时候，她是无比虔诚的。种子就是生命和希望的象征，她重新点燃了生命之火。

以前的Colin是一个每天都郁郁寡欢的病人，不愿意出去面对阳光，用文中的话来说就是“He's a big lad to cry like a baby.”。但是Mary的出现好像是一把钥匙瞬间打开了他封闭的心灵。他们无话不谈——

“‘Do you want to live? ’ inquired Mary.

‘No，’ he answered，in a cross，tired fashion. ‘But I don't want to die.When I feel ill I lie here and think about it until I cry and cry.’”

他找到了活下去的目标，他一点儿也不想死。他讨厌生病的感觉，他以前一直哭一直哭，就是因为病痛折磨着他，他很沮丧，感觉看不到希望。但是有了

Mary，他坚定了要活下去的信念。自从Colin遇到了Mary，他就变成了一个乐于和他人交流的正常孩子。这些改变都让人觉得很欣慰。

再来说Dickon，他是乐观向上和活力满满的。“He's always talking about live things. He never talks about dead things or things that are ill. He's always looking up in the sky to watch birds flying.”乐观的人对待事物的反应都是不一样的，他看着翱翔在天空的小鸟们，会很开心地微笑。他强大的正能量磁场吸引着他身边的人。Mary感受到了这种跳动的生命，从而又去影响了Colin。这三个孩子都在往好的方向发展。作者是这样描写Mary和Colin的变化的——“two ordinary healthy natural ten-year-old creatures”。天真烂漫的孩童时光，真令人羡慕。这就是孩子的魔力，他们可塑性极高，愿意去改变。

读完这几章，我得到了以下的感悟。第一，热情和目标是完成一件事的必要条件。首先我们要去确定一个能够指引的目标，然后我们必须要热爱这件事。第二，父母在和孩子相处的时候不要把自己的负面情绪带到家里来，要尽量保持家庭氛围的融洽，因为这有利于孩子的成长。第三，不要吝啬给予我们的爱，一点点爱都能产生很大的改变。最后，我们要和充满正能量的人相处。

工作室人员分享

我真的很喜欢孩子们的互动。“‘I'll come every day if tha' wants me，rain or shine，’ he（Dickon）answered stoutly.‘It's the best fun I ever had in my life—shut in here an' wakening up a garden.’‘If you will come，’ said Mary，‘if you will help me to make it alive，I'll—I don't know what I'll do，’ she ended helplessly. What could you do for a boy like that？”他们似乎爱上了对方。你今晚感觉不到爱吗？感觉真的很简单，但是很纯洁、很美丽。

他们很年轻，心思细腻，但又体贴。Dickon是一个阳光的男孩，他可以让所有的人开心起来。他说的关于秘密花园的话让我印象深刻。“I wouldn't want to make it look like a gardener's garden，all clipped an' spick an' span，would you？” he said. “It's nicer like this with things running wild，an' swinging an' catching hold of each other.”是啊，应该充满生机，就像他们一样，渴望一起探索。

恰恰相反，Colin病了，他痛苦而冷漠，等待着每个人来取悦他。在第109页上这样写着：“Mary had not known that she herself had been spoiled，but she could see quite plainly that this mysterious boy had been. He thought that the whole world belonged to him. How peculiar he was and how coolly he spoke of not living.”。他不想真正积极地活，但也不想死。但这次，是Mary让他振作起来了。

爱是可以传递的。我还记得一句名言：“I love you not because of who you are but because of who I am when I am with you.”。我爱你不是因为你是谁，而是因为

我和你在一起时的感觉。所以试着做我们自己，同时也试着让别人因自己的存在而感觉幸福。

——李秀文

在这四章中，给我印象最深的是那个可爱的男孩Dickon和Mr. Craven。来自贫困家庭的Dickon从未失去希望，他总是精力充沛、乐于助人。因为他，Mary才有了“第五个”朋友。除了Martha、Martha的妈妈、Robin and Ben，Dickon成了Mary的新朋友。Dickon是一个能使他周围的人感到舒适和高兴的男孩。然而，有一幕让我潸然泪下。他从草地上拾起外衣，从口袋里掏出一个小包裹，包在一块相当干净、粗糙、蓝白相间的手绢里。里面有两片厚厚的面包，中间夹着一片什么东西。“一般都是面包，”他说，“不过今天我还带了一片肥美的咸肉。”他从不抱怨贫穷的生活。他只是习惯了这样的生活。如果现在的人们能像他一样，孩子们能知足懂感恩，我们教师的工作将会更容易开展。更重要的是，Mr. Craven可以接受Martha母亲的建议，尽管他认为“Colin是一个可怜的孩子，他不能给其时间和关心”。因为Mary身边有很多热情的人，他们真的很关心她，所以Mary变成了一个真正的有血有肉的孩子，她会悲伤、紧张、关心，也会去爱。

——宋碧燕

通过这周的阅读，我们终于知道了秘密花园被锁十年之谜。在这个花园里面装着Colin父母的爱情故事，他们的爱情很美好，但是我认为这却对Colin非常不公平。Colin妈妈的过世对于Colin这个小小的男孩来说也是一种莫大的创伤，可是他爸爸却只顾自己沉浸在悲伤之中，甚至因为怕看到Colin触景伤情而有意避开他、忽略他，以至于让Colin在一个父母的爱都缺失的环境里长大。原本他只是失去了母亲，可是因为父亲的自私，Colin变成了父母都缺失了的野孩子，身边的仆人都只是在同情他，没有人给他无条件的包容和爱，更没有人指导他如何成长，就这样他自由发展成了一个古怪的小伙子。

——莫 然

在这几章里，Mary的性格发生了进一步的变化。她从原来非常自我的状态慢慢变得开始考虑他人的感受和对自己的评价了。

“Then Mary did a strange thing. She leaned forward and asked him a question she had never dreamed of asking anyone before. And she tried to ask it in Yorkshire because that was his language，and in India a native was always pleased if you knew him speech. ‘Does tha’s like me？’she said.”

从这一部分可以看出，Mary很在意Dickon对她的看法，也证明Mary走出了孤僻，开始愿意交朋友了。

接着作者在描述Mary的反应时，描述得特别有趣。“Her heart began to thump and she felt herself changing into a stiff，plain，silent child again.”

“Mary put her hand up to her throat because she was afraid he might see the excited lump which she felt jump into it. She came a step nearer to him.”

这一部分对Mary内心反应的描写真的很细微、很生动，她觉得自己又变成了一个呆板、平庸、沉默的孩子。Mary激动得心都快跳到喉咙口了，她怕他看出来，就用手捂住喉咙。这里又表现出了孩童情感的真挚和可爱!

——莫洁文

“He was a funny-looking boy about twelve.He looked very clean and his nose turned up and his cheeks were as red as poppies，and never had Mistress Mary seen such round such blue eyes in any boy’s face.”他看上去非常干净，鼻子向上翘着，脸颊红得像罂粟花，他那双眼睛啊，Mary小姐还从未见过这么圆这么蓝的眼睛。

从作者对Dickon外貌的描述可以看出，Dickon是个身体健康、很讲究卫生的孩子。虽然他生活在一个贫穷的家庭，但是他的父母和兄弟姐妹都很有爱，他的内心也充满了爱，他的心灵自然是健康的，他的身体也很健康。

“Who else could have been charming rabbits and pheasants as the natives charm snakes in India？”从这一句中可以看出，Dickon非常喜欢大自然中的小动物，对动物们很有爱心，小动物们也都喜欢他，他是个心中充满爱的人。

“She wished she could talk as he did. His speech was so quick and easy. It sounded as if he liked her and was not the least afraid she would not like him，though he was only a common moor boy，in patched clothes and with a funny face and a rough，rusty-red head.”

虽然Dickon是个普通的乡下小孩，衣服上还打了补丁，但他不做作、说话爽快、性格开朗、为人真诚、淳朴善良。Dickon的性格和为人对Mary的影响是巨大和深远的，从而使Mary的性格有了很大的改变。

——宋 蕾

我非常喜欢作者表述性格的文字，尤其是作者对于动词和名词的运用。作者运用她独特的写作手法，描述出Mary对他人关心的渴求，以及她想要的自由和让花园富有生机的期待。比如这个例子：“All the pink left Mary’s cheeks. Her heart began to thump and she felt herself changing into a stiff，plain，silent child again.”。

又如这句，“Mary put her hand up to her throat because she was afraid he might see the excited lump which she felt jump into it. She came a step nearer to him.”。Mary用手按住自己的喉咙，因为她害怕他会看到她激动的样子。这个描写太生动了，我几乎能看到Mary那个雀跃的表情。

Dickon和Mary的相遇让我回想起童年时候与小伙伴共度的时光，我们有共同的爱好，在假日的时光里我们会一起玩，还会为对方着想，彼此陪伴地做一些想做的事情。其实当孩子们返璞归真的时候，他们更能洞察事物的本来面貌。

——袁泳施

这几章的文字让我很感动。我能感觉到Mary的心跳，她正急切地等待着“Yes.”的答案。当然，这不是成年人的爱，而是孩子之间最纯洁、最朴素的感情。这意味着Mary完全走出了自己的孤独世界，接受了朋友的陪伴，期望别人也接受她的友善。对于一个叛逆的女孩来说，这真是一个巨大的变化。

当Dickon说“Yes.”的时候，他们开始比以往任何时候都更加努力、更加快乐地改造花园。Mary喜欢和他待在一起。她喜欢他的大嘴巴，还有鼻子。如果你喜欢和一个人在一起，天空就会变得更蓝，一切都会变得更顺利。正如著名作家林徽因所说：“你是人间最美四月天。”Dickon把最美丽的四月带给了Mary。

在接下来的章节里，Mary意外发现了Colin。Colin 独自一人在卧室，与外界隔绝了很长一段时间。他冷漠、孤独，缺乏安全感。他的世界毫无色彩，连他自己都觉得有一天他会死于疾病。Mary帮助他振作起来，带他进入了一个有趣的世界。她给他讲Dickon的事，给他描绘五彩缤纷的花园。Colin 对生活重新燃起了希望。Dickon 改变了Mary，Mary 改变了Colin。快乐和正能量就是这样传播了下去。

——关少娟

“Then Mary realized that somehow she had known at first that he was Dickon. Who else could have been charming rabbits and pheasants as the natives charm snakes in India? He had a wide，red，curving mouth and his smile spread all over his face.

As she came closer to him，she noticed that there was a clean fresh scent of heather and grass and leaves about him，almost as if he were made of them. She liked it very much and when she looked into his funny face with the red cheeks and round blue eyes she forgot that she had felt shy.”

在这几章节中，我印象最深的是Martha与Mary评论Dickon长相的这一段。Martha眼中的Dickon长得不怎么样，鼻子太翘、眼睛圆、嘴巴大，但Mary却认为这些都是Dickon的优点，她都喜欢。这让我想起一句话：情人眼里出西施。由此看来，Mary内心是很喜欢Dickon这个新朋友的，虽说他们才认识不久，但这种“喜欢”有点“一见钟情”的味道。在接下来的故事发展中，相信Dickon对Mary的影响也是很大的。我非常期待在接下来的故事中会发生更加有趣的事情。

——陈雪芬

在第11章里，我看到这样的一段描写："'My mother died when I was born and it makes him wretched to look at me. He thinks l don't know，but I've heard people talking. He almost hates me.' 'He hates the garden，because she died，' said Mary half speaking to herself."

看完这些，我不禁觉得Colin真的很可怜，也很无辜。他觉得自己的爸爸是讨厌他的。妈妈的死跟他的出现有关。我想孩子的内心是疑惑，也是自责的。哪一个孩子不喜欢取悦自己的父母，希望父母爱自己呢？但是在Colin 的身上，他没有感受过母爱，就连父爱，他感受到的仿佛也只有对自己的厌恶而已。他的性格之所以在众人眼中看上去怪异跋扈，恐怕也是环境使然。稚子无辜，我能明白Mr. Craven对亡妻的一往情深，但作为成年人，他的问题是沉迷过去，逃避现实。可是他的消沉也伤害了他的孩子。一切皆是由于爱之深吧。不过，我仍然很欣喜，Colin遇到了可爱的Mary，接下来他一定会在小伙伴的陪伴和帮助下，走出阴霾，拥抱阳光。

——徐 燕

小说内容越来越吸引人，越发有爱而鼓舞人心。第11章让我们对Dickon——the son of the nature有了更深的了解。他健康乐观、积极向上、淳朴善良、细心体贴，在离开秘密花园之前还给Mary留下了一张字条，"A nest with a bird sitting on it. Underneath were the printed letters and they said：'I will come back.'" Dickon指导并带领着Mary耕种秘密花园。这一切改变着Mary，让Mary心中有了爱，她告诉Dickon她喜欢他，还喜欢Martha、Martha's mother、the Robin and Ben Weatherstaff。Mary变得随和亲切，会主动与外界交流，更为让人感动的是她会把心中的爱传递给Colin，给他正能量并鼓舞他。

"Don't let us talk about dying；I don't like it. Let us talk about living. And they laughed so that in the end they were making as much noise as if they had been two ordinary healthy natural ten-year-old creatures—instead of a hard，little，unloving girl and a sickly boy who believed that he was going to die."

其中Mary哄Colin入睡的那一幕颇为温暖。

"'Shut your eyes，' said Mary，drawing her footstool closer，'and I will do what my Ayah used to do in India. I will pat your hand and stroke it and sing something quite low.' 'I should like that perhaps，' he said drowsily.

Somehow，she was sorry for him and did not want him to lie awake，so she leaned against the bed and began to stroke and pat his hand and sing a very low little chanting song in Hindustani. 'That is nice，' he said more drowsily still，and she went on chanting and stroking，but when she looked at him again his black lashes were lying close against his cheeks，for his eyes were shut and he was fast asleep. So she got up softly，took her candle and crept away without making a sound.”

在我看来，我们每个人都想要爱，每个人也都想被爱。那么，就让我们互相关爱而让世界更美好吧。

——李 丹

从这四章里我感觉到了Mary越来越明显的身心变化，仿佛已经从内到外地完全换了一个人，一个自私、脾气暴躁、不讨人喜欢的小女孩开始有了一个个好朋友，也不自觉地开始想要帮助别人，连身体都发生了变化，她自己说长胖了，也有力气了。

“And it was all so alive that Mary talked more than she had ever talked before—and Colin both talked and listened as he had never done either before. And they both began to laugh over nothings as children will when they are happy together.

And they laughed so that in the end they were making as much noise as if they had been two ordinary healthy natural ten-year-old creatures—instead of a hard，little，unloving girl and a sickly boy who believed that he was going to die.

They enjoyed themselves so much that they forgot the pictures and they forgot about the time. They had been laughing quite loudly over Ben Weather staff and his robin，and Colin was actually sitting up as if he had forgotten about his weak back，when he suddenly remembered something.”

一切都那么生机勃勃，Mary从没说过这么多话，也从没这样过。他们两个都开始没来由地大笑，就像小孩们高兴时在一起那样。仿佛他们已经成为两个正常、健康、自然的十岁小生灵——而非一个僵硬、瘦小、无爱心的小女孩，和一个生病的、自认将死的小男孩。他们自得其乐，忘记了图画，忘记了时间。Colin突然记起什么，竟然坐了起来，仿佛忘记了他软弱的后背。

文中提到Mary想要泥土去种东西，代表了她对自然和生活的热爱，这不由得让我想起英美文学中的“泥土”和“土壤”一般都代表了家园，代表一种归属感，可能也在某种程度上代表了Mary此时对这个地方的归属感和热爱。Colin眼中又大、又空、又阴沉的地方在她眼里是一个世界上最美丽的地方，上面长着成千上万可爱的东西，有成千上万的小动物在忙着筑巢、挖洞造穴，相互蹦跳、唱歌、吱吱尖叫。她完全是个热爱生活、热爱大自然的活泼可爱的小女孩。同时我也觉得此时此刻的Mary一定有着某种特有的魅力，能让Colin敞开心扉，忘记自己的病痛和烦恼。

——王之光

I read five chapters yesterday. Mary is so different now. She is very much absorbed about how to make *The Secret Garden* come alive. Finally，she has something interesting to be determined about.

Mary was odd, but now she is more outgoing. She disliked people and things so much, but now the world seemed to be getting nicer for her.

She was even beginning to like to be out of doors. She no longer hated the wind, but enjoyed it. Mary always felt tired and thin before. However, she could run faster and become heavier.

And Mary met Dickon and Colin, who are rather different from each other. She likes Dickon a lot and he seemed too good to be true. Dickon is quite friendly and is like an elder brother for her.

He taught her how to plant seeds and make things grow.

Colin is like a spoiled younger brother for her, given the situation Colin was in. I think it's understandable. And somehow Mary felt sorry for him and she would chant songs for him to make him sleep well. Perhaps Mary is the nicest person he has ever met. That's why Colin likes talking to Mary.

In the next chapters, I look forward to seeing how Mary and Dickon wake up the garden together and how she helped Colin get out of his room.

——麦佩莹

"You can have as much earth as you want," he said. "You remind me of some one else who loved the earth and things that grow. When you see a bit of earth you want, with something like a smile, take it, child, and make it come alive." My feeling: when I will give her the world, she asks instead for some earth.

Mr. Craven is paradoxical. It reminds him of his wife. He gave his wife a whole garden, but didn't accompany with her. Now! He wants to love Mary and give her a family, but he is afraid he can't take good care of Mary. 通过Mary和Mr. Craven之间的对话，我们了解到Mr. Craven对他亡妻的思念。在和Mary的对话中，Mary让他想起了他曾经给了亡妻整个庄园，但却没有陪伴她。Mr. Craven决定要好好宠爱Mary。

——郑剑湘

本章的文字像苏轼的"十年生死两茫茫，不思量，自难忘"那样温暖却又令人心痛。

"'Don't look so frightened.' He (Mr. Craven) exclaimed. 'Of course you may. I am your guardian, though I am a poor one for any child. I cannot give you time or attention. I am too ill, and wretched and distracted, but I wish you to be happy and comfortable. I don't know anything about children, but Mrs. Medlock is to see that you have all you need. I sent for you today because Mrs. Medlock said I ought to see you. Her daughter had talked about you. She thought you needed fresh air and freedom and running about.' "

When he asked Mary if she wanted toys, books or dolls. Mary asked, "might I have a bit of earth?" He gazed at her a moment and then passed his hand quickly over his eyes. "Do you—care about gardens so much?" He got up and began to walk slowly across the room. "You can have as much as earth as you want, you remind me of some one else who loved the earth and things that grow. When you see a bit of earth you want, with something like a smile, take it, child, and make it come alive."

To Mr. Craven: (Mrs. Craven) You left, you took my whole world away, only love for you still lives in my deep heart.

——Ting Feng

Chapter 15-17 of The Secret Garden

导 读

本期分享的内容是*The Secret Garden*的第15章至第17章——"Nest Building" "'I Won't!' Said Mary" "A Tanturm"。"secrets" "conflict"是这几章的关键词。从第15章的secrets shared中体悟到世界万物都有各自的秘密及处理方式，"秘密应该和值得信任的人分享"。以下是第15章中有关不同人之间的秘密的描写段落——

Mary想把花园的秘密告诉Colin，但又不能确定是否该告诉他。

"He was not in the least like Dickon，but he was evidently so pleased with the idea of a garden no one knew anything about that she thought perhaps he could be trusted. But she had not known him long enough to be sure. The second thing she wanted to find out was this：If he could be trusted—if he really could—wouldn't it be ."（P24）

从不和妈妈保守秘密的Dickon为了保护花园的秘密，第一次没有告诉妈妈，妈妈对他有小秘密的反应也是相当自然和充满信任的。

"But I says to mother，'Mother，' I says，'I got a secret to keep. It's not a bad 'un，tha' knows that. It's no worse than hidin' where a bird's nest is. Tha' doesn't mind it，does tha'？'

'It was just like her，what she said，' he answered. 'She gives my head a bit of a rub an' laughed an' she says，'Eh，lad，tha' can have all th' secrets tha' likes. I've known thee twelve years.' "

Dickon、Mary和知更鸟Robin之间的秘密和信任。

" 'Tha' knows us won't trouble thee，' he said to the robin. 'Us is near being wild things ourselves. Us is nest-building too，bless thee. Look out tha' doesn't tell on us.'

And though the robin did not answer，because his beak was occupied，Mary knew that when he flew away with his twig to his own corner of the garden the darkness of his dew-bright eye meant that he would not tell their secret for the world."

从第16—17章的 the conflict of Mary and Colin中能体会到“一物降一物”的道理。

面对Colin的歇斯底里，Mary针锋相对、毫不相让、反唇相讥，反而让无人敢惹的Colin安静下来。

“‘Shall they，Mr. Rajah！’ said Mary fiercely. ‘They may drag me in but they can’t make me talk when they get me here. I’ll sit and clench my teeth and never tell you one thing. I won’t even look at you. I’ll stare at the floor！’

‘What are you？’ said Mary. ‘Selfish people always say that. Any one is selfish who doesn’t do what they want. You’re more selfish than I am. You’re the most selfish boy I ever saw.’

‘You’re not！’ contradicted Mary unsympathetically.

‘I don’t believe it！’ said Mary sourly. ‘You just say that to make people sorry. I believe you’re proud of it. I don’t believe it！ If you were a nice boy it might be true—but you’re too nasty！’”

Colin被Mary冷落后大发脾气时，Mary去劝说Colin。Mary并没有好言安慰Colin，反而大声责骂他，但收到了很好的效果。

“‘You stop！’ she almost shouted. ‘You stop！ I hate you！ Everybody hates you！ I wish everybody would run out of the house and let you scream yourself to death！ You will scream yourself to death in a minute，and I wish you would！’ A nice sympathetic child could neither have thought nor said such things，but it just happened that the shock of hearing them was the best possible thing for this hysterical boy whom no one had ever dared to restrain or contradict.

‘If you scream another scream，’ she said，‘I’ll scream too—and I can scream louder than you can and I’ll frighten you，I’ll frighten you！’

‘You can！’ shouted Mary.

‘Half that ails you is hysterics and temper—just hysterics—hysterics—hysterics！’ and she stamped each time she said it.”

作者把孩子们之间争吵的童真、单纯，及孩子气十足的形象刻画得生动形象，让人倍感亲切。

伏尔泰说过：“每当第一遍读一本好书的时候，我仿佛觉得找到了一个朋友；当我再一次读这本书的时候，仿佛又和老朋友重逢。”读经典作品时，就会有这种感觉。

工作室人员分享

In Chapter 17，“tantrum”翻译过来是“（尤指儿童）耍脾气，使性子”。From the description of this chapter，we feel the temper of Colin，who is easy to get angry，drives mad almost，because he is sensitive，and gloomy，and he thinks he is very ill，and he will die soon. “He’s worked himself into hysterics.” （The nurse） said in a great hurry. “hysterics” 意为“歇斯底里的”，我们通常用angry、mad、crazy来描述愤怒、生气。这个词对我来说也很陌生，我们也可以想象Colin发起脾气来，是真的很可怕。“Facing a mad child，the nurse don’t know how to do，almost everybody has no idea to deal with the situation.So the nurse said to Mary，‘Do go，child，as quick as ever you can.’”对待一个发这么大火的孩子，一般都是成年人去哄，不想也不敢吓到孩子，这里怎么让一个孩子去哄他呢？后面紧接着说道：“It was not until afterward that Mary realized that the thing had been funny as well as dreadful—that it was funny that all the grown-up people were so frightened that they came to a little girl just because they guessed she was almost as bad as Colin himself.”。从这里可以看出，连Mary 事后都明白了事情的可笑又可怕，可笑的是所有的成年人害怕地去找一个小女孩，仅仅因为他们觉得她和Colin一样坏。接下来我们没有看到一个善良且有同情心的小孩的温柔安慰，而是看到了另一个也经常暴躁的小孩的大声呵斥。

——徐 燕

这几章，矛盾冲突的描写具体细致。一方面是Mary和Dickon在秘密花园里快乐地做着园丁，园子在他们的努力下焕发生机。Mary继续改变，她食量变大，身体长胖，脸色变红，性格开朗，对生活充满了热爱。知更鸟在园中筑巢，暗示着Mary的心已经在秘密花园里筑巢，她的快乐来源于此。另一方面，Colin由于长时间被困在房间里，脾气暴躁。他歇斯底里地朝着众人尖叫，发泄内心的压抑，他总觉得背上长瘤，将不久于世。“Do you think—I could—live to grow up？”这样悲观绝望的话出自一个孩子的口，让人心痛。两个小孩内心世界的强烈对比，突显大自然改造人的魔力。在第17章里，Colin发完脾气后冷静地剖析自我。“If he had had childish companions and had not lain on his back in the huge closed house，breathing an atmosphere heavy with the fears of people who were most of them ignorant and tired of him，he found out that most of his fright and illness was created by himself.”这段冲突后的描写说明了Colin迫切需要大自然和玩伴，为后来Colin走出房子，走进秘密花园做了铺垫。本章结尾，“The robin has found a mate—and is building a nest.”一句以类比的写作手法，暗示Colin也有了自己的玩伴和心灵沟通者，那就是Mary。

——关少娟

“‘Tell Colin that I can’t come and see him yet，’ she said to Martha.‘I’m very busy in the garden.’Martha looked rather frightened.

‘Eh！Miss Mary，’ she said，‘it may put him all out of humor when I tell him that.’ But Mary was not as afraid of him as other people were and she was not a self-sacrificing person.

‘I can’t stay，’ she answered.‘Dickon’s waiting for me.’And she ran away.”

这里的小细节很有意思，Mary让Martha给Colin带话说不去看他了，Martha吓坏了，怕Colin生气。而Mary就说她不怕他，而且她也不是一个自我牺牲的人。她不会因为Colin不开心而去改变自己的选择，不会因去迁就他而委屈自己。不得不说，正是Mary这样的不卑不亢，让Colin第一次有了像一个正常人一样被平等对待的感觉，不是畏惧，不是同情，也不是厌恶。这就是Colin从小到大最缺乏的，而后面的争吵与和解也是让他们情感进一步加深的催化剂。

——莫 然

“On that first morning when the sky was blue again，Mary wakened very early... Mary put her hand out of the window and held it in the sun.”

That’s the charm of nature. Sometimes if you stop your steps and spend some time to feel the beauty of nature，life will be much more beautiful. And our mind will be more positive and some trouble from our work，family or life will not be trouble anymore.

I think Mary also felt the charm of the nature. Because she said，“I’m getting fatter and fatter every day.” “Mrs. Medlock will have to get me some bigger dresses. Martha says my hair is growing thicker. It isn’t so flat and stringy.”

——宋碧燕

After a happy date with Dickon in the garden，Mary can’t help running back to share all sorts of nice things with Dickon. On the contrary, Colin was mad at her. They argued badly with each other. Colin was so angry and afraid to lose Mary.Mary was also angry because of his misunderstanding. Actually, it shows that Colin had his own feelings. He was not independent anymore. It was more lively.

——董筱研

Mary忙着和Dickon在秘密花园干活而忘记了Colin，Colin为此而大动肝火和Mary争吵起来，两人互不退让。这一幕充满了童真童趣：

“I’m not as selfish as your fine Dickon is.”

“He’s nicer than any other boy that ever lived. He’s a thousand times better.”

但进一步反映了Colin让人痛惜的悲惨身世。他面黄肌瘦（“It was a poor thin back to look at when it was bared. Every rib could be counted and every joint of the spine."），他郁郁寡欢、忧心忡忡，眼里满是并非他这个年龄应有的绝望。在护士告诉他后背没有lump（肿块）时，Colin猛地咽下一口气。在护士说要是能按伦敦医生说的去做，出去多多地待在新鲜空气里就会活下来时，Colin看到了生的希望。他朝Mary伸出手，"'I'll，I'll go out with you，Mary，' he said. 'I shan't hate fresh air if we can find.' He remembered just in time to stop himself from saying 'if we can find *The Secret Garden*，' and he ended，'I shall like to go out with you if Dickon will come and push my chair.'"。与此同时，Mary对Colin产生了怜悯之心，她顺从Colin的要求，低声地讲述着Colin同样感兴趣的秘密花园。正是Mary让Colin了解了外面的世界是多么让人兴奋，让他重拾了对生活的信心，找回了自己。

——李 丹

"'He always began to think about it when he was cross or tired，' she said to herself. 'And he has been cross today.Perhaps，perhaps she has been thinking about it all afternoon.' She stood still，looking down at the carpet and thinking. 'I said I would never go back again，' she hesitated，knitting her brows. 'but perhaps，just perhaps，I will go and see if he wants me—in the morning. Perhaps she'll try to throw his pillow at me again，but I think I'll go.'"

在Colin发脾气将Mary赶出房间后，她也无法狠心不理他："我是应该去看看，如果他要我去的话。也许他又会用枕头砸我，但我想我还是要去。"

还有，在第17章的结尾，Colin和Mary吵完架后，"His face looked dreadful，white and red and swollen，and he was gasping and choking."。Mary看着Colin那张可怜、疲倦的小脸，红肿的眼睛，便答应Colin这次睡觉时不只是唱歌，还会像第一天那样轻轻地说想象中的秘密花园的样子。Mary抓住Colin的手，慢慢地、轻轻地、耐心地讲起想象中秘密花园的样子，又轻又温柔的声音让Colin安静地睡着了。

我们不难看出，Mary的确已经具备了女性的温柔体贴。在作者的笔下，Mary被一点点地塑造成一个既有女性的温柔体贴，同时又具有像男人一样果敢独立、富有冒险精神的小女孩形象。这也越来越贴近那个时代英国作家们越来越强的女性意识，女主角大都具备了温柔、体贴、果敢、坚强，不依附于任何人的性格品质。

——王之光

在第15章中，"The nurse was just going to give up the case because she was so sick of him，but she says she doesn't mind staying now. 'You've gone on duty with her，' laughing a little."。在Mary的帮助下，Colin已经有所改变。虽然在后面的

章节中，两个被宠坏的孩子彼此成就和成长。虽然Mary是采取以暴制暴的方式，让少爷脾气以及对自己生命产生怀疑的Colin走了出来，最终拥抱生机和活力，但是，这种以暴制暴方式，前提是关心和爱，是友谊和信任的增长。在第15章中，我们看出，Mary 是在意他的感受的，小心翼翼地分享秘密花园，谨慎地介绍Dickon给他，关心他的病情。“The grand doctor had said that he must have fresh air and Colin had said that he would not mind fresh air in a secret garden. Perhaps if he had a great deal of fresh air and knew Dickon and the robin and saw things growing he might not think so much about dying.

Mary看见自己的转变，也想把好的东西分享给Colin。

“Mary had seen herself in the glass sometimes lately when she had realized that she looked quite a different creature from the child she had seen when she arrived from India.

This child looked nicer. Even Martha had seen a change in her. If gardens and fresh air had been good for her，perhaps they would be good for Colin.”

有了这些感情的培养和铺垫，后面两个孩子的沟通中的更多冲突与和解，才有了基础。

——李 玲

我对Mary哄睡Colin的这段话印象最深。Mary说道：“I think the ground is full of daffodils and snowdrops and lilies and iris working their way out of the dark.”（我想地上满是旱水仙、雪花莲、百合花、鸢尾花，在黑暗里起劲地往外长）“And the birds are coming to look at it，because it is so safe and still.”（鸟儿来看秘密花园，因为那里的一切是那么的安全又安宁）。Mary简单的几句话勾勒出秘密花园一派生机勃勃的景象，同时那里也是一片让人感到安全、宁静的乐土。Colin很快睡着了，是因为发脾气累了吗？不！拉着Mary的手，他感到踏实、宁静、无所畏惧；听着Mary讲话，他自己脑海中也慢慢浮现出秘密花园的样子，那个充满生的气息和希望的地方。也许他已经在梦中走进了秘密花园。

在我看来，Mary的存在对于Colin来说，象征着“活着”，有她在，他才有活着的希望和动力。也正是Mary的言语，一次次地给Colin带来生的希望，让Colin忘掉恐惧，让他相信他能活到长大。Colin能遇到Mary，真幸运！但在我们的生活中，却有很多像Colin这样对生活失去信心、失去希望的人。但愿现实中能涌现出更多像Mary这样的人，在别人困惑、失落、无助的时候，勇敢地对其施以援手！

——陈雪芬

We all know that we humans have different sides. Some bright positive sides and some dark negative sides. From Chapter 15 to 17，the story shows me the two kinds of characters collide together and reveals its climax.

In chapter 15，Dickon's affection infected Mary. And she was becoming much brighter. She loved the pretty garden so much that she couldn't help kissing the crocuses. "Mary bent her face down and kissed and kissed them." And Dickon told her affection can make others happy as well. He said， "I've kissed mother many a time that way when I come in from the moor after a day's roaming and she stood there at the door in the sun，looking so glad and comfortable."

But in Chapter 16，facing bad-tempered Collin，Mary stood very strong and stayed true to her own feelings. "Mary was not as afraid of him as other people were and she was not a self-sacrificing person." But later，Mr. Craven's gifts to her replaced her anger with pleasure. "Everything was so nice that her pleasure began to crowd her anger out of her mind. She had not expected him to remember her at all and her hard little heart grew quite warm." When she calmed down she changed her mind and decided to go to see Collin again. "I said I would never go back again." she hesitated，knitting her brows. "But perhaps，just perhaps，I will go and see—if he wants me—in the morning. Perhaps he'll try to throw his pillow at me again，but—I think—I'll go." Hesitated，but she finally made up her mind to see him again.

And of course，they were happy together just like childish children who are good at forgetting bad things. That's sweet.

So my feelings went up and down with their emotion changes. And once again I am reminded that emotions can be infectious，if we can be more positive and show the best of ourselves，we can make a difference to the people around us. "We love life，not because we are used to living but because we are used to loving." So just try to love what we do and be the best of ourselves.

——李秀文

In Chapter 1，Mrs. Medlock had said his father's back had begun to show its crookedness in this way when he was a child. He had never told anyone but Mary that most of his "tantrums" as they called them，grew out of his hysterical hidden fear. Mary had been sorry for him when he had told her. Colin如此地需要Mary，不是因为他吃醋，而是因为他终于找到了一个伴儿，一个和他年纪相当，可以陪他一起聊聊天、说说话，和他一起读书的人。而他的那些所谓的“仆人”，虽然表面百依百顺，但是都希望他早点死，没人愿意理他。像文中所说的：“他耳边偶然听梅得洛克太太和护士的窃窃私语使他产生了自己活不长的想法。”

"'I 'm not as selfish as you，because I 'm always ill，and I'm not sure there is a lump coming on my back.' he said. 'And I am going to die besides.'

'You are not!' contradicted Mary unsympathetically.

He opened his eyes quite wide with indignation. He had never heard such a thing said before.

'You didn't feel a lump!' contradicted Mary fiercely. 'If you did it was only a hysterical lump.Hysterics make lumps. There's nothing the matter with your horrid back—nothing but hysterics!'"

之前仆人对Colin都是百依百顺的，而且经常说他背上长了鼓包将要死了。而这次Mary却来了个一百八十度大转弯，能有一个跟他同样被惯坏了的小祖宗出来治治这个骄横、不可一世的病秧子，还真是救了他一命呢！

——宋 蕾

"On that first morning when the sky was blue again Mary wakened very early. The sun was pouring in slanting rays through the blinds and there was something so joyous in the sight of it that she jumped out of bed and ran to the window. She drew up the blinds and opened the window itself and a great waft of fresh，scented air blew in upon her. The moor was blue and the whole world looked as if something Magic had happened to it. There were tender little fluting sounds here and there and everywhere, as if scores of birds were beginning to tune up for a concert. Mary put her hand out of the window and held it in the sun."

以上是我最喜欢的段落，因为在这个文段中作者对景物进行了很多动态的描写，如"阳光从百叶窗倾斜而入""风吹拂在脸上""鸟儿要开演唱会"等，结合对Mary的细节动作描写"跳下床""打开百叶窗""伸手去感受"等，描写出一个很美并充满喜悦和希望的画面。

——莫洁文

After reading this chapter，I finally understand why Colin is really ill. While checking over Colin's body，the doctor says there is nothing wrong with him. He is just too weak to have a walk. And the doctor suggests the boy has a walk outside to breathe some fresh air. But the maids keep saying that he can't live because of his weak body. Even the boy's back is totally fine，they tell him that there are lumps on it. During the time he growing up，his dad，maids and everybody have thought and told that he would die soon. So what can he do except for believing it? His body is not ill，but his heart，for these wrong comments.Mary is not a friend，but a mentor to him. She brings his new and alive thoughts. She told him that he is not ill but just too weak to walk. And the overwhelming thought also fire up the first fight between them.

——夏丽焱

In this part，we can enjoy the fight between the two cousins（Mary and Colin）. The fights is like a steam clattering along.

"'You are a selfish thing！' cried Colin.

'What are you？' said Mary. 'Selfish people always say that. Any one is selfish who doesn't do what they want. You're more selfish than I am.You're the most selfish boy I ever saw.' 'I'm not！' snapped Colin. 'I'm not as selfish as your fine Dickon is！He keeps you playing in the dirt when he knows I am all by myself. He's selfish，if you like！' ... 'He's nicer than any other boy that ever lived！' she said. 'He's—he's like an angel！' ...

'A nice angel！' Colin sneered ferociously. 'He's a common cottage boy off the moor！'

'He's better than a common Rajah！' retorted Mary. 'He's a thousand times better！' ...

'I won't let that boy come here if you go and stay with him instead of coming to talk to me，' he said.

'If you send Dickon away，I'll never come into this room again！' she retorted. 'You'll have to if I want you，' said Colin."

Enjoy fight，enjoy life！It is fun to have a buddy to fight with.

——Ting Feng

Chapter 18-20 of The Secret Garden

导 读

这一期的内容是*The Secret Garden*的Chapter 18 “Tha'munnot Waste No Time”，Chapter 19 “It Has Come！”和Chapter 20 “I Shall Live Forever”。

这三章讲述了Colin在认识Mary前、认识Mary初期和接受Mary与Dickon帮助后的变化过程。

在认识Mary前，Colin是一个体弱多病、心态悲观、不自信却又渴望与外界联系的孩子。

“The boy had a sharp，dedicate face the color of ivory and he seemed to have eyes too big for it. He had also a lot of hair which tumbled over his forehead in heavy locks and made his thin face seem smaller. He looked like a boy who had been ill，but he was crying more as if he were tired and cross than as if he were in pain.”

长期的隔离照顾导致他看起来像一个生过病的孩子，但他哭得更像是疲倦和生气，而不是痛苦，他的性格也很孤僻。

“‘I wish I was friends with things，’ he said at last，‘but I'm not. I never had anything to be friends with，and I can't bear people.’”

从Colin的这一段内心独白可以看出，他多么渴望与外界产生联系。

在认识Mary初期，Colin表现得很敏感。当Mary关心他时他很开心；当他看到Mary与Dickon玩得很好时又很嫉妒，时常怀疑自己随时要死，甚至歇斯底里地哭。此时，Colin对Mary产生了极大的依赖。

“I hate you when you said he was like an angle and I laughed at you but—but perhaps he is.”

从这里可以看出Colin相当的敏感和不自信。

后来，在Mary的耐心陪伴，在Mary和Dickon的共同帮助下，Colin变成了一个对一切都抱有好奇心且积极乐观的阳光男孩。

“That night Colin slept without once awakening and when he opened his eyes in the morning he lay still and smiled without knowing it—smiled because he felt so curiously comfortable... his mind was full of the plans he and Mary had made yesterday, of pictures of the garden and of Dickon and his wild creatures. It was so nice to have things to think about."

"'Is it?' cried Colin, and his eyes began to search the ivy with eager curiousness."

改变后的Colin睡眠改善了很多，他也感觉到出奇的舒服，开始可以勇敢地去探索外界了。

最后，Colin可以自信地跟Mary和Dickon说："I shall get well! I shall get well! And I shall live forever and ever and ever!"。

读到这里，我们可以感受到此时的Colin和之前那个悲观的Colin有着天壤之别。

那么，小小年纪的Mary是如何使Colin有了这么喜人的变化呢？我们来看看Colin出现以下表现时，Mary是如何应对的。

当Colin自己一个人在房间里哭的时候，Mary来到他身边陪伴他并且跟他聊天；当Colin变得很敏感，对Mary过分依赖时，Mary并没有觉得他厌烦或逃离他，而是依然陪伴着他，表达自己的想法，同时给Colin带来新鲜食物，把Colin负面的注意力转移到正面的事物上；当Colin变得积极、对一切好奇的时候，她带他到外面的世界，引导他多看身边美好的事物。Mary在陪伴Colin的过程中做到了"先接纳后引导"。

"先接纳后引导"其实是教育工作中很重要的一个环节。当我们接纳孩子的时候，孩子才会感受到被尊重，才愿意倾听我们的建议，我们的教育引导工作才能得以进行。否则，成人和孩子之间会在情绪冲突中耗费大量的精力，这样就达不到我们想要的教育效果了。

工作室人员分享

"That night Colin slept without once awakening and when he opened his eyes in the morning he lay still and smiled without knowing it—smiled because he felt so curiously comfortable. It was actually nice to be awake, and he turned over and stretched his limbs luxuriously."

今天我想和大家分享我对上述文段中两次出现的"awake"这个词的理解。在上面文段中，"awake"这个词出现了两次，我认为它们的意思虽然一样，但是不同的时态却反映出Colin前后两种不同的状态。Colin之前总会半夜醒来，很难一觉睡到天亮，"醒来"对于Colin来说是一件痛苦的事情。但认识Mary后，他发现醒来是一件很nice的事情，因为他的生命迎来了"春天"。此篇章名为"It Has Come!"，除了像文中Mary说的那样，秘密花园等来了春天，终将迎来生机勃勃的景象以外，还意味着Colin的生命也将重现生机，他未来的生活也将像秘密花园那样，充满惊喜，充满希望。

——陈雪芬

在这三章中，Mary选择信任Colin的这一段令我感触特别深。内心不断地煎熬，但Mary最终还是选择了信任Colin。她很可能会和Colin分享花园的秘密。她是这样说的——"'Can I trust you? I trusted Dickon because birds trusted him. Can I trust you—for sure—for sure?' She implored."（"我能相信你吗？我信任Dickon，因为小鸟相信他。我能相信你吗？当然——肯定？"她恳求道）。

孩子们是如此的天真无邪，当他们拥有了自己认为可以相信的好朋友时，他们就会把自己珍爱的东西分享给他们。他们选择相信朋友，就不会去隐藏秘密，他们面对朋友时足够坦诚。很多时候，这对你来说不是一件大事，但对孩子来说却是他的整个世界。

Colin看到了Dickon吸引动物的魅力，他被这种活泼吸引住了。Dickon和他的动物给了Colin一个完全不同的世界。

——董筱妍

在这三章中，Mary、Colin和Dickon之间的美好关系让我印象深刻。Mary和Colin能拥有这样一个神奇又温柔的童年玩伴让我羡慕不已。

Dickon在Mary和Colin的生活中简直就是一种特别的存在。在第19章中，Colin初遇Dickon："Colin had never talked to a boy in his life and he was so overwhelmed by his own pleasure and curiosity that he did not even think of speaking."。而Dickon表现是："But Dickon did not feel the least shy or awkward."。Colin长这么大还从来没和男孩子说过话，那席卷一切的兴奋与好奇使他话都说不出来了。而反观Dickon："He had not felt embarrassed because the crow had not known his language and had only stared and had not spoken to him the first time they met. Creatures were always like that until they found out about you."。Dickon丝毫不觉得局促与不安。Dickon进来，带着他最好看的微笑，新生的羊羔在他怀里，红色小狐狸在他身旁轻快地小跑着。"坚果"坐在他左肩上，"煤灰"在右肩上，"果壳"的头和爪子从他外套口袋里探出来。画面感满满的一个平和的阳光男孩。

还有，在第20章里罗奇先生对Dickon的评价让我难忘：

"There really was a sort of Magic about Dickon，as Mary always privately believed. When Mr. Roach heard his name he smiled quite leniently. He'd be at home in Buckingham Palace or at the bottom of a coal mine."（那孩子不管是到了白金汉宫还是在煤坑底下，都是一样自在）。

我眼中的Dickon是个神奇的男孩子，他就像一个会魔法的男孩，不仅是动物和植物们的朋友，也是改变熊孩子Mary与Colin的最主要功臣。我甚至认为Dickon是大自然的化身，他不是真实存在的形象。我对于Mary和Colin能够拥有这样一个神奇又温柔的童年玩伴感到十分羡慕。

——王之光

在这三章中，我关注的是Mary和Colin的变化。Mary，这个刚刚获得了一点点爱的女孩，立即把爱又反哺给了Colin。她对Colin的信任是举棋不定的，但她又强烈地希望帮助他。书中的很多地方都描写了这种情况：

“‘I won’t be long，’ she said. ‘I’m going to Dickon，but I’ll come back. Colin，it’s—it’s something about the garden.’ Mary was so anxious that she got up from her stool and came to him and caught hold of both his hands.

‘Can I trust you？ I trusted Dickon because birds trusted him. Can I trust you—for sure—for sure？’ she implored.

Mary hesitated about two minutes and then boldly spoke the truth.”

Colin这个从出场就让人感到压抑和窒息的人物形象，慢慢开始变得阳光、温暖起来，对生活充满了希望和向往。

“‘Please ask Miss Mary if she’ll please come on，talk to me？’ Think o’ him saying please！”

He looked so strange and different because a pink glow of color had actually crept all over him—ivory face and neck and hands and all. ‘I shall get well！ I shall get well！’ he cried out. ‘Mary！ Dickon！ I shall get well！ And I shall live forever and ever and ever！’”

——郑剑湘

第18章开头Martha 说的一句话，给我触动很大。“Mother says as th’ two worst things as can happen to a child is never to have his own way——or always to have it.” “妈妈说对于一个孩子来说，有两种情况是最要不得的，一种是对他什么都要管，另一种就是什么都不管。”

这句话折射出了当今社会中的两种父母。第一种是为孩子安排好一切，包括生活上无微不至的照顾和决定权上的剥夺。父母以爱为名，什么都干涉。这样的孩子永远是按照父母的意志活着，没有独立生活和独立思考的能力，甚至没有独立的人格。通常说的高分低能者就属于这一类。另一种是什么都不管，比如留守儿童；或者溺爱，任由孩子玩游戏、抽烟、打架。这类孩子通常霸道、自私、缺乏责任感。

所以，Martha的妈妈真的是一个很有教育理念的妈妈。她学历不高，家里经济条件不好，生活在社会的底层，但是培养出来的孩子，即Martha和Dickon都是那么善良、阳光，热爱自然、热爱生活。两个孩子都成为Mary和Colin的心灵引路人。在这点上，她真的很了不起！一个妈妈会不会教育小孩，有时候真的和学历没有关系，和经济没有关系，而是和素养、人品、生活理念及处事风格有关系。

在什么都管和什么都不管之间，应该有个度。度在哪里？什么该管？什么不该管？我想，这是每一个父母都要思考的问题。

——关少娟

阅读了这三章，让人心情愉悦，一切朝着美好的方向发展。在Chapter 18中，我感受到了Mary的善良。原本早餐后先去见Dickon，因为得知Colin发病而果断决定先去看Colin。这一章也让我感受到了Mary的可爱。她学着用约克郡话和Dickon、Colin交流，听起来滑稽可笑，Mary自己也会大笑起来。Chapter 19将Dickon这个动物们的守护神形象描写得淋漓尽致。Dickon了解每一种动物的习性，有一群动物朋友和他形影不离。Mary和Dickon的善良影响着Colin，他们谋划着带Colin去秘密花园并付诸行动。其中让我内心颇为温暖的是Chapter 20里面的两处描写。一处是对去秘密花园沿路风景的描写。“Dickon began to push the wheeled chair slowly and steadily. Mistress Mary walked beside it and Colin leaned back and lifted his face to the sky. The arch of it looked very high and the small snowy clouds seemed like white birds floating on outspread wings below its crystal blueness. The wind swept in soft big breaths down from the moor and was strange with a wild clear scented sweetness. Colin kept lifting his thin chest to draw it in，and his big eyes looked as if it were they which were listening—listening，instead of his ears.”另一处是描写Colin发自内心的呐喊。“And the sun felt warm upon his face like a hand with a lovely touch. He looked so strange and different because a pink glow of color had actually crept all over him—ivory face and neck and hands and all. ‘I shall get well! I shall get well！’ he cried out. ‘Mary！ Dickon！ I shall get well！ And I shall live forever and ever and ever！’”

满园春色因三个孩子而美轮美奂，更加富有生机。

——李 丹

作为老师，我们有很多共同点。我们一大早就起床，照顾学生和家人，晚上很晚才睡觉。通常我们觉得自己太忙太累，没时间做别的事。我们因为站得太久腿都累了，因为说得太多嗓子也疼。我们的脖子、肩膀和背部都很疼，因为我们要准备课程和检查作业。等一下，这些都是我们想象出来的吗？在读完第18到20章后，我突然意识到也许我应该停下来，好好想想，放松一下。上周，我被第17章中的一段话给震惊了，Mary说Colin并没有他想象的那么病态。“If he had ever had any one to talk to about his secret terrors—if he had ever dared to let himself ask questions—if he had had childish companions and had not lain on his back in the huge closed house，breathing an atmosphere heavy with the fears of people who were most of them ignorant and tired of him，he would have found out that most of his fright and illness was created by himself. But he had lain and thought of himself and his aches and weariness for hours and days and months and years. And now that an angry unsympathetic little girl insisted obstinately that he was not as ill as he thought he was, he actually felt as if she might be speaking the truth.”

从第18章到第20章，Colin开始放松自己的警惕，让Mary和Dickon进入他的世界，他自己也试图忘记自己的问题，开始探索外面的世界。他对Craven医生说："When I lie by myself and remember I begin to have pains everywhere and I think of things that make me begin to scream because I hate them so. If there was a doctor anywhere who could make you forget you were ill instead of remembering it I would have him brought here."。最后，在第20章，他情不自禁地感叹道："I shall get well！I shall get well！""Mary！Dickon！I shall get well！And I shall live forever and ever and ever！"。一旦放松自我防卫，我们同样可以自由了。

我这周四和周五晚上去健身房上瑜伽课，感觉很好。更多的运动，更多的汗水，更多的乐趣。一个小小的改变就会有很大的不同。"Life isn't about waiting for the storm to pass，it's about learning to dance in the rain.""生活不是等待暴风雨过去，而是要学会在雨中跳舞。"所以我决定为了更健康、更漂亮，为了更好的心情而锻炼。

——李秀文

在这三章中，我可以从字里行间感受到Colin的希望与喜悦。他的身体和心灵变得越来越强大，而不是像以前一样病恹恹和绝望了。我对下面这个部分印象深刻——"the sun felt warm upon his face like a hand with a lovely touch.And in wonder Mary and Dickon stood and stared at him.He looked so strange and different because a pink glow of color had actually crept all over him—ivory face and neck and hands and all."。我喜欢"a pink glow"这个描述，这表明Colin已不同于过去了。粉红色的光芒意味着他看起来精力充沛，也就是Colin想过好生活的愿望和可能性。Mary和Dickon对帮助Colin改变做出了巨大的贡献，因为他们给了Colin勇气、快乐和信心。当一个人对自己的生活有了希望，自然就会以更乐观的心态去生活。我认识到如果我们都能不遗余力地去帮助和鼓励有需要的人，他或她就不会太悲观。所以，传播积极的精神对每个人都至关重要。

——麦佩莹

Martha妈妈说的话让人非常有共鸣：一个孩子最大的不幸就是不能一直自己做决定，或者一直都是自己做决定。也就是说，一个孩子最大的不幸就是被家长完全控制或者被家长完全放任。这两种状态都是很糟糕的，因为父母的责任是帮助孩子们建立良好的价值观，陪伴他们成长，帮助他们慢慢累积经验去成为自立自强的人，而这两种都不能帮助孩子成长。

而后面说到一直被放任的Colin居然用了please来请Mary去看他，可见Mary的存在就像是填补了Colin父母对他的关心和教育的缺失，她帮助Colin去改变，使他慢慢从一个自以为是的人成为一个更好的人。当然，Mary自己也是这样走过来的，所以就和Colin更有共鸣了。

——莫 然

“Ben说我像他。”Mary说，“他说他敢说我们俩都有同样的坏脾气。我觉得你也像他。我们三个都一样——你、我和Ben。他说我们两个人都不怎么好看，我们就像我们看上去那样酸。但在我认识知更鸟和Dickon之后，我感觉不像以前那么酸了。”他们相似但又不同。Ben因罗宾而变；Mary变了，因为Martha和Dickon；Colin也因为Mary和Dickon而改变。

“当我独自躺在床上，想起我开始浑身疼痛，想起那些让我开始尖叫的事情，因为我太恨它们了。如果哪位医生能让你忘记自己病了，而不是想起病来，我就叫人把他带到这儿来。”他挥动着一只纤细的手，那只手本来应该戴着有皇家印章的红宝石戒指的。“正是因为我的表妹让我忘记了，她才让我变得更好。”我觉得这就是Mary的魔力。她了解Colin，她总是乐于帮助Colin。她治好了Colin的心病。她给了Colin活下去的希望。心情和态度有时比身体健康更重要。

“那是新鲜空气，”她说，“仰面躺下，深呼吸。Dickon躺在荒野上的时候就是这么做的。他说他的血管里有这种感觉，这种感觉让他变得强壮，他觉得自己好像能永远活下去。呼吸它，呼吸它。”

“永远永远！”这让他有这种感觉吗？照她说的做了，一遍又一遍地深深地吸着气，直到他感到有一件全新的、令人愉快的事情发生在他身上。

春天来了，Colin的春天也来了。春天意味着万物苏醒，一切变得更好，充满活力。在某种程度上，这是春天。Colin的新生活才刚刚开始。

——宋碧燕

Mary几次提到Dickon，说明Mary被Dickon的行为和思想深深地影响了。但我们也感受到，Mary又把她得到的帮助和关爱传递给了Colin，Mary对Colin也产生了很大的影响。这些说明帮助和关爱是可以相互传递的。文中有Mary说的一段话，“你吸呀，你吸呀。”然后Colin就说：“可以一直活下去！”于是Colin便照着她的吩咐去做，一次又一次地深呼吸，到后来果真体会到了身上有一种全新的愉快的感觉。Colin这十年间一直处于自闭、孤僻的状态，他害怕开窗，害怕被人看见，总觉得自己要死了。当遇到Mary后，他慢慢变得接受大自然、接受新鲜空气、接受新事物，性格也变得开朗乐观起来，而且有了活下去的勇气。

——宋 蕾

通过之前的阅读，我本以为Dickon只是一个普普通通的小男孩，说着一口浓重的约克郡地方话，对所有人都热情善良。但他其实是一个魔法师，知道如何倾听动物的交流，向大自然和儿童念咒语。在第19章中，是这么写的：

"Even Colin is the rajah to the land of moor, Dickon treats him as a normal boy. He is not a servant to anybody, but a servant to nature. So he knows how to communicate with animals and sew and plant.

Around him are so many gorgeous creatures, so he can easily bring his love to other children whose faces are sore and temper are bad."

权力和地位永远不能让Dickon俯首称臣，只有奇妙的大自然才是他唯一的主人。他用心服侍农田，所以他家的土豆产量永远最高；他用爱倾听鸟儿和松鼠的吵闹，所以他能"听懂"动物间的交流；他尊重每一个孩子，不论年纪大小、地位高低，所以他们才能成为朋友。

因为爱，Dickon听懂了大自然和动物；因为尊重，他交到了Mary和Colin这两个朋友。

——夏丽焱

让我印象深刻的是第20章的几处描写。在这一章里，我们可以看见Colin在Mary和Dickon的帮助下坐着轮椅出了房间。对他而言，这绝对是迈出了人生的重要一步。作者对环境的刻画与描写，就从侧面向我们展示了这份美好。

"Dickon began to push the wheeled chair slowly and steadily. Mistress Mary walked beside it and Colin leaned back and lifted his face to the sky. The arch of it looked very high and the small snowy clouds seemed like white birds floating on outspread wings below its crystal blueness. The wind swept in soft big breaths down from the moor and was strange with a wild clear scented（有香味的）sweetness.Colin kept lifting his thin chest to draw it in, and his big eyes looked as if it were they which were listening— listening, instead of his ears."（Colin身体后仰，抬脸向天，苍穹高耸，雪白的小云朵像白色的鸟儿，伸展着翅膀漂浮在水晶般清澈的天空下。大股的柔风从旷野上荡过来，带着野外的清澈香气。Colin不断鼓起瘦小的胸膛，吸进它，他的大眼睛看上去，仿佛是它们在倾听，而不是他的耳朵）

通过这些文字的比喻和刻画，我们感受到了一幅清晰的画面：三个稚气的孩子，带着探索的、好奇的心，小心翼翼地进入神秘花园。一切都是那么新奇有趣，鸟语花香，大自然如此美好，叫人心情更为明朗。我们不禁和Colin一样非常享受地欣赏着这一切。随着一步步进入花园深处，一个热爱生活、充满阳光的Colin就此诞生。

——徐 燕

Colin对死亡和疾病的思考让他更焦虑。死亡和疾病让我们恐惧，对小孩来说就更自然了。但同时他也开始思考要如何生存下去。他感觉到了自然的力量，这让他开心。我还记得他曾说过："I wish I was friends with things , but I'm not. I never had anything to be friends with and I can't bear people."。"我希望我有朋友，但我没有。从来没有人愿意和我当朋友，我也受不了其他人。"他过去消极地面对生活，对未来一无所求，这让我为他感到伤心。每个人都应该有自己的归属，不是吗？所幸，他遇见了Mary。对他而言，Mary就像是秘密花园的钥匙，她能打开他的心结。

而Mary也逐渐变得强大了，面对悲剧，她并没有展露出消极的一面，而是试着用她的乐观主义带给大家希望。这也帮助了Colin战胜心魔。所以我们永远不要忘记积极的态度，学着打开我们自己的秘密花园，在克服困难的同时，也为他人伸出援助之手。

——袁泳施

This part is like a picture of spring. It is jolly，positive，hopeful and lifeful.

"You smell like flowers and—and fresh things，" he cried out quite joyously. "What is it you smell of? It's cool and warm and sweet all at the same time."

...And then she began to laugh too and they both laughed until they could not stop themselves and they laughed until the room echoed and Mrs. Medlock opening the door to come in drew back into the corridor and stood listening amazed...

That night Colin slept without once awakening and when he opened his eyes in the morning he lay still and smiled without knowing it—smiled because he felt so curiously ...

"Open the window！" he added，laughing half with joyful excitement and half at his own fancy. "Perhaps we may hear golden trumpets！" And though he laughed，Mary was at the window in a moment and in a moment more it was opened wide and freshness and softness and scents and birds' songs were pouring through.

"That's fresh air，" she said. "Lie on your back and draw in long breaths."

"Are you sure you are not chilly，Master Colin？" she inquired.

"No，" was the answer. "I am breathing long breaths of fresh air. It makes you strong. I am going to get up to the sofa for breakfast. My cousin will have breakfast with me."

"I shall get well！ I shall get well！" he cried out. "Mary！ Dickon！ I shall get well！ And I shall live forever and ever and ever！"

心若向阳，万物生光。

——Ting Feng

Chapter 21-23 of The Secret Garden

导 读

今天我们一起来分享*The Secret Garden*的第21章"Ben Weatherstaff"，第22章"When the Sun Went Down"和第23章"Magic"这三章的精彩内容。首先，我们来分析一下故事中Ben Weatherstaff 这个人物吧！

"None as any one can find，an' none as is anyone's business. Don't you be a meddlesome wench an' poke your nose where it's no cause to go. Here，I must go on with my work. Get you gone an' play you. I've no more time."（Chapter 4）

"And he actually stopped digging，threw his spade over his shoulder and walked off，without even glancing at her or saying goodbye."（Chapter 4）

从这两段可以看出来，Ben这个人很倔强、傲慢，脾气也很古怪。

Mary and Dickon wheeled about and looked. There was Ben Weatherstaff's indignant face glaring at them over the wall from the top of a ladder！He actually shook his fist at Mary.（Chapter 21）

从这一段可以看出来，Ben对Mary和Dickon进花园感到很气愤，他本想牢牢守住这个秘密。

"'But no one has been in it for ten years！' cried Colin.'There was no door！'

'I'm no one，' said old Ben dryly.'And I didn't come through the door. I come over th'wall. Th' rheumatics held me back th'last two year'.'

'She was so fond of it—she was！' said Ben Weatherstaff slowly.

'An' she was such a pretty young thing. She says to me once，"Ben，" says she laughin' "if ever I'm ill or if I go away you must take care of my roses." When she did go away th'orders was no one was ever to come nigh. But I come，' with grumpy obstinacy.'Over th' wall I come—until th' rheumatics stopped me—an' I did a bit o' work once a year. She'd gave her order first.'"（Chapter 22）

从这一段可以看出来，Ben是一个对主人忠心耿耿的仆人，虽然主人已经离世，上头命令谁也不许靠近这园子，可是他却不顾风险，偷偷爬墙进来修建园子。

接下来我们一起看一看Colin身上发生的巨大改变。（Great changes that happened to Colin）

第一，在花园里的变化（Changes in the garden）。

“Even his ivory whiteness seemed to change. The faint glow of color which had shown on his face and neck and hands when he first got inside the garden really never quite died away. He looked as if he were made of flesh instead of ivory or wax.”

第二，遇到Ben之后的变化（Changes after meeting Ben）。

“Colin was standing upright—upright—as straight as an arrow and looking strangely tall.”

第三，在Mary帮助下的变化（Changes with the help of Mary）。

“An odd expression came into his face and he began to scratch at the earth. His thin hand was weak enough，but presently as they watched him—Mary with quite breathless interest—he drove the end of the trowel into the soil and turned some over.”

第四，在Dickon帮助下的变化（Changes with the help of Dickon）。

“It seemed very certain that something was upholding and uplifting him. He sat on the seats in the alcoves，and once or twice he sat down on the grass and several times he paused in the path and leaned on Dickon，but he would not give up until he had gone all round the garden.”

最后，我们一起来探讨书中提到的大自然的魔力。

“They always called it Magic，and indeed it seemed like it in the months that followed—the wonderful months—the radiant months—the amazing ones. Oh！The things which happened in that garden！If you have never had a garden，you cannot understand，and if you have had a garden，you will know that it would take a whole book to describe all that came to pass there.”

大自然是万物之源，大自然有着无穷的魅力，有着无穷的力量。就像这个花园，如果能在这里体会四季的变化，大自然的美便能尽收眼底。

Colin妈妈的魔力（Magic：Colin’s mother）

“‘Mrs. Craven was a very lovely young lady，”he had gone on rather hesitatingly. “An’mother she thinks maybe she’s about Misselthwaite many a time lookin’ after Mester Colin，same as all mothers do when they’re took out o’ th’ world. They have to come back，tha’ sees. Happen she’ been in the garden an’ happen it was her set us to work，an’ told us to bring him here.’ Mary had thought he meant something about Magic.”

Colin的母亲是一个美丽优雅、智慧坚韧、无私奉献的女性。文中体现了她温柔体贴、美丽善良、热爱自然的完美形象。

Mary的魔力（Magic：Mary）

"'You can do it! You can do it! I told you, you could! You can do it! You can do it! You can!'

She was saying it to Colin because she wanted to make Magic and keep him on his feet looking like that."

Mary是一个温柔体贴的小女孩，她的鼓励和耐心就像魔力一样唤醒了沉睡的Colin，让他鼓足勇气重新站起来。

Dickon的魔力（Magic：Dickon）

"Secretly she quite believed that Dickon worked Magic, of course, good Magic, on everything near him and that was why people liked him so much and wild creatures knew he was their friend."

一个整日穿梭在沼泽地的小男孩，有一群动物朋友和他形影不离，他了解每一种动物的习性，也会栽培各种各样的植物，他家一块不大的菜地被他打理得井井有条，他还细心地在围起的石墙上栽种了小花，充满情趣。虽然他是一个穷人家的孩子，但是他很善良，他帮助Mary改掉了很多毛病，Dickon让Mary变得健康、开朗。他给Mary讲了许许多多有趣的事情，和Mary一起装扮秘密花园，让花园重现生机。Dickon乐观开朗的性格同时也影响了Colin，让Colin慢慢变得乐观起来。

Colin想到的魔力（Magic that Colin thinks of）

"The sun is shining—the sun is shining. That is the Magic. The flowers are growing—the roots are stirring. That is the Magic . Being alive is the Magic—being strong is the Magic. The Magic is in me—the Magic is in me. It is in me—it is in me. It's in every one of us. It's in Ben Weatherstaff's back. Magic! Magic! Come and help!"

当Colin对周围的一切充满阳光和喜乐时，他重拾了信心，相信自己可以战胜一切困难，勇往直前，这就是自信的魔力。

我的感受（Feelings）

1.Where there is great love, there are always miracles.

2.A confident person will only move forward.

3.In real life, every cause has the confidence to start, and by the confidence of the first step.

工作室人员分享

"'I shall stop being queer,' he said, 'if I go every day to the garden. There is Magic in there—good Magic, you know, Mary. I am sure there is.'

'So am I,' said Mary.

‘Even if it isn’t real magic，’ Colin said，‘we can pretend it is. Something is there—something！’

‘It’s Magic，’ said Mary，‘but not black. It’s as white as snow.’”

我认为从以上对话内容中可以看出，让秘密花园变得如此美丽的魔法是小伙伴对它的爱与照顾。作者想表达的是如果我们每个人心中都有爱，我们也可以拥有“魔法”，让一切都变得美好的魔法。

——陈雪芬

在这三章中Mary最让我印象深刻，在这里我们可以看到Mary 的角色变化：a magic believer—a magic maker—a trainer/teacher。起初Mary就相信魔法，她坚定地告诉其他人Colin能够成功。“‘He can do it！ He can do it！ He can do it！ He can！’ She gabbled over to herself funder her breath as fast as ever she could.”

面对Colin，她非常自信地鼓励着他：“You can do it！ You can do it！ I told you，you could！ You can do it！ You can do it！ You can！”。对Colin来说，她就是魔法制造者。当她发现Colin和Craven的沟通发生了问题时，她就变成了一个老师。她拿自己当例子，“It must have been very horrid to have had to be polite for ten years to a boy who was always rude. I would never have done it.”。Mary教会Colin站在对方的角度考虑问题：“‘If you had been his own boy and he had been a slapping sort of man，’ said Mary，‘he would have slapped you.’”

“For Mary，magic means growth.”魔法给了Colin站起来的力量，所以魔法就是你身边所见之物。而对Mary来说，魔法就是成长。“Perhaps the beginning is just to say nice things are going to happen until you make them happen.”

——董筱妍

这几章让我印象最为深刻的是Colin对魔法的解释。在第21章开头说道：“One of the strange things about living in the world is that it is only now and then one is quite sure one is going to live forever and ever and ever.”。是大自然让性格怪异、体弱多病的Mary和Colin变得美丽、健康。

“I have never seen the sun rise but Mary and Dickon have and from what they tell me I am sure that is Magic too. Something pushes it up and draws it. Sometimes since I’ve been into the garden，I’ve looked up through the trees at the sky and I have had a strange feeling of being happy as if something were pushing and drawing in my chest and making me breathe fast. Magic is always pushing and drawing and making things out of nothing.” “‘Then I will chant，’ he said. And he began，looking like a strange boy spirit. ‘The sun shining—the sun is shining.’”

读到这里，我不禁感慨友情和大自然对孩子成长的奇妙力量。如何让孩子在友情和大自然的滋养下更加顺利地成长，是值得我们思索的问题。

——郑剑湘

这三章是故事的高潮。每个孩子都情绪高昂，深深感受到了自己的巨大变化。Colin一直认为自己会死，但现在宣布，他会活着！作者从三个方面描写了这种变化。

首先，从花园的描述中。“At first it seemed that green things would never cease pushing their way through the earth，in the grass，in the beds，even in the crevice of the walls. Then the green things began to show buds and the buds began to unfurl and show color....”（Chapter 23）花园里的植物顽强地成长，在地里，在草丛里，在花床上，甚至在墙缝里，开始发芽，冒花苞。花园和Colin都经历了他们的艰难时期。但不管有多困难，他们都在为生存而挣扎。这里突显了生命的珍贵和顽强。花园焕发了生机，Colin也是。

其次，从Mary和其他朋友的眼中。“She felt that his Magic was working all the afternoon and making Colin look like an entirely different boy....He looked as if he were made of flesh instead of ivory or wax.”当Colin努力站起来的时候，所有的朋友都感动得哭了。Colin笔直地站着，看上去高得出奇。他那奇怪的眼睛闪着闪电般的光芒。小伙伴们看到这个，惊喜之余，都认为某个地方存在魔法，是魔法治愈了Colin。

最后，从Colin自己本身。“I've seen the spring now and I'm going to see the summer. I'm going to see everything grow here. I'm going to grow here myself.”（Chapter 21）“Being alive is the Magic... the Magic is in me... It is in every one of us.”（Chapter 23）一切都充满生机。Colin开始了新生活。在Mary和Dickon的帮助下，他从黑暗的房间里走了出来。在花园魔法的帮助下，他享受着大自然的美丽和朋友的陪伴。他从游戏中获得乐趣，从种植植物中感受生命的意义和美好。

——关少娟

这三章给我印象深刻的是Chapter 21“Ben Weatherstaff”中花团锦簇、繁花似锦的花园景色的描写。故事跌宕起伏，让人心潮澎湃的情节有以下几处：第一个是Colin询问到一根大树枝被弄断过的老树时，第二个是静默之中Colin突然发现在墙头梯子顶端的Ben时，第三个是Colin站起来的那一刻。还有对Ben看到Colin时一系列的神情描写，细致入微、生动形象。初见Colin时的Ben：“How Ben Weatherstaff stared！His red eyes fixed themselves on what was before him as if he were seeing a ghost. He gazed and gazed and gulped a lump down his throat and did not say a word.BenWeatherstaff passed his hand over his forehead again and gazed as if he could never gaze enough. His hand shook and his mouth shook and his voice shook.”

看到Colin站起来的Ben："What Ben Weatherstaff did Mary thought queer beyond measure. He choked and gulped and suddenly tears ran down his weather—wrinkled cheeks as he struck his old hands together. "

——李 丹

第21章至第23章真让人高兴。一切都变得完美了，花园、Colin、Ben，甚至动物们都在变得更好、更有活力。在第21章的开头，书中说道："That afternoon the whole world seemed to devote itself to being perfect and radiantly beautiful and kind to one boy.（radiantly，我喜欢这个词，很有吸引力，很明亮）Perhaps out of pure heavenly goodness the spring came and crowned everything it possibly could into that one place. More than once Dickon paused in what he was doing and stood still with a sort of growing wonder in his eyes，shaking his head softly."。一切都是那么的美好。

后来Dickon鼓励Colin用腿走路。Ben的出现给了Colin力量，让他终于能用自己的双腿站起来。"His anger and insulted pride made him forget everything but this one moment and filled him with a power he had never known before，an almost unnatural strength."那是一个令人难忘的感人时刻。这提醒我们永远不要低估我们改变自己、让自己变得更好的能力。

Colin很快意识到所有这些伟大的改变都是从好的魔法开始的。有一天他聪明地说："Of course there must be lots of Magic in the world，but people don't know what it is like or how to make it. Perhaps the beginning is just to say nice things are going to happen until you make them happen. I am going to try and experiment."。如果我们能把好的魔法运用到生活中，我们肯定也能成为最好的自己。我很喜欢阅读第23章接下来的部分。

"The Rajah did not object to his staying and so the procession was formed. It really did look like a procession. Colin was at its head with Dickon on one side and Mary on the other. Ben Weatherstaff walked behind，and the 'creatures' trailed after them，the lamb and the fox cub keeping close to Dickon，the white rabbit hopping along or stopping to nibble and Soot following with the solemnity of a person who felt himself in charge.

It was a procession which moved slowly but with dignity. Colin's head was held up all the time and he looked very grand."

我觉得自己就像在看一个童话故事，神奇而甜蜜。在其他人的帮助和支持下，Colin就像一个国王，昂首阔步地前进。很棒，很有趣！

——李秀文

读完这三章后，我对“magic”这个词的内在意思思考了很多。“magic”是小说里的重要艺术主题，贯穿于文本和剧本之中，是推动情节发展的关键。魔法就在我们身边，在秘密花园里，在所有地方。秘密花园的魔法让Colin站了起来并想要活得更好，其中肯定有一个奇妙的魔法和大自然的独特魅力。在这个花园里，Mary学会了独立、善良，Colin也恢复了信心，自我修养和渴望也来自花园。当人类回归到大自然中去，体验大自然的变化时，就能战胜自己的缺陷。

我最喜欢下面的部分：“You learn things by saying them over and over and thinking about them until they stay in your mind forever and I think it will be the same with Magic. If you keep calling it to come to you and help you，it will get to be part of you and it will stay and do things.”（你通过重复说来学习，反复思考，直到它们永远留在你和我的脑海里。我想魔法也是一样的。如果你一直呼唤它来找你、帮助你，它就会成为你的一部分，它会留下来做事情）。

用一句话来表达，就是“念念不忘，必有回响”。这段文字也告诉我们，应该坚守信念，永不放弃尝试。如果我们努力，总有一天会得到回报的。

——麦佩莹

看完了这几章我感到无比的欣慰和感动，这是一个完满的结局。从Colin父亲对Colin的处理方式来看，标签的作用对孩子的影响真的是非常强大的。当Colin不断地被暗示他不正常、他很弱的时候，作为小孩的他就会认为自己就是一个很古怪很弱的孩子。后来，Mary不断跟他强调“你没有问题”，并且陪伴他做到了很多同其他孩子一样能做到的事情时，Colin也深信自己是一个正常的孩子。最后爸爸的领悟令我既欣慰又生气，欣慰的是他终于明白了，Colin不再需要活在他的阴霾里了，生气的是纳闷他为什么要在孩子遭受那么多罪之后才领悟呢！“Mr. Craven then understood the meaning of his dream. His wife’s spirit was，indeed，in the garden，and her good nature was influencing everyone，and teaching forgiveness. His son was a new person.”克莱文先生至此终于明白了梦的真正含义。的确，他妻子的灵魂就在这个花园里，而且她善良的天性影响着大家，教导人们要有宽容之心。

——莫洁文

“And it was like that with Colin when he first saw and heard and felt the Springtime inside the four high walls of a hidden garden. That afternoon the whole world seemed to devote itself to being perfect and radiantly beautiful and kind to one boy. Perhaps out of pure heavenly goodness the spring came and crowned everything it possibly could into that one place. More than once Dickon paused in what he was doing and stood still with a sort of growing wonder in his eyes，shaking his head softly.”

这个情景和之前Mary看到美丽的雨后风景是一样的，当Colin的心态因为Mary的感染而发生变化之后，他眼中的世界也跟着改变了。在他拥有了发现美的眼睛的时候，他才看到了以前从未留意过的美丽风景。并不是以前的春天不美，而是那时候他并没有去享受美的心情而已。

所以真的很希望每个孩子都能遇到可以滋养自己的人，因为拥有丰盈的内心才能看到这个美丽的世界。世界一直都在那里，可是如果内心充满愤恨，再美的风景都会视而不见哦。

——莫 然

没想到两个10岁左右的孩子的思想有时候是那么的成熟，知道假如Colin死了，整个庄园就会是Dr. Craven的了。但在“Magic”这一章中又充分地展示了孩子们天真烂漫的天性和对good magic的深信不疑，这也促使Colin能坚定信念勇敢而自信地活下去。

“Everything is made out of Magic，leaves and trees，flowers and birds，badgers and foxes and squirrels and people. So it must be all around us. In this garden—in all the places. The Magic in this garden has made me stand up and know I am going to live to be a man.”

“When I was going to try to stand that first time，Mary kept saying to herself as fast as she could，‘You can do it！You can do it！’and I did. I had to try myself at the same time，of course，but her Magic helped me—and so did Dickon’s.”

“‘The Magic is in me！’he kept saying.‘The Magic is making me strong！I can feel it！I can feel it！’”

Mary和Dickon的陪伴和不断的鼓励促使Colin向好的方向发展。我个人是很喜欢阅读儿童主题的读物的，因为现实社会中的钩心斗角、尔虞我诈等现象在书中都会被弱化，让人能够在读书中重新洗涤心灵，从而更乐观地面对生活。

——宋碧燕

在第21章“Ben Weatherstaff”中，读到这一段落，我想读者都会情不自禁地屏住呼吸，就像小主人公一般，感叹万物的美丽。

“世间有一件怪事，你只会偶尔觉得，自己会永远活着。

清晨，万物从沉睡中慢慢苏醒，天空从昏暗逐渐亮堂，太阳重复着千万次的升起，你静立着，感受着一切的变化。

傍晚，阳光收缩，树林里开始了光影游戏，金黄，不刺眼的阳光，远处响起声音，但是听不清。

或者，从某人的眼中，你看到了永恒。”

什么样的人，才能感受到大自然的美丽，或者永恒的爱？

一定不是冷漠的人，周遭的日起日落、人来人往，在他看来只不过是乏味的生活，一成不变。可即便生活发生翻天覆地的变化，他也不会快乐，只会满怀怨恨，埋怨命运给的不够多。

只有心怀感恩的人，才能享受当下，感激此刻，自己拥有健康的双眼直视日出，双耳倾听虫鸣，鼻子呼吸空气，双手触碰每一次风的抚摸。

只有心怀感恩的人，才能感受他人的爱，进而反馈自己的爱，让这种关系成为永恒。

——夏丽炎

第21章，初到花园，我们可以想象一个长期关在房间里的孩子，突然来到空气清新、鸟语花香、绿意盎然的花园里会是怎样激动的心情。在这一章里，我们看到了很多对环境和对小动物活动的细节描写。有一句话说，“That afternoon the whole world seemed to devote itself to being perfect and radiantly beautiful and kind to one boy.”，仿佛整个世界都在全心全意地要完美无缺、光彩照人，要对一个小男孩好。

“Dickon pushed the chair slowly round and round the garden，stopping every other moment to let him look at wonders springing out of the earth or trailing down from trees.”多么陶醉的小Colin！甚至后面他还想到了要来点下午茶继续好好享受。直到后来Colin都感叹道：“I don’t want this afternoon to go.”“but I shall come back tomorrow，and the day after，and the day after，and the day after.”“I’m going to see everything grow here. I’m going to grow here myself.”。当Dicken说到你也可以像我们一样在这儿到处走时，Colin是非常激动的，因为他也渐入佳境，觉得自己可以做到别人认为自己能做到的事。对于自卑的人来说，别人的一点点鼓励真的是很有魔力的。

在第23章中，我们看到的是这样一幅画面：

“Colin was at its head with Dickon on one side and Mary on the other. Ben Weatherstaff walked behind，and the“creatures”trailed after them，the lamb and the fox cub keeping close to Dickon，the white rabbit hopping along or stopping to nibble and Soot following with the solemnity of a person who felt himself in charge.”

“‘The Magic is in me！’he kept saying.‘The Magic is making me strong！I can feel it！I can feel it！’”

读完这三章，我了解到Mary和Dickon的“秘密”在于这块属于他们的小天地；Colin的“秘密”在于其实他是能站起来的，还能走得很好；Ben的秘密在于主仆情谊的坚守，多年来默默地护理着这座花园。而文中多次提到的“魔法”到底又是什么呢？孩子们觉得是彼此真的拥有某种超能力。但是我觉得“魔法”就是快乐的传递，因为快乐让一切明媚起来，让脆弱的人变得坚强勇敢，让自卑的人变得自信阳光，大家都在互相影响。我们常说和什么样的人在一起，你就会变成什么样的人，所谓“近朱者赤”，大概也有点相似的意味吧。

——徐 燕

小时候，幼稚地认为魔法就是会帮助我们脱离困境的，但当长大了，好像变了，我好像失去了信念。但读到这一章，我想说Colin口中的魔法其实就是他对于希望的信念。他说：“Everyone thought I was going to die，but I’m not.”（每个人都觉得我要死了，但我就是没有），非常坚定地说自己不会死。“I am not going to be a poor thing. I won’t let people think I’m one. I shall stop being queer.”（我不会是一个可怜的东西，我也不会让别人觉得我可怜。我要正常起来。）他站起来了，他克服了很多困难，他一天天地进步，也相信能改变自己。魔法在他身上好像真的管用，当然还有来自同伴的爱护以及大自然的感染力。显然，他们都是他们生活中的魔术师，他们所坚信的变成了勇气和希望陪伴着他们。因此，如果我们有信念的话，就要坚守我们心中的信念，永不放弃。

——袁泳施

In this part，the kids teach us a lesson that is to **believe，to stick and to insist does work and surely lead to success.**

“‘I go every day to the garden. There is Magic in there—good Magic，you know，Mary. I am sure there is.’ ‘So am I，’ said Mary.”

—To believe

“‘Even if it isn’t real Magic，’ Colin said，‘we can pretend it is. Something is there—something！’”

—To believe

“‘It’s Magic，’ said Mary，‘but not black. It’s as white as snow.’”

“If you keep doing it every day as regularly as soldiers go through drill we shall see what will happen and find out if the experiment succeeds.You learn things by saying them over and over and thinking about them until they stay in your mind...”

—To stick

“‘Then I will chant，’ he said. And he began，looking like a strange boy spirit. ‘The sun is shining—the sun is shining. That is the Magic. The flowers are growing—the root are stirring. That is the Magic. Being alive is the Magic—being strong is the Magic. The Magic is in me—the Magic is in me. It is in me—it is in me.It’s in every one of us. It’s in Ben Weather—staff’s back. Magic！Magic！Come and help！’”

—To stick

“He said it a great many times—not a thousand times but quite a goodly number.”

—To stick

" 'The magic is in me!' he kept saying. 'The Magic is making me strong! I can feel it! I can feel it!' "

—Works

"It seemed very certain that something was upholding and uplifting him..."

"I did it! The Magic worked!"...

—Succeed

——Ting Feng

Chapter 24-27 of The Secret Garden

导读

本周我们分享的内容是*The Secret Garden*的大结局，即最后四章，Chapter 24 "Let Them Laugh"，Chapter 25 "The Curtain"，Chapter 26 "It's Mother! "和Chapter 27 "In the Garden"。

Susan Sowerby这个人，书中有一些句子是描写她的："She had wonderful affectionate eyes which seemed to take everything in—all of them. Unexpectedly as had appeared，not one of them felt that she was an intruder at all. Dickon's eyes lighted like lamps."。在孩子的眼里，她有迷人的双眼，她的脸看上去非常舒服平和。她用她的热情和真诚融入孩子们。"'Even when I was ill I wanted to see you,' he said, 'you and Dickon and *The Secret Garden*. I'd never wanted to see anyone or anything before.'" "Each of them kept looking up at her comfortable rosy face，secretly curious about the delightful feeling she gave them—a sort of warm，supported feeling."孩子们变得非常喜欢跟她待在一起。"'Do you believe in Magic?' asked Colin. 'I do hope you do.' 'That I do，lad,' she answered. 'I never know it by that name but what does th' name matter?'"她发自内心地尊重孩子们，不管他们说的话是荒谬的还是可笑的，她都平等地对待他们。

除此之外，我们还可以从字里行间读到Mr. Craven的变化。"A terrible sorrow had fallen upon him when he had been happy and he had let his soul fill itself with blackness and had refused obstinately to allow any rift of light to pierce through."他过去十年都沉浸在消极的思想里，不让自己走出阴霾，也没有勇气去面对苦难。正如原文所说的："He had been on the tops of mountains whose heads were in the clouds and had looked down on other mountains when the sun rose and touched them with such light as made it seem as if the world were just being born."。经过大自然的洗礼后，他变了。"...the black burden seemed to lift itself again and he knew he was a living man and not a dead one. Slowly—slowly—for no reason that he knew of—he was 'coming alive with the garden'."

有的时候我们需要依靠一些瞬间的信念，才会坚信自己能活到永远。当你看着灰蒙蒙的天空逐渐变红，目睹着朝霞神奇般地变幻，一直到东方的太阳冉冉升起，你的心会平静下来。当你独自一人站在洒满余晖的树林里，你会听到树林好像在轻声地诉说着什么，一遍接着一遍；有的时候，在无比湛蓝的夜空中，满天繁星在等待着，会使人坚信自己会永远活下去。有时则是一个人的目光或声音，会使人有一种坚定不移的信念。

什么是秘密花园呢？我觉得秘密花园是一个关于大自然的，关于音乐的，关于那一片在春日如期而至的玫瑰园，也是关于那些知更鸟快乐歌唱的地方，更是一切和谐美丽的发源地。书中Mary终于找到了属于她的秘密花园。

那秘密花园的钥匙是什么呢？

第一把钥匙是Martha。她把Mary照顾得很好，并跟她成为朋友。她带领Mary和Dickon进入这个房子，并且一直帮助她。

第二把钥匙就是Dickon。他真的好极了。他对一切事物满怀感恩之心，他知道如何享受生活，他总是很乐于助人。

可是也不能忘记Susan，她是第三把钥匙。刚刚我们提到了，Susan做了很多事情，帮助Mary打开心结。“She was full of fun and made them laugh at all sorts of odd things. She laughed as if she could not help it when they told her of the increasing difficulty there was in pretending that Colin was still a fretful invalid.”她用她的真诚去感染其他人，用她的温暖去支持其他人。她教会了孩子们互相尊重、耐心温和的重要性。

“In the first place the boy creature did not come into the garden on his legs. He was pushed in on a thing with wheels and the skins of wild animals were thrown over him.”Chapter 25从知更鸟的角度去描写，这部分让我们了解到Colin在小伙伴们的帮助下变得活泼了，我似乎能看到这个场景。

“‘You are so like her now，’ said Mary，‘that sometimes I think perhaps you are her ghost made into a boy.’ That idea seemed to impress Colin. He thought it over and then answered her slowly. ‘If I were her ghost—my father would be fond of me.’ ‘It might make him more cheerful.’”多么美好的对话。之前肯定不敢相信这话居然会出自Mary和Colin这两个淘气孩子嘴里。他们终于学会了感恩，学会了爱和分享。他们渐渐地向别人敞开心扉，也诚实地把自己的感受分享给大自然。

几天后，Colin在Mary等人的帮助下恢复健康，他真诚地说出这些话：“I shall live forever and ever and ever！”“I shall find out thousands and thousands of things. I shall find out about people and creatures and everything that grows—like Dickon—and I shall never stop making Magic. I'm well！I'm well！I feel—I feel as if I want to shout out something—something thankful，joyful！”。他在不知不觉中，被大自然给治愈了，他勇敢地走出阴霾并且自在地拥抱世界。

“Where you tend a rose，my lad. A thistle cannot grow.”心中有太阳，何处不

光明？相信积极的态度将会帮助我们战胜一切困难！

似乎人们遇到困难的时候，都会想投身大自然去寻找答案，或许这是因为人生而具备这个能力，一个能与大自然和谐共处的能力，一个能与大自然紧紧相结合的能力。一旦我们在心中播种了一朵玫瑰花，我们自己的花园就会被唤醒。可能说不通，但就是这个概念，这就是魔法的力量。

所以秘密花园的第四个钥匙就是大自然。总结一下，要找到我们自己的钥匙，我觉得可以找找这些东西：

1.The beautiful nature around us，telling us how incredibly the harmony and intimacy between human and nature can work.（我们美丽的大自然，它会告诉我们与自然和谐共处将会产生多大的作用）

2.The interpersonal relationship around us，showing how powerful it can be to cure everything.（我们身边的朋友们，他们会帮助我们面临一切困难）

3.The faith and determination to be positive about everything.（充满自信，永远积极）

希望我们都能活在当下，享受生活中的每分每秒，感恩一切好与坏，那么，幸福就掌握在我们自己手中了。

工作室人员分享

让我印象深刻的是第25章“The Curtain”。作者换了一个角度去描写孩子们的活动，那就是知更鸟Robin的拟人化描写。从知更鸟角度看孩子们在花园的一举一动，显得更加有趣活泼。“The robin talked this over with his mate a great deal for a few days but after that he decided not to speak of the subject because her terror was so great that he was afraid it might be injurious to the Eggs.”一开始是警觉，害怕孩子们会破坏它的蛋，到后来的接纳。“Fears for the Eggs became things of the past. On wet days the Eggs’ mother sometimes felt even a little dull because the children did not come into the garden.”

故事到了尾声，意犹未尽，孩子们获得成长。Colin的爸爸也从此释怀。结局无疑是圆满的。秘密花园在快乐中诞生，在悲剧中尘封，又在快乐中开启。而大自然的魅力，让人忘却烦恼。但我们的内心才是真正主宰我们行为的。生活不如意之事十之八九，希望我们都能接纳悲伤，选择快乐，勇敢生活。

——徐 燕

总体来看，最后这四章是轻松愉悦的，每一个读者都会禁不住微笑，被父子重聚的圆满结局而感动。但是在看到Mr. Craven的段落时，我的心情又变得沉重。

一个父亲，因为丧妻之痛，自我惩罚放逐，逃避养育儿子的责任。他不断在外经商和旅行，离开家和儿子，他的身体在路上，但是心却一直记挂着Colin，时刻充满愧疚和自责。

并不是每一个父母，在孩子来到世间的那一刻，都准备好了做一个合格的家长。所以当父亲幡然醒悟，想要赶回家，尽一个父亲的责任时，他又胆怯了，质疑自己，质疑一切是否都太晚。

但是一切都不晚，一个拥抱让这对父子消除了遥远的距离，心又紧贴在一起。因为“爱”永远不会迟到。

——夏丽焱

“One of the strange things about living in the world is that it is only now and then one is quite sure one is going to live forever and ever and ever. Dickon pushed the chair slowly round and round the garden，stopping every other moment to let him look at wonders springing out of the earth or trailing down from trees. It was like being taken in state round the country of a magic king and queen and shown all the mysterious riches it contained.”（Chapter 21）

这一章让我印象最为深刻的是Colin对魔法的解释。当Colin第一次走进秘密花园的时候，他就有这种感觉，相信自己能够永远地活下去，他觉得这是魔法的作用。其实他眼中的“魔法”就是大自然，是大自然让性格怪异、体弱多病的Mary和Colin变得美丽、健康。

“‘I shall stop being queer，’ he said，‘if I go every day to the garden. There is Magic in there—good Magic，you know，Mary. I am sure there is.’

‘So am I，’ said Mary.

‘Even if it isn’t real Magic，’ Colin said，‘we can pretend it is. Something is there—something！’

‘It’s Magic，’ said Mary，‘but not black. It’s as white as snow.’”（Chapter 21）

“They drew the chair under the plum-tree，which was snow-white with blossoms and musical with bees. It was like a king’s canopy，a fairy king’s. There were flowering cherry-trees near and apple-trees whose buds were pink and white，and here and there one had burst open wide. Between the blossoming branches of the canopy bits of blue sky looked down like wonderful eyes.”（Chapter 21）

这一章给我印象深刻的是对花园中花团锦簇、繁花似锦的景色的描写，还有跌宕起伏、让人心潮澎湃的情节。第一个是Colin询问到一根大树枝被弄断过的老树时，第二个是静默之中Colin突然发现在墙头梯子顶端的Ben时，第三个是Colin站起来的那一刻。还有对Ben看到Colin时一系列的神情描写，细致入微、生动形象。

而Susan是12个健康活泼孩子的母亲，在全家只能勉强糊口的情况下，她一直在暗中给予Mary和Colin适时的关心和帮助，设法为Mary和Colin提供食物以满足他们随着身体的日益恢复而逐渐增长的食欲。在小说的结尾处，Susan带着母性的慈爱来到秘密花园，分享孩子们成功转变花园、转变自己后的喜悦。Susan微笑着对Colin说："亲爱的孩子，我相信你的妈妈就在这个花园里，她不会离开这里。你的爸爸一定会回来的。"Susan作为一个母亲，她的母爱的力量不仅使Mary和Colin走上了康复的道路，而且让他们变得开朗、乐观和坚强。

——宋蕾

我印象最深刻的有以下三个场景：

场景一

"她和Dickon都有魔法。"Colin说，"这让她想出做事情的办法——做好事。她是一个有魔力的人。告诉她我们很感激，Dickon——非常感激。"他有时习惯于使用一些相当成熟的措辞。他喜欢他们。他非常喜欢这一点，因此对它进行了改进。

"告诉她，她非常慷慨，我们感激不尽。"

这两个小孩知道Dickon家人多，并不富有，所以他们给Dickon一些钱让他们买东西。"你可以买土豆和鸡蛋，想吃多少就吃多少，而不会觉得像是从十四个人嘴里拿食物吃。"

场景二

"'你正是我想要的，'他说，'我希望你是我的母亲——以及Dickon的母亲！'"

当我读到这一幕时，我的眼睛里充满了泪水。也许因为我也是一位母亲。如果我是苏珊，我也会做苏珊做过的事。

场景三

"我以前很讨厌他，因为他不喜欢我。如果他喜欢上我了，我想我应该告诉他魔法的事。这也许会使他高兴些。"

"假如果我是她的鬼魂——我爸爸就应该喜欢我。"

"你不高兴吗，父亲？""你不高兴吗？我要永远地活下去！"

"现在，我再也不会坐在椅子上了。我和你一起走回去，爸爸——到家里去。"

从这些句子中，我可以看出一个可怜的孩子渴望从父亲和母亲那里得到爱。他期待父亲的爱，虽然他的母亲永远不会再回来了。但是我想他的爸爸会给Colin双倍的爱，Colin也会给他欢笑、快乐和爱。

——宋碧燕

在最后的这几章里，我们看到了每个孩子的成长，以及他们为自己和周围的人带来喜悦后自身发生的变化。

让我印象最深的一个片段就是关于Robin和他的伴侣筑巢并孕育新生命的描写。我感觉这一段是作者对于父母养育孩子的一个美好愿望。因为这个故事里的Mary和Colin都是从小没有得到父母善待的孩子，而这里的Robin和它的伴侣小心翼翼地对待它们的鸟蛋的心情，就像是真人一样，而秘密花园里的其他孩子们也都对这一群小生命充满期待。这就像是一个希望之火，暗示着未来这些得到爱的小朋友们长大之后，也会把他们得到的爱传递给更多的人，特别是他们的下一代。这让我感到非常欣慰和感动。

——莫 然

在最后四章中，整体气氛是轻松的。我能感受到Mary、Colin和Dickon身上的希望和欢乐。还有，我真佩服Dickon的母亲。她对孩子们总是温柔、体贴、慷慨，所以Colin可以从她身上感受到他从未有过的母爱。她甚至体贴地写信、给Craven先生，请他尽快回家。很高兴看到Colin能像其他健康的孩子一样走路、乱跑。更重要的是，父子俩修复了破裂的关系。故事的结尾象征着人物生活的美好与光明。秘密花园使我受益匪浅，这本书让我明白了友谊的价值。活泼的Dickon继续用他那颗真诚的心感动Mary，虽然她以前对一切都感到厌恶。Mary、Dickon和Colin之间的友谊也感动了Colin，他终于重新燃起了生命的火焰和希望。所以只要我们充满信心地面对生活，我们就能创造更加美好的未来。即使我们不能改变世界，至少我们可以改变自己。让我们活在当下，拥有乐观的生活态度！

——麦佩莹

最后三章读起来很愉快，里面有很多感人的时刻。在第24章里，好的魔法帮助孩子们发挥出最好的一面。Colin说：“Perhaps I couldn’t have one （tantrum） at all. That lump does not come in my throat now and I keep thinking of nice things instead of horrible ones.”。对孩子们来说，也许是因为魔法，他们渴望食物、幸福和生活。但在我看来，似乎是因为他们开始从自己的麻烦中解脱出来，他们才能真正拥抱外面的世界。他们开始感激别人。Colin真的感谢了Dickon的妈妈。“Magic is in her just as it is in Dickon，it makes her think of ways to do things—nice things. She is a Magic person. Tell her we are grateful，Dickon—extremely grateful.”最令人惊奇的是，他们开始向Dickon和他的母亲学习，学着关心其他人。他们开始喂养自己，而不是从别人那里得到食物。他们觉得自己做的食物“deliciously satisfying. You could buy both potatoes and eggs and eat as many as you liked without feeling as if you were taking food out of the mouths of fourteen people.”。

之前Colin说“I shall live forever and ever and ever.”，这似乎是一种希望、安慰和鼓励。但这一次Colin带着坚定的信念和肯定意识到他将会好好活着。孩子们的生活充满了希望和可能性。他们与Dickon母亲和Colin父亲的见面，让故事有了令人满意的结局。

最后，我不得不说，我真的很喜欢书中的语言。作者巧妙地运用了比较、拟人和排比等手法，使它很容易阅读和理解。很高兴能读到这本书。

——李秀文

这四章给我印象深刻的是Chapter 27 “In the Garden”，有两次我读的时候不禁流下了眼泪。在读到描写Mr. Craven的内容时，悲伤总会涌上心头，字里行间都透露出他对逝去的妻子深深的怀念和无尽的想念。在妻子离开人世后，Mr. Craven让黑暗塞满了心灵，他荒芜了他的家园，遗忘了他的责任，顽固地拒绝哪怕一隙阳光穿透进来。这种痛彻心扉的感受只有经历过的人才会懂，连儿子都不想理会的行为也只有同样经历的人才能理解。然而，Mr. Craven最终选择了改变，勇敢地走了出来，他回到庄园和儿子Colin重逢时的画面很温馨，让人不禁潸然泪下。除此之外，这一章也能带给读者满满的正能量。它告诉我们生活中的困苦不是永远的，只有自己的心态充满阳光，才能让自己的生活充满温暖与快乐。正如书中的那句话，“Where，you tend a rose，a thistle cannot grow.”（你在哪里种下一株玫瑰，刺蓟草就不能生长）。

——李 丹

阅读最后这几章，就像是经历了一场心灵的洗礼。景物的描写细致生动，同时烘托人物心理的变化，简单的语言蕴含深刻的道理，读起来如沐春风，如饮醇酒，回味无穷。

我一直好奇并且佩服的人物Dickon’s Mum Susan登场了。

“When she found a moment to spare，she liked to go out and talk to him. After supper there was still a long clear twilight to work in and that was here quiet time. She could sit upon the low rough wall and look on and hear stories of the day.” Susan一有空就爱到屋子外面去跟Dickon聊天。晚饭吃过后，天还能蒙蒙亮上好一阵子，有时间可以和孩子聊会天儿，这便是她一天之中能享受到的闲适时光。她会坐在粗石头上、矮墙上，朝四下眺望，听儿子讲一天发生了什么有趣的事情。她喜欢这段时光，短短几行字，就反映出她对Dickon的教育就是陪伴、倾听和肯定。这是最成功的教育方法。当Dickon告诉她，在花园里忙活，小朋友会肚子饿的时候，“Mrs. Sowerby laughed so heartily at the revelation of this difficulty that she quite rocked backward and forward in her blue cloak.” Mrs. Sowerby简直乐不可支，她那穿着蓝罩衫的身体笑得前仰后合。读到这里，我觉得她真是一个性格爽朗、可爱的妈妈。她主动提出由她来准备食物，她用身体力行的善良和慷慨影响着Dickon。

Susan 在秘密花园里的头一次出场，可谓有电视剧里女主角出场的效果，自带光环，也体现了作者对这个人物的喜爱和推崇。“With the ivy behind her，the sunlight drifting through the trees and dappling her long blue cloak，and her nice fresh face smiling across the greenery she was rather like a softly colored illustration in one of Colin’s books. She had wonderful affectionate eyes which seemed to take everything in—all of them.” 这就是一个母亲的形象。从小缺失母爱的Colin第一次看到她就对她说：“You are just what I—what I wanted. I wish you were my mother—as well as Dickon’s.” 这就是Susan的人格魅力和母性光辉的最好体现。

由于Susan的信，Colin 的爸爸终于回来了。庄园，草坪，走出心里阴霾的父亲与走出疾病困扰的儿子并排走着，昂首挺胸，迎接新的生活。这个场景美得如同一幅油画，一幅温暖人心的油画。

悲剧结尾固然深刻，但是happy ending 更符合人的心理需要。这也是*The Secret Garden*经久不衰的原因吧。

——关少娟

读完这三章，仿佛觉得文字是活着的，是充满生机的。我最喜欢最后一章“In The Garden”。开篇的一句话就让我印象深刻：“To let a sad thought or a bad one get into your mind is as dangerous as letting a scarlet fever germ get into your body. If you let it stay there after it has got in，you may never get over it as long as you live.”（听任一种悲观的思想、不良的思想进入你的头脑，就等于听任猩红热病菌侵害你的身体。要是你由它摆布，可能在有生之年，你毫无战胜他的希望）。快乐是自己的，快不快乐只有你自己知道，所以不要假装不快乐，即使你不快乐，也是自己不快乐，别人是不会知道，也不会因此而同情你的。所以活着，就请快乐地活着，为自己，也为身边的人。正如Colin一路的成长蜕变和心境的改变。

另外，深深触动我的一幕是被痛苦绝望折磨的Mr. Craven听从了早已去世的妻子的神秘召唤，重返了花园。

“The place was a wilderness of autumn gold and purple and violet blue and flaming scarlet and on every side were sheaves of late lilies standing together—lilies which were white or white and ruby. He remembered well when the first of them had been planted that just at this season of the year their late glories should reveal themselves.

Late roses climbed and hung and clustered and the sunshine deepening the hue of the yellowing trees made one feel that one，stood in an embowered temple of gold.

The new comer stood silent just as the children had done when they came into its grayness. He looked round and round.

‘I thought it would be dead，’ he said. ‘Mary thought so at first，’ said Colin.

'But it came alive.' "

Mr. Craven的记忆是灰色的。可是当他踏进了花园的门槛，却被活的色彩惊呆了。金色、紫色、蓝色和大红色的野花，白色、红色相间的百合，一丛丛红灿灿的玫瑰，点缀着花园的每个角落。原本已死在Mr. Craven记忆中的花园又活过来了，活的色彩到处飘荡，映衬着幸福的花开。对于Mr. Craven来说，也是他自己从记忆中又活了过来，重获新生，包括Colin和Mary都在这个秘密花园里重获新生！我想可能在我们每个人的心底深处都有一个秘密花园，在那里，善良、乐观、自信就是开启秘密花园的钥匙。

——王之光

"I used to hate it because he was not fond of me. If he grew fond of me, I think I should tell him about the Magic. It might make him more cheerful." "如果他先来喜欢我，我就试着把我的小秘密分享给他。"在这里可以看到Colin有点小别扭，但又渴望父亲的爱。Colin变得一天比一天强壮，他开始对自己有信心，开始觉得快乐。面对截然不同的自己，他内心是很想将这些分享给他的父亲的，希望自己能够第一时间告诉他。这就是亲情吧，无论有什么隔阂，血浓于水，这份爱是无法割舍的。

"I couldn't bear any one else to tell him," said Colin. "I think about different ways every day, I think now I just want to run into his room."

被召唤回来的爸爸，反省了这十年来他所做过的一切，他觉得他做错了，没能及时弥补。"Perhaps I have been all wrong for ten years," he said to himself. "Ten years is a long time. It may be too late to do anything—quite too late. What have I been thinking of! "

父子相见的场面很令人感动："He was a tall boy and a handsome one. He was glowing with life and his running had sent splendid color leaping to his face. He threw the thick hair back from his forehead and lifted a pair of strange gray eyes—eyes full of boyish laughter and rimmed with black lashes like a fringe."。

简单的一句话，十年，Colin终于做回了自己。

" 'Father,' he said, 'I'm Colin. You can't believe it. I scarcely can myself. I'm Colin.' "

——董筱妍

当Colin说他希望Susan是他的妈妈时，一股强烈的悲伤涌上我的心头。Colin从小失去母爱，同时也没有得到父亲Craven先生太多的关注和喜爱。虽然家里有钱，身边有一堆人照顾，但是这一切都无法替代父母的爱。这是造成之前Colin病态心理的主要原因之一。但幸好，Colin在Dickon、Mary、Susan的影响下，重新对生活充满信心。这让我想起了我的学生，我知道我有两个学生也是没有妈妈的，他们的性格也比较孤僻，但我会特别关注他们，希望他们的世界能有更多美好。我认为这本书传达给读者最大的意义是，生命不息，希望永存。只要我们对生活抱有希望，以积极乐观的态度对待生活，生活就会充满阳光。

当我读到前面一段时，Susan说Colin的妈妈也在花园里，我不明白是什么意思，但读到后面一段，提到Craven先生在梦中听到有声音呼唤他去秘密花园，我才明白。Craven先生的内心一直惦记着秘密花园，惦记着他的儿子，正如Colin的妈妈永远活在他的心中一样。

——陈雪芬

In this part the writer tells us how Mr. Carven come to alive.

What was Mr. Carven like fist?

"Most strangers thought he must be either half mad or a man with some hidden crime on his soul. He，was a tall man with a drawn face and crooked shoulders and the name he always entered on hotel registers was 'Archibald Craven，Misselthwaite Manor，Yorkshire，England.' "

"...He had chosen the quietest and remotest spots. He had been on the tops of mountains whose heads were in the clouds and had looked down on other mountains when the sun rose and touched them with such light as made it seem as if the world were just being born."

How did Mr. Carven come alive?

"But the light had never seemed to touch himself until one day when he realized that for the first time in ten years a strange thing had happened.

He was in a wonderful valley in the Austrian Tyrol and he had been walking alone through such beauty as might have lifted，any man's soul out of shadow. He had walked a long way and it had not lifted his. But at last he had felt tired and had thrown himself down to rest on a carpet of moss by a stream. It was a clear little stream which ran quite merrily along on its narrow way through the luscious damp greenness. Sometimes it made a sound rather like very low laughter as it bubbled over and round stones. He saw birds come and dip their heads to drink in it and then flick their wings and fly away. It seemed like a thing alive and yet its tiny voice made the stillness seem deeper. The valley was very，very still.

As he sat gazing into the clear running of the water，Archibald Craven gradually felt his mind and body both grow quiet，as quiet as the valley itself. He wondered if he were going to sleep，but he was not. He sat and gazed at the sunlit water and his eyes began to see things growing at its edge. There had happened to him. Neither does any one else yet. He did not understand at all himself—but he remembered this strange hour months afterward when he was at Misselthwaite again and he found out quite by accident that on this very day Colin had cried out as he went into *The Secret Garden*: 'I am going to live forever and ever and ever! ' "

Mr. Carven came alive.

" 'What is it? ' he said, almost in a whisper, and he passed his hand over his forehead. 'I almost feel as if—I were alive! ' "

——Ting Feng

中篇
A Christmas Carol

◎ 内容简介：

*A Christmas Carol*讲述了冷酷商人Scrooge从来不愿庆祝圣诞节，他没有至亲的家人，也没有什么朋友，无论走到哪里寒气就跟到哪里，人们避着他走路，连狗都不睬他一眼。他对此还十分洋洋自得，认为圣诞节本来就是多余的。圣诞节的前夜，他那已经死去的合伙人Marley从阴间来到他家里，给他讲述了自己死后的悲惨遭遇，告诫他以后不要走自己的老路，以免后悔不及。紧接着三个分别被称为圣诞节的“过去之灵”“现在之灵”和“未来之灵”的鬼魂也来找他，他们一起唤醒了Scrooge的美好人性，让他的人生发生了天翻地覆的变化。

Chapter 1-3 of A Christmas Carol

导读

今天的共读内容是*A Christmas Carol*的第1章至第3章——“Marley’s Ghost” “The First of the Three Spirits” “The Second of the Three Spirits”。本书作者Charles Dickens是19世纪英国最伟大的作家，也是一位以反映现实生活见长的作家。他在自己的作品中，以高超的艺术手法，描绘了包罗万象的社会图景。他的作品一贯表现出揭露和批判的锋芒，贯彻惩恶扬善的人道主义精神，塑造出众多令人难忘的人物形象。他特别关注了英国社会底层“小人物”的生活，深刻地反映了当时复杂的社会现实。*A Christmas Carol*成书于1843年12月。书名的英文原文为*A Christmas Carol in Prose*，*Being A Ghost Story of Christmas*，即“看来是个圣诞鬼故事，实质上却是一首以散文写出的圣诞颂歌”，因此就不难了解Charles Dickens为何把全书分为五节歌，即“Marley的鬼魂”“三鬼魂中的第一个”“三鬼魂中的第二个”“最后一个鬼魂”和“结局”。今天就前三节歌的写作特点，跟大家分享我的读后感受，以及四个特征非常明显的写作手法，它们分别是哥特式写作手法、排比、夸张和对比。

第一个特点是哥特式写作手法。什么是哥特式的写作手法？哥特式小说起源18世纪末19世纪初的英格兰。其模式特征是，故事常常发生在遥远的年代和荒僻的地方，人物被囚禁在狭窄的空间和鬼魂出没的建筑内，悬疑和情感交织在一起。它强调一种神秘、恐怖的气氛。在这本书里，作者创造了Marley 的鬼魂和三个鬼魂。Scrooge被鬼魂带回过去、现在和未来，重新经历过去，预知未来，所见所闻令他大为震惊。Scrooge最终从一个卑鄙、残忍、冷血的人，变成了一个善良、慷慨、愿意与他人分享快乐的人。

我认为最吸引人的场景是鬼魂出现前详细的文字描述。气氛可怕而神秘，但是好奇心迫使你不得不往下读。比如第14页到15页，作者是这样描写Marley的鬼魂出现的：“Without its undergoing any intermediate process of change—not a knocker，but Marley’s face.”。Marley的脸突然出现在门环上，作者先从视觉上进行了描写。读到这里，我想读者和Scrooge 一样，冒出了一身冷汗。接着，作者从听觉上进行渲染。“The sound resounded through the house like thunder. Every room above，and every cask in the wine merchant's cellars below，appeared to have a separate peal of echoes of its own.”楼上的每一个房间和下面地窖里的每一个酒桶，都发出一阵轰隆隆的回声。“...and then he heard the noise，much louder，on the floors below；then coming up the stair；then coming straight toward his door...”（P17）他听到开门的声音，鬼魂到了一楼，上了楼梯，到了房门口。读者能真实地感受到Scrooge 的紧张和害怕。

在描写第一个鬼魂出现的时候，作者又换了一种写法。这次，他着重对主人公的心理进行了描写。

“‘Ding，dong.’‘A quarter past，’said Scrooge，counting.‘Ding，Dong！’‘Half past，’said Scrooge.‘Ding，dong！’‘A quarter to it.’said Scrooge.‘Ding，dong！’‘The hour itself.’”（P29）

因为知道鬼魂来临的具体时间，Scrooge 一分一秒地算着时间，这几声“Ding，dong”写出了他内心焦虑的等待和无比恐惧，心脏跟随钟声加快跳动，无计可施，什么也做不了，只有等待鬼魂的出现。

第二个特点是排比。作者通过大量的排比句式来强调某些情节，使人物更加生动。在第一节歌中，对Scrooge 的描述给我留下了很深的印象。“No warmth could warm. No wintry weather chills him. No wind that blew was bitterer than he. No falling snow was more intent upon its purpose. No pelting rain less open to entreaty. Foul weather didn't know where to have him.”（P5）无论怎样的炎热都不能使他温暖，怎样的酷寒也不能使他发冷，怎样的大风也比不上他的心那样狠，等等。总之Scrooge绝对是一个非常残忍的人，他在意的只有金钱。

第39页，Scrooge的侄子和他的朋友们正在开圣诞晚会。作者没有直接写所有人都到齐了，而是用了以下的句式：

“In came a fiddler ... In came Mrs. Fezziwig... In came the six young followers... In came all the young men... In came the house-maid... In came the cook... In came the boy...”（P39）

这让我想到一个成语“鱼贯而入”，用在这里非常贴切。通过这些排比句子的使用，给圣诞派对营造了热闹的气氛，也表明他的侄子人缘很好，有很多朋友。

第三个特点是夸张。我们一起来朗读这段精彩的文字描写。

No beggars implored him to bestow a trifle，no children asked him what it was o'clock，no man or woman ever once in all his life inquired the way to such and such a place，of Scrooge. Even the blind men's dogs appeared to know him；and when they saw him coming on，would tug their owners to doorways and up courts；and then would wag their tails as though they said，“No eye at all is better than an evil eye，dark master.”（P5）

乞丐都不问他要钱，小孩不向他问时间，男人女人都不向他问路。连瞎子养的狗都似乎认得他，一看见他走过来，就把主人拖进院子里摇着尾巴好像在说："失明的主人啊，生着一双凶恶的眼睛，还不如瞎了好。"这段夸张手法的描写非常生动、幽默，把Scrooge冷漠的形象刻画得生动形象。

第四个特点是对比。作者使用对比的手法贯穿整个故事。举其中几个典型的例子。其一，Scrooge和他的侄子之间的人物性格对比。所有用来描述 Scrooge 的词都是负面的，如吝啬、冷酷、孤独、自私等；相反，描写他侄子的词都是阳光的，如开朗、大方、活跃、热爱生活等。

我特别喜欢"tight-fisted hand"这个词。形容Scrooge吝啬，作者不用mean，而是用了紧紧握住的手来比喻他连一个便士都不舍得给别人，就如汉语里的"铁公鸡"，形容他一毛不拔，很生动。其二，Scrooge 和他前女友的对比。他的前女友拥有一个幸福的家庭，疼爱她的丈夫，成群的子女，家里充满欢声笑语。而他什么也没有，没有家人，没有爱人，没有朋友，只有孤独。其三，鬼魂拜访Scrooge前后，Scrooge的人生观对比。刚开始他对圣诞节的态度是"Out upon merry Christmas！"。这句译成中文就是一句粗口："去他妈的圣诞节快乐！"因为他不舍得给别人礼物，不想跟别人分享。这时候的他是冷血的。第一个鬼魂带他看到曾经的自己时，他的心境是"But fell upon the heart of Scrooge with softening influence and gave a freer passage to his tears."。他是感动的，看到别人曾经帮助过作为孩童的自己，他后悔没有帮助站在他店门口寻求帮助的孩子。这时，他有同情心了。看到别人办派对，他受到感染。"Scrooge had acted like a man out of his wits. His heart and soul were in the scene."这时候的他又是开心的。当看到前女友的幸福生活时，他悲伤、后悔，想要逃离，不敢再多看一眼。第二个鬼魂带他看了他侄子对他的评价，大家还是愿意跟他一起过圣诞，他感受到了亲情，从而变得感恩。一个冷血的人终于有了正常人的喜怒哀乐的感受，对比非常强烈。

引用他侄子老婆的一段话作为结语：

"It is a fair，even-handed，noble adjustment of things，that，while there is infection in disease and sorrow，there is nothing in the world so irresistible contagious as laughter and good humor."

圣诞节原本的意义，就是和身边的人分享爱和欢乐。

工作室人员分享

*A Christmas Carol*这部作品，在我看来，真是一本"活见鬼"的小书。读完第1至3章后，我认为这部小说最为突出的特点是情节怪诞，描述了人与鬼魂的沟通联系，通篇都有冥俗对话的情节，而每一次作者都赋予它们不同的内容与功能。

第一次是Marley的鬼魂与主人公Mr. Scrooge的对话。Scrooge一开始并不相信自己遇见的鬼魂，为了证实自己的感觉，他竟然敢要弄鬼魂。他邀请Marley坐在壁炉对面的椅子上，又让他瞧瞧是否能看见一根牙签。这些细节描写让人感到十分滑稽。鬼魂告诉Scrooge，从今天起连续三天每次钟敲 1点的时候就会有一位鬼魂到来。这次对话对后续故事的发展起到了推动的作用。

第二次是主人公与“过去的圣诞鬼魂”的对话。

“Suddenly Scrooge realized they were standing on an open country road，with fields on each side. London，the fog，and the darkness had all disappeared，and it was a clear，cold，winter day，with snow on the ground. ‘Good Heavens！’ cried Scrooge. ‘I was born near here！I remember it well！’ The spirit looked kindly at the old man. ‘How strange that you’ve forgotten it for so many years！What is that on your face? Are you crying? ’ Scrooge put a hand over his eyes. ‘It’s nothing—I’ve got a cold，that’s all. Take me where you want，spirit！’ ”

鬼魂领着他走上一条开阔的乡村小路，来到一所学校。Scrooge认出，那正是自己幼年时所在的学校……不知不觉中，鬼魂唤起了Scrooge泯灭已久的天真，他一点一滴重新找回了童年的天真和爱心……

第三次是主人公与“现在的圣诞鬼魂”的对话。

“ ‘Spirit，’ said Scrooge quietly，‘take me where you want. Last night I learned a lesson which is working now. If you have anything to teach me tonight，let me learn from you.’ ‘Touch my robe！” said the spirit，and Scrooge obeyed.”

从以上这段对话可以看出，主人公Scrooge对于鬼魂的出现已经不再有恐惧和害怕的心理了，他更加坦然地接受了鬼魂以及他将要看见的东西。

——陈雪芬

读完本期内容，我认为Mr. Cratchit 一家非常温馨有爱。全家只能分享一个布丁，但是没人说出来，还一直赞美Cratchit太太布丁做得好。这就是我们普通人家的快乐，家人在一起就是财富。Scrooge 在鬼魂拜访后，有了很大的改变。他希望能为唱圣诞颂歌的小孩做些什么，希望能为自己的员工做些什么。文章首尾呼应，这些情节都为后来主人公的反省做了铺垫。他的变化主要有：

1. 对给他唱圣诞颂歌的小孩的态度的改变

“ ‘I wish...’ muttered Scrooge. He didn’t finish his thought. He put his hand in his pocket and looked about him. He rubbed his eyes dry. ‘It’s too late now.’ ”

2. 对他自己的员工的态度改变

“ ‘No，’ said Scrooge. ‘No，not really. I just wish I could say a word or two to my clerk just now. That’s all.’ ”

首尾呼应，前面所发生的场景都在为Scrooge后面的自我反省做铺垫。当过往之神带他回到他做学徒时候的店时，他碰到了Mr. Fezziwig，那时恰逢圣诞前夕，他们一起欢歌笑语。那个鬼神故意说，“ ‘A small matter，’ said the Ghost， 'to make these silly fools so full of gratitude.'"但是Scrooge很生气地反驳，"'It isn't that,' said Scrooge angry at the remark. He sounded more like his former self, not his later self. 'It isn't that, Spirit. He has the power to make us happy or unhappy. He can make our hearts light or heavy. Say that his power lies in words and looks. The happiness he gives is quite as great as if it costs a fortune.'"

当他说完这句话后，我觉得非常诧异，因为在第1章的描写中，可以看出Scrooge每天的快乐只有算钱，他不需要别人的陪伴，也不会轻易地被他人的快乐所感染。但是当他梦回以前，他便马上体会到了一点点的快乐都可以创造出巨大的财富。

——董筱妍

*A Christmas Carol*的前三章主要讲述了如下几个情节：Scrooge的冷漠以及他被Marley纠缠，"过去之灵"和"现在之灵"两位圣诞鬼魂的来访。

我对第1、2章的感触比较大，作者生动地描绘了Scrooge的外貌和心理特征。由于其心灵长期自我封闭，他的眼睛布满红色，嘴唇呈蓝紫色，嗓音高而暴躁。即使室外骄阳似火，他的办公室也如同冬天一样寒冷阴暗。他对于外甥的新年邀请进行了无情的回绝，他对待募集善款的爱心人士给予了怠慢驱逐。他没有朋友，没有访客，孩子们从不敢接近他。他的这种冰冷与麻木已经到达了极致，甚至连乞丐都不愿向他乞讨，就连盲人的狗也似乎深知其秉性，对其避而远之。主人公的形象被刻画得淋漓尽致。我们可以看出主人公对待亲情是冷漠的，对待爱情是不屑的，对待社会是冷酷的。

我喜欢第1章中作者借他侄子的口对圣诞节的描述：

"the only time I know of, in the long calendar of the year, when men and women seem by one consent to open their shut-up hearts freely, and to think of people below them as if they really were fellow-passengers to the grave, and not another race of creatures bound on other journeys. And therefore, uncle, though it has never put a scrap of gold or silver in my pocket, I believe that it has done me good, and will do me good; and I say, God bless it!"（据我所知，在漫长的一年当中，只有这个时节，男男女女才似乎不约而同地把他们那紧闭的心房敞开，把那些比他们卑微的人真的看作是走向坟墓的伴侣，而不是走向其他路程的另一种生物。圣诞节虽从来没把丝毫金银放进我的口袋，我还是相信它的确给了我好处，而且以后还会给我好处。所以我说，上帝保佑它！）在我看来，这是对圣诞文化的一种很好的解读：人们在这美好的时刻，打破人与人之间心灵的隔阂，分享喜悦，共同对生活怀揣美好的期待。

——王之光

读一本书之前，对其背景知识的了解非常重要。因此，在开篇章节，我查阅了有关*A Christmas Carol*一书的资料，尤其是其经久不衰的原因及相关时代背景。1843年至1848年，除了1847年外，每年圣诞节Dickens都要发表一部中篇小说，后来这五篇小说结集成*Christmas Books*。第一篇*A Christmas Carol*在其中最为著名，这几篇圣诞故事篇幅不大，情节也不复杂，但要论受欢迎程度，却是毫不逊色。有人说过这样的话，英国四分之三的人不仅知道*A Christmas Carol*是谁的作品，还能清清楚楚地说出故事中的人物来，Dickens凭借这部作品，把自己和圣诞节牢牢联系在了一起。资产阶级革命和工业革命一度让圣诞节传统日渐衰弱，老百姓不再像过去那样重视这一节日。*A Christmas Carol*成为超级畅销书之后，改变了这一状况。可以说，是Dickens重新“发明”了圣诞节。*A Christmas Carol*是一篇“非典型”的圣诞故事，与英国当时那些说教色彩浓重的圣诞故事相比，*A Christmas Carol*借用了鬼怪故事的外壳，但内容既不可怕也不血腥，反而亦庄亦谐，虚实相生，许多地方令人读了会心一笑。另外，此书也有浓重的自传色彩。

小说结构非常齐整，在人物刻画方面更是生动形象。不光主人公的形象让人印象深刻，配角们也是千姿百态。Dickens塑造的人物仿佛漫画人物，他擅长抓住人物的一两个特点加以艺术化的夸张。“童心”或许是人类最为宝贵的东西之一，是Dickens开出的解救社会问题的良方。Scrooge的财富虽然在一天天变多，但是他的灵魂却在一天天地变得空洞。他的侄子和下属虽然并不富裕，却始终保持着赤子之心，活得远比Scrooge快乐。

Scrooge的外貌描写也令人印象深刻：“He was a hard，clever，mean old man，Scrooge was！There was nothing warm or open about him．He lived a secretive，lonely life，and took no interest in other people at all．The cold inside him made his eyes red，and his thin lips blue，and his voice high and cross．It put white frost on his old head，his eyebrows and his chin．The frost in his heart made the air around him cold，too．”

——莫洁文

这部文学作品滋润着我们的内心，慰藉着我们的心灵。阅读时我会无意识地与主人公一起欢笑，一起悲伤，一起经历，一起感悟。它让我进一步领悟到生命和生活的意义，更深地懂得什么是爱，什么是善，什么是恶。在第1章里，作者将Scrooge冷漠无情、自私吝啬的一面描写得淋漓尽致：圣诞节要给不工作的职员们发薪水，他为此感到不值；有人请他为穷人捐款，却被冷酷赶走；侄子邀请他参加晚宴，却受到他的刻薄对待。“He was a tight-fisted hand at the grindstone. A squeezing，wrenching，grasping，scraping，clutching，covetous，old sinner！Hard and sharp as flint，from which I had ever struck out generous fire；secret，and self-contained，and solitary as an oyster.” “External heat and cold had little influence on

Scrooge.No warmth could warm，no wintry weather chill him. No wind that blew was bitterer than him，no falling snow was more intent upon purpose，no pelting rain less open to entreaty.”这些描写让人印象深刻。

——李 丹

坦白地说，如果让我自己选的话，我决不会选择读这本书。因为我不喜欢任何关于鬼怪的恐怖书籍。所以一开始，在我内心深处，我是抗拒读这本书的。但是当我一点点地读下去，不去想那些可怕的鬼魂形象时，我意识到我甚至喜欢它。特别是当Scrooge 看到他过去的快乐时光时，他冰冷的心开始融化。当他看到弟弟自己在老板家和其他工人玩得很开心时，他意识到“这不是钱的问题”。Scrooge热情地回答，他说话的方式和年轻时一样，而不是现在这个老人。“不，鬼魂，你看，我们的雇主可以让我们高兴或者悲伤。他的话，他的外表，所有这些都是如此重要！他给我们的快乐就像金钱一样珍贵！”

后来，Scrooge开始关心别人。当现在的灵魂告诉他：“If his life does not change soon，he will die before next Christmas. What does that matter? There are too many people in the world，so it’s a good thing if some of them die．”。甚至他自己也被自己这些话的残忍震撼了。

当Scrooge的侄子和他的朋友们玩游戏，祝他圣诞快乐、新年快乐时，他也加入了他们，并对他们心存感激。此时此刻，他的生命似乎又复活了。他开始真正地重生了。

幸亏读了这本书，让我可以从日常生活中抽身出来，回顾一下自己的生活。有时候，我们可能会被金钱或名誉所蒙蔽，但我们应该永远把最重要的东西放在心里，比如亲爱的家人、朋友和我们周围的人。我们知道，每个人都有各自不同的生活，而生活就是我们每天所做的选择。所以我们最好明智地选择，做最好的自己。善待他人，忠于自己。“Live beautifully，dream passionately，love completely.”美好的生活，充满激情的梦想，完全的爱。

——李秀文

这个故事我之前看过电影，不过小说的描写真的比电影好看多啦！语言特别生动，很有意思！其中有一小段对话就是侧面描写了Scrooge的固执和冷血无情，内容是他不想和侄子一家过圣诞节，只想自己待着，然后还嘲笑侄子竟然会爱上别人。看到他这爱怼人的性格，我就能猜到他小时候肯定是很缺爱才会有这样的反应的。看来这次又是讲一个可怜之人变成可恨之人的悲惨故事。

——莫 然

“Now，dear reader，if you had been watching Scrooge at this moment，you might think it was strange to see Scrooge's cold eyes shine and his soft smile, when he heard the boys say 'Merry Christmas! ' After all, you and I both know that Scrooge didn't care about Christmas. He hated Christmas! What was the good of Christmas, as he always liked to say? "(Chapter 2)

读到这里，我感到无比惊奇。当他听到男孩子们说"圣诞快乐"时，他那冷酷的眼睛放射出光芒，脸上带着温柔的笑意。这说明Scrooge本来是很善良的，但因为受到环境的影响，变成一个非常小气、吝啬、刻薄的商人。昔日鬼魂带领他回忆往事，触动他的心灵，让他记起其实他内心还是善良的。

"'What do you mean? ' 'What is the matter? ' asked the ghost of Christmas past.

'It's nothing.' said Scrooge. 'It's not important.There were some little boys who came to sing a Christmas song at my office door last night.I wish I had given them something, that's all.' "(Chapter 2)

Scrooge说道："没事，昨天晚上有几个男孩来我的办公室门外唱圣诞欢歌，我真希望当时给他们点什么。"往事唤醒了他的良知，年轻时的他是个多么快乐、乐于帮助别人的人。现在他也想主动帮助别人、施舍穷人，让别人快乐也让自己快乐。

——宋 蕾

Ebenezer Scrooge是个十成的吝啬鬼。伦敦的圣诞前夕，吐气可成冰，他宁愿自己挨冻也不愿意在办公室烧煤，给秘书取暖。从这个细节可以看出，Scrooge不是一般的吝啬，他不仅对别人抠门，对自己也不手软，简直把金钱当作他的生命在珍惜。但是，物质至上的他，只是拥有了账目上不断增长的数字。从过去到现在，他不断地抛弃爱他的妻子、家人，宁愿与冰冷的金钱相伴，度过一个个孤独的圣诞节。

反思现代社会，总是流行着这样一种声音："有钱不能为所欲为，但没钱是万万不行。"钱，真的是第一位吗？不，因为视钱财如生命而走向悲剧结局的例子还少吗？为钱财，抛弃人民公仆良知的贪官，住进了铁栅栏。钱，只是一串串"零"，增加再多，没有"一"也是毫无意义。那么，最重要的是什么？我猜，文豪Dickens会在最后的两章中，用幽默的文字，给我们揭晓深刻的回答。

——夏丽焱

在这一部分里，有一段关于Scrooge青年时期的场景让我印象颇深。鬼魂带着Scrooge来到了他曾经打工的地方，老板夫妇在圣诞节来临的时候，会慷慨地支付一点钱举办小聚会，请人表演，跟员工一起庆祝节日。"'a small matter' said the Ghost, 'to make these silly folks so full of gratitude.' It isn't that's aid Scrooge, heated by the remark，and speaking unconsciously like his former not his latter self. It isn't that Spirit. He has the power to render us happy or unhappy：to make our service light or burdensome a pleasure or a toil. Say that his power lies in words and looks；in things so slight and insignificant that it is impossible to add and count them up：what then？The happiness he gives，is quite as great as if it cost a fortune.”可见，当初的快乐是多么简单纯粹，大家都没那么功利，但是在追逐金钱的道路上，离初心也越来越远。这里Scrooge开始有了一点人性的回归，让他想到自己作为雇主又是怎样对待下属的。

接下来去的是一个Scrooge不愿意面对的时刻，在他追求名利的时候，和曾经心爱的女孩也是渐行渐远，选择离开了她。这些过往的经历，是在提醒Scrooge曾经的纯粹与美好是存在过，也是他人性中最初美好的样子。在第3章中，我们感受到了Scrooge人性的一些回归。他会渴望温暖以及别人对他的评价，也会开始关心别人。Scrooge作为可恨之人也是有可怜之处的。人还是不要迷失自我，迷失在物质的浮华中，要时常回头看看来时的路，这样就会更感恩现在拥有的，会更容易收获快乐。

——宋碧燕

At first，the Ghost led Scrooge，the main character，saw how the people celebrated Christmas.

"Here，the flickering of the blaze showed preparations for a cosy dinner，with hot plates baking through and through before the fire，and deep red curtains，ready to be drawn to shut out cold and darkness. There all the children of the house were running out into the snow to meet their married sisters，brothers，cousins，uncles，aunts，and be the first to greet them. Here，again，were shadows on the window—blind of guests assembling；and there a group of handsome girls，all hooded and fur-booted，and all chattering at once，tripped lightly off to some near neighbour's house...

A light shone from the window of a hut，and swiftly they advanced towards it. Passing through the wall of mud and stone，they found a cheerful company assembled round a glowing fire. An old，old man and woman，with their children and their children's children，and another generation beyond that，all decked out gaily in their holiday attire."

We can also sense the atmosphere of warmth，pleasure and happiness by staying with families on Christmas.

To us，very often，festival is a time to be with families. It may just mean：

一灯，一窗，一归途；一茶，一饭，一家人。

——Ting Feng

Chapter 4-5 of A Christmas Carol

导 读

在第4章“The Last of the Spirits”中，第三个鬼魂即未来鬼魂出现了，它什么话也不说，只是带着Scrooge去看那些尚未发生但将来会发生的事情的幻影。在未来，Scrooge死了，但是人们对他的死去漠不关心。Scrooge死亡的时候，身边没有家人和朋友，被剥光了衣服躺在空屋子里，没有蜡烛和鲜花。“Joe and the women had disappeared，and Scrooge was standing in a dark room. Opposite him was a bed，with no blankets or curtains. A light shone down from above，on to the body of a dead man，covered with a sheet. ‘How sad，’ thought Scrooge，to die with no friends or family around him！To lie in an empty room，with no candles or flowers，and robbed of his clothes！”一位年轻的妇女对于他的死去甚至感到高兴，因为她的家人不再需要还钱给Scrooge。“‘He is dead，Caroline，’ answered her husband. ‘thank God for that！’ cried the young woman from her heart. The next moment she realized what she had said. ‘Oh，I didn’t mean that. I’m sorry if anyone dies.’ ‘Perhaps the person who inherits his business will give us more time to pay the money back. And we’ll have the money by then. Tonight we can sleep well，Caroline！’”

第三个鬼魂让Scrooge看到了他的死亡给别人带来的是幸福，而不是悲伤，甚至连他的坟墓都是脏乱不堪的。Scrooge对此感到难过和恐惧，他对着第三个鬼魂乞求，希望鬼魂给他机会改变，他愿意通过改变自身来改变这悲惨的下场。

在最后一章中，Scrooge醒来时很高兴，因为他发现自己还活着，圣诞节还没结束，他庆幸仍有机会去改变未来的事情，当然他首先要改变自己。他给他的职员Bob送去了一只大的火鸡，他和他的侄子及家人一起开心地度过圣诞节……多亏了几个鬼魂，Mr. Scrooge一夜之间变得和以前完全不一样了，从此以后圣诞节他一直过得很快活。

最后两章的内容并不难理解，我想和大家分享的主要有以下三点。

第一，作者对于未来鬼魂的外貌、性格特征的刻画都十分生动形象，总的概况为“黑、沉默”，给人一种阴森恐怖的感觉。“It was shrouded in a deep black garment, which concealed its head, its face, its form, and left nothing of it visible save one outstretched hand. But for this it would have been difficult to detach its figure from the night, and separate it from the darkness by which it was surrounded." 从以上句子中，我们可以了解到这个未来的鬼魂全身都是黑的，十分神秘的样子。再如："He felt that it was tall and stately when it came beside him, and that its mysterious presence filled him with a solemn dread. He knew no more, for the Spirit neither spoke nor moved." "The Spirit answered not, but pointed onward with its hand." "It gave him no reply. The hand was pointed straight before them." 。鬼魂无声的动作和对Scrooge冷漠的态度，让人觉得更加诡异。"Although well used to ghostly company by this time, Scrooge feared the silent shape so much that his legs trembled beneath him, and he found that he could hardly stand when he prepared to follow it." Scrooge对这个鬼魂的恐惧胜过前面所有的，他连站都站不直。读完这几段，我顿时感到毛骨悚然，这个未来的鬼魂太吓人了。

第二，我想谈谈我对Bob家庭的看法。我认为Bob之家是一个充满爱的家庭！在面对小蒂姆的不幸时，他们感到无比伤痛，但他们不会忘记这个何等有耐心、何等彬彬有礼的孩子，他们会带着对小蒂姆的爱，继续好好活下去。

"'It's just as likely as not,' said Bob, 'one of these days; though there's plenty of time for that, my dear. But however and whenever we part from one another, I am sure we shall none of us forget poor Tiny Tim—shall we—or this first parting that there was among us?'

'Never, father!' cried they all.

'And I know,' said Bob, 'I know, my dears, that when we recollect how patient and how mild he was; although he was a little, little child; we shall not quarrel easily among ourselves, and forget poor Tiny Tim in doing it.'

'No, never, father!' they all cried again.

'I am very happy,' said little Bob, 'I am very happy!'

Mrs. Cratchit kissed him, his daughters kissed him, the two young Cratchits kissed him, and Peter and himself shook hands."

Bob和他其余几个孩子的对话让我深受感动。

第三，让我印象最为深刻的是Mr. Scrooge身上发生的变化。过去，他过得不开心，为人自私自利，毫无怜悯之心，唯一能让他充满热情的只有金钱。他和他周围的人时刻保持距离，他待人冷漠，脾气也很差。没有人对他有好感，甚至有很多人很讨厌他。但是后来，受教于三个鬼魂后，Scrooge变得开心多了，他对周围的人友好又慷慨大方，他常常关心和帮助身边的人，助人为乐和充满慈爱之心的他过得比以前快乐多了。我们可以从以下一些词句中了解并体会到Mr. Scrooge的变化。

1. happy（开心的）

"I am as light as a feather，I am as happy as an angel，I am as merry as a school boy. I am as giddy as a drunken man. A merry Christmas to every-body！A happy New Year to all the world！Hallo here！Whoop！Hallo！"（我整个人像羽毛那么轻盈，像天使那样快乐，和小男生一样开心。祝世上每一个人圣诞节快乐，祝愿全世界新年快乐！）

"Really，for a man who had been out of practice for so many years，it was a splendid laugh，a most illustrious laugh. The father of a long，long line of brilliant laughs！"（对于一个若干年没有笑过的人来说，这笑太开怀了。这是一长串开怀大笑的开始！"）

从以上句子可以看出，Mr. Scrooge的心情特别好！

2. friendly to people（对人很友好）

"'Do you know the Poulterer's，in the next street but one，at the corner？' Scrooge inquired.

'I should hope I did，' replied the lad.

'An intelligent boy！' said Scrooge. 'A remarkable boy！Do you know whether they've sold the prize Turkey that was hanging up there？Not the little prize Turkey；the big one？'

'What，the one as big as me？' returned the boy.

'What a delightful boy！' said Scrooge. 'It's a pleasure to talk to him. Yes，my buck！'"

Mr. Scrooge用了"intelligent、remarkable、delightful"这三个褒义词来赞美小男孩。

"Scrooge regarded every one with a delighted smile. He looked so irresistibly pleasant，in a word，that three or four good-humored fellows said，'Good morning，sir！A merry Christmas to you！' And Scrooge said often afterwards，that of all the blithe sounds he had ever heard，those were the blithest in his ears."他对每个人都微笑着。当别人和他说"圣诞快乐"时，他觉得那是他听到过的最美妙的声音。

3. generous（慷慨大方的）

Mr. Scrooge很大方地赠予Bob一家一只大火鸡，还不打算告诉Bob是他送的。

"Come back with the man，and I'll give you a shilling. Come back with him in less than five minutes，and I'll give you half-a-crown！"

"I'll send it to Bob Cratchit's！" whispered Scrooge，rubbing his hands，and splitting with a laugh. "He shan't know who sends it. It's twice the size of Tiny Tim. Joe Miller never made such a joke as sending it to Bob's will be！"

“去把那只火鸡买下来，并让店主送到这里。你和店主一起回来我就给你一个先令。如果在5分钟之内回来，我就给你三个先令！我要把这只火鸡送给Bob一家！他永远也不会知道是谁送去的。”之后，Mr. Scrooge又遇到了曾经到他办公室为穷人讨要钱财的老先生。他主动走上前向老人道歉，并承诺该给的钱一先令都不会少。

4. get close to the people（**平易近人**）

“He went to church，and walked about the streets，and watched the people hurrying to and from，and patted children on the head，and questioned beggars，and looked down into the kitchens of houses，and up to the windows：and found that everything could yield him pleasure.” Mr. Scrooge去做了礼拜，给孩子钱去买糖果，他发现他一生中从未这样幸福过。

5. merciful，warm-hearted（**慈爱的、热心肠的**）

“‘Now，I’ll tell you what，my friend，’ said Scrooge，‘I am not going to stand this sort of thing any longer. And therefore，’ he continued，leaping from his stool，and giving Bob such a dig in the waistcoat that he staggered back into the Tank again：‘and therefore I am about to raise your salary！’

‘A merry Christmas，Bob！’ said Scrooge，with an earnestness that could not be mistaken，as he clapped him on the back. ‘A merrier Christmas，Bob，my good fellow，than I have given you for many a year！I’ll raise your salary，and endeavors to assist your struggling family，and we will discuss your affairs this very afternoon，over a Christmas bowl of smoking bishop，Bob！Make up the fires，and buy another coal-scuttle before you dot another I，Bob Cratchit.’”

Mr. Scrooge要给Bob先生加薪，他承诺要帮助Bob全家，他还让Bob给火里多加些木柴，这些举措与之前Mr. Scrooge刻薄、冷漠、吝啬的形象形成了巨大的反差。

故事的结局是美好的，Mr. Scrooge改变了自己，他成了一个“好人”。“Scrooge was better than his word. He did it all，and infinitely more；and to Tiny Tim，who did not die，he was a second father. He became as good a friend，as good a master，and as good a man，as the good old city knew，or any other good old city，town，or borough，in the good old world.”

那么，“好人”应该具备哪些特征呢？我认为，*A Christmas Carol*这本书告诉我们，“好人”就应该是“待人友好、慷慨大方、乐于助人，对人有怜悯心、同情心及慈爱之心的人”。在我看来，与其说是上帝拯救了Mr. Scrooge的灵魂和未来，不如说是他自己拯救了自己。

当然，这本书也让我们了解到什么是圣诞精神。我认为包括以下三点：

1. Christmas is a time to be with family and friends，like our Spring Festival.

2. Christmas is a time to bring happiness and bless to everyone.

3. Christmas is a time to be generous to the poor.

All in all, the center of Christmas Spirit is humanitarianism. The spirit of Humanitarianism is hidden in everybody's heart. We can use it to love, to forgive others. As long as we dig it out and use it to help others, we will be a good man.

工作室人员分享

看了一系列场景之后再看到自己的坟墓，Scrooge的心凉了，他知道自己的未来就会是这样，死得很惨，很悲凉，没有人关心他是怎么死的，都觉得他死得活该。他内心极度恐慌，他不断地求助于鬼魂，说他已经改过自新，一定会改变，一定会对他人行善的。

带着泪迹斑斑的脸和惶恐的心情，他回到了现实生活中，看到自己没有死，仍在现实中活着时，他万般高兴，可以说胜过一个小学生。他立即改变了他的生活状态，对人友善，救济穷人，善待朋友家人，不再那么看重钱。并且在圣诞这一天做了很多令他人和自己都开心的好事，过了一个非常快活幸福的圣诞节。

这部经典名著和佛教的《地藏经》在写法上很有相似之处。佛经中赞扬了地藏菩萨在修行过程中有代表性的事迹，例如婆罗门女救母、光目女救母的故事。介绍了地狱的状况，解释了众生在生时、死时、忏悔时、为救拔亲人眷属苦难时的种种方法。佛教讲的是因果报应，警示人们要知因果，积德行善。

*A Christmas Carol*传播了圣诞精神。什么是圣诞精神？“反思自我，祝福他人”，让自己和别人在这个节日里都快快乐乐的。从反思而来的自信，通过分享带来的快乐，通过播散博爱让所有的人都幸福，通过秉持善良期待未来的美好生活。

——宋 蕾

读完*A Christmas Carol*，仿佛经历了一场心灵的洗礼。通过Scrooge这个人物形象，我对人生观、价值观有了更深刻的理解：正是金钱和贪欲让曾经纯真善良的人变成了可悲的守财奴. 然而善良和博爱的力量是巨大的，可以让Scrooge改过自新，重新认识生命的意义。这对我们当前的生活也有很好的启示意义。无论过去我们多么无知、迷茫，只要我们有勇气去重新选择今天的生活，并愿意改变自己，像Scrooge那样，我们便将有权获得幸福。任何人都不是完美的，每个人都会犯错，重要的是我们要懂得重新认知世界、认知自己。

在*A Christmas Carol*这部小说中，Scrooge的转变是上帝对他的救赎，更是他自己对自己的救赎。而在生活中，或许每个人都是自己的上帝。

——关少娟

Scrooge看到他衰老之后卧病在床，连圣诞节也没有亲人朋友来看望他的孤苦景象。三个鬼魂的造访唤醒了Scrooge人性的另一面——同情、仁慈、爱心、喜悦。 Scrooge固有的自私及冷酷消失殆尽，从此变成了一个乐善好施的人。在第5章中有两段描述给我留下了深刻的印象。第一个是Scrooge买了一只特别大的火鸡并叫人给Bob家送去。“The chuckle with which he paid for the Turkey，and the chuckle with which he paid for the cab，and the chuckle with which he recompensed the boy，were only to be exceeded by the chuckle with which he sat down breathless in his chair again，and chuckled till he cried.” Scrooge从中感受到了帮助别人能带给自己的快乐。第二个是Scrooge去拜访侄子，在街上逢人便招呼“圣诞快乐”，而人们也都报以和善的微笑。“He dressed himself ‘all his best’，and at last got out into the streets，waling with his hands behind him，Scrooge regarded every one with a delighted smile. He looked so irresistibly pleasant，in a word，that three or four good-humored fellows said ‘Good morning，sir！A merry Christmas to you！’ And Scrooge said often afterwards，that of all the blithe sounds he had ever heard，those were the blithest in his ears.”

在我看来，我们的生活中也有类似故事中“鬼魂”一样关心我们、鼓励我们，会指出我们的错误并帮助我们去改正的人，他们是我们的父母、好朋友等。多亏了他们，我们才能过着幸福的生活。当然，我们也应该记得要心存感恩，友好地对待身边的每个人。

——李 丹

在过去的章节中，Scrooge目睹了自己的死亡，感受到了周围人的冷漠。他开始改变自己。他试图对周围的人更慷慨、更友善。他帮助那些需要帮助的人，并与他自己的亲戚和朋友重新建立联系。就这样，他终于开心起来了。他有一个美妙的晚会，美妙的游戏和美妙的幸福！我感到幸运的是，他终于能意识到自己的幸福了。从他的经验中我也意识到，付出比索取更快乐。送上玫瑰，手捧芬芳。“Life is too short and precious so make it count.” 生命太短暂、太珍贵，所以要珍惜。

——李秀文

在这本书中，三个鬼魂是重要人物。过去的圣诞鬼魂、现在的圣诞鬼魂和未来的圣诞鬼魂给了Scrooge一些影子。这些阴影让他意识到一些事情。最后讲述了在三个鬼魂的来访后，他的一些巨大变化。

他终于知道他之前是错的，而这些阴影改变了他的生活。他醒来后发现鬼魂在一个晚上拜访了他。他买了一只大火鸡，把它送给Bob，并给了募捐者一大笔钱。小蒂姆后来也健康了。Scrooge再也没有见过鬼魂，因为他让圣诞节的精神活在了他和每个人的心里。

我认为作者试图告诉我们，我们的未来取决于我们现在的行为。我们应该更加关注那些真正珍贵的东西，比如亲情和对世界的同情心，用热情、慷慨和善意对待你周围的人。而且做人不能自私自利，要多为他人着想，正所谓“我为人人，人人为我”。

——麦佩莹

“‘If he wanted to keep them after he was dead，a wicked old screw，’ pursued the woman，‘why wasn’t he natural in his lifetime? If he had been，he’d have had somebody to look after him when he was struck with Death，instead of lying gasping out his last there，alone by himself.’

‘It’s the truest word that ever was spoke，’ said Mrs. Dilbert. ‘It’s a judgment on him！’”

在这一段，作者给我们展示了Scrooge死后的凄凉画面：孤独一人，无人料理，无人悲伤，家中财物被盗，甚至还有些人觉得他有这样的结局是罪有应得。这个画面让我想到了“完美受害者”理论。该理论就是：因为这个受害者不是完美的，所以他成为受害者是活该，是自找的。

在这里，Scrooge孤独地死在家中也是一个偶然+一个悲剧，他是受害者。可是那些去他家偷东西的人却用他平时性格不好，没人照顾他，所以他的死就是上帝对他的惩罚，他有罪等这样莫须有的理由为自己的偷盗行为开脱。在这里，我想发表我的看法：虽然冷漠无情的确可能让Scrooge孤独终老，但这不是什么罪过，每个人都有选择自己活法的权利，他既不偷也不抢，就算真的孤独终老，也不应该被人拿这个说事儿，说他的死是活该。

——莫 然

Chapter 5 “The last of the Spirits” 向我们展示了两组画风对比强烈的画面。一个是Scrooge死后的凄凉，无人过问。在他死后，人们没有悲悯，只有不屑与嫌弃，甚至还变卖他的一些遗物，连身上穿的衣服都不放过。此时的Scrooge绝望地向鬼魂恳求：“‘If there is any person in the town，who feels emotion caused by this man’s death，’ said Scrooge quite agonized，‘show that person to me，Spirit，I beseech you.’”结果看了一圈下来，“The only emotion that the Ghost could show him，caused by the event，was one of pleasure.”。此时这种黑色幽默也让人忍俊不禁。Scrooge只能无奈地说：“Let me see some tenderness connected with a death.”。

接下来鬼魂带他看的是他属下Bob的孩子。Tiny Tim过世时，一家人为之悲伤，被人铭记的画面，对比强烈。

"'No, never, father!' they all cried again.

'I am very happy,' said little Bob, 'I am very happy!'

Mrs. Cratchit kissed him, his daughters kissed him, the two young Cratchits kissed him, and Peter and himself shook hands. Spirit of Tiny Tim, thy childish essence was from God."

我们感受到的是当亲人逝去，家人的悲伤和缅怀，还有美好的祝愿。这两个画面，让主人公Scrooge受到了很大的冲击。

在Chapter 6 "The End of It"里，Scrooge被看到的一切吓出了冷汗，惊醒后发现这是一场梦。幸好是一场梦，一切都还来得及。接下来Scrooge一改往常，主动和一个男孩搭讪，乐意给一点小费让小男孩帮他做事。

读完之后，感受到作者构思的巧妙，也引发自己关于人生的一些思考。如果能让我们看看自己的将来，或许我们会把现在过得更有意义，会更加珍惜一些东西。读书不仅是在读着别人的故事，品尝作者给予的鸡汤，也真的是给自己的生活以警醒与启发，让浮躁的内心获得启迪和平静。

——徐 燕

在经过"过去之灵""现在之灵""未来之灵"的轮番刺激下，Scrooge看到了童年时的欢乐，穷人间的友善，自己以后的惨状，他终于做出了改变，用慷慨、友爱、宽容之心代替了那颗冷漠、吝啬、封闭的心，并得到了人们的赞赏与喜爱。书中对他内心独白的描写生动形象：

"'How sad,' thought Scrooge, 'to die with no friends or family around him! To lie in an empty room, with no candles or flowers, and robbed of his clothes! To know that nobody loves him, because he loved nobody in his life! Money can't buy a happy life, or a peaceful death!' He looked at the spirit, whose hand was pointing at the man's covered head. It would be easy to lift the sheet, and see who the man was. But for some reason Scrooge could not do it. 'I will remember the past, and think of the future. I will be good to other people. I will keep Christmas in my heart, and will try to be kind, and cheerful, and merry, every day. Oh, tell me I can clean away the writing on this stone.'"

"Scrooge did everything that he had promised, and more. To Tiny Tim, who did NOT die, he became a second father. He became as good a friend, employer and man, as anyone in London or in the world."

——郑剑湘

*A Christmas Carol*让我感受到人性的本质。其实人之初，性本善，是自私自利把我们慢慢地腐蚀。正如书中所看到的未来，你做了善事，心中快乐，你做了恶

事，像书中的Marley，肩负沉重的铁链，灵魂得不到安息。*A Christmas Carol*让我感悟到了圣诞节的意义，如果世界上能多些如书中的“鬼魂”一般的人，把那些自私自利的人们的心灵转变，让我爱人人，人人爱我，这个世界将会变得多么美好。

在读*A Christmas Carol*原著前，我读过故事的简介并看过电影，但还是原版书籍里对故事主人公人物特点的勾画更为深刻，描述风格更为犀利！

——莫洁雯

*A Christmas Carol*的第一个目的是向读者介绍圣诞节是个感恩和帮助他人的节日。Scrooge先生同三个鬼魂的历险，惊险刺激。但这本书的目的不只是如此浅显，Dickens写这本书还有更深层次的目的，是为了揭示当时英国社会穷人的生活现状。书中有一场非常深刻的对话，现实的鬼魂怒斥主人公没有行善事，可他狡辩自己努力经商交税，英国政府用这笔钱修建了大量福利院和救济所，拯救了很多孤儿和穷人。可鬼魂反问道：“你是指监狱和囚犯工厂？”这也暗示着当时的福利院和救济所没办法拯救孤儿和穷人，最终他们还是被送进了监狱和囚犯工厂。

严苛的法律只能惩罚小偷、妓女、杀人犯，福利院收容所只能保留他们的肉身，使其成为劳动力，但是没办法培养出会计、律师、科学家。穷人的命运被那些贵族牢牢把控，永无出头之日。

——夏丽焱

“He wondered what would happen if this man could rise now. What would he think? He lay in the dark without a man，woman，or child to grieve. No one cared he was gone. No one but the cat scratching at the door and the rats stirring beneath the hearth begging to be let in. Why were they so restless now? Scrooge didn’t dare to think.”跟着最后一个鬼魂，Scrooge看到了自己死后的惨状。路人开他玩笑，没有怜悯之心。那些佣人分光他的物品，他死后都不能体面地离开……他躺在黑暗中，没有一个男人、女人或是孩子为他哀悼。没有一个人在乎他的离世，只有老鼠和猫在身边闹。这一段描写，让我觉得Scrooge既可怜又无可奈何。因为是他自己造成了如今的局面，生前为人吝啬自私，没有人情味，死后就显得格外孤独和凄凉。“restless”这个单词用得巧妙：Scrooge生前不喜欢圣诞节，因为觉得麻烦，他也不喜欢别人麻烦他；死后就真的没有人吵他，只有老鼠在上蹿下跳。

“His hands were busy with his garments turning them in and out.‘I don’t know what to do！’he said，laughing and crying in the same breath.‘I’m as light as a feather. I’m as happy as an angel. I’m as merry as a schoolboy. Merry Christmas to everybody！Happy New Year to all the world.’”（我就像羽毛一样轻飘飘的。我

就像天使一样乐呵呵的。我就像学童一样喜洋洋的。祝每个人圣诞快乐！祝全世界新年快乐）

Scrooge从梦境中醒来，如获重生。他完全变了一个人，之前阴郁吝啬，而现在快乐得就像一个孩子。他感恩世界，感恩所有人，他不再讨厌圣诞节。

“The church steeple rang out. Ding，dong，bell. Bell，dong，ding. Hammer，clang，clash！Oh，glorious！Glorious！”Scrooge的心境不同了，他对圣诞欢歌的感受都发生了变化。“glorious”一词体现了他当时的心情，并真正地点题“欢”歌。他从不知道就这么简单地走走路能给他带来如此多的欢乐。

——董筱妍

这两章作者让吝啬鬼身处他死后的场景，看到了死神，这让他害怕极了。这个场景也慢慢地唤醒他，唤醒他内心中一些好的品质，比如对他人的同情心，他的善良和对别人的爱。他也终于明白了三个鬼魂出现的意义，他终于意识到他之前所犯的错误和愚蠢的做法。最终，他用行动去证明他的确想改变自己了。当我们面对死亡的时候，不管是谁的死亡，我想都会引起我们的反思。反思什么呢?比如，我本来应该要做得更好，我本来应该要对别人更好，我本应该对这世界更友善。所幸，像吝啬鬼一样，我们都有改变的机会，但要获得这个机会可能需要花费我们一生的时间，或者需要我们付出沉重的代价。因此，活在当下吧！学会谦卑待人，把握住爱的时间，常怀感恩之心，不要爱得太迟。

——袁泳施

这个星期，我读完了这本书，给我留下深刻印象的是Scrooge的巨大变化，特别是最后一个鬼魂给他看的他死后的情景。没人在乎他的死，两个为他洗衣服和做家务的女人甚至偷了他的衣服卖了钱，让他光着身子死去。就这样结束他的生命，真是太遗憾了。Scrooge希望看看是否有人会关心他的死。鬼魂告诉他，只有曾向他借过钱的一对夫妇在乎他，怕他会要求他们把钱还给他。多么可怜又可悲的Scrooge啊，没有朋友和家人在身边而孤单地死去！躺在一个空房间里，没有蜡烛和鲜花，死后连一点体面都没有，光着身子走！没有人爱他，因为他一生中没有爱过任何人！金钱买不到幸福的生活，也买不到平静的死亡。

从那之后，Scrooge决定改变，因为他从鬼魂那里知道了自己可怕而无望的结局！他答应对别人好。他要把圣诞节记在心里，每天都试着做个善良快乐的人！

当他回到现实的时候，在圣诞节当天，他很高兴。真的，对于一个这么多年没有笑过的人来说，这是一种绝妙的笑声。它是一长串精彩笑声的源头！能重活一遍，心境改变了，他看到的一切都变得奇妙。他从窗户往外看。没有雾，晴朗、明亮、寒冷的天气，金色的阳光，蓝色的天空，清新的空气，欢快的钟声。

他帮助他周围的人。他在圣诞节把火鸡送给了Bob！下午他去了侄子家。他经过侄子家门口好几次才鼓起勇气去敲门。后来他被侄子带进了起居室。最后，他们度过了一个愉快的圣诞之夜。

Scrooge做了他所承诺的一切，甚至做得更多。他成了一个好人、好的雇主和好男人。看到他的变化，有些人笑了，但他不在乎。他的内心在笑，这对他来说已经足够好了。他再也没有和鬼魂交谈过，但圣诞节过得很愉快，他过上了幸福的生活。这是我们都想要的。

——宋碧燕

*A Christmas Carol*的后两章主要讲了“未来之灵”的来访和Scrooge改过自新感悟到人生真谛的故事。

我深深地感觉到这本书有着一种温暖人心的力量。小说通过奇异而充满快乐的圣诞节，改变了吝啬鬼的人生轨迹，也使很多人对这个节日有了新的诠释，并为之感动。整本书给了我们一个很好的价值观，让人获得快乐幸福或许只用一件小东西或者一个小举动就能实现，这就是善行的力量。我尤其喜欢文中的这段文字：

“Best and happiest of all，the Time before him was his own，to make amends in!

‘I will live in the Past，the Present，and the Future.’ Scrooge repeated，as he scrambled out of bed. ‘The Spirits of all Three shall strive within me. Oh，Jacob Marley，Heaven，and the Christmas Time be praised for this. I say it on my knees，old Jacob，on my knees.’

He was so fluttered and so glowing with his good intentions，that his broken voice would scarcely answer to his call. He had been sobbing violently in his conflict with the Spirit，and his face was wet with tears.”

当醒来后发现一切只是个梦，而自己还躺在床上，活在人世间的时候，他激动不已，因为“所有的事物之中，最好的最幸福的事情是，他将来的时间是属于他自己的，使他可以改过自新”。

这本书对我们当前的生活也有很好的启示意义，无论过去我们多么无知、迷茫和负有偏见，只要我们有勇气去重新选择今天的生活，并愿意改变自己，像Scrooge那样，我们就有权获得幸福。任何人都不是完美的，每个人都可能犯错，就像每个人都可能会改正一样。在小说中，Scrooge的转变是上帝对他的救赎，同时更是他自己对自己的救赎。而在生活中，或许每个人都是自己的上帝。

——王之光

In the end of the story，Scrooge saw his own future：

“He lay，in the dark empty house，with not a man，a woman，or a child，to say that he was kind to me in this or that，and for the memory of one kind word will be kind to him. A cat was tearing at the door, and there was a sound of gnawing rats beneath the hearth-stone. What they wanted in the room of death, and why they were so restless and disturbed, Scrooge did not dare to think."

"...when old Joe, producing a fiannel bag with money in it, told out their several gains upon the ground. 'This is the end of it, you see! He frightened every one away from him when he was alive, to profit us when he was dead! Ha, ha, ha!'

'Spirit!' said Scrooge, shuddering from head to foot. 'I see, I see. The case of this unhappy man might be my own. My life tends that way, now.'"

By reading the story, we learn a lesson:

Why do we live, to please ourselves as well as others.

—Ting Feng

下篇
The Book Thief

◎ 内容简介：

*The Book Thief*是澳大利亚作家Markus Zusak创作的长篇小说，首次出版于2005年。该小说以“死神”的视角用第一人称来描述故事，并用稍带揶揄的口吻叙述着第二次世界大战背景下一个女孩成长的故事。1939年的德国，9岁的小女孩Liesel和弟弟被迫被送往Munich远郊的寄养家庭。弟弟不幸死在了路上。在冷清的葬礼后，Liesel意外得到她的第一本书*The Grave Digger's Handbook*。这将是14本给她带来无限安慰的书之一。这个孤苦的孩子，父亲被纳粹抓走，母亲随后也失踪了。在苦难的日子里，Liesel每晚抱着*The Grave Digger's Handbook*入睡，噩梦不断。养父为了让她安睡，便为她朗诵*The Grave Digger's Handbook*，并开始教她识字。在养父的引导下，她学会了阅读。尽管生活艰苦，她却发现了一个比食物更难以抗拒的东西——书。她忍不住开始偷书，并用偷来的书继续学习认字。从此Liesel进入了文字的奇妙世界。这个被死神称为“偷书贼”的可怜女孩，在战乱中的德国努力地生存，并不可思议地帮助了周围同样承受苦难的人。

Part One of The Book Thief

Arrival on Himmel Street—Growing up a Saumensch

导读

本期开始我们一起读经典名著*The Book Thief*。今天我们共读第一部分的前两个小节，“Arrival on Himmel Street”和“Growing up a Saumensch”。

1939年的德国，9岁的小女孩Liesel和弟弟被迫被送往Munich远郊的寄养家庭。6岁的弟弟不幸死在了路途中。在冷清的葬礼后，Liesel意外得到她的第一本书*The Grave Digger's Handbook*。

这将是一本给她带来无限安慰的书。她是个孤苦的孩子，父亲被纳粹带走了；母亲随后也失踪了。在会弹奏手风琴的养父的帮助下，她学会了阅读。尽管生活艰苦，她却发现了一个比食物更难以抗拒的东西——书。她忍不住开始偷书。Liesel，这个被死神称为“偷书贼”的可怜女孩，在战乱中的德国努力地生存着，并不可思议地帮助了周围同样承受苦难的人。

Author profile and writing background

Markus Zusak was born in Sydney, Australia, on June 23, 1975. He grew up listening to his parents' stories of their childhoods in Vienna and Munich during World War II.

One story his mother often told was about watching a group of Jews being marched down the street on their way to the concentration camp in Dachau.

An old man was struggling to keep up with the rest of the group. When a boy ran up to the man and offered him a piece of bread, the man fell to his knees, crying and kissing the boy's ankles. Then German officers took the bread from the man and whipped the boy.

This scene became the basis for “*The Book Thief*”. In the book, it is the main character's foster father who offers the old man the bread and is whipped by the officer. Zusak has said the story symbolized everything that is both beautiful and horrible about humanity.

By the time *The Book Thief* opens, in 1939, Hitler had been self-declared "führer", or leader, of Germany for more than four years. Anyone with Jewish blood was removed their civil rights. Communists, Socialists, and anyone else considered an enemy of the Nazi Party was arrested and sent to labor camps in Dachau.

Main characters

Death: The narrator of the story. Death collects so many souls.

Liesel Meminger: a nine -year-old girl who loses her brother and is given over to foster parents in Molching. She is lonely and misses her mother and brother so much. But she represses it and tries her best to fit in the new family.

Hans Hubermann: Liesel's step father. Hans is patient and gentle with Liesel, and is the first adult who is able to win her trust. He is constantly motivated to help others, and his strong sense of right and wrong causes him to act against his own best interests.

Rosa Hubermann: Liesel's stepmother. Unlike her husband, Rosa first looks cold and impatient. The story reveals, however, that beneath her tough exterior she is in fact kind and caring through her treatment of Liesel and willingness to take in Max.

Plots

When Liesel arrives in Molching, she has at least some inkling that she is being saved, but that is not a comfort. If her mother loves her, why would she leave her here on someone else's doorstep? ...The fact that she knows the answer—if only at the most basic level—seems beside the point.

Her mother is constantly sick and there is never any money to fix her. Liesel knows that. But it doesn't mean she has to accept it... Nothing changes the fact that she is a lost, skinny child in another foreign place with more foreign people, alone.

The Book Thief is a nine-year-old girl, Liesel Meminger. She and her younger brother, Werner, are traveling by train with their mother towards Munich, where they will live with a foster family. As *The Book Thief* dreams of Adolph Hitler, Werner dies suddenly. Liesel and her mother get off the train with Werner's body at the next station and bury him in the town. One of the grave diggers drops a book, and Liesel, who has been digging in the snow, picks it up. Liesel and her mother continue on to Munich, then to a suburb called Molching. Liesel's new foster parents live on Himmel Street, in Molching.

Liesel's stepfather, Hans, is a house painter who wins her over by teaching her how to roll cigarettes for him and playing his accordion for her. After a few weeks, Rosa Hubermann instructs Liesel to call her and her husband Mama and Papa. Liesel complies.

工作室人员分享

Rosa 和Hans 用不同的方式爱着Liesel.

I think both Hans and Rosa loved Liesel in their different ways. Rosa loved Liesel although she was constantly shouting abuse and beating her with a wooden spoon. She never called Liesel by her name. When Liesel finally had a bath，after two weeks of living on Himmel Street，Rosa gave her a big hug and asked her to call her Mama. She said，"I'm Mama Number Two".

For Hans，when Liesel refused to have a bath，Hans，described as a house painter and accordion player，acted more kindly. He taught Liesel to roll a cigarette. He is a gentle man with a remarkable amount of integrity and bravery—Hans' compassion sets a strong example for Liesel，who is soothed by his presence.

——王之光

After I read this book，I found the most impressive part is Death and Rosa Hubermann.

Death is the narrator of the book. It is through his eyes that we witness the unfolding of the lives of the people on Himmel Street. Death doesn't like his work，but he knows it is his duty，so he keeps on taking souls with him. He tries to appreciate the colors of the world，they are his focus as he takes the souls，because he cannot stand to see the grief of the those left behind.

Rosa Hubermann is a woman who is angry with the world. Rosa makes everyone march to her tune. Her way of showing endearments is to call those she loves pigs and others assholes. She has a very colorful vocabulary and uses it to its fullest effect.

Death goes on to explain in detail the story of *The Book Thief*，Liesel Meminger. Liesel and her brother，Werner，were being taken，by their mother，to Munich. She was going to turn them over to foster parents，so they could have a better life than what she would be able to give them.

Werner was buried in an unknown town. His mother and sister，along with the two grave diggers were in attendance. The young apprentice grave digger dropped his book and Liesel took it. This was the first book she stole. It was a guide to being a grave digger.

She was turned over to Hans and Rosa Hubermann，who lived in the town of Molching on Himmel Street. Hans seemed kind，but Rosa was an angry woman.

We learn that Liesel's father was a communist，which caused problems for her mother，because others did not want to be associated with a communist. Liesel and her brother were being given up to foster parents，because their mother was ill and couldn't take care of them.

Rosa Humbermann was an ill-tempered woman who called Liesel Saumensch，which means female pig. She called everyone a pig and an arschloch which is an "asshole". She for all her crude ways did love Liesel.

Hans Hubermann was a gentle man，who was a painter by trade and made extra money by playing the accordion. He was kind to Liesel and made her feel safe. After a few months，Rosa told Liesel to call her Mama and Hans Papa.

——宋碧燕

"××× How it happened ×××

There was an intense spurt of coughing.

Almost an inspired spurt.

And soon after—nothing.

When the coughing stopped，there was nothing but the nothingness of life moving on with a shuffle，or a near-silent twitch. A suddenness found its way onto his lips then，which were a corroded brown color and peeling，like old paint. In desperate need of redoing."

让我印象深刻的是这一段，描写小男孩快要死了的一瞬间，作者描写得细致入微、生动逼真，让人不禁感受到人有时很坚强但同时也很脆弱。

"For Liesel，there was the imprisoned stiffness of movement and the staggered onslaught of thoughts. Es stimmtnicbt. This isn't happening. This isn't happening.

And the shaking.

Why do they always shake them?

Yes，I know，I know，I assume it has something to do with instinct. To stem the flow of truth. Her heart at that point was slippery and hot，and loud，so loud so loud."

这一段作者描写了主人公Liesel的弟弟死的一刹那，Liesel失去亲人的痛苦以及她的悲痛心情。人世间最伤心的事莫过于亲人离世，九岁的小女孩Liesel经历了人世间的悲欢离合，品尝了人世间的苦难，在以后人生道路上会变得更加勇敢坚强。

——宋 蕾

It is a story about separation and death caused by war. As a mother，I can't help putting my feet into the mother's shoes and feel a strong sense of desperation. "The new family could at least feed the girl and the boy a little better，and educate them properly."（P25）This is her menial hope. However，God let her down by taking her son away. Just a few words are used to describe the mother directly. "There was woman wailing... She climbed down into the snow，holding the small body... the body in her mother's arms... the body was getting heavy."（P22）"How could that woman walk? How could she move？"（P25）But from these short sentences，I can feel that her sadness deep in her heart is too heavy for a mother to bear. Who is willing to send her own children to a foster family unless there is no hope to live on? How could a mother stand the pain of burying her little child? However，she experiences both. She has to manage to get through it. She is numb finally. During the war，there were so many mothers losing their children and so many children died from hunger or left their parents. Everyone struggled to live. This was the darkest time in human history. The writer wrote this book，I think，to emphasize the value of life and to call on all people to cherish our peaceful life today.

——关少娟

第24—25页的内容让我印象深刻。在埋葬了弟弟之后，Liesel和妈妈继续坐上火车前往Munich寄养家庭。

"Mother and daughter vacated the cemetery and made their way toward the next train to Munich. Both were skinny and pale. Both had sores on their lips. Liesel noticed it in the dirty，fogged-up window of the train when they boarded just before midday. In the written words of *The Book Thief* herself，the journey continued like *everything* had happened."

这个everything用了斜体来向我们表达女孩内心这样的一种感受，那就是她仿佛经历了世上一切悲欢离合，出发时三个人，下车时已是天人永隔，现在只是两个人的旅途。亲眼看见弟弟的死亡与埋葬，对小主人公Liesel来说太过残酷，也让人感受到揪心之痛。

"When the train pulled into the Bahnhof in Munich，the passengers slid out as if from a torn package. There were people of every stature，but among them，the poor were the most easily recognized. The impoverished always try to keep moving，as if relocating might help. They ignore the reality that a new version of the same old problem will be waiting at the end of the trip—the relative you cringe to kiss. I think her mother knew this quite well. She wasn't delivering her children to the higher echelons of Munich，but a foster home had apparently been found，and if nothing else，the new family could at least feed the girl and the boy a little better，and educate them properly."

这段文字背后，也让我们感受到无助母亲对待孩子们的一份良苦用心。

我们知道与战争有关就注定是一个悲剧的故事，也许Liesel身边的人来来去去，终将离开，我们将见证很多的生离死别。但还是觉得阅读这本书真的让人着迷。

——徐 燕

From the beginning of the book，I realize the story is narrated by a special character—the Death. And the author uses plenty of unique metaphors and descriptions of the characters，which makes the story more attractive to me.

In Chapter One，on the train to Himmel Street，Liesel saw her brother die and had to bury him in the snow with her mother and two grave diggers. Liesel was filled with sorrow and desperate in her heart. I also notice a detail description of this sentence：“She realized her mother had come back for her only when she felt the boniness of a hand on her shoulder.” I think the word “boniness” shows the impoverished condition of Liesel's family. And that's why she's given to a foster family.

Speaking of her foster parents，Hans and Rosa，they have very different personalities. Hans is a man with patience and gentleness while Rosa is a woman who is good at being furious. She even called Liesel “Saumensch”，which had a bad connotation on her. “But she did love Liesel. Her way of showing it just happened to be strange.” In other words，we know her bark is worse than her bite.

——麦佩莹

Hello，good evening my dear friends. It feels like a great honor and privileged to read this book，*The Book Thief* by Markus Zusak，an international bestseller with lots of international awards. And I do agree with most of the praise for the book in the front of the book. The book is stunning，fabulous，gripping and touching，which can keep me into the night feverishly reading.

And for the content，the writer successfully creates a hook in the beginning of the book，which can arouse my interest and curiosity to keep on reading for more.

I am really impressed by the language itself in the book. And here I definitely agree with what *Time*（the magazine） said about the book. “Zusak doesn't sugarcoat anything，but he makes his ostensibly gloomy subject bearable ... with grim，darkly consoling humor.” I am kind of obsessed with its narration in the book. It tries hard to be neutral. But you can still sense its irony and humor. School Library Journal starred the book “an extraordinary narrative”.

I really appreciate the following narration. “A reassuring announcement，please be calm despite the previous threat. I am all bluster. I am not violent. I am not malicious.

I am a result." It's clear. And very neutral but full of humor.

Another paragraph, "the guards were tall and short. The tall one always spoke first. Though he was not in charge. He looked at the smaller round one the one with the juicy red face." Juicy red face. Quite interesting.

Another description about Liesel's Foster mother. "She is good at being furious, in fact you could say that Rosa Hubermann had a face decorated with constant fury. That was how the creases were made into the cardboard texture of her complexion." Anything ugly can be expressed in a humorous way.

And what the narrator said really inspired me. "My one saving grace is distraction. It keeps me sane, it helps me cope, considering the length of time I've been performing this job (the dead). The trouble is who could ever replace me? Who could step in while I take a break? The answer, of course, is nobody. Which has prompted me to make a conscious, deliberate decision to make distraction my vacation. Needless to say, I vacation in increments (counting the dead?) in colors." The heroine Liesel also made reading her vacation a break from the cruel world.

I am reminded that Life sometimes can be unbearably hard and tiring. Life is not always promised to be pleasant. But we still have to cope with it. So we'd better learn to enjoy it. How? Make distraction our vacation. Let's live positively with a sense of humor. Let's make a difference together.

——李秀文

阅读这两个小节时的心情多半都是沉重的。走投无路的母亲被迫把9岁的Liesel和弟弟送给Munich远郊的人家收养。6岁的小男孩却不幸死在途中，这便成为Liesel 终生摆脱不了的噩梦。文章画面感强，很容易让读者感同身受。其中的一些描写直扣人心。比如说在简单操办完弟弟的葬礼后，描写Liesel的那一段。"The girl, however, stayed. Her knees entered the ground. Her moment had arrived. Still in disbelief, she started to dig. He couldn't be dead. He couldn't be dead. He couldn't... Within seconds, snow was carved into her skin. Frozen blood was cracked across her hands. Somewhere in all the snow, she could see her broken heart, in two pieces. Each half was glowing, and beating under all that white." 失去了弟弟，又要面对和母亲的离别，只身一人来到养父母家。作者将养父母的形象描写得生动形象，一个大嗓门整天骂骂咧咧叫她"小母猪"却心地善良的养母，以及一个眼睛里散发着温暖光芒的养父。相信在接下来的章节中，养父的温柔会更暖人心，Liesel的坚强会更让人感动。

——李 丹

At the first chapters, the author tries to brush over the seriousness of the situation, somehow I was touched by the descriptions of the book. And I think probably Liesel has died at the beginning of the book. Death is not something special or surprising. Everybody dies. Liesel, when she was still little, had witnessed her brother's death. In her inner mind, she has died because of everything.

"The girl, however, stayed.

Her knees entered the ground. Her moment had arrived.

Still in disbelief, she started to dig. He couldn't be dead. He couldn't be dead. He couldn't—

Within seconds, snow was carved into her skin.

Frozen blood was cracked across her hands.

Somewhere in all the snow, she could see her broken heart, in two pieces. Each half was glowing, and beating under all that white. She realized her mother had come back for her only when she felt the boniness of a hand on her shoulder. She was being dragged away. A warm scream filled her throat."

From which I also learn the bitterness of losing someone you love.

However, the sadness didn't end after her brother died. Maybe from that moment, Liesel died in her heart too.

Although she knew nothing about words, she kept the first book very well, because that's about the last scene when she was with her family. And it was also the beginning of her love for reading.

——袁泳施

我是从第1页开始读*A Book Thief*这本书的，书的一开头就讲到“Here is a small fact. You are going to die.”。我预感这本书的内容可能会让人感到很悲伤。文中的“I”，是死神，以他的视角用第一人称去讲述“偷书贼”的故事，因此，我在想，偷书贼是不是一直都在与死神打交道，但是又一次次幸运地活了下来？读完前面35页，我的心情是很压抑、很悲伤的。尤其是上面这段文字，深刻细致地描述了Liesel弟弟葬礼结束后，Liesel是多么的伤心欲绝。Liesel不愿离开，她无法接受弟弟已经离开的事实，她开始挖地，文中讲到她感到刺骨的冰冷，双手的血液仿佛也结冰了，她的心被撕成了两半。读到这里，我也觉得很“冷”，感同身受。我在想如果我的至亲去世了，我也会不顾冰冷地去挖地。后来，Liesel的妈妈也不得不离开她。我在想，当时是怎样一个悲惨的世界啊！我很期待后面的内容，希望后面的内容不再那么令人悲伤。

——陈雪芬

*The Book Thief*这本书用了大量色彩和四季的变化去反映人物内心的心情，作者通过运用比喻的修辞手法，以“颜色”“天空”“云朵”“文字”等生活周遭的事物，衬托当时战争的残酷，从而突出人物的性格。我很喜欢作者用“颜色”贯穿整个故事情节。故事一开始和书本的页面一样净白，待主角进入故事，书本颜色、天空色彩更迭、爸爸Hans眼睛的银色光泽、手风琴上的黑白琴键、遍地血流成河的鲜红、Liesel老年死时的午后蓝……在书中看到了成千上万的奇幻色彩，每个色彩都有其象征意义。（P4）“the question is，what color will everything be at that moment when I come for you? What will the sky be saying? Personally，I like a chocolate-colored sky. Dark，dark chocolate. People say it suits me. I do，however，try to enjoy every color I see—the whole spectrum...”（我逼近你的那一刻，天下万物呈现出什么样的色彩？天空出现哪种讯息？我自己最喜欢巧克力色的天空，很深、很深的巧克力色，人家说这种颜色适合我。不过，我还想尽量欣赏我见到的每一种色彩，光谱中所有的颜色……）颜色舒缓了我的压力，放松了我的心情。

——郑剑湘

故事的开头发生在一辆通往Himmel Street的火车上。快十岁的Liesel本来是和她的弟弟、妈妈一起去养父母的家。在经历了一些变故之后，只剩下她成功到达。令我印象深刻的是书中25页关于火车车站的描写。

无论是在西方还是在东方，车站都代表着离别，车站上，形形色色的人，各行各业各类层次的人在里面不停地穿梭着，车站是最不缺少人烟的地方。这一段中重点描写穷人在车站时的情景。文章中提到“The impoverished always try to keep moving，as if relocating might help.”。穷人在火车站中不停地中转，车站就好像是他们奔赴新生活的美好承载。就像Liesel一样，她的妈妈病了，没办法抚养她和弟弟，不得已才将他们送去养父母家。火车的终点就是她的新生活。

第二个令我印象深刻的是在第2章中关于洗澡的描写。新家的陌生让她坐立不安，所以她一直都不肯洗澡，她的养母是一个性格很直率的人，就会用方言骂她。但是，她的养父却是一个相貌平平但很温柔的人。他教她roll a cigarette，两个人静静地坐在月光下。养父的平和和从容让她很快镇定下来。这就是温柔的力量吧。

There is nothing stronger in the world than gentleness.

——董筱妍

“To most people，Hans Hubermann was barely visible. An unspecial person. Certainly，his painting skills were excellent. His musical ability was better than average. Somehow，though，and I’m sure you’re met people like this，he was able to appear as merely part of the background, even if he was standing at the front of a line. He was always just there. Not noticeable. Not important or particularly valuable.

The frustration of that appearance, as you can imagine, was its complete misleading, let's say. There most definitely was value in him, and it did not go unnoticed by Liesel Meminger. (The human child—so much cannier at times than the stupefying ponderous adult.) She saw it immediately.

His manner.

The quiet air around him.

When he turned the light on in the small, callous washroom that night, Liesel observed the strangeness of her foster father's eyes. They were made of kindness, and silver. Like soft silver, melting. Liesel, upon seeing those eyes, understood that Hans Hubermann was worth a lot."

I think the description is very vivid and makes me think of some of my students who are so colorful inside but too shy to show themselves.

I think Hans also has a very colorful soul and maybe Liesel will be influenced by him and change herself in some way.

——莫 然

On a snowy gray morning in 1939, a woman took her daughter, the main character, and son to Munich, where the girl and the boy would soon be given over to foster parents in order that the children could live on. While on the train, the boy died. The woman buried the boy half way. The girl, Liesel, experienced the whole thing. Finally, Liesel was sent to the foster family sadly and alone. Although she was told thousands of times that she was loved. She refused to accept it. So in Liesel's heart, nothing could changed the fact that she was a lost, skinny child in another foreign place, with more foreign people. Alone. At first, Liesel had a hard life in the foster family. Foster mother called her pig. She didn't have a bath for two weeks. She had nightmares every night. Luckily, her foster papa was really kind to her. When she refused to take a bath, he said gently "leave her to me" and they played with tobacco and the cigarette papers. He didn't forced her to take a bath at all. Of these two parts, what impressed me most is Liesel's three WHYs. The three WHYs show Liesel felt lonely, helpless sad...

——Ting Feng

The Woman with an Iron Fist—The Other Side of Sandpaper

导读

本期的分享内容是*The Book Thief*第一部分的第3至6小节——“The Woman with an Iron Fist”“The Kiss”“The Jesse Owens Incident”和“The Other Side of Sandpaper”。

这周的四个章节，每个章节都在侧重介绍一个人物，我们一起来看看吧！

首先是“The Kiss”这个章节。

“Insane or not，Rudy was always destined to be Liesel's best friend. A snowball in the face is surely the perfect beginning to a lasting friendship.”（P48）

“In fact，Rudy Steiner was one of those audacious little bastards who actually fancied himself with the ladies.Every childhood seems to have exactly such a juvenile in its midst and mists.He's the boy who refuses to fear the opposite sex，...and he's the type who is unafraid to make a decision.”（P49）

根据这些句子，我想用下面四个形容词来概括Rudy：naughty、naive、narcissistic、determined。他的自恋和坚定让我觉得他更多了一分可爱。

接着就是“The Other Side of Sandpaper”。

“He ran a hand through his sleepy hair and said，‘Well，promise me one thing，Liesel. If I die anytime soon，you make sure they bury me right.’she nodded，with great sincerity.”（P66）

“‘Papa！’she whispered.‘I have no eyes！’He patted the girl's hair. She'd fallen into his trap.‘With a smile like that，’Hans Huberman said，‘you don't need eyes.’He hugged her and then looked again at the picture，with a face of warm silver.”（P68）

根据这些句子，我想用下面四个形容词来概括Hans：humorous、highlyesteem、optimistic、positive。Hans就是一个很让人喜欢的角色。

在“The Woman with an Iron Fist”中，Rosa被塑造出来的形象是愤世嫉俗的、经常很抓狂的。

在“The Jesse Owens Incident”中，一个不谙世事的男孩和一个残酷的现实，形成了鲜明的对比。

还想跟大家分享一下我很喜欢的一个段落：

"'Hundred meters,' he goaded her. 'I bet you can't beat me.' Liesel wasn't taking any of that. 'I bet you I can.'

'What do you bet, you little Sau mensch? Have you got any money?'

'Of course not.Do you?'

'No.' But Rudy had an idea.It was the lover boy coming out of him. 'If I beat you, I get to kiss you.' He crouched down and began rolling up his trousers.

As they walked back to Himmel street, Rudy forewarned her. 'One day, Liesel,' he said, 'you'll be dying to kiss me.'"（P53-55）

在这个部分当中，我感受到了Rudy对Liesel的心动，他们之间的情感在一步步升温。

在"The Woman with an Iron Fist"中，我留意到一些幽默的描述：

"When a woman with an iron fist tells you to get out there and clean spit off the door，you do it. Especially when the iron's hot."（P44）

"A man known primarily as 'Pfiffikus'—whose vulgarity made Rosa Hubermann look like a wordsmith and a saint."（P46）

关于Liesel的变化，文中有一个鲜明的对比。比如，之前在学校她是不合群的，年纪比其他小孩大，但懂得太少，总是想在人群当中消失。在爸爸的帮助下，她日渐进步，现在能赶上进度了，就不觉得自己是怪胎了。所以有了爸爸在身边，她的生活变得好过些了。我打心底为Liesel感到高兴，她的生活正在一步一步地走向光明。

在读完四个章节后，我有一些感悟。我更加深刻意识到种族平等、人人平等是非常重要的。幸运的是，我们没有生活在那个可怕的年代，而是生活在一个安全平等的社会，没有战争，没有硝烟，有的只是满满的幸福感。同时，在养育孩子方面，我们应该对孩子更细心、更温柔。与此同时，在他们的成长过程中，要花更多的时间去陪伴。还要忠于自己的决定，保持积极和自信的生活态度！祝愿我们的世界变得越来越美丽！

工作室人员分享

在"The Woman with the Iron Fist"这一章中，首先，我感受到了浓浓的生活气息。女主人公Liesel因为不会阅读和写字，在学校无所适从，在家也没有人能够教她。然后笔锋一转，描写了她养父母拌嘴的日常。Mama说Papa教不了Liesel，因为他四年级就没上学了。Papa就腹黑地回复Mama才读了三年级。养父母之间的日常拌嘴非常可爱。

其次，我觉得很生动的地方是在41页对养母Rosa的描述。就算是夜晚的厨房，它都是很热闹的，因为Rosa一直在说话，与人争辩，不停地在抱怨。但是Rosa手上也一直没停，一直在打铁。这一段形象生动地描写了一个劳动女性的日常。

最后，在这四章中我见证了Liesel和Papa的关系慢慢亲近的过程。一开始Papa夜晚的陪伴，逐渐建立起父女之间的信任，再到后面父女俩之间有了小秘密——一起读一本书。这过程是多么温馨啊！

——董筱妍

这几章中，我最喜欢的一章是《砂纸的背面》，Liesel和Hans相处的点点滴滴让我感动。此时在我眼中Hans举止沉静、和蔼可亲，眼睛里充满了慈爱，闪着柔光。Hans会在Liesel做噩梦的时候到床边爱抚她。更让我感动的是，Hans无意间发现了她的书，他并没有因为这是一本*The Grave Digger's Handbook*而忽视地扔掉它，反而同意读给她听。Hans自己的阅读能力也不怎么样，他同样对这本关于掘墓人的书感到困惑，但还是开始给Liesel读。Hans发现Liesel自己不会读任何单词，于是他开始用砂纸和画家的铅笔教她字母表。

在我看来，这本书最初对小女孩来说是对母亲和弟弟的纪念，前面的章节提到过the book's meaning，（1. The last time she saw her brother. 2. The last time she saw her mother.）。接下来，这本书好像又变成了小女孩和养父之间的一种联系，或许这本书里并没有特别吸引人的故事，应该也没有任何优美的词句和意境，但是我们可以想象这本书为小女孩打开了一个全新的世界。正是因为生活中的点点滴滴，让她感受到了人与人之间的脉脉温情，也得到了无尽的勇气与希望。

——王之光

Liesel的第一位领读人是她的养父Hans。Hans是从“一战”的战场上捡了一条命回来的老兵，也是一位会拉手风琴的粉刷匠。他22岁的时候，在法国的战场上，有一个比他大一岁的战友教会了他拉手风琴。在战役中，他躲过了一劫，成为唯一的幸存者。Liesel因亲眼看见了弟弟的死亡，接着成了弃儿，她心里对生活存在着渴望。在遇到Hans之前，她过着卑微的生活，虽未死，生活却如同死水一般。Hans或许听懂了Liesel午夜噩梦中的每一声尖叫，那是对死的恐惧和对生的绝望。Hans因为文字，成为战争的幸存者。作为幸存者的他，又用文字，拯救了Liesel。他们之间传递的，不只是生命，还有通过文字、书籍传递的爱。

——郑剑湘

这几章能引起我共情的地方有很多。下面我挑了感受最深的几点来跟大家分享。

“Hello，stars.”（P45）

Liesel初到养父母家，养母虽然心善，但脾气暴躁，整天喋喋不休地谩骂。街道的居民有些也不好相处，甚至有人往别人门上吐痰。这是一个社会底层的劳动人民家庭。Liesel离开亲生父母，亲眼看见弟弟的死亡，入住新家庭，适应一个全新并且压抑的环境，对于小小年纪的她，太不容易了。晚上清洁门上的口水，抬头看到星星，她跟星星打招呼。这是艰难环境下，一次呼吸自由空气的机会，这是一个短暂的、美好的瞬间，这句“Hello，stars.”说明了女主角是坚强的，对待生活是积极向上的。

“‘Don’t ask him for help，’ Mama pointed out，‘That Saukerl，’ Papa was staring out the window，as was often his habit.‘He left school in fourth grade.’

Without turning around，Papa answered calmly，but with venom，‘Well，don’t ask her，either.’ He dropped some ash outside.‘She left school in the third grade.’”（P39）

这两句对白太接地气了。当谈到孩子教育问题的时候，妈妈说爸爸帮不上忙，他只有四年级水平。爸爸说妈妈更帮不上忙，她只有三年级的水平。读到这里，我忍不住大笑。这对父母太可爱了。但是后来证明，没读过多少书的他们却养育出了优秀的“偷书贼”。对于孩子来说，比起有学历的父母，有爱的父母更重要。

关于 Rudy，我的脑海里时不时浮现出一个全身涂满黑炭的小男孩。Rudy模仿Owens跑步夺冠这个情节实在太出彩了。这个男孩子活泼开朗，鬼点子多，聪明，模仿能力强。他涂好黑炭后，还要往口袋里装几块黑炭，随时准备补妆。像极了我们化好妆出门逛街，还要往包里放口红的样子。很幸运，Liesel 交到了Rudy 这个好朋友，他们一起游戏，一起上学。上学的路上，Rudy给Liesel介绍路上遇见的人和事。我们能感受到他们之间的童真童乐。他们还一起挑逗Pfifikus. 书中是这样描述这个人物的：“The old man simultaneously straightened and proceeded to swear with a ferocity that can only be described as a talent.”（P53）。他在骂人方面是一个天才，脏话连篇。即便如此，Liesel 还是会还口。“‘Pfiffikus，’ she echoed，quickly adopting the appropriate cruelty that childhood seems to require. Her whistling was awful，but there was no time to perfect it.”这段描写让我想起了童年类似的经历。我们上学要路过一片田野，田野上有时候会晒着腌好的白萝卜，就摆放在稻草上。我们几个调皮捣蛋鬼会偷来吃。萝卜又脆又甜，在物质比较匮乏的年代，这是小孩的美味了。农村里的老太太，不是所有的都是慈祥的。有一个特别厉害，骂人就跟Pfifikus一样毒。她发现我们偷了她的萝卜，就大声地问候我们祖宗十八代，声音大得全村都听得到。可是我们依然偷，拿了就跑，她追不上我们。现在想想那时候我们太调皮了。后来读高中了，我们买糖给她吃，以此弥补我们童年时犯的错误。

Rudy 可谓是Liesel青梅竹马的朋友，他是Liesel灰暗童年里的一笔亮色。虽然Liesel对于Rudy提出的亲吻的请求，回答是“Not in a million years.”“你做梦吧，想都别想”，但这正是两小无猜的乐趣和美好的回忆啊！

——关少娟

阅读这几节给我留下深刻印象的有两个人，一个是Liesel的养父Hans Hubermann，另一个是Liesel的同学Rudy Steiner。Liesel是不幸的，但她又是幸运的，因为她遇到了一个真正爱她、懂她、会拉手风琴、有一双闪着银光眼睛的养父，还有看似粗俗可笑但却善良的养母。我们不难从字里行间体会到她内心感受到的幸福。比如说Liesel做噩梦时，养父安抚她的相关描写："He came in every night and sat with her. The first couple of times，he simply stayed —a stranger to kill the aloneness. A few nights after that，he whispered，'Shhh，I'm here，it's all right.' After three weeks，he held her. Trust was accumulated quickly，due primarily to the brute strength of the man's gentleness，his thereness. The girl knew from the outset that Hans Hubermann would always appear midscream，and he would not leave."。除此之外，还有在"The Other Side of Sandpaper"这一小节里描写养父用午夜的课堂引领她进入文字世界的场景，使她在悲惨恐怖的环境下也能获得心灵的安宁而且变得更坚强。至于Rudy，Liesel的同学，带着她上学，并成为她最好的朋友。Rudy性格开朗，怀揣着要成为世界上跑得最快的人的梦想，因此他将自己全身涂成黑色，在一个漆黑的夜晚在运动场上跑步。这滑稽的情景历历在目。Rudy喜欢调皮捣蛋，却对Liesel非常友好，他和Liesel比赛跑步，为的是赢得Liesel的一个吻，显然在Rudy心中，Liesel是美好的象征。也正是因为有了这样的朋友，Liesel体会到了朋友的价值，获得了宝贵的友谊。

——李 丹

这一段描写让人感觉很温暖。我喜欢接下来的叙述。在第36页，Liesel的养父"Hans Hubermann came in every night and sat with her. ... After three weeks，he held her. Trust was accumulated quickly，due primarily to the brute strength of the man's gentleness，his thereness."。一个有趣的词"there"和"ness"合起来就有了"thereness"，它只是意味着"在那里"。叙述者总结道："Not leaving：an act of trust and love，often deciphered by children."。后来，关于舒适的身体气味的描述让我印象深刻。"Hans Hubermann sat sleepy-eyed on the bed and Liesel would cry into his sleeves and breathe him in. Every morning，just after two o'clock，she fell asleep again to the smell of him. It was a mixture of dead cigarettes，decades of paint，and human skin."听起来很矛盾。"dead"和"decades"意味着老旧，而"human body"意味着生命。虽然Liesel梦到了她死去的弟弟，但是这气味给她带来了生机。"At first，she sucked it all in，then breathed it，until she drifted back down."

这让我想起了我的父亲。我小的时候，我父亲就是我的超人。我喜欢他身上的味道。在他的怀抱里我感到安全。有时仅仅是"在那里"，就可以给孩子安慰、关心和爱。"Thereness"很重要。

Liesel对Rosa的描述很有趣和幽默。“she was always talking，and when she was talking，it took the form of schimpfen. She was constantly arguing and complaining. There was no one to really argue with，but Mama managed it expertly every chance she had. She could argue with the entire world in that kitchen，and almost every evening，she did.”这有点儿夸张了。但也许因为作者是个男人，他对母亲这个角色的印象才如此可笑却又令人厌恶吧？也许我们应该多注意一下自己的形象，待人处事要表现得更加明智和善良。

——李秀文

天无绝人之路，故事发展到这部分终于可以让读者从压抑中抽离回来一些了，Rudy和Liesel养父的出场给读者带来了一点希望和温暖，Liesel养母的出场也把读者的注意力从残酷的战争中转移到战争时代人们的家庭生活中。

“Possibly the only good to come out of these nightmares was that it brought Hans Hubermann，her new papa，into the room，to soothe her，to love her.”也许这些噩梦带来的唯一好处就是把Hans——她的新爸爸带进了房间，来安慰她、爱她。上帝还是给了Liesel一点补偿，给她安排了一个充满爱的养父。

Rudy，一个可爱的男孩。“In fact，Rudy was one of those audacious little bastards who actually fancied himself with the ladies.”（事实上，Rudy是一个大胆的小混蛋，他幻想自己能和女士们在一起）“Insane or not，Rudy was always destined to be Liesel’s best friend. A snowball in the face is surely the perfect beginning to a lasting friendship.”（不管是不是疯了，Rudy注定是Liesel最好的朋友。打在脸上的雪球肯定是持久友谊的完美开端）。Liesel在非常灰暗的阶段遇上了一个活泼积极的“小混混”，对她来说也是一件挺好的事情。

——莫洁文

在这几章里，令我印象最深刻的情节就是养父在战场上跟自己的队友学手风琴。由此我才知道，虽然战争本身是很残酷的，会造成很多的流血和牺牲，但是去参加战争的大部分人也都不过是普通人，他们甚至根本不愿意打仗，只想早点结束战争回家陪家人。而且在这里关于手风琴的描写总让我感觉是个伏笔，估计后面这个手风琴会有大用处。除了手风琴之外，还有一个令我印象深刻的片段就是养父陪Liesel读书了，养父并没有因为Liesel拿着一本奇怪的《掘墓人手册》而打击奚落她，反而非常耐心地教导她去读书，成为Liesel的启蒙老师。我想我们作为教师，面对基础比较差的孩子，如果也能抱着这样宽容和耐心的态度，也许可以帮助他们更好地找到学习的乐趣吧。

——莫 然

今晚有三件事想与小伙伴们分享。

第一，是Liesel和Hans。

这是一个小女孩的故事，她的生活被她弟弟的死所颠覆，她的母亲把她留在养父母家照顾。Liesel经常做关于她弟弟的噩梦，Hans会来到她的房间让她平静下来，他还会在早上为她拉手风琴。后来，当Hans发现她有一本书时，他和Liesel进行了一场有趣的谈话。

“这是你的吗？”

“是的，爸爸。”

“你想看吗？”

“是的，爸爸。”

一个疲惫的微笑。

一双仿佛正在熔化的银色眼眸。

“好吧，那我们最好读一读。”

然后他们开始了每天午夜的阅读课。

她也被送去了学校，但一切都很糟糕，因为她已经九岁，但不会认字。学校安排她和年纪小的孩子们在一起，这样她虽然可以学习阅读，这对她来说很尴尬，但她确实在试着阅读。

第二，是Rosa。

Rosa把时间花在抱怨所有的事情上，尤其是那些雇她洗衣服的人。Rosa和她的邻居也有不和，每次经过Rosa家的时候，她的邻居都会在她的门口破口大骂，并且把痰吐在Rosa家的门上。我觉得她的邻居也是个奇葩，很幼稚。

第三，是Rudy。

在隔壁男孩Rudy朝Liesel扔雪球后，Liesel和他成了朋友。Rudy告诉她在社区里要远离谁，要信任谁。他也是她的犯罪搭档，比如那天他们在赛道上比赛，两人都因为赛道太湿而变成了泥人。

Liesel开始适应新环境，交了新朋友。我非常高兴能看到她的转变，从类似自闭中走出来接受新的一切。

——宋碧燕

陪伴，就是对孩子的爱。

许多父母认为，给自己的孩子提供充足的食物、大房子和优质的教育，就是一个负责的父母。不可否认，上述条件确实是现代社会中培养人才的重要因素。

但是，我必须指出，有了这些还远远不够。不论父母在儿童成长过程中提供多少物质，如果缺乏信任和爱，儿童就永远无法成长为一个有责任感并成熟的人。

在本书中，小主人公为什么乐意喊Hans“爸爸”。原因也在此，Hans用他的爱与信任治愈了Liesel的恐惧，换来了她的爱。

——夏丽焱

在这几章中，描述了Himmel Street 上的普通百姓平凡简单的生活，有争吵，有寒暄，有小朋友们的嬉笑打闹，也有家庭里夫妻间、亲子间的吵架拌嘴。在这几章中，我们了解了Hubermann夫妇，以及Rudy是如何与Liesel成为朋友的。作者形容养母是"the woman with an iron fist"，但文中描述的却是一个有温度的刀子嘴豆腐心的妇人，这个比喻很有趣。

在Chapter 3中，关于《掘墓人手册》这本书的前后描写让我印象深刻。关于手风琴对Liesel的意义："The sound of the accordion was，in fact，also the announcement of safety. Daylight. During the day，it was impossible to dream of her brother. She would miss him and frequently cry in the tiny washroom as quietly as possible，but she was still glad to be awake."（对于一个小女孩来说，太难了，与弟弟的死别，与妈妈的生离，噩梦缠绕，让她会不禁尿床）。

"On her first night with the Hubermanns，she had hidden her last link to him—*The Grave Digger's Handbook* —under her mattress，and occasionally she would pull it out and hold it. Staring at the letters on the cover and touching the print inside，she had no idea what any of it was saying. The point is，it didn't really matter what that book was about. It was what it meant that was more important.

THE BOOK's MEANING

1. The last time she saw her brother.

2. The last time she saw her mother.

Sometimes she would whisper the word Mama and see her mother's face a hundred times in a single afternoon. But those were small miseries compared to the terror of her dreams. At those times，in the enormous mileage of sleep，she had never felt so completely alone. "

虽然这是主人公心底的痛，但是我们也庆幸她还是找到了一个好的寄养家庭。所有宁静的生活都是在二战的背景下存在的，这注定是一个悲伤的故事，越是这样有趣生动，在死神的诉说中，结局恐怕越会叫人悲伤。如果说*The Secret Garden*是欲扬先抑，那*A Book Thief*便是欲抑先扬，读起来让人有种莫名的心痛与感动。

——徐 燕

Liesel遇见了Rudy，一个可爱的男孩。"In fact，Rudy was one of those audacious little bastards who actually fancied himself with the ladies."不知怎的，Rudy对Liesel好像有些特别的感觉，可能因为第一次见面是在跟他喜欢的足球

有关的场合；可能是因为在她脸上的那个泥雪球让他印象深刻；也可能是因为Liesel想打败他的决心；也可能是因为这让他想起他的偶像Jesse Owens的事件，“The moon was down into the sky and the clouds were stitched around it.”，他们一样无畏。Rudy也是一个没心没肺的简单孩子，面对目标，有一股冲劲儿。他也自信地跟Liesel说：“You will be dying to kiss me one day.”（终有一天你肯定会忍不住亲我的）。所以Liesel这个小女孩，身边也有了这样一个乐观积极的小伙伴。她还有papa，他用他的画作教她字母，教她写字，安抚她度过每个担惊受怕的夜晚，让她感到安心和快乐。这些都太难得了。“With a smile like that，you don't need eyes. He hugged her. What a day！”

——袁泳施

Part One—Two of The Book Thief

The Smell of Friendship—The Joy of Cigarettes

导 读

这一期我们一起品读书本第一部分的“The Smell of Friendship”“The Heavyweight Champion of the School-Yard”“A Girl Made of Darkness” “The Joy of Cigarettes”。在这四个章节里，作者给我们呈现的是四个故事：和爸爸一起读书，校园里的一场“战役”，主人公Liesel的第二本书，还有就是关于礼物。

字里行间，我们继续感受着在小镇上发生的日常生活，而且透过文字，我们对人物的性格也有了愈加深刻的感受。文中的描写温暖人心，如以下文字所描绘：

“As they walked toward Frau Diller’s，they turned around a few times to see if Mama was still at the gate，checking on them. She was. At one point，she called out，‘Liesel，hold that ironing straight！Don’t crease it！’

‘Yes，Mama！’

A few steps later： ‘Liesel，are you dressed warm enough？！’

‘What did you say？’

‘Saumensch dreckiges，you never hear anything！Are you dressed warm enough？It might get cold later！’

Around the corner，Papa bent down to do up a shoelace. ‘Liesel，’ he said，‘could you roll me a cigarette？’

Nothing would give her greater pleasure.” （P70）

从对话中我们可以感受到Rosa的“刀子嘴豆腐心”。在这一章节里，我们知道Rosa是一个强悍的妻子，Hans是一个“妻管严”。夫妻间的对话就显得非常有趣。“‘I’m asking you，I’m begging you，could you please shut your mouth for just five minutes？’ You can imagine the reaction.”（P72）

夫妻间的打趣拌嘴，让Liesel逐渐敞开心扉，融入新的环境，并且与身边的人愈加亲近。

正如在“The Joy of Cigarettes”这个章节里所描述的，养父母的生活本就捉襟见肘，还想着给Liesel准备生日礼物——书，养父没能来得及给妻子买一双她心爱的鞋子，但是这位善良而又极易满足的妻子却丝毫不计较。

“A few nights later，however，Hans Huberman came home with a box of eggs.‘Sorry，Mama.’He placed them on the table.‘They were all out of shoes.’

Mama didn’t complain.

She even sang to herself while she cooked those eggs to the brink of burndom. It appeared that there was great joy in cigarettes，and it was a happy time in the Huberman household.”（P90）

这真是一对善良有爱的夫妻，在这样的大背景下，这些淳朴的百姓显得那样可爱与宝贵。

“The Heavyweight Champion of the School-Yard”，在这个章节里，Liesel性格中倔强、不服输的一面向我们展示得淋漓尽致。起初只是在一次朗读练习中，Liesel有些自信地认为可以发挥得很好，殊不知自己掌握的那点儿有限的文字或者知识，还不足以应付这个“艰巨”的任务。她没有退缩，硬着头皮，乱说一通，迎来的自然是小伙伴的一片嘲笑。这个倔强的“女汉子”为了捍卫自己的尊严，直接和其中一位带头嘲笑她的同学打了一架。“She stood up and took the book from him，and as he smiled over his shoulder at some other kids，she threw it away and kicked him as hard as she could in the vicinity of the groin. Well，as you might imagine，Ludwig Schmeikl certainly buckled，and on the way down，he was punched in the ear. When he landed，he was set upon. When he was set upon，he was slapped and clawed and obliterated by a girl who was utterly consumed with rage. His skin was so warm and soft. Her knuckles and fingernails were so frighteningly tough，despite their smallness.‘You Saukerl.’Her voice，too，was able to scratch him.‘You Arschloch. Can you spell Arschloch for me？’”（P78）

Liesel就是这样有些粗鲁，却非常勇敢要强。在战火纷飞的年代，有些人选择唯唯诺诺，有的人选择迎难而上，活也要活得漂亮。

但就是在这样的一个背景之下，作者会冷不丁地在行文之中冒出一些叫人沮丧的文字。

“She even sang to herself while she cooked those eggs to the brink of burndom. It appeared that there was great joy in cigarettes，and it was a happy time in the Hubermann household.

It ended a few weeks later.”（P90 Chapter 10）

“Like most misery，it started with apparent happiness.”（P84 Chapter 9）

“The beginning of September. It was a cool day in Molching when the war began and my workload increased.

The world talked it over."（P73 Chapter 8）

以死神的视角，我们一边感受幸福温暖的同时，也感受到战火下生活的压抑，及其带来的痛苦的蔓延。比如，"A Girl Made of Darkness"中有对德军的这样一番描述：

"The Germans loved to burn things. Shops，synagogues，Reichstags，houses，personal items，slain people，and of course，books. They enjoyed a good book-burning，all right—which gave people who were partial to books the opportunity to get their hands on certain publications that they otherwise wouldn't have."

可见战争的可怕。而胆大的Liesel敢在这样的环境下，扒开火堆，从而得到了自己的第二本书——多么的讽刺和凄凉。所有的见闻与经历冲击着Liesel，也让读者对主人公的命运产生强烈的好奇。

当读完这四章之后，我们不禁感慨，生命是宝贵的，我们应该珍惜所拥有的；当我们遇到困难的时候，还是要勇敢面对，努力去克服，如此，我们才能收获成长与幸福；动荡年代的人们能够活着已是幸运。愿世界和平，愿每个人都能过得幸福、快乐。

工作室人员分享

在这几章内容当中，令我印象最深刻的是对Liesel打架的情景描写，作者对Liesel的动作和语言描述得很生动细致，让人看完觉得很解气。我认为Liesel是非常勇敢的，她真的很生气愤怒，换作别人，明知道自己不会阅读，也许会觉得很惭愧、很尴尬，但是Liesel面对别人的嘲笑时能勇敢地做出反击，我很欣赏她这种行为，虽然打架是不对的。

此外，我印象最深的还有第86页，当中描写到Liesel和爸爸已经读完A Grave Digger's Handbook第十一章，还剩最后一章时，爸爸已经很困了，上下眼皮在打架，但是Liesel 还恳请爸爸继续把书读完。爸爸没有拒绝，反而长舒了一口气，继续给Liesel读书至天亮。这体现了爸爸对Liesel浓浓的父爱。

最后，我想请教大家，第87页中描写到爸爸读完书后说了一句话："Look at the colors. It's hard not to like a man who not only notices the colors，but speaks them."我不理解爸爸话中的man是指谁，爸爸说这句话有什么深层的意思吗？

——陈雪芬

书中第78页提到，当Liesel被一个叫Ludwig的小男孩所羞辱时，其他孩子都在旁边看热闹，直到看着她大发雷霆。这时Rudy建议她要冷静下来，但是她说你说起来容易，你又不傻。这句话真的很令我震惊，她所说的让我想起了那些在学习方面有困难的孩子。其他人会觉得学习并不是一件难事，然而那些孩子并不这样认为。他们确实在学习中非常努力，但是收获并不明显。所以作为教师，我们应该如何帮他们解决困难呢？这个问题对我来说，还需要更多的思考。

书中接下来提到Liesel的圣诞节礼物——两本书。她的养父把那些肮脏的香烟全都卷起来，然后把它们卖出去，八根香烟换一本书。Liesel对她的礼物非常满意，因为这些礼物蕴含着爸爸对她的爱。看到这样的场景，妈妈有点小嫉妒了。几个晚上以后，爸爸带了一些鸡蛋回来给她，因为鞋子都卖光了。刀子嘴豆腐心的妈妈，开心地煮了那些蛋。是彼此的爱维系着这个家庭。

——董筱妍

我最喜欢的一章是“The Joy of Cigarettes”，其中的两处情节让我感到温暖。

第一处是Hans为Liesel读书的情节。这天，Liesel和Hans已经读完了*The Grave Digger's Handbook*的三个章节，还剩最后一章“Respecting the Graveyard”。这时已是凌晨三点了，Liesel貌似想一口气读完最后这章，可是Papa，“his silver eyes swollen in their tiredness...”（爸爸的银色眼睛已经满是疲倦……）。虽然如此，在Liesel的请求下，Hans还是为她读完了最后一个章节，此时，天已将近破晓。

第二处在第88页。“To her surprise，on Christmas Eve，after sitting in church at midnight with Mama，Papa，Hans Junior，and Trudy，she came home to find something wrapped in newspaper under the Christmas tree.‘From Saint Niklaus，’Papa said，but the girl was not fooled. She hugged both her foster parents，with snow still laid across her shoulders.”

可见，小姑娘与养父之间，慢慢有了一种亲昵与默契。父亲阳光而乐观，在战争的阴云中努力让家庭中有一点阳光。他与小姑娘之间几乎建立了一个属于两个人的秘密地下读书会。我们也有理由相信，养父每天坚持熬夜陪她阅读，教她识字和坚持阅读的行为本身，就会使文字呈现出更大的触及心灵深处的魔力。

——王之光

Rudy与Liesel之间“友谊之花逐渐开放”。邻居Rudy为Liesel带来快乐，坚守秘密、追求梦想的行为让Liesel感受到友谊的珍贵，Liesel逐渐克服了内向的问题，性格逐渐转为开朗乐观。

Rudy是Liesel的邻居和同学，当得知Liesel刚刚被Hans一家收养时，他早上便主动来打招呼，带着Liesel上学，并成为Liesel最好的朋友。Rudy性格开朗，也调皮捣蛋，却对Liesel非常友好。书中很多章节描写他们之间的友谊。他和Liesel比赛跑步，为的是赢得Liesel的一个吻，显然在Rudy心中，Liesel是美好的象征。在阅读测试中，Liesel测试失败，其他同学嘲笑Liesel，说她是最蠢的人，要求Liesel读文字给大家听，以此来羞辱Liesel，而Rudy却对Liesel说“Don't listen to them.”。他这么做的目的就是安慰Liesel，让她建立起对自己的信心，克服自卑心理。正是有了这样的朋友，Liesel才体会到了朋友的珍贵。同时，Rudy也是一个心怀梦想的人，他想像黑人欧文斯一样成为世界上跑得最快的人。为此，他将全身涂黑，迎风飞奔，只可惜家庭并不能忍受他这样的张扬性格。Rudy这样外向的性格也深深影响着Liesel，Liesel脸上的笑容越来越多，也更愿意融入集体的环境之中。

后来，得知Liesel家藏了一位犹太人时，Rudy按照他的约定坚守着这个秘密，他可以不顾一切地跳入水中去捞被河水冲走的书，时刻守护Liesel，种种行为都让Liesel感受到他们之间友谊的可贵。

我觉得，一位好的朋友就如一盏明灯，指引着一个人的人生之路。Rudy就是深深影响着Liesel的榜样，让Liesel逐渐开朗乐观，并载梦前行。

——郑剑湘

I really appreciate the languages of this book. It may touch you all of a sudden and cause you to tear. Also，it may make you laugh to tear. For example，

“Liesel，are you dressed warm enough？”（P70）

Liesel 和爸爸要去送洗好的衣服。前一秒钟，妈妈还在喋喋不休地唠叨、谩骂，用词十分不雅。突然，这样一句问候，虽然分贝一如既往的高，哪怕Liesel走远了，没有听清楚。妈妈的爱，我相信Liesel一定能感受得到。作为读者的我是突然被温暖到了。不得不佩服作者成功地塑造了一个刀子嘴豆腐心的妈妈形象。

“Why did he have to die？”（p80）

Liesel先被老师责罚，后与同学打架。小小的身体爆发了巨大的能量，一连把两个人打趴下了。可是在回家的路上，她却在雨中痛哭。“in a hurry of thoughts，a culmination of misery swept over her—the failed recital of *the Grave Digger's Handbook*，the demolition of her family，her nightmares，the humiliation of the day—and she crouched in the gutter and wept.”所有的委屈随着泪水和雨水倾泻而出。如果读到这里，你还没被触动的话，那么接下来，她的一句“他为什么会死？”一定会让你理解这个小孩心里承受了多么大的痛楚。死亡，是一个成年人都无法接受的事实。可是小女孩亲眼看见了弟弟在她面前死去！弟弟的死，是Liesel无法释怀、无法放下的。她喜欢阅读*The Grave Digger's Handbook*，一是因为她爱阅读；更重要的是，这本书是在弟弟的坟墓附近捡到的，是关于掘墓的。她阅读的时候也许能感觉到书与弟弟存在某种关联，能给她带来一定程度的慰藉。

“Just don't kick me in the egg.”（P80）

Liesel 哭的时候，Rudy没有打扰，而是默默陪伴。等Liesel 哭完了，他跟她开玩笑，说了这一句。我初读时没有反应过来，觉得奇怪，Rudy没有带着鸡蛋啊。难道我读漏了某些内容？后来一想，in 后面加身体部位，原来这句话是说：不要踢我的下身。“egg”这个词太形象了。我刚被感动得要哭，一下子又被逗笑了。这就是作者用词的魅力。这种语言是我们在教科书里接触不到的，只有原

版小说中才有，其实它更地道。

——关少娟

这几个章节让我进一步感受到了养父母对Liesel无微不至的关爱。养父带着Liesel前往Amper-upstream，养母在大门口喊道："Saumensch dreckiges，are you dressed warm enough? It might get cold later."。在我看来，养母简单的一句问候特别暖心，而养母口中的"肮脏的小母猪"也是贬词褒义，更多地体现了她对Liesel的疼爱。养父一直陪伴在Liesel身边，耐心地教Liesel读书写字，在河边、在地下室、在午夜的床边，离平安夜还有一个星期的某个午夜，养父陪伴Liesel读完*The Grave Digger's Handbook*。圣诞节到来时，养父用烟叶卷烟，然后拿到集市上跟吉卜赛人换来两本书*Faust the Dog*和*The Lighthouse*，作为圣诞礼物送给Liesel。

养父母的关爱融化了Liesel心中的坚冰，让她敞开了封闭的内心，心中多了份温暖和满足。在"The Smell of Friendship"这一节中有段描写体现了Liesel内心的温暖和满足。

"Sitting in the water，she imagined the smell of it，mapped out on her papa's clothes. More than anything，it was the smell of friendship，and she could find it on herself，too. Liesel loved that smell. She would sniff her arm and smile as the water cooled around her."

在Liesel看来，烟草味混合着油漆味就是爸爸的味道，是充满爱的味道。Liesel闻着这味道，用心地回味着来自爸爸的爱，发自内心地笑了。

在"The Heavyweight Champion of the School-yard"这一节中，我感受到了Liesel性格的另一面，也让我进一步感受到Rudy对Liesel的关爱。有一段描写让我印象很深刻。放学时，Liesel因纷繁的思绪和一连串悲惨的往事袭上心头而情绪失控，伤心欲绝地蹲下大哭。

"Rudy stood there，next to her. It began to rain，nice and hard. One sat painfully now，among the falling chunks of rain，and the other stood next to her，waiting. When finally she finished and stood herself up，he put his arm around her，best-buddy style，and they walked on."

伤感的场景中却有着满满的关爱。快乐向上的Rudy在心智上启迪着Liesel，让她克服了内向，逐渐开朗起来。

——李 丹

我还是被书里这部分的黑色幽默逗乐了。我发现Liesel很敏感却很勇敢，她的养母很严厉却很可悲。

其中对学生们阅读测试时的描述是如此生动，我都能感觉到Liesel当时的感受。"Throughout the test，Liesel sat with a mixture of hot anticipation and excruciating fear. She wanted desperately to measure herself, to find out once and for all how her learning was advancing...." "Each time Sister Maria looked at her list, a string of nerves tightened in Liesel's ribs. It started in her stomach but had worked its way up. Soon, it would be around her neck, thick as rope."这种感觉令人窒息。就像等待高考结果的感觉一样，对吧？当修女玛利亚没有邀请她读书时，她试着站在课室的前面，想象着"herself reading the entire page in faultless, fluency-filled triumph."。即使在她失败了，其他孩子羞辱了她之后，她的愤怒和凶猛还是没有爆发出来。所以最后当她宣布"I'm not stupid."时，没人争论，我觉得这部分很幽默。

Rosa粗鲁的语言让人觉得她难以接近。跟很多底层忙于生计的妇女相似，也许是因为长时间的辛苦劳累，她一直都很孤独。她没有读书，也不会演奏任何音乐，她一直在抱怨，但在她内心深处，她很容易被取悦。在第90页，当Hans交换了一些烟草，带着一盒鸡蛋回家时，Rosa甚至开心地对自己唱歌。

——李秀文

在这四章中，我印象最深刻的是"The Heavyweight Champion of the School-Yard"。Liesel终于到了她应在的年级，不用觉得自己太高大了。虽然她的写作和阅读确实在进步，但她仍然不如其他孩子。我不喜欢Mary修女说"l am afraid you can not do it."，这不是一个好老师应该说的话。我认为作为一名教师，我们的学生最需要的是我们的鼓励和认同，而不是我们的否认。"The girl cleared her throat...snickering."我能想象那种情况。看到Liesel想象自己完美、流畅、胜利地读完整页书，感觉很有趣。这意味着她渴望在他们面前展示自己的进步。不幸的是，她最终失败了。幸运的是，她身边有Rudy。"When finally she finished and stood herself up, he put his arm around her..."这句话让我比以前更崇拜Rudy了。他真是一个好伙伴、好朋友。我也相信Liesel总有一天会在阅读方面成功的!

——麦佩莹

在这部分，作者更多地描述了Liesel在养父养母家中的生活，其中有不少令人感到很温暖的温馨画面。这种家庭温暖跟战争的残酷形成了强烈的对比。

"'Saumensch dreckiges, you never hear anything! Are you dressed warm enough? It might get cold later!' Around the corner, Papa bent down to do up a shoelace. 'Liesel,' he said, 'could you roll me a cigarette?' Nothing would give her greater pleasure."（"见鬼，你什么也没听到！你穿得暖和吗？过一会儿可能会冷！"走到拐角处，爸爸弯下腰来系鞋带。"Liesel，"他说，"你能给我卷一支香烟吗？"再没有比这更使她高兴的了）

"There was a wooden-planked bridge. They sat maybe thirty meters down from it，in the grass，writing the words and reading them aloud，and when darkness was near，Hans pulled out the accordion. Liesel looked at him and listened，though she did not immediately notice the perplexed."（那里有一座木板桥。他们坐在离它大约三十米的草地上，一边写着字，一边大声朗读。夜幕降临时，Hans拿出手风琴。Liesel看了看他，听了听，虽然她没有立即注意到那天晚上爸爸弹琴时脸上困惑的表情）

这些画面都令人感到温暖！

——莫洁文

这几章很好看，故事从日常生活慢慢进入战争阶段，虽然没有直接写战争，但是从爸爸的accordion expression就可以侧面看出战争的残酷。

一开始爸爸妈妈的互动也很有意思，妈妈的各种碎碎念和吐槽像极了生活中妈妈的样子，非常有代入感，包括她吐槽爸爸会教Liesel什么，自己都没啥文化呢，吐槽Liesel不好好听她说话，爸爸和Liesel读书的时候也一直在叨叨叨，以至于爸爸都受不了她了，不过最后的结果是把两父女赶到地下室去读书了……这些细节都是特别生活化的，人物刻画也很生动。

后来二战开始了，爸爸的眼神又忧郁了，而且Liesel在学校的生活也出现了问题……她虽然每天都在努力学习阅读，但还是跟不上其他同学……在朗读测试的时候，她一个字都读不出来，只好背诵了她偷的那本书上的内容……同学们都笑了……甚至还有一个男生专门跑过来取笑她，虽然她揍了他一顿，甚至把其他同学都震慑住了。读到这里，我真心佩服Liesel。Rudy安慰她，而且Rudy是一边安慰她，一边有点怕她会迁怒打他，这里太喜感了。所以逆境有时也不完全是坏事，可以帮助人分清谁是真心对自己好的人，还可以锻炼自己解决问题的能力。不过看到后面书里突然转折说"很多痛苦都是从快乐开始的"，我就整个人都不好了……感觉准备开虐了。以至于后来读到Hans用卖烟的钱给Liesel买书作为圣诞礼物等比较欢快的情节时，我也隐约感觉到忧伤，都不敢开心，总觉得要发生什么不好的事情。

下面几个小片段我印象很深刻：

"They sat maybe thirty meters down from it，in the grass，writing the words and reading them aloud，and when darkness was near，Hans pulled out the accordion. Liesel looked at him and listened，though she did not immediately notice the perplexed expression on her papa's face that evening as he played.

There had been a change in him. A slight shift.

She saw it but didn't realize until later，when all the stories came together. She didn't see him watching as he played，having no idea that Hans Hubermann's accordion was a story. In the times ahead，that story would arrive at 33 Himmel Street in the early hours of morning，wearing ruffled shoulders and a shivering jacket. It would carry a suitcase，a book，and two questions. A story. Story after story. Story within story.”

这个关于accordion故事的伏笔特别有意思，特别是最后那个“Story after story. Story within story.”，让人充满了好奇，很想知道这个手风琴到底还有什么故事，而这个故事肯定是可以丰富对Hans的人物刻画的，因为雁过留声，发生过的事情就会在人的身上留下痕迹。很期待后面作者讲手风琴的故事。

还有妈妈说爸爸好臭，一身烟味和煤油味，而Liesel却很喜欢，觉得那是友谊的味道，这个细节我也特别喜欢。有时候喜欢一个人真的会觉得他的汗都是香的，这真的太真实了。

“Like most misery，it started with apparent happiness.”

这句话看得我差点把书给丢掉，有种“暴风雨前的平静”的那种感觉，接着立马风雨欲来，心里不免有点担忧。

——莫 然

这周，看完*A Book Thief*的部分章节，有一些场景给我留下了深刻的印象。

第一个场景：一天晚上，Liesel醒来发现自己尿床了。爸爸走进她的房间，看到她尿床后帮她换了床单。作为一个养父，我认为Hans是一个善良、脾气好、可爱的人。因为Hans和Rosa的爱，Liesel的生活不再黑暗。他们帮助Liesel很好地适应了当地的生活。

尽管她仍然会做噩梦，会梦到她的弟弟，会想念她的母亲，但现在她得到了安慰。

第二个场景：1939年10月，Liesel在学校的学习水平开始上升。11月，学校对全班学生的阅读能力进行测试，除了Liesel，每个人都被叫到了。她要求轮到她，可是当轮到她的时候，她还是看不懂上面写的字。在学校里，她被其他孩子嘲笑为笨蛋，她痛打了嘲笑她的同学。虽然老师罚她站在走廊里，但同学们都不敢再笑她了。我能看到Liesel的勇敢。正因为如此，Liesel的命运与其他女孩不同。

第三个场景：在她偷第二本书之前，Liesel和她的家人在庆祝圣诞节。她很惊讶地在平安夜发现了送给她的礼物。是两本书，她很高兴，因为她和爸爸已经读完了第一本书。Liesel发现爸爸通过卖他自己的香烟来买书送她。随着阅读能力的提高，她很高兴有了这些书，并且读了很多遍。在这个贫穷的家庭，他们没有更多的钱买礼物，但是Hans给了Liesel两本书，Liesel非常感激。另一面，尽管Rosa会抱怨她的丈夫一点都不好，她觉得如果Hans爱她，他就会用一些烟草换她急需的新衣服或更好的鞋子，但Rosa没有阻止Hans给Liesel买书。由此我们也可以看出Rosa是爱Liesel的。

我这周读所有章节时有很多快乐的时刻，我的心情也随之雀跃。

—— 宋碧燕

"He walked into the kitchen and said，'Sorry，Mama，she's not going with you today.' Mama didn't even bother looking up from the washing bag. 'Who asked you，Arscblocb? Come on，Liesel，' 'She's reading，' he said. Papa handed Liesel a steadfast smile，and a wink. 'With me. I'm teaching her. We're going the Ampere-upstream，where I used to practice the accordion.' Papa grinned and pointed at the girl. 'Book，sandpaper，pencil，' he ordered her，'and accordion！' once she was already gone. Soon they were on Himmel Street，carrying the words，the music，the washing. Around the corner，Papa bent down to do up a shoelace. 'Liesel，' he said，'could you roll me a cigarette？' Nothing would give her greater pleasure."

"They sat maybe thirty meters down from it，in the grass，writing the words and reading them aloud，and when darkness was near，Hans pulled out the accordion. Liesel looked at him and listened."

爸爸乐观、幽默风趣，就连教孩子读书也不是一板一眼的，都会引导孩子带着乐趣去读书。爸爸带着Liesel到安伯河旁边的草地上写单词，大声朗读，Liesel认真聆听他弹手风琴，而她最喜欢做的事就是帮爸爸卷烟。不知不觉中，他们已经建立了深厚的感情，爸爸对Liesel无微不至的关爱和细心耐心的教导，让这个饱受风霜的女孩有了依靠和安全感。

"In one of their basement session，Papa dispensed with the sandpaper（it was running out fast）and pulled out a brush. There were few luxuries in the Hubermann household，but there was an oversupply of paint，and it became more than useful for Liesel's learning. Papa would say a word and the girl would have to spell it aloud and then paint it on the wall，as long as she got it right. After a month，the wall was recoated."

Hans家没有什么富余的物件，油漆却是管够，它将在Liesel的学习中派上大用场。养父用家里能派上用场的油漆和刷子帮助Liesel读书写字，这种独特的学习方式不仅增添了乐趣，而且提高了学习效率，同时增进了父女之间的感情。

"'You stink，' Mama would say to Hans. 'Like cigarettes and kerosene.'

Sitting in the water，she imagined the smell of it，mapped out on her papa's clothes. More than anything，it was the smell of friendship，and she could find it on herself，too. Liesel loved that smell. She would sniff her arm and smile as the water cooled around her."

"你臭死了，"妈妈对Hans说，"全身都是烟味和煤油的味道。"然而Liesel却爱上了这种味道，那是友谊的味道，她在自己身上也能闻得到。Liesel和养父之间已经建立起了深厚的友情，这里不仅是友情，更是亲情，她爱她的养父，也爱上了他身上的味道，所谓"爱屋及乌"就是这个道理吧！

——宋 蕾

Liesel与Papa相处的画面让我动容。Liesel听着Papa的琴声，Papa在墙上教她读和写，“从学校回家的路上，从小河边到家里的地下室，从好日子到糟糕的时候”，papa都陪在她身边，我替她感到开心。“between school and home，from river to the basement，from good days to the bad. With an oversupply of paint，Liesel could use it well until she got it right.”当她成功写出字来的时候，她肯定乐开怀。虽然Papa和Mama文化程度不高，但他们其实很会教小孩。Papa和Mama的相处方式也让我们沉浸其中，他们爱着彼此，也非常关心Liesel。圣诞节时，当Mama告诉Liesel Papa是怎么得到这些书作为她的礼物时，“Mama only handed him one of her trademark looks of disgust，but when she got the eggs from papa by cigarettes，she felt so much joy.”。Mama嘲笑式地看着Papa，满满的温情。生活中其实有很多细节等着我们去发现，去感受生活的温度。这样的生活虽然简单但很深刻，也是Liesel最大的幸福来源。

——袁泳施

In these Chapters，the writer shows Liesel’s happiness in Molching to us.

Her foster father began to teach her to read. She got great interest in reading even though they had to read in the basement. We can imagine how dim and moist the basement was. In school，she had a fight with one of the kids because she was laughed at and provoked as a new comer to the place. She showed her power and from then on，no one dare to bully her，she got friendship from the kids. Then in the next chapter，she got her second book The Shoulder shrug while Nazi Germany was burning. In order to get the book，she risked to burn herself from the burning pile and as a result she got all dirty. What a book lover！Liesel received a great Christmas gift—two books. Even though she still had nightmares about her brother and missed her mother，there were comforts for her after she had settled into life in Molching pretty well. She finished reading *The Grave Digger's Handbook*，escaping the ire of Sister Maria，receiving two books for Christmas from her foster father. From these chapters，I learn that we should learn to enjoy life even if life is hard.

生活若苦，便要学会苦中作乐。

——Ting Feng

Part Two of The Book Thief

The Town Walker—100 Percent Pure German Sweat

导 读

今天品读的是*A Book Thief*第二章“The Town Walker” “Dead Letters” “Hitler’s Birthday，1940” 和 “100 Percent Pure German Sweat” 四个小节。

在“The Town Walker”小节中给我留下深刻印象的人物是养母Rosa，其中有三处描写。第一处是养母Rosa对Liesel说的一番话：“From now on you’re going to pick up and deliver the washing for me. Those rich people are less likely to fire us if you’re the one standing in front of them. If they ask you where I am，tell them I’m sick. And look sad when you tell them. You’re skinny and pale enough to get their pity.”。这一番话展现了Rosa以家庭为中心，在生活艰难时期设法维持一家子生活的心理。第二处是有关Liesel独自去收送衣物的描写：“Overall，Liesel enjoyed it. There was no share of the pay，but she was out of the house，and walking the streets without Mama was heaven in itself. No finger-pointing or cursing. No people staring at them as she was sworn at for holding the bag wrong. Nothing but serenity.”。这段描写充分展示了Rosa爱唠叨、强悍的性格特点。第三处是养母Rosa和养父Hans夜晚的对话：“The night she wrote the letter，she overheard a conversation between Hans and Rosa.‘What’s she doing writing to her mother?’Mama was saying. Her voice was surprisingly calm and caring. As you can imagine，they worried the girl a great deal. She’d have preferred to hear them arguing. Whispering adults hardly inspired confidence.‘She asked me，’ Papa answered，‘and I couldn’t say no. How could I?’ ‘Jesus，Mary，and Joseph.’Again with the whisper.‘She should just forget her. Who knows where she is? Who knows what they’ve done to her?’”从中我们可以感受到Rosa刀子嘴豆腐心和一心想保护Liesel不受伤害的善良。

在“Dead Letters”这一节，我想和大家重温的人物是Liesel。作者描写了Liesel渴望写信给母亲，盼望收到母亲的来信以及被养母Rosa打骂的场景。Liesel动笔写第一封信时感觉有太多的事情要讲给母亲听，花了3个小时，前后修改了

6次，不怕一切困难坚持给母亲写信，在地下室写了第五封信然后邮寄出去。接下来就是每天去邮箱寻找母亲的来信，从一月到四月，天天如此；养父看在眼里痛在心里。最让我揪心的是作者描写Liesel被养母打骂的那一场景："What came to her then was the dustiness of the floor，the feeling that her clothes were more next to her than on her，and the sudden realization that this would all be for nothing—that her mother would never write back and she would never see her again. The reality of this gave her a second Watschen. It stung her，and it did not stop for many minutes.The red marks grew larger，in patches on her skin，as she lay there in the dust and the dirt and the dim light. Her breathing calmed，and a stray yellow tear trickled down her face. She could feel herself against the floor. A forearm，a knee. An elbow. A cheek. A calf muscle.The floor was cold，especially against her cheek，but she was unable to move. She would never see her mother again.For nearly an hour，she remained，spread out under the kitchen table，till Papa came home and played the accordion. Only then did she sit up and start to recover."外貌描写、动作描写加上心理描写足以表达Liesel内心的痛苦和绝望，让人不禁想到一句话："想念是世界上没有解药的毒药。"

"Hitler's Birthday，1940"和"100 Percent Pure German Sweat"两个小节主要谈论了那个时期众人对Hitler的崇拜，并为他庆祝生日。纳粹分子十分野蛮，采用惨无人道的方法对付敌国的人、资讯、文化。他们严加控制和屠杀犹太人。这一节中也提到了Hans的儿子是Hitler的忠实追随者，但Hans却展示了对犹太人的友善。这两节中也有一些有趣、温馨的场景描写。

"In the Hubermann household that morning，all was typical. 'That Saukerl's looking out the window again，' cursed Rosa Hubermann. 'Every day，' she went on. 'What are you looking at this time？' 'Ohhh，' moaned Papa with delight. The flag cloaked his back from the top of the window. 'You should have a look at this woman I can see.' He glanced over his shoulder and grinned at Liesel. 'I might just go and run after her. She leaves you for dead，Mama.' 'Schwein！' She shook the wooden spoon at him.

Papa continued looking out the window，at an imaginary woman and a very real corridor of German flags."

读完这几章的内容，我的感受是：有了爱、善良、宽容、知识，就没有逾越不了的困难。

工作室人员分享

这几段讲述的是Liesel因为私自拿钱去寄信被养母打了，但让她感到痛苦绝望的是她知道永远都见不到她的妈妈了。文中对Liesel被打后的动作、表情及思绪的描写让我潸然泪下。多么可怜的孩子！养母的道歉未能让她从冰冷的地板上站起来，除了养父的手风琴乐声。“黑暗与光明，有什么区呢？”在Liesel心中，那个情境中的一切都是黑色的，尽管灯是亮着的。养父的音乐也是黑色的，但能让Liesel感到安慰，为什么呢？我想，正是养父的陪伴给了Liesel慰藉，因为养父懂得她的痛苦与悲伤。这就正如当你伤心难过的时候，有个朋友能在身边陪你一起哭。

——陈雪芬

令我印象深刻的是Liesel挨打的情节。Liesel为了寄信给生母偷偷从洗衣费中抠出钱来，还是被 Rosa知道了。养母非常生气，拿木勺狠狠地打她，这是给她的身体带来的直接疼痛。“Redmarks like footprints, and they burned.”当她解释道那些钱是用来寄信的，Liesel如当头一棒，突然醒悟：“...her mother would never write back and she would never see her again.The reality of this gave her a second Watschen.It stung her，and it did not stop for many minutes.”。这个残酷的现实是给她的第二顿痛打——对她心理的打击，深深地刺痛着她的心。紧接着，Liesel的哭这一段的描写更是令人心碎。身体的疼痛，昏暗的灯光，浑浊的眼泪，冰冷的地板，她再也见不到生母了。当Liesel回忆起这个事情，她的记忆都是黑色的。dark room，black tear，she was beaten in the dark，a cold dark kitchen floor，这些关于黑色的记忆给Liesel带来了无比的疼痛。色彩描写令人感同身受。

——董筱妍

After reading Hitler’s Birthday，1940，I lost in thought about politics and races. Papa’s son came back and had an intense conflict with his father. The son said，“Well, have you even tried again? You cant just sit around waiting for the new world to take it with you. You have to go out and be part of it—despite your past mistakes.” Papa looked up. “Mistakes? I’ve made many mistakes in my life but not joining the Nazi Party isn’t one of them...”

I was deeply touched by Papa’s words. He is not well-educated or wealthy，but he is a man of great wisdom. In his time，the government and many of the nations looked down upon Jews even persecuted them. However，Mr. Hubermann was brave and kind enough to paint houses for them at the risk of being punished. In his eyes，all the human beings are equal，no matter where he is from and no matter what race he belongs to. He is a man that is worthy being respected by us.

Ignoring futility，Papa walked to the doorway and called out to his son. “Coward? I’m the coward? ” ... a father catch up his son and grab hold of him，begging him to stop. From these sentences. I can feel Mr. Hubermann’s complex emotions at that moment. He loved his son，he knew that it was dangerous for his son to be in the party. But he couldn't change his son's radical idea. Instead, he was regarded as a coward. Feeling sad, angry and helpless, what he could do was just to let his son go.

In my opinion, racial discrimination is an excuse that the invaders uses to invade and occupy other countries and nations. Who gave the right to Germans to kill Jews? Who proved that Germans were smarter and nobler than Jews? Massacre is retrogression of human civilization.To be strong and to be the strongest in the world is the only way for a nation to live in this world. I am proud because I am Chinese. It is everyone's duty to maintain peace and reject war.

——关少娟

For this part of the book, I was deeply impressed by Liesel's dead letters to her mother and the comparison between Liesel's birthday and Hitler's.

As a mother of two children, I'm really touched by Liesel's deep love for her mother. Even her foster parents pitied Liesel, who could not get in touch with her mother. They were all haunted by some unknown questions.On Page 96, it says "In bed, Liesel hugged herself tight. She balled herself up. She thought of her mother and repeated Rosa Hubermann's questions. Where was she? What had they done to her? And once and for all, who, in actual fact, were they? "

The feelings were getting so strong that Liesel couldn't help mailing the letters with a little of the washing and ironing money.And that was her precious birthday present for herself.

"When her birthday came around, there was no gift. There was no gift because there was no money, and at the time, Papa was out of tobacco." As the war continued, life was getting harder and harder.Yet, when it came to Hitler's birthday, children wore uniforms and had a bonfire party. The comparison was quite clear. Different people had different attitude toward the war.But people were living in poverty and great tension. Like the fire, exciting but destructive.It seemed it can destroy everything just within a minute. It felt like the eclipse before dawn.

——李秀文

I finished reading the four chapters with a heavy heart. Each part makes good bedding for the next part.When Liesel finally accepted the fact that she would never hear from her real mother, she was overwhelmed by sadness. She was beaten in the dark, even Papa's music was the color of darkness. Even papa's music. From the sentences, I can feel the despair inside Liesel's heart, no matter how comforting papa's music was before.

I also feel sorry for Hans because he and his son stood in different positions which led to a terrible quarrel between them，His son Junior fought mercilessly against Hans. The word “coward” hurt the old man deeply.Even Rosa didn’t admonish him at all，which was rare. And I noticed a word “communist”. I think this word will tell us about what really happened to Liesel’s father and mother. I’m curious. We may find out soon.

——麦佩莹

Last week，all of us were pleased with Liesel’s happiness.However，nobody can escape from the suffering in the world，especially for poor Liesel.I felt really sad for her when she wrote letters to her birth mother who would never read the letters in fact.

The part which impressed me most is “No matter how many times she tried to imagine that scene wist the yellow light that she knew had been there，she had to struggle to visualize it. She was beaten in the dark，and she had remained there on a cold，dark kitchen floor. Even Papa’s music was the color of darkness. Even Papa’s music.”

The strange thing was that she was vaguely comforted by that thought，rather than distressed by it. From this part，we can see how tough Liesel’s life was. However，we can also see she had a very strong will which attracted readers too.

——莫洁文

“ ‘From now on you’re going to pick up and deliver the washing for me. Those rich people are less likely to fire us if you’re the one standing in front of them.If they ask you where I am，tell them I’ m sick.And look sad when you tell them.You’re skinny and pale enough to get their pity.’

‘Herr Vogel didn’t pity me.’

‘Well.’ Her agitation was obvious. ‘The others might. So don’t argue.’

‘Yes，Mama.’

For a moment，it appeared that her foster mother would comfort her or pat her on the shoulder.

Good girl，Liesel. Good girl. Pat，pat，pat.”

这个片段让我印象很深刻。这里Liesel本来想要点零用钱，但Rosa不给，而是教她自己去挣钱，甚至教她装可怜，去算计那些有钱人。而在这里Liesel想到了自己的亲妈，想象她会拍拍她、安慰她。老实说我看到后面就感觉这里又是一个伏笔，是在为后面她亲妈的死做铺垫。

——莫 然

Due to the war，Rosa started to lose customers for her clothes washing business. She decided to have Liesel pick up the laundry，because she thought the people would be less likely to fire a little girl. In other words，it meant their life would be much harder.

At school，Liesel had an assignment to write two letters，so she decided to write to Rudy and her birth mother. This caused concern between Rosa and Hans，because they did not know what happened to Liesel's mother. Liesel heard them whispering about her mother and became concerned about her mother's safety.

Because Rosa was losing customers due to the war，Liesel didn't receive a birthday present. After receiving no reply to her letters，Liesel decided to give herself a present，by taking some money to buy a stamp and mailing the five letters she had written her mother.

Rosa beat her when she found out the reason for the missing money. Rosa was sad about the circumstance surrounding Liesel's mother，but all Liesel could see was the darkness of the situation around her.Because she knew her mother would never write back and she would never see her again. Rosa said sorry to Liesel，but in Liesel's heart，tears were dark；the scene was dark；the kitchen was dark；even Papa's music was dark！How hopeless Liesel was.

I was so sad that Liesel's father disappeared，her mother also left her and her poor brother was dead. Though Liesel's foster family treated her well，they were also full of sadness and privation. If there was no war，maybe their life will be better and Liesel will have a poor but happy family. So I am so grateful for the stability in our country.

——宋碧燕

Molching，like the rest of Germany，was in the grip of preparing for Hitler's birthday. This particular year，with the development of the war and Hitler's current victorious position，the Nazi partisans of Molching wanted the celebration to be especially befitting. There would be a parade. Marching.Music.Singing.There would be a fire. While Liesel walked the streets of Molching，picking up and delivering washing and ironing，Nazi Party members were accumulating fuel.A couple of times，Liesel was a witness to men and women knocking on doors，asking people if they and any material that they felt should be done away with or destroyed. "Any materials，" it requested，"from such times—newspapers，posters，books，flags—and any found propaganda of our enemies should be brought forward to the Nazi Party office on Munich Street." Everything was in place to make April 20 magnificent.It would be a day full of burning and cheering.

倘若一个国家发生战争，整个社会陷入狂热，你还能分清是非吗？在纳粹德国，真的所有人都痛恨犹太人吗？还是他们只是麻木地跟从，为了让别人觉得自己不是一个异类，而对无辜的陌生人施以迫害？这种狂热已成为一种思想，这种思想却演变成了极端的个人崇拜。就是对Hitler的极端崇拜，盲目的服从，才让人们做出了如此骇人听闻的恶行。

"'So have they let you in yet?' 'In what?'

'Take a guess—the party.'

'No，I think they've forgotten about me.'

'Well，have you even tried again? You can't just sit around waiting for the new world to take it with you. You have to go out and be part of it—despite your past mistakes.'

Papa looked up. 'Mistakes? I've made many mistakes in my life，but not joining the Nazi Party isn't one of them. They still have my application—you know that—but I couldn't go back to ask. I just...'

'You've never cared about this country，" said Hans Junior. "Not enough，anyway.'

But Hans Junior wasn't finished. He stepped closer and said， 'You're either for Fubrer or against him—and I can see that you're against him.You always have been.' 'It's pathetic—how a man can stand by and do nothing as a whole nation cleans out the garbage and makes itself great.'

'You coward.' He upturned them into Papa's face，and he promptly left the kitchen and the house."

小Hans对父亲是很有偏见的，他觉得父亲是个袖手旁观的人，甚至说他是懦夫。因为父亲没有加入纳粹分子，就认为他不是真正的德国人，甚至认为爸爸之前是犯了错误才没有入党的。这个错误应该指的是别人涂抹在犹太人商店墙上的脏话，爸爸给粉刷掉了。其实小Hans也是受害者之一。在二战时的纳粹德国，人们盲目追随元首，已经进入一种狂热的状态，人们的思想已经麻木了。书中说，"水晶之夜"前夕，所有犹太人的商店被砸，墙壁被人恶意涂抹，这位油漆匠免费帮犹太人刷墙，在所有人都避之唯恐不及的时候，Hans却勇敢地站了出来。那他的下场是什么？下场就是被拒绝加入纳粹党。可以感到在Hans的内心里，他不仇视犹太人，他认为每个人都有平等的权利，他是一位刚正不阿的人，但同时也是个很矛盾的人。比如书中说道："For a while，he remained silently at the table after the eating was finished. Was he really a coward，as his son had so brutally pointed out? Certainly，in World War I，he considered himself one.He attributed his survival to it.But then，is there cowardice in the acknowledgement of fear? Is there cowardice in being glad that you lived?"。

——宋 蕾

I want to share something about argument between Hans and his son. Hans Junior accused his father of being disloyal to Germany and asked why Liesel wasn't reading Hitler's book.Hans Junior then called his father a coward for doing nothing while a whole nation cleans out the garbage and makes itself great and stormed out.

Hans'character becomes more complex as it is revealed that he is not a member of the Nazi Party, his application having been tabled because of his willingness to paint Jewish homes and cover up Jewish graffiti. As a result, Hans' business suffers despite his talent, his standing in the community becomes threatening despite his affability, and his relationship with his son is ruined despite their former closeness.

在我看来，从这一章开始Hans的性格变得更加复杂，人物形象也更加饱满。他被揭露不是纳粹分子成员，原因是他愿意粉刷犹太人的家园和掩盖辱骂犹太人的涂鸦导致他的申请被搁置了。结果，尽管Hans很有才华，但他的生意还是受到了影响；尽管他是和蔼可亲的，但他在社区中的地位受到威胁；尽管他和儿子以前很亲密，但他们的关系还是恶化了。小Hans完全被灌输了纳粹思想，他认为爸爸在战争面前是个懦夫。我认为Hans作为一名父亲，他深知战争的残酷，但又不得不面对，他不满战争给他的生活带来的一切磨难。这让我开始感到，在战争面前，每个人都是弱小和无助的。

——王之光

"You're either for the fubrer or against him—and I can see that you're against him. You always have been.It's pathetic—how a man can stand by and do nothing as a whole nation cleans out the garbage and makes itself great. You coward."

小Hans对父亲的控诉，与其说是儿子不认同懦弱的父亲，不如说是狂热的德国纳粹分子对中立派的孤立。我不禁疑惑：到底什么是懦弱 ，什么又是勇敢？如果Hans先生也像他儿子一样加入纳粹，驱赶犹太人，征服他国，就是勇敢吗？不，勇敢才不是人云亦云或随大流。

勇敢是，即便亲人朋友都在批评、反对你，但是你仍然坚持自己。这让我想起一件证明自己"勇敢"的事情。我和朋友去长隆乐园，朋友刺激我去玩大摆锤，说那样才能证明我是个勇敢的女汉子。当时我看到一些小孩子，个头只有我肩头高，都敢玩第二遍时，我决定要征服大摆锤，结果两分钟后，还是它征服了我。我差点哭着下来，缓了半天腿才不抖。当时的我，明知道这是个错误的决定，但是在朋友的支持和周围人的刺激下，我还是效仿了。这不是勇敢，而是冲动。这也是读完这几章，让我感触颇多的情节。

——夏丽焱

After reading these four chapters，I feel sorry about what Liesel has experienced. The atmosphere is sad，hopeless，even a little ironic. In these four chapters，three scenes impress me a lot. After writing five letters（“Even when Liesel retreated to the basement to write her fifth letter to her mother—all but the first one yet to be sent”），even it would make Rosa angry，she insists to save money to post the letters.

Rosa在不知情的情况下，痛打了Liesel一顿，当她得知真相，她说：“I’m sorry，Liesel.”。Liesel knew her well enough to understand that it was not for the hiding. The red marks grew larger，in patches on her skin，as she lay there，in the dust and the dirt and the dim light，Her breathing calmed，and a stray yellow tear trickled down her face.She could feel herself against the floor.A forearm，a knee. An elbow.A cheek. A calf muscle. The floor was cold，especially against her cheek，but she was unable to move. She would never see her mother again.

dead letter 意味着石沉大海，有去无回。She has to accept the truth that she won’t see or connect with her mother again. We can feel a hopeful girl turning to be a hopeless girl. From the description，we can feel how sad she is！后文中多次出现的dark、darkness，不仅是挨打的那个夜晚的黑，更反映了她的内心，她的世界变成了黑色。真的令人怜悯！

The second scene that impressed me a lot is the talk between Hans Huberman and his son Hans Junior. The young man was a Nazi.

“‘You’ve never cared about this country，’ said Hans Junior.‘Not enough，anyway.’”

“‘You’re either for the Fubrer or against him—and I can see that you’re against him.You always have been.’‘It’s pathetic—how a man can stand by and do nothing as a whole nation cleans out the garbage and makes itself great.’‘You coward.’ He upturned them into Papa’s face，and he promptly left the kitchen，and the house. Ignoring futility，Papa walked to the doorway and called out to his son.‘Coward? I’m the coward?！’ He then rushed to the gate and ran pleadingly after him. They could hear nothing，but the manner in which Hans Junior shrugged loose was loud enough.”

这段对话，让人感受到的其实是父亲的心痛与无助。

在“100 percent pure Germany Sweat”里多处讽刺地描述了对战争的看法。大家焚烧着书籍，高呼着Hitler万岁时，死神说：“Personally，I can only tell you that no one died from it. Or at least，not physically. There was，of course，the matter of forty million people I picked up by the time the whole thing was finished. Birds above did laps. They circled，somehow attracted to the glow—until they came too close to the heat. Or was it the humans? Certainly，the heat was nothing."。显然火焰的热度比不上人类的狂热。逐渐地，我们开始真正认识到战争的残酷与无情。

——徐 燕

After reading these parts, I had complicated feelings about the main characters, Liesel, mama and papa. Liesel actually had complex feelings to her mama, anyway. She followed her orders for mama took care of her. She helped deliver the ironing and washing.She listened to her cursing or anything else.But inside her heart, she was afraid of mama. She told Rudy, "It's not so bad for you—you don't have to face my mama." So papa said "What do you want to write a letter to her for? You have to put up with her every day." When she said she wanted to write a letter for her mama.And when it comes to her writing to her real mother, she spent six drafts perfecting the letter, she wanted to tell her mother everything about her.I can't help crying for her at that time. She's just a kid in need of her mother's love and care. But somehow she had to hide her feelings and swallow her sadness. When hearing mama and papa whisper about her, after mama found out she used the money, "She didn't whine or moan or stamp her feet. She simply swallowed the disappointment." That reminds me of the saying, those who suffered a lot at early ages can become independent and mature very early. Maybe for Liesel, she had to do so.Hopefully, papa and Rudy and the books can be her best friends.

——袁泳施

Liesel给妈妈写信的迫切和期盼。

"It took three hours and six drafts to perfect the letter, telling her mother all about Molching, her papa and his accordion, the strange but true ways of Rudy Steiner, and the exploits of Rosa Hubermann. She also explained how proud she was that she could now read and write a little. The next day, she posted it at Frau Diller's with a stamp from the kitchen drawer. And she began to wait."

然而在写信的当晚，她听到一向都恶狠狠大声说话的养母在低声和养父说话："She should just forget her. Who knows where she is? Who knows what they've done to her? "

Liesel听到有关生母消息时，感到绝望、无助和孤独。"In bed, Liesel hugged herself tight. She balled herself up.She thought of her mother and repeated Rosa Hubermann's questions. Where was she? What had they done to her? And once and for all, who, in actual fact, were they? "

死神接着把故事向前跳了。几年后，养父向 Liesel 诉说知道这些信是寄不去又不知道该怎么办时的彷徨。

——郑剑湘

In these Chapters，the writer shows what Liesel did，saw，and felt in Molching. As World War II went further. Life for people in Germany appeared to be hard.The part The Town Walker began with the rot started with the washing and it rapidly increased. Some customers of Rose could no longer afford to have their washing and ironing done.In order to save their business，Rose asked Liesel alone to pick up and deliver the washing and to tell the customer that she was sick to get their pity. In the middle of January，schoolwork turned its attention to letter writing. Liesel decided to write her birth mother a letter.And she took some money from the washing and mailed the letter to her mother. She got a good beat for it. She waited for a reply from her mother throughout March and well into April.She checked the mailbox each day. But all turned to disappointment. On Hitler's birthday in 1940，with the development of the war and Hitler's current victorious position，the Nazi partisans of Molching prepared the celebration to be especially befitting. They had parade. Marching. Music. Singing and a fire. Liesel joined the crowd.When the audience shouted"Heil Hitler！"she thought of her starving mother，missing father and dead brother.

What impressed me most in this part was the description about Liesel's beat. Her foster mother was so angry because of the missing money that she gave Liesel a good beat. After the beat，Rose said，"I'm sorry，Liesel."From Rose，we know how hard life was and how deep she loved Liesel.

——Ting Feng

Part Two—Three of The Book Thief

The Gates of Thievery—The Mayor's Library

导读

本期的分享内容为第二至第三部分的"The Gates of Thievery""Book of Fire""The Way Home"和"The Mayor's Library"。这部小说主要是关于Liesel的成长过程的，它向我们展示了Liesel鲜活的生活。这四章的主要内容可以概括为：成长、隐忍、坚强和渴望。在我看来，这四章主要通过焚书事件、火中偷书和初入市长夫人的书房三个主要事件描述了Liesel的心理成长和世界观的逐渐变化。而重要的角色之一也出现在这个部分——市长的妻子。我认为是她在颠沛流离的艰难时期为Liesel打开了新世界的大门。

在第十六章"The Gates of Thievery"，焚书事件的后续，Liesel看着书的残骸和四处飘散的灰烬，痛苦地想起了爸爸的失踪和妈妈的离去都跟共产主义分子有关，陷入沉思的她在做一道加法题：共产主义分子+ 盛大的篝火 + 一堆杳无回音的信 + 亲生妈妈的遭遇 + 弟弟的夭折=元首。随后她反问Hans，自己的妈妈是不是元首带走的，吃惊的Hans回答说："我想可能是的。"

"'I hate the Fubrer,' she said.'I hate him.' He clenched his eyes. Then opened them. He slapped Liesel Meminger squarely in the face. Don't never say that! His voice was quiet, but sharp.

'Good.' He placed her back down. Now, let us try... At the bottom of the steps, Papa stood erect and cocked his arm... With absolute miserly, she repeated it.'Heil Hitler.' It was quite a sight—an eleven-year-old girl, trying not to cry on the church steps, saluting the Fubrer as the voices over Papa's shoulder chopped and beat at the dark shape in the back—ground."

一阵愤怒袭上Liesel心头，她说："我恨元首，我恨他。"惊恐的爸爸用掌掴耳光的方式提醒Liesel不能说出招致祸患的话，他还执意教Liesel练习"Heil—Hitler！"Liesel站起身，也伸出手臂，带着所有的痛苦，她重复道"Heil—Hitler！"这个场面令人难过，一个十岁大的女孩，站在教堂的台阶上，强忍住眼泪，向元首致敬。她的声音越过了爸爸的肩膀，凌乱地散落在背后的黑暗之中。对于孩子来说，违背内心感受而不得不对现实采用隐忍的态度是一件多么艰难的事，但是Liesel做到了。在我看来是因为她把书当成一种寄托，一种沉默的精神享受，当然她更不希望对她好的人因言获罪。

在第17章“Book of Fire”中，Liesel从纳粹分子的篝火堆里发现了没烧着的书，她忍着烫偷了出来。Liesel不明白自己行为的真正后果，但在这里她表明，她愿意为一本书冒险。在我看来，此时此刻书籍对她来说已经变得如此珍贵，这也可以被看成是她第一次反抗Hitler的一种形式。

第18章 The Way Home，Liesel在忐忑和欣喜中又收获了一本书*The Shoulder Shrug*。Hans发现了Liesel偷书的行为后有这样一段对话，这为以后的故事埋下了伏笔。“‘Listen，Liesel.’ Papa placed his arm around her and walked her on.‘This is our secret，this book. We'll read it at night or in the basement，just like the others—but you have to promise me something.’ ‘Anything，Papa.’ The night was smooth and still. Everything listened.‘If I ever ask you to keep a secret for me，you will do it.’ ‘I promise.’”养父Hans在那个非常困难的时期，竭尽所能地引导和陪伴着Liesel读书。也正是因为养父Hans在Liesel偷书后给予理解与关怀，宽广仁慈的胸怀给Liesel搭起了安全的避风港，才使得这个小女孩在那个专制蛮横的强权时代里做出了如此勇敢的事情。此时他们分享了共同的秘密，互相支持，他对Liesel的爱让我感受到了温暖和大爱。

在第19章‘The Mayor's Library’里，Liesel担心要把洗好的衣服交给市长的妻子，并担心她会因为偷窃而受到惩罚。起初，她假装市长家里没有人，但Rosa让她回去了。这时，另一个重要人物出现了。“The mayor's wife，who never spoke，simply stood in her bathrobe，her soft fluffy hair tied back into a short tail. A draft made itself known. Something like the imagined breath of corpse.”作者用这几处简单的描述向我们呈现了一个麻木、有距离感且沮丧的女人。在我看来，她同时代表了富人阶层的良知，她自己也承受着失去孩子的痛苦，她没有告发Liesel偷书，而是邀请Liesel在她庞大的图书馆中阅读，从而为她打开了新世界的大门。

这是Liesel最重要的时刻之一。在此之前，Liesel只把书看作是随意被偷走或赠予的物品，但现在她看到了一种特殊的奢侈品，那就是把数百本书都整理好并安全地存放起来。当Liesel被领进书房的时候，那是多么令人震撼的一幕啊！

“‘Jesus，Mary...’ She said it out loud，the words distributed into a room that was full of cold air and books. Books everywhere！Each wall was armed with overcrowded yet immaculate shelving. It was barely possible to see the paintwork. There were all different styles and sizes of lettering on the spines of the black，the red，the gray，the every-colored books. It was one of the most beautiful things Liesel Meminger had ever seen....

She walked over and did it again, this time much slower, with her hand facing forward, allowing the dough of her palm to feel the small hurdle of each book. It felt like magic, like beauty, as bright lines of light shone down from a chandelier. Several times, she almost pulled a title from its place but didn't dare disturb them. They were too perfect.

作者的描写非常细腻和温暖，仿佛梦境般美妙的场景，对于Liesel来说这是她第一次真正意义上主动接触到经典书籍，她有了那种小心翼翼、屏住呼吸，但又压抑着内心狂喜的心情。从此，她打开了人生新世界的一扇大门。

读了这四章，我有如下几点感悟：

1.父母是孩子的第一任老师，家庭是孩子的第一堂课。

2.人生的所有经历，无论是成功或失败，快乐或痛苦，都将对个人的成长产生影响。

工作室人员分享

"Every minute, every hour, there was worry, or more to the point, paranoia. Criminal activity will do that to a person, especially child. They envision a prolific assortment of caught out. Some examples: People jumping out of alleys. School teachers suddenly being aware of every sin you've ever committed. Police showing up at the door each time a leaf turns or a distant gate slams shut. For Liesel, the paranoia itself became the punishment, as did the dread of delivering some washing to the mayor's house.

She's going to torture me, Liesel decided. She's going to take me inside, light the fireplace, and throw me in, books and all. Or she'll lock me in the basement without any food."

以上两段文字描述了Liesel偷书后害怕的心情。Liesel这次偷书被人看到了，她好像患了妄想症似的，总是幻想各种被人抓住的情景。后来去市长家，当市长夫人托着一堆书叫Liesel进屋看看时，Liesel还是很害怕，甚至幻想着市长夫人叫她进屋是要折磨她，把她和书都扔进火炉里，或者关到地下室里不给她饭吃。"For Liesel, the paranoia itself became the punishment." "这种妄想已经成为一种惩罚。"我认为这句话写得很贴切，虽然Liesel没有因为偷书遭受到肉体上或金钱上的惩罚，但是她精神上有太多恐惧和担忧，这样的描述和那些潜逃的罪犯的心情是一样的，终日惶恐不安。但是，后面Liesel还是勇敢地踏进了市长的家，这一点反衬出她对书那强烈的渴望。

——陈雪芬

Liesel看到了市长夫人的书架，面对琳琅满目的书，Liesel感觉一切都很梦幻。文中是这样描述的："on the spines of the black，the red，the gray，the every color the books. It was one of the most beautiful things that Liesel had ever seen."。各种颜色的书是Liesel看过最好看的事物。这是视觉的描写。

得到夫人的允许，Liesel伸手触碰那些神圣的书。"it sounded like an instrument or the notes of running. She used both hands. She raced them." 这是听觉和触觉的描写。

再一次重复刚刚的动作，Liesel慢慢地用心去感受这些书，她的动作是无比虔诚的，你会感受到Liesel对知识的绝对信仰。

作者从视觉、听觉和触觉等一系列描写入手，生动形象地刻画出了一个对书本着迷又胆怯的小女孩的形象。这让我们读者可以通过这些丰富生动的描写更好地去感受Liesel，同时也为下文做好铺垫。

——董筱妍

从不说话的市长夫人看出了Liesel喜欢书，一天她把Liesel领进了自家的书房。小女孩不禁惊呼，她看到了梦想中的情境，竟然有一个地方有这么多的书："Jesus，Mary..." She said it out loud，...It was one of the most beautiful things Liesel Meminger had ever seen.With wonder，she smiled.That such a room existed！Even when she tried to wipe the smile away with her forearm，she realized instantly that it was a pointless exercise. She could feel the eyes of the woman traveling her body，and when she looked at her，they had rested on her face.这一段描写，非常生动形象地写出了Liesel对书本的酷爱之情。

——郑剑湘

这四章中给我留下深刻印象的是"The Mayor's Library"，我从中品味到了市长夫人的宽容、仁慈和偷书贼Liesel对书的渴求、热爱。从几处有关市长夫人的外貌描写（never spoke、in her bathrobe、soft fluffy hair、chalky hand and wrist、cold-fingered、looked vulnerable等）中可以揣测出她是一个饱受命运摧残的人，但她还是不动声色地消化了自己的苦难，在黑暗中给了Liesel微光。在这一章里还有很多对Liesel不同心理的描写，有担心市长夫人会告发她偷书的忐忑，有随之而来要去市长家收送衣服的恐惧。"The great door was like a monster."间接描写出Liesel来市长家时内心的极度恐惧。之后一次去市长家，看到市长夫人不像平日那样手里拎着袋子，而向她伸手示意进屋时，"'I'm just here for the washing.' Liesel's blood had dried inside of her. It crumbled. She almost broke into pieces on the steps."。在市长夫人抱着一摞书让Liesel进屋看看时，"She's going to torture me，Liesel decided. She's going to take me inside，light the fireplace，and throw me in，books and all. Or she'll lock me in the basement without any food."。有

以为自己侥幸逃脱的喜悦。“For quite a while，Liesel remained，facing the blanket of upright wood. She took the first few steps backward，calulating. She turned and handled the remainder of the steps normally，taking the last three all at once. She even allowed herself a laugh.”还有见到满屋子书时的惊愕和兴奋。此外，本章节里还有一些细致入微的动作描写，将Liesel对书的痴迷、视书为宝的一面刻画得生动形象。She ran the back of her hand along the first shelf，listening to the shuffle of her fingernails gliding across the spinal cord of each book. It sounded like an instrument，or the notes of running feet. She used both hands. She raced them. One shelf against the other. And she laughed. Her voice was sprawled out，high in her throat，and when she eventually stopped and stood in the middle of the room，she spent many minutes looking from the shelves to her fingers and back again.”读完这一章，感触很深，市长夫人的宽容让Liesel在苦难中体会到了人性的温暖和宽容的力量。黑暗中，这世上总会有人会悄悄地点燃一抹微光，照耀着你前行。

——李 丹

在这一部分，Liesel对书籍的热爱令人印象深刻、令人着迷，对Liesel感情的描写非常细致。当我读到它的时候，我情不自禁地在脑海里想象当时的情景。

在第120页，Liesel从篝火中偷走了那本火之书。书里是这样描述的：“when she reached her hand in，she was bitten，but on the second attempt，she made sure she was fast enough. She latched onto the closest of the books... Smoke lifted from the cover as she juggled it and hurried away. Her head was pulled down，and the sick beauty of nerves proved more ghastly with each stride.”。作者甚至把Liesel的感受和燃烧中的书的温度结合起来。后来，她有了被忽视的兴奋！“the book felt cool enough now to slip inside her uniform... by the time she made it back to Papa，the book was starting to burn her. It seemed to be igniting.”在这里，“igniting”是描述Liesel感情的完美词汇。这种激动点燃了她。但是当她发现有人看到她时，“the book was truly burning her.”“She winced... Beneath her shirt，a book was eating her up.”。这些生动的描写让读者真切地感受到Liesel偷书时的紧张心情。

当不得不面对市长夫人，以为自己可能会受到惩罚时，偷书贼Liesel走进了一个装满书的房间，而且描述得很棒！她想：“it was one of the most beautiful things she had ever seen.”“With wonder，she smiled. ... even when she tried to wipe the smile away with her forearm，she realized instantly that it was a pointless exercise.”。最后，她的紧张被感激所取代。她的秘密很安全，生活也充满了快乐。

有时候我们的经历会影响我们的喜好。有些东西可能不贵，但对我们很有价值。因为不同的经历，生活是丰富多彩的，我们是独一无二的。好好享受这段旅程，不要回头。We are beautiful in our own ways.我们各具自己独特的美。

——李秀文

当我读到Hans扇了Liesel一巴掌的时候，我非常震惊！在前几章里，他是那么温柔体贴。是什么使他的行为变得令人担忧？我想这就是我们通常讲的——爱之深责之切。这不一定是个不适当的举动，在某种程度上是可以理解的。Hans不想让Liesel因为她所说的话而陷入危险的境地。难道他不明白她的感受吗？不。如果这对她意味着不可预知的危险，那就不值得在公共场合说出来。在某种程度上，我有点认同Hans。我可能会做和Hans一样的事。同时，它也给了我一些思考。作为成熟的父母，当不好的事情发生时，我们应该试着冷静和理性地对待我们所做的和所说的。如果这意味着伤害孩子的心，那就不要这样做。试着做孩子的榜样。我意识到市长夫人看到Liesel偷了一本书，却没有揭发她，这让我有点困惑。我不知道她的意图。但我确实能感受到Liesel看到一屋子书时的兴奋，也许她会经常来这个“图书馆”。我开始期待接下来的章节会发生什么。

——麦佩莹

当Liesel问起她的妈妈是否是共产党员，表达讨厌Fubrer时，养父突然一改平时的慈爱变得非常严肃甚至严厉。“He clenched his eyes.Then opened them.He slapped Liesel Meminger squarely in the face.‘Don’t ever say that！’His voice was quiet，but sharp.As the girl shook and sagged on the steps，he sat next to her and held his face in his hands.”（他紧闭双眼，随后睁开。他掴了Liesel一记耳光。“千万别这么说！”他的声音很平静，但很尖锐。女孩颤抖着瘫倒在台阶上，他坐在她旁边，用手捂着脸）。这段文字把养父当时的情绪状态描写得细致入微。在当时的大环境中，Liesel的想法可能会使她陷入危险中，养父的一巴掌背后正是因为他对Liesel的紧张和保护，可他打完后马上用手捂着脸，这也看得出他马上对打的那巴掌感到后悔。从这里，我依然可以看到养父对Liesel浓浓的爱护。到后面部分，Liesel终于找到机会潜入市长夫人的书房了，我们可以看得出来，市长夫人意识到Liesel偷了一本书，但是她并没有揭发她。我认为市长夫人的做法是非常艺术的，她保护了Liesel的自尊心和对阅读的热情。也许作为市长夫人，她也希望自己能够为战争中的孩子做点事情。

——莫洁文

“He clenched his eyes. Then opened them. He slapped Liesel Meminger squarely in the face.“Don’t ever say that！”His voice was quiet，but sharp.As the girl shook and sagged on the steps，he sat next to her and held his face in his hands. It would be easy to say that he was just a tall man sitting poor-postured and shattered on some church steps，but he wasn't. At the time，Liesel had no idea that her foster father，Hans Hubermann，was contemplating one of the most dangerous dilemmas a German citizen could face.Not only that，he'd been facing it for close to a year."

这一大段文字让我印象很深刻，因为Hans第一次动手打了Liesel，而他却不能直接告诉Liesel原因。作者在这里又埋了好几个伏笔，一个是前面的lie，一个是后面说他面临危险，基本上从这里我们就能猜到Hans后面肯定会遭遇麻烦。

"'Looks like，' Papa suggested，'I don't need to trade any more cigarettes，do I？Not when you're stealing these things as fast as I can buy them.' Liesel，by comparison，did not speak. Perhaps it was her first realization that criminality spoke best for itself. Irrefutable."

这里也让我有点儿印象深刻，因为Hans用开玩笑的口吻和Liesel讨论她偷东西的行为，而Liesel也第一次想到她这个行为是偷窃，是犯罪的行为，第一次有了负疚感。

——莫 然

Hans发现Liesel坐在教堂的台阶上，看着人们从篝火中把一切清理干净。Liesel一直在思考她听到的事情，问Hans她的母亲是不是共产主义者。他告诉她他不知道，但接着Liesel问他元首是否要为她母亲被带走负责。他告诉她他是这么想的，Liesel回答说她恨元首。Hans扇了她一耳光，告诉她再也不要在公共场合说那样的话。这是Hans第一次如此严厉地扇Liesel耳光。因为政治是残酷的，有时一个词就能杀死一个人或整个家庭。她意识到她永远不会看到她的母亲了，因为她的母亲是一个共产主义者。她恨Hitler，但Hans告诉她，她必须把这些感情藏在心里。

当他们两人离开城镇广场时，Hans受到了一个朋友的欢迎。就在他们说话的时候，Liesel走到火炉边，注意到几本没有被烧毁的书。她抓住机会，抓起了一本书。一系列的动作描写生动地展现了Liesel偷书时的果敢和志在必得！她试图以生动而笨拙的方式偷这本书。Liesel知道有人看到她偷书，因为书本冒出的烟出卖了她，但她和Hans依然神情自若地走回家，尽管书在她的衣服里继续燃烧着。

在这一部分，我喜欢书中描述的成功小偷的四个主要特征：潜行、神经、速度、运气。这部分幽默诙谐，使这本书更有趣，也减少了悲伤，尽管这本书的背景是在Hitler血腥和残酷的政治统治下的战争年代。

Liesel和她的父亲从镇广场的篝火旁走回家，她给爸爸看了她偷的书。她爸爸没有生她的气，但要她保证再也不偷书了。他还要求她答应为他保守秘密：

"If I ever ask you to keep a secret for me，you will do it."（Hans Hubermann，The Way Home，P127）

故事发展到此，Hans预料到Max会来他们家。他必须确保Liesel会保守这个秘密，这样全家和Max才会安全。Liesel没有让Hans失望，因为她永远不会做任何危及她妈妈和爸爸的事情。这时，她已经爱上了他们俩。

——宋碧燕

"The heat was still strong enough to warm her when she stood at the foot of the ash heap.When she reached her hand in，she was bitten，but on the second attempt，she made sure she was fast enough.She latched onto the closest of the books.It was hot，but it was also wet，burned only at the edges，but otherwise unhurt.

Smoke lifted from the cover as she juggled it and hurried away.Her head was pulled down，and the sick beauty of nerves proved more ghastly with each stride.There were fourteen steps till the voice.

'Hey！' That was when she nearly ran back and tossed the book onto the mound，but she was unable.The only movement at her disposal was the act of turning.

In the previous moments of stupendous danger，Papa had said goodbye to Wlofgang Edel and was ready to accompany Liesel home.

'Ready，' she answered.They began to leave the scene of the crime，and the book was well and truly burning her now. *The Shoulder Shrug* had applied itself to her rib cage.

As they walked past the precarious town hall shadows，*The Book Thief* winced. 'What's wrong？' Papa asked. 'Nothing.'

Quite a few things，however，were most definitely wrong：Smoke was rising out of Liesel's collar.A necklace of sweat had formed around her throat.Beneath her shirt，a book was eating her up."

以上几个片段描述了Liesel偷书后紧张的心情。即使书在那堆灰烬里已经烧焦了，但她还是鼓足了勇气去伸手拿那本发烫的书。当她偷完书准备走时，封面冒出了烟。她低着头，每走一步神经都愈发紧张。后面有人喊了一声，她吓得想跑回去把书扔进灰烬里，但是她又不甘心。当她知道只是两个负责收拾场地的人在聊天时，她才松了一口气，她悬着的心才落了地。在这一章的最后，当爸爸问她："出什么事啦？"她说："没什么事。"其实当时她怀里烧着的书已经烫得她生疼，她的领口正在往外冒烟，脖子正在冒热汗，但是她也不想把偷书的事告诉她的爸爸。可见，她偷书后心情是多么的紧张和焦虑。

——宋 蕾

读完这一章，我内心充满了好奇和恐惧。Liesel终于进入了市长的房子，我也很替她担心，担心她可能会被发现，会产生很严重的后果。作者很擅长制造紧张的氛围。与此同时，我看着Liesel走进去——琳琅满目的书籍，整齐的书架子，我也兴奋起来了！但最让我疑惑的是市长夫人的表情，难道那个表情意味着接下来会发生一些不好的事情吗？

纵观这几章，印象最深刻的还是Liesel对书本、对阅读的热爱。当她走进书房，“She almost pulled a title from its place but didn't dare disturb them. They were too perfect.”太热爱书以至于她不敢碰，不敢打扰它们，因为它们太完美无瑕了。她偷了一本书，那本书就像是火焰之书，开始燃烧她，但并没有让她停下来。我想那是因为书本就像她生活中的明火，尽管会受伤，但她也需要那一束光，她非常渴望它。书本也好，手风琴也好，都是人们在战乱时期的心灵慰藉。

——袁泳施

On the celebration of Hitler's birthday，in 1940，Liesel realized the Fubrer caused all her misfortune. She felt angry and said “I hate Fubrer." These words frightened her foster father，he was so afraid that he slapped Liesel and told her never to say that again sharply and imploringly. While Liesel and Papa getting out of the square，she got her fourth book The Shoulder Shrug which wasn't burnt up in the bonfire. Later Liesel was let into a book palace—the mayor's library by his wife.

In this part，what impressed me most was the slap from papa when Liesel said “I hate Fubrer”

—I hate Fubrer.

— “Pa！” Don't ever say that！（papa slapped Liesel）

—Papa?

—You can say that in our house，but you never say it on the street，at school，at the BDM，never！Do you hear me?

—Are we still friends?

The writer described how fearful，helpless and painful Hans was through their talk. He slapped Liesel because he could do nothing to help her，to protect her except stopping her from saying that again. The slap was beat on daughter，but hurt dad's heart.

——Ting Feng

Part Three of The Book Thief

Enter the Struggler—The Struggler Continued

导 读

本期品读内容为"Enter the Struggler" "The Attributes of Summer" "The Aryan Shopkeeper" "The Struggler Continued"四个章节。

这部分的主要人物有两个，一个是奋斗者Max，另一个是偷书贼Liesel。他们两人身上有着惊人的相似点，那就是书中的三个词：starving、childhood trusted friend、lucky。

对于奋斗者Max来说，一个犹太人，他躲在黑暗中，忍饥挨饿，奄奄一息。幸运的是，他儿时最信任的朋友 Walter 及时救了他。Walter 设法给 Max 带来了一点食物、水和火车票。又一次，运气站在了Max这边，他成功地登上了火车逃离了。但这部分也有它的特别之处，那就是字里行间充满着紧张感和淡淡的忧郁感。

然而，描写小偷Liesel这部分却很轻松而且充满乐趣。尽管他们都很饥饿，Liesel仍然热爱读书，她依然喜欢和儿时最信任的朋友Rudy踢足球。他们如此饥饿，以至于抓住了另一个偷窃的机会，那就是偷苹果。幸运的是，他们成功地偷了一些苹果，尽管Liesel因为吃太多而生病了。这部分非常好玩，惊险刺激但又充斥着苦中作乐的味道。

在阅读这两部分的过程中，我深深感受到了这两部分之间的强烈对比。一个压抑沉重，另一个轻松愉快。更重要的是，我深深地感受到一种强烈的危机感。就好像它在不断酝酿着、酝酿着，酝酿着一些可怕的东西。市长夫人失去儿子的深切悲痛，使整个事件变得灰暗。所有这些迹象都告诉我们，更糟的灾难还没有到来。

本书的这一部分看似有三个不同的部分，但实际上它们却是连贯而密不可分的一个整体，有着共同的美好部分，而且文笔优美，令人着迷。

这部分再一次提醒我：Peace and friends are so precious that we should always stand strong to keep them.（和平与朋友是如此珍贵，我们应该永远坚强地维护他们）。

工作室人员分享

“The point is，Ilsa Hermann had decided to make suffering her triumph. When it refused to let go of her，she succumbed to it. She embraced it.

She could have shot herself，scratched herself，or indulged in other forms of self-mutilation，but she chose what she probably felt was the weakest option—to at least endure the discomfort of the weather. For all Liesel knew，she prayed for summer days that were cold and wet. For the most part，she lived in the right place.”

这几个章节中，我印象最深的是第146页第2段，Liesel 不小心触碰到市长夫人隐藏在内心的悲痛，但市长夫人却很愿意说说她儿子的事，虽然作者目前没有详细说明市长儿子的死因。我认为市长夫人在某种程度上来说还是挺坚强的。“When it refused to let go of her，she succumbed to it. She embraced it.”当她无法让苦难从她生命中消失时，她只有接受它、拥抱它。也许这是一种无奈的选择，但在我看来这是积极面对苦难的态度。市长夫人没有选择自杀、自虐，而是继续忍受这糟糕的天气，即继续活下去。我认为“糟糕的天气”意指当时那种处于战争中的恶劣环境。我想Liesel能从市长夫人身上看到与自己相似的一面，也能从市长身上学到点儿东西。

——陈雪芬

在“The Attributes of Summer”这一章节中，Liesel花了一整个夏天的时间在不同的地方读书和玩耍。她的暑假是多么的多姿多彩、有滋有味啊！Liesel的爸爸和她每天晚上一起阅读书本。即使当她爸爸睡着了，她自己还是会继续遨游在书籍的海洋中。有时候她看着爸爸的睡态就会放下手中的书，静静地观察爸爸。似乎这就是她感受爸爸和了解爸爸的一种方式。当Liesel对她的爸爸说：“好好睡吧，我觉得很温暖。”这让我想起了之前那段日子，Liesel刚到这个新家，夜夜被噩梦缠身，那时侯是爸爸彻夜的陪伴给她带来了新生。现在Liesel也慢慢长大了，她也会反过来用她的方式去安慰爸爸了。尽管我们都知道他们之间是没有血缘关系的，但Hans对Liesel无私的爱是超过任何一段血缘关系的，Liesel也能完完整整地感受到这份爱。

——董筱妍

读到这里，书中爱意满满的画面在不知不觉中慢慢地减少了。在这几章中，“The Attributes of Summer”让我印象深刻。作者对Liesel和Rudy的描述让我感受到了夏天的明媚和耀眼。作为Liesel的同龄人之一，从不掩饰对Liesel喜爱之情的Rudy一如既往地站在Liesel身边支持和陪伴她。他们之间油然而生懵懵懂懂的感情，更多的应该是一种友情。作者用了大量的笔墨去描写这两个人的相处，他们一起踢足球、跑步、偷苹果，Rudy无不坚定地站在Liesel左右。当Liesel和Rudy在一起时，我看到了战争中德国青年人的成长与青春勇气。我想Liesel在Rudy心中应该是一个美好的象征，而Rudy让Liesel感受到了友谊的珍贵，Liesel正在一点点地变得开朗和乐观。两个小朋友美好的情感让我感受到，即使战争再惨绝人寰，人性中的美好和青春也永不会褪却光芒。

——王之光

二战时期的德国孩子，因为饥饿，会时不时地去偷点吃的，如偷别人家果园里的苹果。在“The Attributes of Summer”这一章中，偷苹果那一节让我联想到童年和伙伴们偷邻居家的橘子、桃子的情节，鲁迅在《社戏》一文中也写到了童年时偷邻居家豆子煮着吃的乐趣，是不是每个童年都有这么一个乐趣？

“Their first adventure is stealing apples from an orchard surrounded by barbed wire. They are successful，and Liesel eats so many apples that she throws up later at dinner time. Rosa is furious，but Liesel has the happiness of a full stomach.More stealing begins，and again it feels （to the reader at least）like subversion—all the food is going to Hitler’s war，but there are still growing children who need to eat. Liesel clearly isn’t bothered by stealing，but she is still figuring out her inner moral compass in such a perverse society.Again Liesel can find childlike happiness in small things. She and Rudy become partners in crime for the first time，and they enjoy the stealing.”

这一段的童真童趣让人回味无穷、忍俊不禁。

——郑剑湘

“ struggler”这个词让我感动和震惊。战争期间，每个人都在挣扎求生，人们因为缺少食物而忍饥挨饿。Rudy 说“I am starving.”，我快饿死了。可是没有什么可吃的，除了豌豆汤。饥饿最终迫使孩子们去偷东西。我肯定他们不想当小偷，但他们别无选择。几个苹果可谓是一顿大餐，大到让他们称之为“奢侈品”。Liesel尝到糖果的时候，眼睛里充满了阳光。在这段艰难时期，只要一点点食物就能让孩子们开心。最让我感动的是，在饿肚子的情况下，Liesel对阅读和书籍的渴望并没有改变，反而比以前更加强烈了。待在市长书房里的每一刻，都是令人愉快的。她会坐在一小堆书旁边，每本书都读上几段，试图记住她不认识的单词。

本章节中出现了一个新的角色——Max，一个犹太人。为了不被纳粹分子抓住和杀害，他不得不躲在一个小黑屋里。当他想上火车，逃去更安全的地方时，我和他一样紧张。幸运的是，他通过了检查。Hans会帮助Max吗？同为一个书迷，Max会对Liesel产生什么样的影响？他们会成为好朋友吗？我期待下一章节的内容。

——关少娟

让我印象深刻并乐在其中的章节是“The Attributes of Summer”。这一章让我再次感受到了养父Hans陪伴Liesel夜读的温暖；市长夫人允许Liesel在她书房看书的体贴入微。我们读懂了市长夫人心中的伤痛，书中的描写特别触动人心。当苦难不愿放过她的时候，她就俯首称臣，她就拥抱苦难。除了这些，这一章还带着我们一同感受Liesel、Rudy和伙伴们踢足球、偷苹果吃的童真童趣。尤其是对偷苹果的相关描写充满乐趣。由6到15岁孩子组成的小团伙，有团伙老大Berg，有行动前Berg的发号施令：“One，don’t get caught on the fence. Two，one in the tree，one below. Someone has to collect. Three，if you see someone coming，you call out loud enough to wake the dead—and we all run.”。有老大Berg对Liesel和Rudy行动后的点评：“Not bad. Not bad at all. Good work.”。Liesel和Rudy成功地做了apple thief，每人分到6个苹果，狼吞虎咽地吃到呕吐。但在他们看来，那是让人满足而快乐的呕吐。“The Aryan Shopkeeper”一章也同样给我留下了深刻印象，我深深地感受到了Liesel和Rudy的可爱至极和深厚情谊。“They shared a piece of candy by trading sucks. Ten sucks for Rudy. Ten for Liesel. Back and forth. By the time they were finished，both their mouths were an exaggerated red，and as they walked home，they reminded each other to keep their eyes peeled，in case they found another coin. In Rudy’s opinion，this is the good life.”

——李 丹

这是一个相当大的变化。我今天读了几页书，感觉情绪有点低落。透过书页，我注意到两个可怜的人物。他们是Max和市长夫人。让我从Max开始吧。多么可怜的犹太人啊！他只能待在一个小储藏室里，独自坐在他的手提箱沙发上。他被孤独、恐惧、饥饿和疲劳笼罩了很长一段时间，甚至想被拖出来结束这一切。我觉得Max这本书的名字就像他现在的处境——挣扎。他不知道自己属于哪里，也不知道自己的未来会是什么样子。也许他甚至看不见前面的光。

我希望Max的脸刮得干干净净，前途一片光明。我想提的下一个角色是市长夫人。她允许Liesel和她一起在房间里看书。我曾经想知道她到底为什么要那么做。通过阅读第144页的这句话——“She usually paid more attention to what was next to her，to something missing.”，我意识到她失去了一个人——他的儿子。也许他的儿子也像Liesel一样喜欢读书，所以当她看到Liesel读书时，她能感觉到她的儿子还在这里。我不禁感叹，生活在战争环境中的人们是多么不幸啊！

——麦佩莹

战争对孩子来说是残酷的，父母在教育孩子上也常常遇到很无奈的情况。大家都明白为人应该友善、诚实、正直，等等，但是在连温饱问题都难以解决的战争环境中，这些都没有用，有时候不得不通过偷或者抢来满足自己的需求。幸运的是，故事中的这些人物Liesel、养父、养母和Rudy依然保持着心底的那份善良，彼此之间相互陪伴、相互鼓励。文中时常会出现一些温馨的画面，比如Liesel会和养父一起进行睡前阅读，沟通中总会互相关心、互相安慰。Liesel和Rudy两个小朋友在互相陪伴中也给彼此带来了一些小幸福。正如标题所说的struggler，战争中的老百姓都是挣扎者，为好好地活着而挣扎。老百姓对美好生活的向往和战争的残酷形成了强烈的对比，这更令人觉得难受！

——莫洁文

这几章让我印象深刻的是一个小结，介绍这个夏天Liesel做了什么事情的，介绍第一件事时用到了这样一个细节："Each night，when she calmed herself from her nightmare，she was soon pleased that she was awake and able to read."。

这个细节我很喜欢，因为之前Liesel是很害怕噩梦的，可是现在因为和爸爸相伴阅读，她不再害怕了，而是对生活充满了期待，每天醒来都很开心，因为可以阅读。这时候，阅读已经成为她的精神支柱了。

我想到了最近的很多青少年自杀的新闻。那些孩子的人生可能远没有Liesel那般坎坷，但是他们为什么会做出那样决绝的选择呢？可能就是因为没有像Liesel那样找到内心的精神支柱吧。

——莫 然

在这些章节中，我印象最深的是：几周后的一天，市长夫人邀请Liesel到她家里。Liesel以为她有麻烦了，但市长夫人却带她去看了她家的大图书馆。看到这么多的书，Liesel感到震惊。我仍然记得那一幕：

当市长夫人走了过来，以一种难以置信的脆弱而坚定的姿态站在那里时，她用腹部撑着一摞书，从肚脐一直撑到胸部的顶端。她在那可怕的门口显得那么脆弱。又长又轻的睫毛，还有最轻微的表情，这个表情意味着过来看看的意思。

市长夫人什么也没说，只是坐在女孩旁边，看着她安静地读书。大多数时候，她要么盯着什么，要么什么都不看，我想她心里想的都是她死去的儿子。我们可以看出她是个悲伤的妈妈，因为Liesel"只看到了一个悲伤的女人，她喜欢看一屋子的书。这是她的所有。那是她那个夏天生活的第二部分"。

在斯图加特镇，一个名叫Max的犹太人坐在手提箱上等了好几天，等着有人来把他带走。最后，他被摇醒，被告知有一张伪造的身份证放在一本书里等着他。这本书里还包括一张地图、一个方向和一把钥匙。帮助他的人也给了他少量的食物。即将会帮助Max的人是Hans。

夏天到了，Liesel通过踢足球、看偷来的书、在市长的图书馆看书和偷苹果来打发时间。她很享受和市长夫人在一起的时光，因为她被允许看越来越多的书。这几个章节的内容还是比较欢快的，虽然在欢快中也夹杂着一些隐隐的悲伤，希望作者能给多一点时间让这些处在战争年代的孩子们感受到应有的童年快乐。

——宋碧燕

Liesel came back out and would somehow always end up opposing Rudy.They would tackle and trip each other，call each other names. Rudy would commentate：“She can’t get around him this time，the stupid Saumenscb Arscbgrobbler.She hasn’t got a hope.” He seemed to enjoy calling Liesel an assscratcher.It was one of the joys of childhood.

我想分享一下这几章当中相对比较轻松愉快的场景。比如“The Attributes of Summer”一章中Himmel Street soccer中的一段。Liesel和Rudy在足球场上，他们会互相较劲、互相嘲讽，Rudy有时候会现场解说：“这回，他肯定过不了人，这头愚蠢的小母猪，只会挠别人的屁股。”他们之间的这种相互打趣，大大增加了彼此之间的友谊，使得感情更加深厚了，这也算是童年的一大乐趣吧。

“Two Debutant Apple Thieves，Whispering

‘Liesel，are you sure？Do you still want to do this？’

‘Look at the barbed wire，Rudy.It’s so high.’

‘No，no，look，you throw the sack on.See？Like them.’

‘All right.’

‘Come on then！’

‘I can’t.’Hesitation.‘Rudy，I—’

‘Move it，Saumenscb！’”

这是Liesel和Rudy偷苹果前的一段对话，特别纯真也特别有趣。在拿到苹果之后，他们狼吞虎咽地吃下了所有的。他们从来没有体验过这样的奢侈，也知道可能会撑得恶心。可见在战争年代，可能连吃到一个苹果都觉得是一种享受，恨不得一下子吃个够。当爸爸妈妈问她为什么吐得这么厉害的时候，她一句话也没有说。她却在心里面回答：“那是苹果啊！”不敢和家里人说偷了苹果，心里却是无比高兴的。战争很苦，但是童年的那些童趣却磨灭不了。

——宋 蕾

读完这四个故事，我被两个关于吃的情节震撼了。

第一个情节是，Max把面包分成三份，把其中两份放在一边。我本以为，已经挨饿好几天的他会一口气吃完所有面包。但他没有，而是仅仅吃了三分之一。

从这个细节更能看出，Max是一个自律到极点的人。为了躲避德国宪兵的搜查，他可以不吃不喝，躲在储藏室，甚至悄无声息好几天。所以难怪他拿到食物，不是张嘴就塞肚子，而是先分好，预备好之后的口粮。

第二个情节是Rudy和Liesel轮流吃一颗糖。Rudy先舔糖果十下，然后Liesel舔十下，轮着来。两个小孩轮流吃一个糖，对我来说，即便是再好的朋友，都有点不敢尝试。然而这两个小伙伴却说这是完美的生活。

快乐是多么简单啊！可是成年人的快乐，总是需要物质作为附加条件，升职加薪才值得高兴，比别人过得好才开心。多想拥有儿童的快乐，它是那么单纯美好。和心爱的人一起分享，即便只是一颗糖，也好开心。

——夏丽焱

有家人和朋友陪伴的Liesel，日子过得异常开心，还有她最忠诚的朋友——书本。一些细节让我印象深刻。比如当Liesel和爸爸一起阅读后，Liesel看着爸爸睡觉的画面，温馨而动人。Liesel用她自己的方式去安慰爸爸，也了解爸爸的感受，这是多么难能可贵啊！她也让爸爸感到非常窝心。有了爸爸妈妈的爱，她变得更加温柔和善良了。

当我读到Liesel和可爱的Rudy在一起的童趣时，我忍不住露出微笑。可能就像是“seeking happiness in suffering”一样吧，他们的相伴比珍宝还要来得珍贵，在战争年代，彼此的陪伴已经是最好的礼物了。换句话说，他们彼此治愈着对方的心灵。就像我们小时候，物质比较匮乏，人与人之间的感情简单而纯粹，一颗糖果都可以让孩子的心被点亮。所以心态最重要，找寻快乐的能力也非常重要。

——袁泳施

The further the story goes on，the harder the life for the people was. In Enter the Struggler，the writer pictured for us how Max deal with the food the visitor brought him. Max divided the bread into three parts and set two aside. The one in his hand he immersed himself in，chewing and gulping，forcing it down the dry corridor of his throat. Later in Attributes of Summer，even though the color of life was greyer and greyer，the writer still tried to describe the hard life in bright color—joy. Another of the joys，of course，was stealing. In fairness，there were many things that brought Rudy and Liesel together，but it was the stealing that cemented their friendship completely. It was brought about by one opportunity，and it was driven by one inescapable force—Rudy’s hunger. The boy was dying for something to eat. At last the depressing pea soup and Rudy’s hunger finally drove them to fruit thievery.

Because of the war，People were plunged into an abyss of suffering lucky for us to live in a peaceful world. Let’s cherish our life.

——Ting Feng

Part Three—Four of The Book Thief

Tricksters—A Good Girl

导读

本期我们一起品读*The Book Thief* 的第三至四部分的四个小节："Tricksters" "The Struggler，Concluded" "The Accordionist" "A Good Girl"。

现在我们来品读每个小节：

Tricksters

故事回到Rudy和Liesel继续他们的犯罪生活。这一次Rudy决定抢劫每周五下午给当地牧师送食物的Otto Sturm。他们设法偷走了食物，一伙人分享了。

在偷土豆的时候，Rudy被铁丝网缠住了，一个挥舞着斧头的农民向他逼近，最终获救。

Rudy和Liesel卖了一些栗子给别人，然后把钱花在店里买了混合糖果。

The Struggler，Concluded

Max又害怕又疲惫，但他还是强迫自己继续走，直到到达他的目的地——Hans的家。Max走到前门时松了一口气，但也有些害怕。如果这是错的房子或是更糟的陷阱呢？那么，他会怎么做呢？让这些人为他冒生命危险，他也感到内疚。他从拳头里拿出了前门的钥匙。

在房子里，Max问了Hans两个问题："你是Hans吗？""你还会拉手风琴吗？"这两个问题与Hans的战争经历有关。他在德国军队服役时遇到了一个名叫Erik的德国犹太人。是Erik教Hans如何拉手风琴，并成为Hans最好的朋友的；也是Erik救了Hans的命。

那一天，这位中士需要一个字写得好的人，Erik主动推荐了Hans，从此他远离了那次的战斗。虽然他们俩都不知道，那天每个参战的人都会死。

The Accordionist

战争结束后，军队决定不把Erik的手风琴寄回去，因为它太大不能邮寄，而是把它给了Hans。战后，Hans试图把它归还给Erik的妻子，但她不想要。为了报恩，Hans告诉她，如果她或她的儿子需要什么，就告诉他。他不知道二十年后，Erik的儿子Max会接受他的提议。Max的朋友在1939年6月16日第一次联系到Hans，这一天永远地改变了Hans的生活。Hans受到了当地纳粹分子的监视，因为他加入得很晚，还做了一些他们不赞成的事情，但尽管如此，他还是决定帮助Max。

A Good Girl

Liesel和Rudy学会了偷他们想要的食物。Hans开始帮助战争伙伴的儿子，他是犹太人。Liesel和Hans正以自己的方式学习打破规则，帮助自己和他人。

Max来到了Hans的家。他只有24岁，害怕、疲倦得无法形容，他只想知道自己是否安全。然后他发现Liesel穿着睡衣站在门口看着他。他又害怕起来，但Hans让他放心，他没什么好担心的，因为Liesel是个好女孩。

纵观每个小节内容，我开始明白为什么Hans不愿意加入纳粹分子，并不与他所在城镇的其他人一起虐待犹太公民。他把自己的生命归功于Erik，一个德国犹太人。Erik和Hans是朋友，这对他们来说是最重要的。Hans欠Erik一个人情，他忘不了Erik为他所做的一切，他感觉亏欠了Erik的儿子，因此他会尽他所能去救Max。

这就是死神给读者的故事梗概。死神是这本书的叙述者，这本书完全是从死神的角度出发来叙述文章故事的。他在这里告诉我们这本书是关于Liesel、Liesel的书、Hans、Erik和Hans共用的手风琴、纳粹、犹太人Max的。

Hans是一个善良的男人，他对一个孤独的小女孩表现出了极大的耐心和同情。他轻声地和她说话，为她拉手风琴。他花时间教她读书，并和她一起分享她在学习上的成功。

Hans也是一个言出必行的人，在他承诺尽其所能帮助Erik的家人之后，他收留了他的儿子，让自己的家人陷入了危险。在纳粹分子的恐怖统治下，他冒着生命危险把一个犹太人藏在家里。他觉得这是他欠Erik的债，因为Erik救了Hans的命。Erik那天的行为使他自己失去了生命，而Hans却得以继续活下去。

Liesel也是一个忠诚的朋友，她与Rudy和Max的友谊证明了这一点。当他们抢劫农民时，她和Rudy站在一起，Rudy差点被抓住，但是Liesel没有舍弃Rudy，尽管很害怕被抓住，但仍然尽力帮助Rudy脱险。

Max是Erik的儿子，Erik救了Hans的命。Max是一个德国犹太人，只想活下去，但他为自己可能会连累母亲和其他家庭成员而感到非常内疚。他知道他们很有可能最终会被关进集中营，所以Max只能逃。而他的逃亡也使他面临着更多的内疚，他又把Hans一家的生命置于危险之中。他知道如果他在他们家里被抓，那么，他们所有人都会被送进集中营或马上被杀掉。

他真诚地感谢他们为他冒了这么大的风险，同时他也为把他们置于危险之中而感到很抱歉。

可惜在Hitler冷血残酷的统治下，从1937年春天至1938年结束，德国的所有犹太人基本全部被屠杀了。这是人类历史上的一段黑暗岁月。人人生而平等，虽然大家都懂这句话，但是古今中外又有多少的生命还没有绽放就已经凋零。

通过对故事内容和人物特征的分析，结合当时残酷的大环境，我由衷地感到：

1.种族平等很重要。对我们来说，生活在一个更安全、更平等的社会里是幸运的。祝愿我们的世界变得越来越美好！

2.小小的帮助可能会有大大的回报，所以不要吝啬于帮助别人。

3.忠于自己的决定，对生活保持积极乐观的态度。

工作室人员分享

在这几章中，令我印象深刻的是“The Accordionist”这一章。死神将故事带回了第一次世界大战，当时Hans正在法国作战。他和一个名叫Erik的犹太人成了朋友，犹太人朋友教会他拉手风琴，并在战场上救了Hans的命。而在这几章中一个新的人物Max正式登场了，他是Hans的犹太人朋友留下的儿子。Max有幸得到朋友的帮助，几经周折最终来到Hans家避难。事实上，Hans和Rosa的处境是极其艰难的，一个犹太人凌晨出现在家里，在这个纳粹主义诞生的地方，他们一定经历了极度的不安、恐慌和焦虑，但他们还是接纳了Max。我想在这一章中，手风琴似乎又被赋予了一个深刻的情感蕴意。初期，手风琴一直陪伴着Liesel展开了她在天堂街的新生活，让Liesel在冰冷陌生的新环境中感受到了温暖和安宁；而此时它象征着Hans在乱世之下依旧不忘老朋友承诺的忠诚。

——王之光

Liesel和Rudy继续和他们的朋友从农民那里偷东西。除了苹果，他们还开始偷洋葱和土豆。他们还设计了一个从Otto那里偷东西的计划。Otto每周五给牧师送食物。他们和其他人分享偷来的这些东西，他们又偷了一个农民的东西。Liesel和Rudy每人吃一个栗子，然后卖掉剩下的，再回到 Frau Diller 的店里，买了各种各样的糖。“...Liesel and Rudy continue to steal from farmers with their gang of friends. In addition to apples，they begin stealing onions and potatoes，too. They also devise a plan to steal from Otto Sturm，a boy from school who delivers food to the priests every Friday. They share these goods with the rest of the gang，and Arthur also tells them that they should take the basket back to Otto...”

这一章的描写说明了Liesel、Rudy还有Arthur是如何理解做一个有道德的小偷的。他们对道德与不道德的小偷的认识，与小说后面出现的帮派新领袖形成了鲜明的对比。Liesel明白偷窃有对有错，Arthur也是。他们回到店里买东西，也表明了他们对抗Hitler的胜利。

——郑剑湘

“The Struggler，Concluded”一章虽然只有短短几页，却发人深省。

“Everything stiffened. Glowing pockets of streetlights. Dark，passive buildings. The town hall stood like a giant ham-fisted youth，too big for his age.”作者通过对周围环境的描述，渲染了一种沮丧和恐惧的气氛，衬托了逃亡中Max的心境。他打了个冷战，警告自己“Keep your eyes open.”。我能感受到 Max 的焦虑和恐惧。他一直很警惕，以免在路上被抓。同时，他还有罪恶的刺痛感。他怎么能这么做，让别人为他冒生命危险？他怎么能这么自私？他挣扎着活下去，从不放弃任何希望。然而，这绝对会给那些救他的人带来麻烦。他很善良，不想伤害别人。但他该怎么办呢？所以他陷入矛盾中。作者细腻的描写，把我们带进了Max的内心世界，让我们感同身受。

Max处境的危险，反面衬托了Hans的伟大。Hans为了报答当年战友的救命之恩，如今亦用生命来保护战友的儿子。Hans是一个知恩图报的人。

——关少娟

正如那句名言所说：“A friend in need is a friend indeed.”。在阅读这部分内容时，我再一次不禁想起这句话。在偷窃行动中，Liesel坚决帮助Rudy脱险。“instinctively，Liesel ran back.... Liesel arrived and started pulling at the fabric of his pants. Rudy’s eyes were open wide with fear.‘Quick，’he said，‘he’s coming.’”Liesel是如此的勇敢和忠诚，以至于她可以不惜一切代价去救她的朋友。她是个好女孩。她的养父Hans也是一个好人。他们有很多共同点。即使事关生死，Hans仍然选择帮助他的朋友。他没有对犹太人抱有任何偏见。他努力保持中立，以避免战争。在他的朋友，一个名叫 Erik Vandenburg 的德国犹太人的帮助下，他两次幸运地逃避了死亡。这种说法既有趣又幽默。但Erik没有Hans那么幸运。他在战斗中牺牲了，把手风琴留给了Hans，Hans继续保持中立，幸运地远离了纳粹分子。承诺就是承诺。Max向Hans求助。Hans和Erik的友谊触动了我的心。既然Liesel和Hans有很多共同点，他们肯定会帮助Max。当然，接下来的故事会越来越精彩，让我们继续往下读吧。

——李秀文

战争对人性有很大的考验。Max是犹太人，在逃亡中极需帮助，但自己也深知可能连累朋友。“Glowing pockets of streetlights. Dark，passive buildings. The town hall stood like a giant ham-fisted youth，too big for his age. The church disappeared in darkness the farther his eyes traveled upward. It all watched him. He shivered. He warned himself.‘Keep your eyes open.’Come on，just thirteen more. As an estimate，he completed ninety sets，till at last，he stood on the corner of Himmel Street.”这一段描写将Max对黑暗环境的恐惧和强烈的求生欲形成强烈的

对比，体现了Max不言败及坚韧的一面。“Of course，there was also the scratchy feeling of sin. How could he do this? How could he show up and ask people to risk their lives for him? How could he be so selfish? ”（他怎么能这样做呢？他怎么能让人为他冒生命危险呢？他怎么能这么自私？）这一段描写了Max内心的挣扎。幸好Hans为了报答当年战友的救命之恩，毅然地决定保护战友的儿子。读到这里，我不禁感慨Hans真是有情有义！同时，我也开始为这家人担忧起来，毕竟这么做很有可能惹上杀身之祸。

——莫洁文

在这几章里，我印象最深刻的是养父Hans的一诺千金。这也让一开始我觉得手风琴可能是一个伏笔的想法得到了印证：果然手风琴的背后就是养父对昔日老战友的承诺，他会善待老战友的亲人。就那么一句口头的诺言，一个只要他不承认就可以烟消云散的诺言，却被他如此尽心尽力地践行到底。他深知自己只是一个粉刷匠，能力有限，但是在周围都在排挤甚至抓捕犹太人的环境下，他还能信守对昔日战友的诺言，二话不说把Max带回家，放在地下室把他保护了起来，实属不易。相比之下，他们街区里的几个犹太人只是因为自己的种族，明明没有做任何坏事，店铺就被别人扔石头。不得不说，在那个德国纳粹疯狂给人们洗脑的大环境下，能保持清醒的头脑而不受影响真的很不容易。

——莫 然

He carried the accordion with him during the entirety of the war. When he tracked down the family of Erik Vandenburg in Stuttgart upon his return，Vandenburg’s wife informed him that he could keep it.Her apartment was littered with them，and it upset her too much to look at that one in particular.

The others were reminder enough，as was her once-shared profession of teaching it.

“You know，” Hans explained to her，“he saved my life.” The light in the room was small，and the air restrained. “He—if there’s anything you ever need.” He slid a piece of paper with his name and address on it across the table. “I’m a painter by trade.I’ ll paint your apartment for free，whenever you like.” He knew it was useless compensation，but he offered anyway.

我想说一说Hans这个人物。Hans是个正直、善良、懂得感恩、信守承诺的男子汉。他的一举一动让我都非常感动。

回国后，他找到了Erik的家人，并给他的妻子弹奏曲子。他想尽他所能来帮助Erik的妻子，虽然他仅仅是一个粉刷匠，虽然他也想要报答他的妻子，但是也于事无补。

“After lodging his form at the Nazi headquarters on Munich Street，he witnessed four men throw several bricks into a clothing store named Kleinmann’s. It was one of the few Jewish shops that were still in operation in Molching，Hans moved closed and stuck his head inside.‘Do you need some help?’‘I will come tomorrow，’he said，‘and repaint your door.’Which he did.It was the second of two mistakes.”

少数几家仍在营业的犹太人开的商店被几名男子扔砖头，玻璃砸得满地都是。“肮脏的犹太人”这几个字写得歪歪扭扭。Hans为人正直、善良，虽然当时纳粹分子这样仇视犹太人，Hans表面上还是会追随大众的潮流，但他还是义无反顾地去帮助犹太人，始终忠于自己内心的想法。

——宋 蕾

英国有一句谚语“Never judge a book by its cover.”，字面意思是“不要根据一本书的封面来判断它里面的内容”。人们多用这个说法来强调在对人和事物做评价时，不要以貌取人，不能光看表面，只凭外表不能看出一个人或一件事情的真实情况。Hans并没有因为他人的相貌或者身份而评判一个人，他只是追随自己的内心去对待每一个人。所以他没办法加入纳粹去痛恨犹太人。虽然这个决定给他带来了灾难，但是他从来没有后悔过。因为自己的善良和良知，他收留了逃亡的犹太男孩Max。

——夏丽焱

让我印象深刻的是“A good girl”这个章节里对犹太人Max现状的一些描写。

“‘Liesel’s papa walked to the front door and opened it. Cautiously，he looked outside each way，and returned. The verdict was‘nothing’.

Max Vandenburg，the Jew closed his eyes and drooped a little further into safety. The very idea of it was ludicrous，but he accepted it nonetheless. Hans checked that *The Curtain*s were properly closed. Not a crack could be showing. As he did so，Max could no longer bear it. He crouched down and clasped his hands.

The darkness stroked him. His fingers smelled of suitcase，metal，Mein Kampf，and survival.”

Max就是这样过着战战兢兢的生活，暗无天日，怕被人发现。这种挣扎的心理实在是太不容易了，让人真的感到非常同情。在那个时代，犹太人不得不面对随时失去生命的危险，他们不能光明正大地行走在街道，只能过着东躲西藏的日子。多么无奈和叫人同情啊！同时，我也不禁对我们现在的生活多出一份感恩，感恩我们现在平凡却安宁的生活。作者的这段文字描写也是画面感极强，无需刻意煽情，简单的陈述却字字扎心。

——徐 燕

Hans和Erik的友谊让我印象深刻。Erik的去世让Hans难以接受，虽然嘴上说一些话如“He taught me to play.”安慰了Erik的妻子，但Hans的内心比谁都难受。Erik曾经救过他一命，“He obviously thought that today wasn't the appropriate time for his friend to die.”。显然，他觉得今天不是一个他朋友要死去的日子。毕竟，如此善良的人怎么会就这样离开他了。在我的记忆里，Hans非常在意他的手风琴，并视其为珍宝。现在我意识到他肯定是把手风琴当作Erik，他最好的朋友，这也是Erik留给他的最后一件东西，所以Hans每天都把它带在身边陪着他。无法想象Hans一个人活下来有多痛苦，但他又不得不坚强起来去帮助Max渡过难关，正是这一切，见证了他作为一个朋友、作为一名父亲的善良、诚实和可靠。所以才有Liesel前后的变化，他是让家庭的氛围得以缓和的一个角色，他也充当着本书一个调和剂的角色。

——袁泳施

As the story goes further, I feel harder to breathe. Children were driven to steal from produce on the farm to goods. As for their behaviour, they sense complex feelings. On the one hand, they feel guilty, on the other hand, they feel happy without suffering from hunger. In their own words, “we might be criminals, but we are not totally immoral.” The writer described their feeling through their conversation.

For a long time, they walked in silence. (They were both deep thinking and they were deep sorry for what they had done.)

—Do you feel bad?

—About what?

—You know.

—Of course I do, but I'm not hungry anymore, and I bet he's not hungry either (try to reduce guilt).

—He just hit the ground so hard (hurt others).

—Don't remind me.

Liesel lives in gradual awakening. She has a deep understanding of the hard situation and the war. She is growing up quickly.

——Ting Feng

Part Four of The Book Thief

The Short History of the Jewish Fist Fighter—The Sleeper

导 读

本期的共读内容为“The Short History of the Jewish Fist Fighter” “The Wrath（愤怒）of Rosa” “Liesel’s Lecture” “The Sleeper”。

The Short History of the Jewish Fist Fighter

在这一章里，作者主要介绍了Hans犹太人老战友的儿子Max，他走投无路来投奔Hans了。Max虽然幼年丧父，很小就搬去了叔叔家和6个堂兄弟姐妹一起生活，但是他依然坚强地长大了，而且十几岁的他是那样年轻气盛，是那样无所畏惧，是一个靠拳头走天下的热血少年。

这里的几处细节描写也是很有意思的，一个是当Max和别人打拳击的时候被打到嘴巴里都是鲜血，可是却发现“He tasted it，and it tasted good.”。他完全没有因为拳击可能让自己流血受伤而害怕，相反地，他觉得这热血沸腾的感觉相当好，甚至有种视死如归的疯狂。那Max为什么会有这样的想法呢？原来是因为他的叔叔是个特别委曲求全的人，遇到什么事情都不抗争，让他看着觉得很憋屈，所以他立志长大之后一定不会像叔叔那样憋屈地活着。可惜世事弄人，因为纳粹的统治，犹太血统成了原罪，现在的他只能找地方躲起来苟且偷生。

The Wrath of Rosa

在这一章里，我们可以看到Rosa作为家里脾气最暴躁又喜欢唠叨的人的另一面。

一开始看到这个标题，我还以为Max这个不速之客突然来到Hans家里会让Rosa暴怒。毕竟Hans一直都是那么温柔和富有同情心，所以他接受Max算是在我们的意料之中，可是平时经常念叨Hans老是做老好人的Rosa居然也在短暂的思想斗争之后一脸庄重（原文用了“grave”这个词，意思是“庄严的”）地接受了Max，还问他要不要多吃点，还是挺出人意料的。后来看到Max因为太久没吃东西所以吃得太急把食物打翻了，以为Rosa会发火，但她还是只说了一句“Move.”，然后就默默收拾东西去了。

Liesel's Lecture

在这一章里，Rosa和Hans很认真地和Liesel交代了Max的来历。让我觉得感动的是，Rosa和Hans都没有把Liesel当作小孩子，而是把她当作一个平等的人，很认真地和她谈话，从手风琴开始一点一点把过去的故事和承诺都告诉了她，并且告诉她因为Max是犹太人，现在的环境之下窝藏犹太人就和窝藏罪犯一样，必须保密，甚至不惜威胁Liesel，如果她不好好保密的话就把她的书全部找出来烧掉，于是Liesel一边忍不住流眼泪，一边郑重地承诺"I will keep a secret."。

The Sleeper

在这一章里，我们看到了从Liesel的视角对Max的观察。Max已经完全没有了原来那个年少气盛的拳击手的痕迹，一来到Hans家地下室就足足睡了3天，以至于Liesel总是忍不住去看他是不是还有呼吸，而这几天的观察竟然让Liesel发现了这个陌生人和自己的相似之处，因为他们都会做噩梦。不得不说人总是很容易就会在人群之中发现自己的同类，可能这就是同类相吸吧。不过后来等Max真的醒来后反而把Liesel吓了一跳，她立马大叫papa，这个初次见面也是挺有戏剧化的。

这几章让我感受最深的就是：

人们总是可以在人群中准确认出和自己相似的灵魂。

工作室人员分享

我终于读懂了Max，让我惊讶的是，原来Max从很小年纪就经历了那么多的苦痛。其中大多都是关于家人的，印象最深的应该是他叔叔的死吧。"He kept to himself and scarified everything for his family."叔叔是一个伟大的愿意为家庭付出一切的人，可他的付出没有得到回报。当Max看着叔叔在床上睡去，他就发誓他以后一定不要这样死掉。我想这也是Max不屈不挠的原因。因为他有太多东西要去争取了：他跟Walter之间的斗争、他的民族和纳粹的斗争以及他自己与死亡之间的斗争。最折磨人的便是无法帮助家人逃脱的无助感以及当只有他被救下来的释然，"His body felt like it was being screwed up into a ball，like a page littered with mistakes. Like garbage."。其中的矛盾让他痛苦，每次都让Max回忆起那段痛苦的往事。我期待下一章，但又很害怕战争的来临。

——袁泳施

犹太拳手的历史令人着迷，但又苦乐参半。Max年少的时候，最喜欢的就是打架了。在和对手的第一次较量之后，"A trickle of blood was dripping from Max's mouth. He tasted it，and it tasted good."暴力的种子似乎在Max的生活中找到了生根发芽的土壤。后来他的叔叔，"Worked quietly away for very little reward and sacrificed everything for his family，died of something growing in his stomach."。从此Max决定"he would never allow himself to die like that."。他发誓："When death captures me，he will feel my fist on his face."。而死神甚至喜欢他的"愚蠢"勇气和精神，他说："Personally，I quite like that. Such stupid gallantry. Yes. I like that a lot."。

作品中对于Max青少年时变化的叙述准确而生动。他在争斗中努力驱散青少年的狂躁能量。Max "enjoyed the tight circles and the unknown." "The bittersweetness of uncertainty：To win of to lose. It was a feeling in the stomach that would be stirred around until he thought he could no longer tolerate it. The only remedy was to move forward and throw punches."他就像一只被困在笼子里不安分的狮子，但又无路可逃。当时很黑暗，一切都不确定，只有战斗才能让他远离忧虑和恐惧。通过这种方式，他和对手建立了深厚的友谊。对于我来说，虽然他们的兄弟情谊和我们的姐妹情谊是如此不同，但是我惊讶地发现，我竟然觉得他们的打斗很有趣。"there was new blood in him—the blood of victory—and it had the capability to both frighten and excite."他们互相争斗，互相帮助。

Hans给了Liesel一个严厉的警告，一个令人印象深刻的教训。我突然想起，有时候有些事情必须先变得糟糕才能变好。经历了痛苦才懂得快乐和感恩，经历过惩罚才懂得遵守纪律的必要性。这也是教育的双面性。教师的工作是世界上最艰巨，但也是最重要的。

——李秀文

这四个章节主要围绕着Max来讲。我知道Max的生活很悲惨，他2岁时父亲去世，9岁时母亲身无分文。他的叔叔在他13岁时就去世了。他的生活充满了不确定性和压力。并且，他对离开家人感到内疚，他不得不躲藏了6个多月。他只能待在储藏室里，从一个房间换到另一个房间，躲藏在无尽的黑暗中。幸运的是，他有一个叫Walter的朋友能帮他一起渡过难关。

过去他们常常打架，发誓要把对方打倒。我仍然记得书上对他们打架的生动描述。的确，生活是不可预测的！

Liesel的演讲也给我留下了深刻的印象。为了让Liesel明白这个问题有多严重，Hans不得不对她很严厉，告诉她最坏的结果，尽管这可能会让她伤心。但这就是现实！我想Liesel和Max一定会成为好朋友，因为他们都是带着不安和焦虑来到Himmel Street的，而且他们都做噩梦。他们之间有着很多共同点。

——麦佩莹

在这几章中，我被Max颠沛流离的逃亡生活所震惊，我对于他的遭遇深感同情。

"When Max heard the news，his body felt like it was being screwed up into a ball，like a page littered with mistakes. Like garbage.

Yet each day，he managed to unravel and straighten himself，disgusted and thankful. Wrecked，but somehow not torn into pieces."

Max藏起来了，但是他托朋友每天去看看他的家人。一天，朋友告诉他，开门的是陌生人。那么，他的家人去哪里了？逃亡了？被抓了？甚至被杀了？Max，经历着这种亲人分离的痛苦，他的身体仿佛被揉成一团，像一张被画得乱七八糟的纸，像一堆垃圾。垃圾是什么？是被遗弃的东西。然而，他还是坚强的，每天都试着让自己解脱并振作起来而不崩溃。

Max被好心的Hans收留了。有一段描写他做噩梦的话。

"Sometimes，close to the end of the marathon of sleep，he spoke. There was a recital of murmured names... Family，friend，enemy.

They were all under the covers with him，and at one point，he appeared to be struggling with himself. 'Nein.' he whispered. It was repeated seven times. 'No.' "

他在梦里像是和自己争辩。不！不！不！这个字被重复了7遍。一个"不"字，让我们听到他不想逃亡，不想跟家人分离，不想受国人纳粹分子的迫害，不想遭受杀戮，不想过胆战心惊的生活，不想偷偷摸摸地东躲西藏的心声。我们可以想象他内心对战争的痛恨，可以体会他的痛苦和无奈。

——关少娟

Max竟然是一个拳击爱好者，还是一名出色的街头拳击手，真是令人吃惊啊！之前的故事里，他躲在储藏室，担惊受怕，不敢出声或者移动。饿了好几天，一拿到面包没有直接吃，而是先分成三份。他谨慎又自律，同时还是一个内心充满恐惧的年轻人。但是逃亡之前的他是另一个样子，充满活力，无比坚强。即便和比他强大数倍的对手同台比赛，他也能咬牙承受重击，还能不停地挥舞拳头，给予对手还击，并且十分享受搏斗的过程。

我不禁思考，到底是什么让一个健壮的拳击小伙变成了在黑暗中东躲西藏的"小老鼠"呢？那是战争，它让年轻犹太人丧失勇气和力量，为生存而奔逃；它让年轻德国宪兵失去良知，夺走弱者生命；它让光明变成黑暗，美好变成残缺，生命变成死亡；让疲于在战争中回收灵魂的死神叹气，不想再次发生战争。

——夏丽焱

这几章主要描述了Max的命运。Max是一名犹太人，一名热爱拳击的年轻小伙子。"When he was younger，he grew to love nothing more than a good fistfight. A trickle of blood was dripping from Max's mouth. He tasted it，and it tasted good." 在面对他叔叔的死亡时，他曾经质疑过自己对拳击的热爱，但是他仍旧无法否认自己对拳击的热爱。"Where's the fight? he wondered. Where's the will to hold on? 'When death captures me，' the boy vowed，'he will feel my fist on his face.

Personally，I quite like that. Such stupid gallantry. Yes. I like that a lot.’”

但是生活在纳粹统治下的德国，犹太人的命运太悲惨了。Max无法继续与别人打拳击比赛，没有女孩愿意跟他在一起。“What could he offer those girls? By 1938，it was difficult to imagine that life could get any harder.”他不得不离开家人，变得无家可归。到后来，他的家人也遭遇了不测。“When Max heard the news，his body felt like it was being screwed up into a ball，like a page littered with mistakes. Like garbage.”而他的生命安全也受到威胁，就连向别人求助，都要小心翼翼。“We don’t know what might happen. I might get caught. You might need to find that place... I’m too scared to ask anyone for help here. They might put me in.”

但是令人欣慰的是，Max得到了Walter和Hans Hubermann一家的帮助。战争是残酷的，它能摧毁人的事业、家庭、生命，但是它却无法磨灭掉所有人的亲情和友情。

——陈雪芬

这几章让我体会到了书中人物之间的深厚情谊并为之感动。有Max和Walter之间的不打不相识，由夹杂着恨意的惺惺相惜转变成真挚的友谊，到最后Walter拼尽全力帮助Max逃亡。有Max和家人之间的深厚情谊，离别时母亲将那张陈旧的能带给Max最后希望的纸片塞进他的口袋，其他的家人纷纷给他塞了些钱和值钱的小物件，而Max仓皇离家时没来得及回头看家人一眼，无尽的悔恨成为他生命中最深的痛楚。“They left，without looking back. It tortured him. If only he’d turned for one last look at his family as he left the apartment. Perhaps then the guilt would not have been so heavy. No final goodbye. No final grip of the eyes. Nothing but goneness.”有Hans和Max父亲之间生死之交的深厚情谊，Max的父亲在一战的时候救了Hans一命，因此Hans愿意豁出自己的性命来保护这位年轻的犹太人。“A promise is a promise.” “Liesel’s Lecture”这一章通过大量的语言描写、动作描写让我们更深地体会到Hans一家豁出性命来保护Max的情意。尽管恐惧在黑暗中闪烁，Hans和Rosa却把这些非理性的情绪压在心底。初来乍到的Max经常从噩梦中惊醒，就如同几年前的Liesel一样，关于这些噩梦的交流，成为Liesel和Max友谊的开端。相信接下来的内容会让我为这两人的深厚情谊而感动。

——李 丹

“As expected，it was a Nazi in uniform.

‘Never.’

That was Max’s first response.

He clung to his mother’s hand and that of Sarah，the nearest of his cousins. ‘I won’t leave.If we can’t go，I don’t go，either.’

He was lying.

When he was pushed out by the rest of his family，the relief struggled inside him like an obscenity. It was something he didn't want to feel，but nonetheless，he felt it with such gusto it made him want to throw up.How could he? How could he?

But he did.

'Come on.' Walter pulled at him as the rest of the family said their goodbyes and gave him money and a few valuables："It's chaos out there，and chaos is what we need."

They left，without looking back.

It tortured him.

If only he'd turned for one last look at his family as he left the apartment. Perhaps then the guilt would not have been so heavy.No final goodbye.

No final grip of the eyes.

Nothing but goneness."

这一段描写让我印象非常深刻，我非常同情Max的遭遇。他是一位犹太男孩，在他很小的时候就深深地爱上了打拳。他有一个不幸的童年。当他两岁的时候，他的爸爸就在战争中不幸遇难身亡了。在他9岁的时候，他的妈妈彻底破产，卖掉了音乐教室，搬到了叔叔家过日子。

当他13岁时苦难再次降临，他的叔叔也死了。在战争年代，像别的家庭一样，家人围坐在他叔叔的床边，看着他向命运低头。

让我印象深刻的是Max的逃跑和躲藏。他的拳击对手同时也是他的好朋友Walter，从中帮助了他。Walter把他藏身于一间储藏室，就在Walter前些年干活的一栋大楼里。每一天Max都在厌恶和庆幸中折磨自己，他疲惫不堪，但好在没有崩溃。

Max离开家后，一直感到很愧疚。一方面，他觉得是他抛弃了家人；另一方面，他又不想被纳粹分子迫害。他匆匆离开家，都没有好好看看家人，甚至都没有和家人说再见，而这一直折磨着他。战争给犹太人带来了无尽的痛苦和灾难，让他们流离失所、无家可归。

——宋 蕾

在本期的第一章节，我们终于迎来了Max的出场。他是一个犹太男孩，也是个年轻的拳击手。他看起来很瘦，但是非常有力量。文中是这样描写他的长相的："Skinny as a whittled broom handle."。对于犹太人的性格，文中说道："Jews preferred to simply stand and take things. Take the abuse quietly and then work their way back to the top."。但是不像普通的犹太人，Max非常热衷于拳击。他有着一个不幸的童年，小时候他亲眼看见了他叔叔的死亡。小小的他想知道

"Where the fight is? Where's the will to hold on? "。他发誓"when the Death captures me he will feel my fist on his face."。他能在这个年纪说出这样的话，是非常令人惊讶的。Max对生死有着自己独特的理解。从他说的这些话中，我能够感觉到他内心的力量是非常强大的，而且他对生命是非常虔诚的。他永远不会向命运低头。作为一个拳击手，你会想当然地认为他是足够强壮和勇敢的。但事实上，作为犹太人，他仍然害怕纳粹的迫害。这让我想起另一本书——《安妮日记》。纳粹分子侵入荷兰时，安妮和她的家人为了活下去，在一个暗无天日的地下室躲了两年。当我在阅读那本书的时候，透过安妮的文字能够深刻地体会到纳粹对犹太人的迫害和残忍。

——董筱妍

在这部分，回顾Max的生活是必要的，以便我们理解他是如何最终站在Hans家里的。

Max在贫穷中长大，由于父亲的去世，家里没有钱，最后搬到了叔叔家里。Max的堂兄教他如何打架，这成了Max最喜欢的活动。他与Walter是通过打架认识的。他和Walter打过几次架，大部分时间都是Walter赢，但最终他们成了朋友。这里有种不打不相识的感觉，可能这就是男人之间独特的交友方式吧。这也让我想起羽毛球坛的"超级丹"和李宗伟。

纳粹掌权后，是一名纳粹士兵Walter把Max藏了起来，并帮他找到了Hans。是Walter和Hans做了安排，使Max得以前往Hans家。当Max和Walter一起离开去寻找安全的地方时，他不禁对自己离开母亲和堂兄弟独自逃生的行为产生负罪感。

Rosa走进厨房，发现一个陌生人和她丈夫坐在一起。她想知道他是谁。那个年轻人狼吞虎咽地吃着，然后把食物吐了出来。对于一个习惯了食物太少的胃来说，太多的食物反而不能适应。这个陌生人闯入了Rosa的生活，她很担心，但并没有生气，也没有和Hans争论。这里特别表现出她的善良和对丈夫的宽容。

第二天早上，Liesel被带到地下室和爸爸谈话。Hans是耐心和民主的。他向她解释了Max是谁，以及爸爸如何欠了Max爸爸的一条命。他还解释了她若把这件事告诉别人的严重性。爸爸告诉她，如果她不守秘密，他会把她所有的书都烧掉，然后会有人来把Liesel带走。因为他知道书对Liesel来说是最重要的。他还告诉她，Max、妈妈和他自己也会被带走，再也不会回来。Liesel听后哭了起来，但Hans必须让她明白，把Max留在家里的秘密是一定要保守住的。这是一件非常重要和严肃的事情。当他确信她理解了之后，他和妈妈拥抱了她。

Liesel已经观察Max三天了，她意识到他也会做噩梦。她还意识到，他们俩都是在危难中来到Hans家的，并受到了欢迎。就像书上说的，"一切都很好。但这也太可怕了"。其实他们两个人是同病相怜的，Liesel的爸妈是共产主义者，Max

是犹太人，这两种人在当时都是不被统治者欢迎的，因此他们都受到了迫害，只不过是种族歧视的矛盾更加尖锐罢了。

——宋碧燕

这个故事又回到了过去，讲述了Max的一生。他小时候喜欢打架。他小时候和表兄弟们打过架，11岁的时候第一次真正打架。13岁的时候，Max看着他的叔叔死于胃病，他对自己看起来如此顺从感到失望。到后来，Max被迫和家人告别离开，躲在朋友 Walter 曾经工作过的一间空储藏室里，他感到绝望，同时也被仍然想活下去的内疚感折磨着——选择逃跑和生存，而不是留下来和他的家人一起被捕。

而如今，Max为了活命来到了Hans家中。Max满脸愁云，痛苦不堪。Max的痛苦不仅来自对自己生命的恐惧，还来自把他人置于危险之中的内疚。

Max的种种经历，让他的人物形象更加鲜明地跃然纸上，也能让读者更好地理解Max这样一个前后完全不一样的矛盾体：一个从发誓要战斗到最后，有着不顾一切的勇气，坚信生比死好，连死神都不得不佩服、尊敬的年轻战士，到现在因迫害和恐惧而支离破碎、萎靡不振的胆小鬼。

——郑剑湘

这部分对Max的成长经历展开了描述，Max在成长中因战争而承受的生离死别和痛苦实在令人压抑和难受。正是因此，Max对战争是深恶痛绝的；也正是因此，Max才形成了不屈不挠的性格。文中有一段对Max噩梦的描写令我印象深刻。“有时，在漫长的睡眠即将结束时，他会说话。大家低声念了几个名字：家人、朋友、敌人。他们都和他一起被窝在被子里，有一次，他似乎在和自己做斗争。‘不行。’他低声说。重复了七次‘不’。”可见战争对Max的巨大伤害，战争是他无法摆脱的噩梦，现在这种逃亡的状态也让他陷入自我斗争中，让人感到窒息！

——莫洁文

In this part，the writer brought us back to Max's journey of fight，fleeing，hiding and how Hams helped Max. What impressed me most was how Hans told Liesel the consequence of Max's visit.（**skillful**）

He began the lesson with his accordion，World War One，Erik and Hans，the visit to the fallen soldier's wife，Max's appearing.（**why he takes such risks to help Max**）

Remember the fuhrer's birthday.（**protect herself**）

“Liesel，if you tell anyone about the man up there，we will all be in big trouble.

At the very least，mama and I will be taken away.

For starters，1 will take each and every one of your books—and I will burn them！I'll throw them in the stove or the fireplace.

Next，they'll take you away from me，do you want that?

They'll drag that man up there away，and maybe Mama and me too—and we will never，ever come back."（**serious consequence**）

The writer describe Hans's shadow with the word "giant". "In the basement，the lamplight is burning，it magnifying his shadow. It turned him into a giant on the wall." Here，"GIANT" has two meanings，one is the shadow，and the other is Hans' lofty character. It's really a good writing.

——Ting Feng

Part Four—Five of The Book Thief

The Swapping of Nightmares—The Floating Book（Part I）

导读

本期的内容是“The Swapping of Nightmares”“Pages from the Basement”“The Floating Book（Part I）”。书中这几章中配了很多有意思的插画，都是选自Max在地下室创作的画册。首先是“The Swapping of Nightmares”，这一章节可以分成三个部分——Max住在地下室时窘迫的处境，Hans对Max的改变，Liesel和Max之间的相处。我们都知道Max终于找到了Hans，并且住在他家的地下室，地下室的居住环境是非常恶劣的。但是他很卑微地说道：“If there was one place he was destined to exist，it was a basement or any other such hidden venue of survival.”。他解释道他生来就是一个犹太人，在他的看法里面，犹太人只能住在地下室或者其他用来躲藏的地方。第二点他认为犹太人现在代表着世界上最惨的群体。对于这样的现状，他无能为力且感到落寞。他最喜欢说的口头禅是“Thank you.”和“I'm sorry.”。你会发现这两句话，简简单单地就能描写出Max现在的一个心境——永远觉得自己低人一等，时刻在说“很不好意思，很抱歉给你们家带来的麻烦”“谢谢，谢谢你能收留我”，但是他一直都觉得他不会被困太久，他当然想要走出去。但是他又会否定自己。由此可见，他的内心是挣扎的。Max觉得活下去的最低代价是牺牲他的罪恶感和羞耻感。罪恶感指的是他要去麻烦Hans一家人，而羞耻感就是作为一个活生生的人，他不得不活在阴暗的角落里面，所以这是他付出的代价，并且他还牺牲了他的自由。

接下来就是Hans一家人对Max的改变。当时所有人都是不能收留犹太人的，而且纳粹分子一直在不停地搜查。之前的Hans，在我看来是有一点懦弱无能的，他的妻子Rosa虽然很强悍，但是面对这样的情况也是非常无助的。因为这个普通的家庭需要冒着极大的风险去收留Max。为了活下去，他说只要能给一点吃的就行。但是，Rosa说：“会尽我所能把你喂饱的。”虽然Rosa以前都是那种粗枝大叶、大大咧咧型的，但是这里你会发现她是心地善良的老实人。书中有一个场景描写他们的争吵，因为一家人都要对这个秘密守口如瓶。但是对于Max的日常生活起居，他们照顾得非常到位。每天都有人在特定的时间段给Max送吃的，甚至Rosa还会给他倒一些热水洗澡。接下来，Liesel觉得她妈妈身上发生了改变。因为之前她就是一副市井妇女的形象，每天靠洗衣服养活一家人。但是书中这样写道："She was a good woman for a crisis."，就是她碰到这样的紧急情况立马就拿定了主意，这与她老公内心的慌乱、纠结、复杂形成了一个鲜明的对比。

第三部分就是Max和Liesel之间的相处。我把他们两个形容为soul mate。第一个原因是她爸爸跟Max说"She is like a good fist-fighter."，他的女儿也像一个很棒的拳击手。第二个原因是他们两个都喜欢看书。Max住在地下室都能用读书来慰藉自己和平复自己的心灵。第三个原因是他们两个晚上都会做噩梦，都会梦到逝去的家人。

第二个章节，书中给我们展示了很多Max画的插画。有一幅图，画了Max的生日。Max和Liesel友情的转折点是在Max生日的那一天，Liesel给他送了一份礼物，这让Max非常感动。然后还有一幅图上有他写在地下室墙上的四个单词——day、light、water和movement。在这四个最简词里面，Max总结道，Liesel是他珍贵的朋友；她的出现像是一束阳光照耀着他；她像水一样在他现在的生活中不可或缺；因为有Liesel陪他在地下室走动，让他看到了一丝活力。通过这些描写，你会了解到，其实Max不光会打拳看书，他还会创作非常可爱的小漫画。

在第三个章节"The Floating Book"里面，气氛马上不一样了。前一段在描写可怜的Max，但是当Liesel和他成为好朋友后，你会感觉到事情一点点地在发生转变。但是这一章节却有对Rudy死亡的预告。这一章的内容非常少，但是给人的冲击是非常大的。首先这一章是以死神的口吻写的，他觉得Rudy不该死，上天不能抢走这样一个热血男孩。Rudy面对喜欢的女孩子时会开玩笑，也会在她难过的时候安慰她。读完这一章节，我内心非常伤感。

最后，用两句谚语总结我对这三个章节的感受。"A good friend is like a mirror." "A true friend reaches for your hand and touches your heart." 这两句话可以充分地表达在这样的战乱时期Liesel和Max之间珍贵的友谊。

工作室人员分享

书中这一部分变得更加有趣和感人。Liesel和她的家人生活在紧张和谨慎之中，而Max却生活在内疚和羞耻之中。但是作者是如此伟大，以至于他可以用幽默感来粉饰它。Liesel的养母Rosa是个应对危机的好女人。"What shocked Liesel most was the change in her mama. Whether it was the calculated way in which she divided the food，or the considerable muzzling of her notorious mouth，or even the gentler expression on her cardboard face，one thing was becoming clear. She was a good woman for a crisis." Max刚来的时候，Liesel试图否认他的存在。然后她发现他们有很多共同点。最后，他们成了好朋友。太贴心了，Max给Liesel做了一份迟

到的生日礼物——一本书。

令人惊讶的是，书中Max的形象是一只大鸟，仅仅因为Liesel说他的头发看起来像羽毛。Liesel是他最好的女性朋友。然而，我被死神关于Rudy死亡的消息震惊了，尽管他试图幽默地告诉我们他也感觉到很遗憾很难过，他说："even death has a heart."。

Rudy和Liesel在一起时是那么的可爱和幸福。突然之间，我无法接受Rudy会死掉的信息。当然，这扣人心弦的情节也成功地激起了我继续阅读的兴趣。

——李秀文

Max的一生都是悲惨的，自小就失去了父亲，作为一个犹太人在当时的大环境中是在夹缝里求生存。虽然有他不打不相识的拳击朋友的掩护和帮助以及Hans一家的照顾和帮助，以及最后和Liesel成为朋友，但是他活得太卑微了。他说得最多的是"I'm sorry." "Thank you."。他也对Liesel坦白"I'm selfish." "leaving people behind. Coming here. Putting all of you in danger..."。他的人生写照是："To live. Living was living. The price was guilt and shame."。

接着就是死神告知Rudy的死，这让所有人都很伤感，这样一个阳光男孩应该有更好的未来，有更长的人生轨迹。甚至死神都觉得不应该是这样。最让我觉得遗憾的是：一直以来Rudy都希望Liesel能给他一个吻，但是等Rudy死后Liesel才实现了Rudy的愿望。Rudy的灵魂在看着："*The Book Thief* on her hands and knees, next to his decimated body. He'd have been glad to witness her kissing his dusty, bomb-hit lips."。作为无神论者，我觉得凡事都应该把握现在和当下，有些东西过去了就永远都无法挽回，愿我们的人生少些追忆和遗憾。

——宋碧燕

我觉得好的作品就是能让人去体验自己没有机会体验的人生。

这几章看完之后，我就觉得完全进入了Max的角色，也通过很多细节去理解作为战乱年代的犹太人的辛酸，能感觉到他的自责、自卑还有感恩。他觉得自己活着都是一种罪恶，只会给别人带来不幸，但是又没有勇气去死，就这样苟且偷生，一直活在痛苦和矛盾中。从这个人物的个人心路历程出发，我们就可以以小见大地看到战争的残忍足以把一个人的所有棱角磨平。在战争面前，每个人的生命都显得那么脆弱，那么渺小，那么无助！

——莫 然

Max制作了两本小册子送给Liesel。

这两本小册子，都是以他自己的经历作为蓝本创作的。与其说它是写给Liesel的，不如说是写给Max自己的。他以寓言的形式，告诉Liesel真实世界的残酷和文字的力量。在和Max相处的两年中，Liesel有三次刻骨铭心的经历，使她充分感受到了文字和书籍的力量。

第一次是Max昏迷时。因为潮湿阴冷的地下室环境，Max生了一场大病，整整昏迷了将近半个月。在Liesel读完四本书之后，Max终于苏醒。第二次是遭遇轰炸时。在躲避炸弹轰炸的地下室，Himmel 的人们无不因死亡的威胁而战栗。Liesel在黑暗中用读书来安抚大家。所有人都在Liesel的阅读声中平静了下来。当大家走出地下室时，每个人都来感谢Liesel转移了他们的恐惧。第三次是面对邻居阿姨的示好时。邻居阿姨原本和Liesel的养母Rosa是死对头，只要经过Hans家，邻居阿姨必定要往Hans家的大门上吐一口仇恨的痰。可是，在地下室听了Liesel读书之后，邻居阿姨竟然主动冰释前嫌，甚至在听闻小儿子的死讯之后，依靠Liesel的读书声获得了暂时的平静。

——郑剑湘

"During that week，Max had cut out a collection of pages from Mein Kampf and painted over them in white. He often hung them up with pegs on some string，from one end of the basement to the other. When they were dry，the hard part began. He was educated well enough to get by，but he was certainly no writer，and no artist. Despite this，he formulated the words in his head till he could recount them without error. Only then，on the paper that had bubbled and humped under the stress of drying paint，did he begin to write the story. It was done with a small black paintbrush.

There were practice versions on the pages of the Molcbing Express，improving his basic，clumsy artwork to a level he could accept. As he worked，he heard the whispered words of a girl.

When he was finished，he used a knife to pierce the pages and tie them with string.The result was a thirteen-page booklet that went like this."

这一章节，Max的突然闯入，使得Liesel刚开始无法接受他的到来，又要为他的到来保守秘密。但是因为两个人都喜欢读书，而另外一个相似之处，是都会做噩梦。他们彼此感受和传递着内心的痛楚和对生活的无奈，产生共鸣，慢慢地建立了深厚的友谊。

让我印象深刻的是在Liesel生日那天，她收到了爸爸妈妈的礼物——一本书*The Mud Men*，而Max则尴尬地站在角落里，用很微弱的语气说了一声"祝你生日快乐"。他本知道自己没有什么礼物送给她，他还说谎话："我真不知道，不然我也能送你点礼物。"然而Liesel却走过去拥抱了他并说了一句："谢谢你，Max。"之后Max却给了她一份特殊的礼物作为回报。我觉得这份礼物意味深长，Max把自己从小到大的人生经历写成了一本小册子，小册子的标题是*The Standover Man*。Max觉得，在他的一生中，他都害怕那些俯视他的人，直到他遇到了Liesel，他才感觉到温暖。小册子当中的这些人生经历一直折磨着他，甚至让他感到愧疚和耻辱。但是他愿意和Liesel分享他的感受，这是多么难能可贵的友谊。一个人如果能把自己内心深处的痛楚毫无保留地和别人分享，那就说明他对对方有足够的信任。

一个德国人和一个犹太人之间的友谊，说明种族没有界限，种族之间应该是平等、友爱和互助的。在战争年代，这应该是Liesel收到的一份最珍贵的生日礼物了。

——宋 蕾

战争打响，生活已经完全发生改变，但Liesel一家又不得不表现坦然，“that was the business of hiding a jew or of hiding the nightmares that once tortured Max and Liesel.”。因为在战争中收留一个犹太人毕竟不是一件容易的事情。战争见证了很多人的死亡，也让Max的梦想变成了一个泡影，“The Jewish rat，back to his hole.”。他没有选择，为了保护自己、保护家人。“Jewry was more than ever a label—a ruinous pieces of dumbest luck around.”但两个孩子居然勇敢地向对方“分享”自己的噩梦，不难想象，让我们去“重温”痛苦时刻是艰难的，有些画面历历在目。“it was like a timetable train，at a nightly platform，pulling on memories behind it. There’s lots of dragging；a lot of awkward bounces，not to mention the pages from basement.”就像是一部火车，停在记忆的月台，很多凌乱的声音，碎片漫天飞，人们无所适从地胡乱逃跑。还有，Rudy去世了，他明明是那个给大家希望和自信的人啊！他的逝去就像是当前平和生活的终结，让人心碎。

——袁泳施

“It would be nice to say that after this small breakthrough，neither Liesel nor Max dreamed their bad visions again. It would be nice but untrue. The nightmares arrived like they always did，much like the best player in the opposition when you’ d heard rumors that he might be injured or sick—but there he is，warming up with the rest of them，ready to take the field. Or like a timetabled train，arriving at a nightly platform，pulling the memories behind it on a rope. A lot of dragging. A lot of awkward bounces.”

在“The Swapping of Nightmares”这一章节里，Max和Liesel说出了自己所梦到的东西——Max梦到自己挥手离开，Liesel梦到一列火车和她死去的弟弟。读到这里，我很难想象他们当时是以一种怎样的心情去互换梦境的。人们总是说“日有所思，夜有所梦”，他们梦境中的东西其实就是深藏在他们内心深处的伤痛。正如作者所描述，噩梦就像是对方球队里最棒的队员，随时准备上场；也像是一列按照列车时刻表运行的火车，停靠在夜晚的站台，后面用一根绳子，牵引着好多回忆，一长串的回忆，引发一连串可怕的碰撞。读到后面，我明白了，他们找到了与自己有"共同点"的朋友，他们之间是信任的。在那个动乱的年代，Max能与Hans一家相处，让我感到一丝慰藉。

——陈雪芬

这周读完三节故事后，我对当时寒冷的天气感触特别深。

作者对德国寒冷冬天的生动描写是："outside，a mountain of cold November air was waiting at the front door each time Liesel left the house. Drizzle came down in spades. Dead leaves were slumped on the road."。看到这里，我都忍不住打了个寒颤，结冰的雪花，冻人的寒风，让我想起了2008年的冰灾。当时城里没电，外头零下几度，爸妈都不敢让我出门，而且城里不像农村可以烧柴取暖，我只能躲在被窝里，缩成一团。

但是，我是因客观条件不允许我取暖，Max却是主动选择待在地下室，苦苦挨冻。当然一方面是为了保护Hans一家人，不让外人发现自己。可是我相信更深层次的原因是，他用这种方法惩罚自己，没有和家人挥手告别，就急匆匆地逃生，所以他会用一生来赎罪。"To live. Living was living. The price was guilt and shame."

——夏丽焱

读到"The Swapping of Nightmares"这一章节的开头，我不禁在想到底是什么让犹太人处于如此难以忍受的境地。为了生存，犹太人只能待在地下室或其他隐蔽的地方。犹太人甚至没有资格感到寒冷和孤独，因为他们总是处于最低的地位，而活着的代价就是内疚和耻辱！Max总是因Hans感到内疚，因为他知道他们会被牵连进来。虽然他在一个安全的地方，但他从不感到安全。他不能。多么可怜啊！我对Max深表同情。更不用说我读了这本13页的小册子后的悲伤了。我一页一页地读着，泪水在眼眶里流淌。尤其是这部分："Tell me what you dream of. So I did."。然后，这张全家人的照片深深地打动了我的心。Max非常想念他的家人和朋友。这本小册子是他能给Liesel的最好礼物。然而，这意味着很多。他用这本小册子告诉Liesel他的艰难生活、他的噩梦、他的感受和他们的共同点。这本小册子我一遍又一遍地读，读了四遍。也许the Standover Man指的是帮助Max的人。最后，我真的不想Rudy死去。太伤心了！

——麦佩莹

这三章故事让我们的心情跟着温暖，也跟着难过。我们为Liesel和Max有了交流而振奋；我们感动于小人物Hans夫妇在这个动乱的年代里，愿意收留这样一个危险的犹太人，并且那么坚定地去做这件冒着生命危险的事情。

文中是这样描述的："Every morning when Liesel left for school，or on the days she ventured out to play soccer or complete what was left of the washing round，Rosa would speak quietly to the girl. 'And remember Liesel...' She would point to her mouth and that was all. When Liesel nodded she would say 'Good girl，Saumensch. Now get going.' True to Papa's words，and even Mama's now，she was a good girl. She kept her mouth shut everywhere she went. The secret was buried deep."。

Hans夫妇为Max解决了温饱问题，Liesel给他带去的是心灵的慰藉，是读书让他们有了些共同语言。他创作的这个小册子，其中的文字给了Liesel力量，也给了她未来成为一名作家的一些启发吧。而作者的文字也颇有深意，孩子们探险般地从家里出来踢球，可见在当时战火弥漫的情况下，人们生活的那种小心翼翼。

——徐 燕

阅读了这几章，内心的感受是复杂的，有感动，有辛酸，还有温暖。为Hans一家豁出自己的性命去保护Max，而且竭尽全力去照顾Max而感动；与此同时，也因Max的逃亡生活而感到辛酸。书中的几处描写特别感动人。

"To live. Living was living. The price was guilt and shame."（P208）

"In the morning，he would return to the basement. A voiceless human. The Jewish rat，back to his hole."（P215）

"During the nights，both Liesel and Max would go about their other similarity. In this separate rooms，they would dream their nightmares and wake up，one with a scream in drowning sheets，the other with a gasp for air next to a smoking fire."（一个在汗湿的床单上发出尖叫声，另一个则在炉火旁喘着粗气）（P219）

这几章中也有几处温暖人心的场景。Liesel捡起垃圾桶中的*Molching Express*将其带回家拿给Max看，想着让Max做点填字游戏来打发时间。在Liesel12岁生日那天，她收到了自己心仪的礼物——*The Mud Men*，她拥抱了妈妈和爸爸，然后，又走过去拥抱了Max。感受到温暖的Max决心要给Liesel一点回报，用心制作了一本名为*The Standover Man*的十三页的小册子（booklet），并把它作为一份迟到的生日礼物送给了Liesel。图文并茂的小册子讲述着Max自己，其中有些句子让我印象很深刻。"Many years later，I needed to hide. I tried not to sleep because I was afraid of who might be there when I woke up. But I was lucky. It was always my friend. Now I think we are friends，this girl and me. On her birthday，it was she who gave a gift to me. It makes me understand that the best standover man I've ever known is not a man at all." 在"the Floating Book （Part I）"这一章里，作者提到了"A small announcement about Rudy，his death."，语言描写得很伤感，正如作者所说的"Even death has a heart."。这世上总会有人悄悄地点燃一抹微光，为你提供一点

光亮而足以惊天地泣鬼神。

——李 丹

在这几章中，我印象较深的有两个情节：

第一处在第219页。Max和Liesel都做噩梦，在Liesel眼里，Max跟她一样失去了母亲，也会像她一样在睡觉时抱着一本书做噩梦。同病相怜的两人很快就成了好朋友。他们会分享心事，Max给Liesel讲他和家人挥手告别，Liesel则告诉Max关于弟弟的事。如果说Hans教会Liesel识字，伊尔莎给了她阅读的机会，那么我想，Max则教会了Liesel用想象力和文字创造传奇。Max会让Liesel给她讲述外面的故事，那些干巴巴的单词经过想象力的润色，变得像书中的句子那样优美、生动。它们给了Max想象的空间，让他能再次感受外面的世界。

第二处在第220—221页。“The only thing that changed was that Liesel told her papa that she should be old enough now to cope on her own with the dreams. For a moment，he looked a little hurt，but as always with Papa，he gave the right thing to say his best shot...”当Liesel告诉爸爸自己已经长大了，可以独自应对那些噩梦了，有那么一瞬间，他有一种受伤的感觉，但爸爸总归是爸爸，他的话讲得总是很得体。他说：“哦，感谢上帝。”他似笑非笑地说：“至少我可以睡个安稳觉了。”有种吾家有女初长成的味道，老父亲的小伤感被刻画得自然而又淋漓尽致。

——王之光

Part Five of The Book Thief

The Gamblers（A Seven-Sided Die）—Rudy's Youth

导 读

本期共读内容是“The Gamblers（A Seven-Sided Die）”“Rudy's Youth”，我主要从两个章节的summary及analysis进行分享。

The Gamblers（A Seven-Sided Die）

Introduction部分：死神为提前告知了故事的结局而抱歉，但他还是觉得对神秘的事物更感兴趣。这里他想先解释为什么*The Whistler*这本书会在河里。他把这一章分成了几个部分，每个部分都以投掷到骰子上的数字作为标号，这也说明了把犹太人隐藏在自己家里其实就是一场赌博。在这一章中，作者采用倒叙法，并通过象征手法来展开故事，以赌博象征Hans夫妇隐藏Max的危险——这与Liesel偷书的感觉相似，但要可怕得多。

The Haircut：场景又回到了现在，Max想要理发，Rosa和Hans在争论谁来做这件事，但Max却要求Liesel来剪。Liesel剪下他“鸟窝似的”头发，并马上烧毁了剪下的头发。如果有任何蛛丝马迹，显示Max待在他们家里，都是非常危险的，哪怕像剪头发这样看似平常的事情。

The Newspaper：后来在市长的图书室里，Liesel想告诉Ilsa自己家的地下室里有个犹太人的事情。Ilsa 再次提出给她*The Whistler*这本书，但Liesel拒绝了。在回家的路上，她在垃圾桶里翻找上面有 Max喜欢的填字游戏的报纸。Liesel坐在地下室读书，而Max在做填字游戏。他们很少说话，但是他们因为共同对文字的热爱而心灵相通。就像和赫尔曼夫人的关系一样，Liesel也是通过书籍和文字与Max变成朋友关系的。也像和赫尔曼夫人一样，他们之间的交流不是通过交谈而是通过书籍和文字。

The Weatherman：一天，Liesel冲进房子，吹嘘着她在足球比赛中所进的球，然后又跑去地下室告诉Max。Max让她也描述一下外面的天气，Liesel不经意间用了富有诗意的语言描述天空。Max在墙上画了一幅有太阳和两个简笔小人的画，并写下了Liesel刚刚说的话。Liesel像死神一样，用诗意的语言描绘天空的颜色，

Max像死神一样，画出了文字的意境。这是死神对人类美好景象的描绘。

The Boxer：Max除了时间什么都没有，活下去似乎只是一种惩罚。他只能开始锻炼，幻想和Hitler在进行拳击比赛。人群都支持元首，他们嘲笑Max是犹太人。他们两个开始打起来，起初Max让Hitler打他。然后他站起来了，一拳打在Hitler的下巴上，把他打翻在地。Hitler站起来，转向人群，发表演讲，要求人群和他一起爬上拳击台，因为犹太人已经毁坏了一切，所有德国人被鼓动登上了拳击台，击败了Max。Liesel递给他一个填字游戏，中断了他的幻想。哪怕是在Max的想象中，Hitler都在用语言来获取权力和煽动仇恨，Hitler再次成为邪恶和痛苦的代言人。幻想也象征着Max的困境，他的同胞们都反对他、恨他，他独自一人生活在这样的国度中，唯一的安慰就是Liesel的友谊和鼓励。

Rudy's Youth

与此同时，Rudy一直在参加Hitler青年团，结果并不理想。他的烦恼来自听力有问题的Tommy和专横的青年团头目Franz之间的矛盾。Tommy因为听不清命令，总是搞乱行进路线，Franz因此嘲笑他。Rudy为了帮助Tommy，反而导致Franz对他们的惩罚，让他们在泥地里跑圈、做俯卧撑。之后他们告诉了Liesel这件事情，Tommy竭力向Rudy道歉，表示感谢。Rudy请求Liesel吻他，尽管他的处境很可怜，但还是遭到Liesel拒绝。将来Liesel也许会意识到，正是这些日子，满足了他们偷窃的欲望。Rudy在形成自己的道德准则的同时，Liesel也是如此。Rudy天生脾气暴躁，但他却为了帮助弱者（Tommy）而使自己处于危险之中。Franz这一形象代表的是一类残忍的、没有同情心，但又有权力的人物。就像Hitler一样，Franz用他的力量，即使很小，也给那些比他弱的人带来了痛苦。

我很喜欢的两句话：

I have hated words and I have loved them，and I hope I have made them right.（我讨厌过文字，我也喜爱过文字，我希望我能把它们运用得恰到好处）

Not leaving：an act of trust and love.（不离开：是信任和爱的表现）。

工作室人员分享

"As we speak，he is plotting his way into your neighborhood... Will you stand out there，powerless? Or" —and now he stepped one rung higher— "will you climb up into this ring with me? " Max shook. Horror stuttered in his stomach.Adolf finished him. "Will you climb in here so that we can defeat this enemy together? " In the basement of 33 Himmel Street，Max Vandenburg could feel the fists of an entire nation. One by one they climbed into the ring and beat him down. They made him bleed. They let him suffer. Millions of them—until one last time，when he gathered himself to his feet...

——陈雪芬

“Gambling is by hiding a Jew and this is how you live. Living in the basement for a long time，Max had to get his hair cut.He passed the scissors to Liesel. Liesel cut the feathery strands，Max said，‘Thanks，Liesel.’His voice was tall and husky，with the sound in it of a hidden smile. A hidden smile means a lot—hidden in the basement，hidden under the common people，hidden feelings... He expressed his feeling simplistically.”l feel heartbreaking by reading this. Humans should have equal rights to show their feelings. But because of the war Max can’t.

In Mid-May，her soccer team had trounced Rudy’s. Liesel was excited and willing to describe what the weather was like outside for Max. Her description was cute—the sky is blue today，Max and there is a big long cloud，and it’s stretched out，like a rope. At the end of it，the sun is like a yellow hole... Through her words，Max seemed to feel the sun. So he wrote down they walked on a tightrope to the sun. A tightrope means their heart got closer. He found himself more interested in life again. He took up exercising to kill the time. At the same time，this reminded him of the boxing game and he still dreamed of beating the Nazi.

——董筱妍

这几章的阅读让我再次想起了自己一直以来都很喜欢的一句话：“有时候，我们总觉得，在黑暗中只有自己在踽踽独行，没有人会理睬你，更不会有人与你感同身受；而其实，这世上总会有人，悄悄地点燃一抹微光，为你提供一点光亮。”在我看来，对Max而言，Liesel就是那个点燃微光、提供光亮的人。Liesel给Max剪头发，毫无避讳地翻垃圾桶给他找报纸看，和Max一同安静地享受阅读，这些场景温馨而美好。“Liesel would usually sit on some drop sheets，she would read while Max completed those crosswords. They sat a few meters apart，speaking very rarely，and there was really only the noise of turning pages.”（P248）除此之外，Liesel还会给Max描述每天的所见所闻——比赛的进球、天空的颜色。可以说，是Liesel让Max重新对生活产生了兴趣。Max在墙上画了长长的云朵和两个朝太阳走去的人——Liesel和他自己，在地下室练习做俯卧撑为了尽快恢复体能，甚至开始幻想自己和元首打了一场拳击赛。作者详细地描写了这场幻想中的拳击赛，我们从中可以感受到Max对拳击的如痴如醉，好胜、倔强的一面，也能感受到当时那种背景下犹太人的窘迫地位。

在“The Showdown：June 24”这一章，作者描写得也很详细，通过环境描写、外貌描写、心理描写、动作描写、语言描写，将Liesel因为市长夫人执意送书随即取消洗衣服的业务而失望至极、怒不可遏的一面描写得淋漓尽致。给我印象特别深的是这一段：

“Liesel stopped breathing. She was suddenly aware of how empty her feet felt inside her shoes. Something ridiculed her throat. She trembled. When finally she reached out and took possession of the letter，she noticed the sound of the clock in the library. Grimly，she realized that clocks don't make a sound that even remotely resembles ticking，toking. It was more the sound of a hammer，upside down，hacking methodically at the earth. It was the sound of a grave. If only mine was ready now，she thought—because Liesel Meminger，at that moment，wanted to die."（P259）

——李 丹

For this part of the book，I am once again struck，moved and angered.

On the one hand，I'm struck by how surprising Max's new dream was. He pictured his fight with Hitler！And the fight was so brutal. It says，"Max could feel the fists of an entire nation. One by one they climbed into the ring and beat him down. They made him bleed. They let him suffer... Nothing but dark. Just basement. Just Jew." The Jews were just like animals being hunted by the people around. How miserable their life was！

On the other hand，I am struck by how brave and powerful Liesel could be again. The first time I was struck by it was when she hit a naughty boy for calling her stupid. This time I was struck by how angrily she reacted to the mayor's wife. Liesel revealed the ugly brutal truth and threw it at the mayor's wife's face. She informed her，"It's about time that you do your own stinking washing anyway. It's about time you faced the fact that your son is dead. He got killed！He got strangled and cut up more than twenty years ago！... He's dead！He's dead and it's pathetic that you sit here shivering in your own house to suffer for it. You think you're the only one？" The words were ugly but true.

I am deeply moved by the wonderful cozy connection between Liesel and Papa. She was both angry and guilty about the ugly truth she told the mayor's wife. However，they could always find comfort when they were together.

I am once again angry with Rudy's death. Cuz deep down in my heart，I think Rudy was a brave，upright and loyal boy. The part that he stood by Tommy's side once again proved his great character. He deserved a much better ending.

——李秀文

"'Mistakes？' Papa looked ready to tear his own hair out by that stage，but his voice became a barely audible whisper.'Who the hell's going to see him？' He motioned to speak again but was distracted by the feathery appearance of Max Vandenburg，who stood politely，embarrassed，in the doorway. He carried his own scissors and came forward，handing them not to Hans or Rosa but to the twelve-year-old girl.She was the calmest option. His mouth quivered a moment before he said，‘Would you？’

Liesel took the scissors and opened them. They were rusty and shiny in different areas. She turned to Papa，and when he nodded，she followed Max down to the basement.

Thursday was the only delivery day left for Liesel Meminger now，and it was usually able to provide some sort of dividend. She could never dampen the feeling of victory each time she found a Molching Express or any other publication. Finding a newspaper was a good day. If it was a paper in which the crossword wasn't done，it was a great day. She would make her way home，shut the door behind her，and take it down to Max Vandenburg.‘Crossword？’he would ask.‘Empty.’‘Excellent.’ The Jew would smile as he accepted the package of paper and started reading in the rationed light of the basement. Often，Liesel would watch him as he focused on reading the paper，completed the crossword，and then started to reread it，front to back...”

这几章让我感觉到很多细节都显示出Liesel和Max的关系越来越近了，他们之间有种惺惺相惜的感觉，Max很信任Liesel，愿意和她说话，而Liesel也经常想着Max，会给他带报纸，还会想着他睡觉的时候老是不踏实，甚至是睁着一只眼睛睡的。这份感情在这个时候显得多么可贵。不过这也让我担心，总觉得有什么可怕的事情可能要发生。

——莫 然

※※※A Triple Tiered Problem※※※

1.Tommy Muller's ears.

2.Franz Deatscher—the irate Hitler Youth leader.

3. Rudy's Inability to stay out of things.

‘Well，’he asked.‘What can you say for yourself？’

Tommy's twitch only increased，in both speed and depth.

‘Are you mocking me？’

‘Heil，’twitched Tommy，in a desperate attempt to buy some approal，but he did not make it to the‘Hitler’part.That was when Rudy stepped forward. He faced Franz Deatscher，looking up at him.‘He' got a problem，sir—’

‘I can see that！’

‘With his ears，’Rudy finished.‘He can't—’”

给我印象深刻的是“Rudy的青春”这一章节。Tommy的耳朵感染得很严重，严重到彻底影响了他的听力。列队前进时，他听不清头头喊的指令。Tommy反反复复地在列队中出错，因此Franz也就是青年团的头头彻底受够了。他开始骂Tommy，“你这个蠢货，你在搞什么鬼？”Tommy是个天生胆小怕事的孩子，他胆怯地往后退，左脸开始猛烈地抽搐。Franz问道：“怎么？”“你还有话要说？”“你是在嘲讽我吗？”Tommy的抽搐变得越来越频繁、越来越猛烈。他胆怯地想说“Hitler万岁”，但说“万岁”时，Tommy嘴角抽搐，“Hitler”这个词怎么也说不出口。Rudy不顾个人安危，挺身而出帮助Tommy，却遭到了Franz严厉又残酷的惩罚。然而，这件事之后，Rudy并没有责备怨恨Tommy，当Tommy说“都是我的错”时，Rudy却摆摆手，还说了一句“Tommy，please！”Rudy脸上挂着一种奇特的心满意足的神情。可以看出Rudy是一个为了朋友两肋插刀、很有正义感的青年。

——宋 蕾

There are several parts in the gamblers that impressed me. The first one is the newspaper and the weather report. Liesel was willing to look for a newspaper in the garbage for Max each Thursday for the past few months. It’s the only way that Max could learn something about the outside world. Being down in the basement，the minutes were cruel and the hours were punishing for him. The newspaper and the weather report were the least diversions for Max. And the crossword is also a good way to bring closer the relationship between Max and Liesel. They are getting closer day by day. When I read these sentences— “he always slept fully clothed，shoes included，just in case he needed to flee be again. He slept with one eye open.” I felt sad for Max again.The description of his condition is so vivid，fully reflects his dilemma.The second part is the wall painting and written words of Max— “It was a Monday，and they walked on a tightrope to the sun.” I think tightrope means their dilemma and the sun indicates his eager for living decently. I quite like the meaning behind the painting. And I also find that Max’s dream of fighting Hitler is interesting.He imagined Hitler being beaten up and bleeding. Even though it is just his imagination，he got his own satisfaction. He needed it.

——麦佩莹

From Page 258 to 263，the power of words to impel violence is explored in this part. Liesel’s tirade against Ilsa is perhaps her cruelest moment. Liesel tells Ilsa，who has suffered for years over the death of her son，to get over it and pictures Ilsa’s face as bloodied and battered from this verbal abuse. Liesel was genuinely angered about Ilsa’s firing Rosa，and did not regret what she said，though she later told Hans that she was going to hell.

Liesel家洗衣店的老顾主Ilsa因为外界的压力，停止了和Liesel家洗衣店长期以来的生意关系，这对Liesel家打击很大，因为这几乎是她家全部的生活来源，Liesel因此痛骂了她。在我看来已经到了口不择言的地步。Liesel对Ilsa解雇Rosa感到真正的愤怒，她并不后悔她所说的话，尽管她后来告诉Hans，她要下地狱了。这让我感受到在战争环境下，人与人之间那种相互帮助又互相残杀的复杂情感，这也让我觉得很难过。

——王之光

“The Gamblers”这章中有太多令人感动的情节和发人深省的历史重现。本章详细描写了Max和Liesel的关系随着故事的发展，由疏远、畏惧到同情、关心再到亲密，一步一步地推进。这种亲密是由于有着相同悲惨的命运而带来的惺惺相惜，以及有着对阅读的同样热爱而产生的心灵依托。“They sat a few meters apart，speaking very rarely，and there was really only the noise of turning pages... Max and Liesel were held together by the quiet gathering of words.”（P248）他们是因为分享无声的文字走到一起的。“Hi，Max.” “Hi，Liesel. ”“Bye，Max. ” “Bye，Liesel.”他们之间的话很少很少，但是读者能从这只言片语中感受到他们在无声阅读中交流了很多很多。

Liesel在生活上也非常乐意跟Max分享感受，比如赢了球赛，“she then rushed down to the basement to decribe it below to Max，who put down his newspaper and intently listened and laughed with the girl.”。从“rush”这个词，我们仿佛看到一个喜悦地奔跑着的少女，急切地想把她的快乐传递给她的心灵友人。而对于Max，Liesel就是黑夜里的阳光，是他孤独单调生活里的慰藉和希望。“Initially，he tried to resist，but it was harder every day that the girl appeared，each time with a new weather report，either of pure blue sky，cardboard clouds，or a sun that had broken through like God sitting down after he’d eaten too much for his dinner. ”（P250）由此可见，Liesel是隐藏于地下室的Max和外面自由生活联通的纽带。所以她对于Max来说，是不可抗拒的诱惑。

Max听了Liesel的天气报告后做的画，可以说是地下室里的伊甸园。蓝天、白云，连着太阳的纽带，还有并肩而走的Max和Liesel。然而现实是Max只能在幻想中与元首抗争。幻想和现实一样，他们实力悬殊。书中用了对比的手法。“He simile loudest when the ring announcer listed his achievements，which were all vociferously applauded by the adoring crowd.”（P251）元首有随从，有华衣，有强大的支援。而Max，“No robe. No entourage.Just a lonely young Jew with dirty breath，a naked chest，and tired hands and feet.”。Max被打得鲜血直流，然而，他还是说：“Come on，Fubrer.”。他还是会找到机会，出其不意给予反击。“Max stepped aside and plunged him into the corner. He punched him seven times aiming on each occasion for only one thing. The mustache."（P253）Max在向世人证明，他虽然身处困境，但是不放弃生命，不放弃希望。事实也是如此。他吃着简单的食物，蜗居地下室，然而他还能坚持锻炼身体，在微弱的灯光下坚持阅读。我们不由得钦佩这位坚强的勇士，他富于韧性的生命可以给每一个身处绝望的人极大的鼓励！

——关少娟

That reminds me of one sentence before，"Living was living.The price was guilt and shame." For Jewish boy Max，living in the basement with Germans is part of his gambles. But he dared to fight and was eager to win. He trained himself so hard dreaming to defeat Hitler. I admired his courage despite his situation. "As for you，my Jewish chum，I'd watch mystery very closely if I were you. Very closely indeed." It would be suicidal to resist when overwhelming Hitler and his people，he realized. "He punched him seven times，aiming on each occasion for only one thing." Thankfully，Liesel was there for him holding the crossword. I feel complicated reading this. I'm glad they met each other，and I am heartbroken that they are put in such a situation. What's more，the weather man in Mid-day is also impressive. How difficult can it be for us to see the sky and the sun and how the clouds go like? But for Max，it can be tough. "I don't know how you scored it in the sun，or of the clouds have covered everything？" He asked. Reading the wall-written words by Max，"It was a Monday，and they walked on a tightrope to the sun." Maybe the sun is like a bright future，or a better one. The point is，their arms balanced.They are together.

——袁泳施

What impressed me most is that how Liesel acted when she was informed they were fired by the mayor's wife. The writer pictured deeply the changes of her feeling from sadness to anger like this. Her sadness left her and she was overwhelmed with anger. "That bastard mayor，" "the pathetic woman. You think you can buy me off with this book？You give me this Saumensch of a book and think it'll make everything good when I go and tell my mama that we've lost our last one？While you sit here in your mansion？It's about time，that you do your own stinking washing anyway. It's about time you faced the fact that your son is dead. He got killed！He got strangled and cut up more than twenty years ago！Or did he freeze to death？Either way，he's dead！He 's dead and it's pathetic that you sit here shivering in your own house to suffer for it. You think you're the only one？" But after she came home，she lied to her mama that they lost the last customer all because of her fault. She want to make mama feel better by giving her a good beat. But on the contrary, mama accepted the fact of losing the last customer, the hard time of life instead of beating her.People need to hug together to warm each other during the hard time.

——Ting Feng

Part Five of The Book Thief

The Losers—Three Acts of Stupidity by Rudy Steiner

导读

这一期的内容是*The Book Thief*的“The Losers”“Sketches”“The Whistler and the Shoes”“Three Acts of Stupidity by Rudy Steiner”这几个章节。

在“The Losers”这一章里讲述了Liesel和Rudy偷窃的过程：他们首先试图获得Viktor的信任，然后把握偷窃的机会，接着走了十里路才偷到了几个苹果，结果却被Viktor发现了，得到了被吃了半个的苹果作为回报，Rudy为此感到非常生气，想要反抗，不料被Viktor打了。在当时战乱的环境中，老百姓的生活是很艰难的——连冒险去偷都偷不到什么东西！

在这一章里，Viktor的性格勾画得生动形象。

“‘No crime in wanting a little more，’ he claimed，lying back in the grass with a collection of boys assembled around him.‘Wanting more is our fundamental right as Germans. What does our Fubrer say？’ He answered his own rhetoric.‘We must take what is rightfully ours！’ At face value，Viktor Chemmel was clearly your typical teenage bullshit artist. Unfortunately，when he felt like revealing it.”这里描述Viktor是典型的暴力！强而有力的Viktor打败了固执的Rudy。

“Sketches”这一章讲述了Max是如何用文字记录他的经历和制作安排表的。

在“The Whistler and the Shoes”这一章里，描述了Liesel和Rudy因为饥饿决定再次去偷东西，这次定位在市长家。但神奇的是，Liesel要偷的并不是食物，而是书。

“She didn’t care about the food. Rudy，no matter how hard she tried to resist the idea，was secondary to her plan. It was the book she wanted. *The Whistler*. She wouldn’t tolerate having it given to her by a lonely，pathetic old woman. Stealing it，on the other hand，seemed a little more acceptable. Stealing it，in a sick kind of sense，was like earning it.”在Liesel心中，书本是高于一切的。

在“The Whistler and the Shoes”这一章里，Liesel并没有偷任何的食物反而

偷了一本书，因此被冠以“偷书贼”的绰号。

“It was the first time Liesel had been branded with her title，and she couldn’t hide the fact that she liked it very much. As we’re both aware，she’d stolen books previously，but in late October 1941，it became official. That night，Liesel Meminger truly became *The Book Thief*.”虽说Liesel被取了“偷书贼”的绰号，但是她却对“偷书贼”这个称号相当满意!

在“Three Acts of Stupidity by Rudy Steiner”这一章里，总结了Rudy的性格特点。

RUDY STEINER，PURE GENIUS...

1. He stole the biggest potato from Mamer’s，the local grocer.

2. Taking on Franz Franz on Munich Street.

3. Skipping the Hitler Youth meetings altogether.

Rudy，纯粹的天才……

1. 他从当地的杂货商Mamer那里偷了最大的土豆。

2. 在Munich大街和Franz Franz较量。

3.完全不参加Hitler青年团的会议。

工作室人员分享

“‘No crime in wanting a little more，’he claimed，lying back in the grass with a collection of boys assembled around him.‘Wanting more is our fundamental right as Germans. What does our Fubrer say？’He answered his own rhetoric.‘We must take what is rightfully ours！’”

在这篇文章中，出现了一个新的人物——Viktor Chemmel。他的出场给我们留下了非常深刻的印象。文中的他就是那种有着茂密的头发、眼睛浑浊的不良少年。他很贪婪，想要更多。他对自己的德国人身份非常自信。他想当然地认为他想要什么就可以去掠夺，而且他非常的盲目自大。

“Say what you will about Viktor Chemmel，but he certainly had patience and a good memory. It took him approximately five months to turn his statement into a true one.”

Rudy因为一个烂苹果和Viktor打了一架。Viktor比Rudy强壮，所以Rudy被打败了。但是Rudy并没有认输。显然，Viktor一直惦记着Rudy，因为他不想让任何人凌驾于自己之上。“你以后会为此付出代价的”，从这句话中，你会了解他的报复心有多大。

“It was the first time Liesel had been branded with her title，and she couldn’t hide the fact that she liked it very much. As we’re both aware，she’d stolen books previously，but in late October 1941，it became official. That night，Liesel Meminger truly became *The Book Thief*."

根据这段文字，我们终于知道为什么 Liesel被称为“偷书贼”了。Rudy需要一场胜利，他们得偷点东西回来。他们去市长家参加舞会。市长解雇了Liesel的妈妈。“And she wouldn’t tolerate having it given to her by a lonely，pathetic old woman.For her，stealing it was like earning it.”

他们在一起度过了一个特别的夜晚——偷书。另外还有一个情景描写，你会觉得很好笑——在偷书过程中，因为太紧张，Liesel忘记了她的鞋子。于是Rudy冒着生命危险又返回去取鞋。多么甜蜜的友情!

——董筱妍

“The Whistler and the Shoes”这一章节的描写继续表现Liesel、Rudy对偷窃行为的理解。

直到秋天，Max、Liesel、Rudy 继续着各自的活动，但是当Franz让 Rudy 在满是泥巴的地里做俯卧撑的时候，这种安静的局面发生了变化。一天，Rudy 脏兮兮地回到家，告诉 Liesel 他需要“胜利”——偷点东西。起初他们毫无头绪，但后来Liesel决定带Rudy去市长家报复他们解雇了Rosa。Liesel希望窗户是开着的，但那天却是关着的。他们第五次来的时候，窗户开了，Liesel决定进去。Rudy认为他们应该偷食物，但Liesel其实只是想要*The Whistler*这本书。偷窃更像是赚钱，而不是出于同情让市长夫人给她。Liesel 决定一个人进去，她把鞋子给了Rudy。Rudy提醒她去找吃的，但Liesel没有理会。

到目前为止，Rudy和Liesel的经历使他们认为偷窃是一种积极的行为——对他们来说，这意味着控制疯狂的、放肆的世界的一小部分。偷窃对他们来说不是犯罪，而是一种拥有自我权利的行为。Liesel想偷赫尔曼夫人给她的书，因为偷书更像是“赚钱”。如果市长夫人出于同情把书给了Liesel，感觉就像是在同情她，但是偷书却是Liesel 给自己的权利。

——郑剑湘

上周，我强调了Liesel和Max的关系。在这三章里，我想集中讨论Liesel和Rudy。他们一起经历了困难时期，就像俗话说的“A friend in need is a friend indeed.”。Rudy被Viktor欺负了。他的膝盖压住了Rudy的胳膊，双手掐住了他的喉咙。“‘You’re hurting him.’Liesel said.‘Am I？’Viktor was smiling again. She hated that smile...Liesel took Rudy’s hand and they left.”（P275）显然Viktor比他们俩都强壮，他粗鲁、残忍、不讲道理。冒着被打败的危险，Liesel还是勇敢地站在Rudy身边，为他说话。我不禁钦佩她保护朋友的勇气。后来，Rudy邀请Liesel偷点东西，尝尝胜利的滋味。他们决定从市长家里偷一本书。两个朋友合作得很好。一个从窗户悄悄进入房间，另一个站岗。Liesel如愿以偿地得到一本书。不幸的是，她把鞋子落在了现场。Rudy得回去拿。他们的偷窃行动充满了曲折。阅读的同时也替他们担心。我喜欢这一章的文字和细节描述。

——关少娟

这几章的阅读让我印象深刻的是“The Whistler and the Shoes”。体现了两个人物对Liesel的爱。Liesel最好的伙伴——阳光而又热心肠的Rudy，对Liesel的爱意贯穿通篇。他5次陪伴Liesel去市长家偷窃，在我看来，Rudy心中明白Liesel想偷窃的东西。在意识到Liesel的鞋子落在市长家时，Rudy果断冒险回头去拿。一系列的描写是这样的：“Rudy’s face whitened.—Rudy searched desperately around himself，begging against all reality that he might have brought them with him.—‘Dummkopf，’ he admonished himself，smacking his ear. He looked down shamefully at the sullen sight of Liesel’s socks. It didn’t take him long to decide on making it right. Earnestly，he said，‘Just wait，’ and he hurried back around the corner.—Rudy’s triumphant face was held nicely up as he trotted steadily toward her. His teeth were gnashed into a grin，and the shoes dangled from his hand.‘They nearly killed me，’ he said，‘but I made it.’”。最后，Liesel被Rudy冠上了一个自己心仪的名称——book thief。另一个对Liesel的爱温暖如初的是市长夫人。当Liesel对她产生误会去她书房偷书时，她不着痕迹地虚掩窗户，让Liesel尽情偷书。这种含蓄而深沉的爱也着实让人心动。正如一句话所说的，心中有爱，可以温柔岁月，也可不负相遇。

——李 丹

“The Losers”一章中的几段文字让我看到一个在战争年代出现的活灵活现的乱世枭雄。当然Viktor的形象也没有那么高大，但是从他的言行举止中可以明显感觉到他是一个因为活得很无聊所以要通过冒险来找点乐子的人，同时还能顺便欺负一下弱者。

老实说，这个反面人物的出现让我意识到，同样是在乱世中，有的人因为有人性而处处受挫，反而是像Viktor这样的坏人可能在那个年代活得很好，所以他反而很容易成为一个逍遥自在的人。

——莫 然

这周，从第272—299页，Viktor成为偷东西团队的组长，他很小气，他偷东西是因为他喜欢。农民们收成不好，这意味着这个群体的收获很少。Rudy和Liesel分到的是一个苹果。当Rudy抱怨时，Viktor把吃了一半的苹果扔向他们。Rudy因为表达了自己的不满而遭到了报复，Viktor把他的鼻子弄出血了。Viktor把Liesel和Rudy赶出了队伍，但在他们离开之前，Rudy朝Viktor的脚上吐了口水和血。5个月后，他让Rudy为他的行为付出代价。Viktor当然是有耐心和良好的记忆力的，但他不是一个好的领导者，他只关心自己，他不会为他的伙伴付出任何代价。

然而，还有许多不好的事情等着Rudy。Rudy是个好孩子，但有一点调皮，正因为他的调皮，经常给他带来麻烦。第一个问题发生在1941年11月，地点是Mamer's。Rudy总是很饿，他偷了商店里最大的土豆。这引起了商店里其他顾客的愤怒，Mamer想要报警并把Rudy交给他们，但在学校老师的帮助下，他只是被扔出了商店。

他也可能有点目中无人，这给他在Hitler青年会议上带来了麻烦。他经常因为一些鸡毛蒜皮的小事，例如忘记Hitler的生日而受罚。一天，他在街上发现了Franz，就朝他扔石头。作为报复，Franz把他扔到人行道上，Rudy的眼睛被打青了，肋骨骨折，还被剪了个很丢人的发型。

在这几章里，我只能看到Rudy的坏运气。他真可怜。

——宋碧燕

"He had what he called just a small ration of tools:

A painted book.

A handful of pencils.

A mindful of thoughts.

Like a simple puzzle，he put them together.

The desecrated pages of *Mein Kampf* were becoming a series of sketches，page after page，which to him summed up the events that had swapped his former life for another.

He resolved that when the book was finished，he'd give it to Liesel，when she was old enough，and hopefully，when all this nonsense was over.

From the moment he tested that pencils on the first painted page，he kept the book close at all times.Often，it was next to him or still in his fingers as he slept."

1914年的夏天，自从Max来到Hans家里的地下室，他没有一直沉沦下去，除了每天做做俯卧撑和仰卧起坐，他还给这一年的夏天留下了文字和色彩。在他最孤独的时候，各种想象喷涌而出，他选择用笔写下一个个完全不同的故事，这些故事有着真实的触感，其中描绘的事件将他过往的人生彻底重写。他始终保守这个秘密，没有和任何人说起，包括Liesel。他下定决心，等到故事画完，等到Liesel足够成熟，等到一切荒诞不经都结束，他要把它送给Liesel。而且他常常将它放在手边，连睡觉时都不松手。看到这一幕，我非常感动，一个人在如此悲凉无助的情景下，仍然能镇静下来写写自己的过往，叙述自己的人生，希望生活能留下自己的足迹。更让我感动的是他想把他的人生故事赠予Liesel，一个无比纯真善良的女孩，由此可知Liesel在Max心中占有多么重要的位置，他们的深厚友谊让人羡慕和感动。

——宋 蕾

在这四个小节中，Liesel终于看到了成长前的黑暗。从gambler开始，生活就像掷骰子，结果总是让人失望。

Liesel本来好好地享受着和市长夫人的阅读时光，结果因为市长一个提倡节约的演讲，市长夫人就取消了Rosa的洗衣服务。Liesel刚被拒绝的时候还很懵，过了一会儿才用语言狠狠地反击了她。包括后面她去市长家偷东西，Liesel也不认为是偷，而是去取回原本属于自己的东西。

面对成年，世界的黑暗，Liesel一直在反抗，用语言诅咒，用偷窃证明，自己仍然是那个单纯的孩子。

——夏丽焱

Rudy时而是冲动的、愚蠢的，也有男孩的淘气，但与此同时，他更是一个善良和忠诚的朋友。在“The Losers”这个章节里，Rudy有他的性格，他不是一个失败者。由于太过冲动，他被Viktor揍了一顿，他把Viktor当作他的劲敌；但那是因为Viktor也有不当的行为，Rudy还是为了正直而站了起来。他是非分明、勇敢无畏，怎么会是一个失败者呢？“Once was immoral. Twice was complete bastard.”当Liesel的鞋子落在市长的图书馆那儿，他一开始“admonished himself，smacking his ear”，当作听不到，把耳朵捂住，然后没多想，还是冒着被抓住可能会把命都丢了的风险，去帮Liesel捡回了鞋子，后面回来时还骄傲地说“I made it！”，我搞定啦。我想Liesel跟我一样，不会忘记他这张骄傲的脸吧！所以虽然他很淘气，但那也是这个年龄特有的，他更多的是一个可靠的队友。在那天最后，他对Liesel说：“晚安，偷书贼。”我想那时候Liesel肯定是笑着回应他的。

——袁泳施

Part Five—Six of The Book Thief

The Floating Book（Part Ⅱ）—Thirteen Presents

导读

今天我们一起来读*A Book Thief*的“The Floating Book （Part Ⅱ）” “Death’s Diary：1942” “The Snowman” 和 “Thirteen Presents” 这四个章节。

“The Floating Book （Part Ⅱ）”讲述了Viktor为了报复Rudy和Liesel往冰凉的河水里扔书的故事。“Death’s Diary：1942” 讲述了战争制造了更多的尸体和出窍的灵魂。“The Snowman” 这一节既带给我们快乐，又带给我们担忧。“Thirteen Presents” 讲述了Max昏迷不醒，卧病在床，Liesel给她准备了生活中看似很不起眼的礼物，期盼有一天他能够醒过来。

让我们一起进入第一个故事“The Floating Book（Part Ⅱ）”。

“‘I’ll tell you what，’ he said. ‘For fifty marks，you can have it back.’

‘Did I ask you to speak？’

‘No，’ he said. ‘I will do anything I want，’ and he proceeded to the river.

‘Tell me，’ Viktor said. ‘Who was the last Olympic discus champion，in Berlin？’”

可以看出Viktor是一个十足的混蛋，他非常粗鲁无礼。

“The water toppled. Viktor Chemmel did the spin.

The book was released gloriously from his hand. It opened and flapped，the pages rattling as it covered ground in the air.

Viktor shook his head. ‘Not enough height. A poor throw.’ He smiled again. ‘But still good enough to win，huh？’”

这一段讲述了Viktor扔书的一个场景。从他说的话中可以看出，Viktor是一个报复心理很强也是一个仗势欺人的人。

“‘This is between us.’ Rudy tried to reason with him. ‘It has nothing to do with her.Come on，give it back.’ Rudy rushed at him now. ‘Come on，Viktor，don’t do this to her.It’s me you are after.I’ll do anything you want.’”

这段场景描述了Viktor想要欺负Liesel，Rudy毫不犹豫地出手相救，可以看出Rudy非常关心照顾Liesel。

“Soon，he peeled off his coat and jumped in，wading to the middle of the river.

Liesel，slowing to a walk，could see the ache of each step. The painful cold.

Another note of interest is that Rudy did not attempt to leave the devastatingly cold water as soon as he held his book in his hand.For a minute or so，he stayed.”

这一段文字描写的是非常感人的一幕，是Rudy不顾一切下到冰冷刺骨的河里为Liesel捡书的一个场景。

接下来让我们一起进入第二个故事：“Death’s Diary：1942”。

这个故事是用死神的口吻描述战争给人类带来的痛苦和不幸的。书中这样写道：战争制造了更多的尸体和出窍的灵魂。这种事情靠几枚炸弹、几间毒气室，或是几声遥远的枪声就能办到。如果没能把事情办妥，至少也能让人类流离失所，我所到之处都是无家可归的人。

※※※AN ABRIDGED ROLL CALL FOR 1942※※※

1.The desperate Jews—their spiris
in my lap as we sat on the roof,
next to the steaming chimneys.

2.The Russian soldiers—taking only.
Small amounts of ammunition，relying on the fallen for the rest of it.

3.The soaked bodies of a French coast—Beached on the shingle and sand.

我引用的这部分是书中这一章缩略版的1942年的花名册。通过死神的口吻来描写战争的残酷和无情。

“They say that war is death’s best friend，but I must offer you a different point of view on that one. To me，war is like the new boss who expects the impossible. He stands over your shoulder repeating on thing，incessantly：‘Get it done，get it done.’ So you work harder.You get the job done.The boss，however，does not thank you.He asks for more.”

在这一段文字中，死神把战争比喻成了老板，这位老板压榨自己的员工，深刻地描述了死神的心理状态——以无数人的死亡为代价来换取个人的利益。从表面上来看，死神的心态是镇定自若、毫不动摇的，其实他的内心是不安的、迷惘的和饱受摧残的。

“She’s carrying some snow down to a basement，of all places.

Handfuls of frosty water can make almost anyone smile，but it cannot make them forget.

Here she comes.”

这一段是这一章的最后一部分，也是一个伏笔。战争的悲痛是让人们难以忘却的，是深刻的，也是刺痛的。因此我们可以感受到二战的背景下残酷的社会情境。

接下来让我们一起进入第三个故事“The Snowman”。

这个故事既有让人开心的一面，也有让人担心的一面。

“All things being fair，she first threw a snowball at Max and collected a reply in the stomach. Ax even threw one at Hans as he made his way down the basement steps.

‘Arschlocb，’ Papa yelped. ‘Liesel，give me some of that snow. A whole bucket！’ For a few minutes，they all forgot.They were only humans，playing in the snow，in a house.”

这一段描述是非常暖心的一幕，他们在一起打雪仗。Liesel一家人大喊大叫和大笑。他们都是战争当中的普通人，有着普通人的快乐。

“‘A snowman，’ Liesel replied. ‘We have to make a snowman.’

Papa called out to Rosa.

Once she recovered，she came down and helped them.She even brought the buttons for the eyes and nose and some string for a snowman smile.Even a scarf and hat were provided for what was only a two-foot man of snow.”

这一部分也是暖心的一幕。Liesel一家在开心地堆雪人。

“She stepped closer，afraid of the answer. ‘Is he alive？’

The bun nodded.

Rosa turned then and said something with great assurance. “Now listen to me，Liesel.I didn’t take this man into my house to watch him die.Understand？”

Liesel nodded.

‘Now go.’

In the hall，Papa hugged her.

She desperately needed it.”

这一段描述是让人揪心的一幕。Max病倒了，他们把他抬到了Liesel的床上，Liesel担心地问：“他还活着吗？”说明Liesel非常担心和焦虑。但是Liesel的妈妈却坚定地说：“我既然把他留在我们家，就不会眼睁睁地看他死掉。”爸爸紧紧地抱住Liesel，一家人都在为Max担心。这一幕非常感人，Max和他们一家没有血缘关系，就凭Max的父亲曾经在战场上救过Hans的命，他们就一定不会放弃Max。从这些画面当中，我们可以看出，妻子善良、坚定和从容，丈夫体贴细心。

※※※MAX VANDENBURG’s VISITOR※※※

让我们一起进入第四个故事“Thirteen Presents”。

一个压坏的球、一条丝带、一颗松果、一枚纽扣、一块石头、一根羽毛、两份报纸、一张糖果包装纸、一朵云、一个玩具兵、一片神奇的叶子、一本读完的书和一层厚厚的哀愁。

这些礼物有一些共同的特点：都是被人们遗弃和扔掉的垃圾，但是在Liesel眼中却是珍贵的礼物。

“Later，he suggested that perhaps she could read to him.

From that day on，Liesel read *The Whistler* aloud to Max as he occupied her bed.”

这一段文字描述的是一个温暖的场景。Max昏迷不醒，Liesel的爸爸建议她给Max读*The Whistler*。从那天起，Liesel就开始给Max读书。但是过程并不那么顺利，好些页都粘在一块儿，Liesel只好不停地跳过这些章节。书还没有干透。即便如此，她也努力地读下去。这本书整整有三百九十六页。即使有那么多的不便，Liesel仍坚持给Max读书，希望有一天他能醒过来。

“In the outside world，Liesel rushed from school each day in the hope that Max was feeling better. ‘Has he woken up？’ ‘Has he eaten？’

‘Yes，Mama.’ She was about to open the door. ‘But you’ll come and get me if he wakes up，won’t you？’”

这一段文字描述的也是非常温暖的场景。Liesel急切地盼望Max能够醒过来。

“ ‘I’m sorry，’ she said，‘it’s not much.But when you wake up，I’ll tell you all about it.I’ll tell you it was the grayest afternoon you can imagine，and this car without its lights on ran straight over the ball. Then the man got out and yelled at us.And then he asked for directions. The nerve of him...’

Wake up！ She wanted to scream.Or shake him.She didn’t.”

在这13个礼物当中，其中最让人感动的就是被碾碎了的球。想想连Rudy都说要这个破球有什么用呢，可见，这个球是不值钱的，是被抛弃之物，但在Liesel那里，这个球是她花心思送给Max的，因为这个球的背后有个故事，Liesel想把这个故事分享给Max。

“Lightly，he tapped her skull with his knuckles. ‘Memorize it.Then write it down for him.’

‘...It was like a great white beast，’ she said at her next bedside vigil，‘and it came from over the mountains.’

She imagined the vision of it passing from her hand to his，through the blankets，and she wrote it down on a scrap of paper，placing the stone on top of it.”

Liesel想送给Max一朵云。但是这朵云怎么能作为礼物送给Max呢？Liesel把它记在心里，然后通过反复地修改和补充，写下来送给他。这份礼物是Liesel费尽心思通过讲故事、通过读书想唤醒Max的意识。这些东西虽然不值钱，但是背后都有一些动人的故事，对于Liesel来说都是弥足珍贵的。

My feelings：

1.life is precious. Love the people around us，and cherish what we have.

2.Be brave when we have difficulties，and try to overcome them wisely.

3.Wish the world peace，and everyone can live in happiness.

结束语：读书如行路，历险毋惶恐。（《清诗铎·读书》）

工作室人员分享

“He continued down the water’s edge，showing her the book’s location. ‘Over there！’ He stopped，pointed，and ran farther down to overtake it. Soon，he peeled off his coat and jumped in，wading to the middle of the river.

Another note of interest is that Rudy did not attempt to leave the devastatingly cold water as soon as he held the book in his hand. For a good minute or so，he stayed. He never did explain it to Liesel，but I think she knew very well that the reasons were twofold.”

在这一章节中，我印象最深刻的是Rudy尽他最大努力去抓取漂浮在河面上的那本书——*The Whistler*。Rudy想都没想就一头扎进河里，即使当时的河水很冰冷，因为他很清楚那本书对于Liesel来说是多么的重要。Rudy跳下河的那一刻，根本没有考虑过自己的人身安全，他把那本书看得比他自己的生命还重要。Rudy总是会尽自己所能地保护Liesel。而这次Rudy成功地为Liesel拯救了她心爱的书，他感到如此的高兴和自豪以至于他拿到书后还不愿上岸。他太可爱了！如果这世上有一个甘愿为自己上刀山下火海的男人，那是多么幸福的一件事啊！我想我一定要把Rudy和Liesel的故事讲给我的丈夫听，呵呵！

——陈雪芬

这几章中，我最喜欢的章节是“雪人”，尤其是第312页到313页中的这段文字给我留下了深刻的印象。

“Melt it did，though，but somewhere in each of them，that snowman was still upright. It must have been the last thing they saw that Christmas Eve when they finally fell asleep. There was an accordion in their ears，a snowman in their eyes，and for Liesel，there was the thought of Max’s last words before she left him by the fire.”

不过，它最后还是融化掉了，但在他们每个人的内心深处，一直有一个雪人站着。平安夜的晚上，他们进入梦乡时，雪人一定是陪着他们的。他们的耳朵里传来的是手风琴的声音，眼前晃动着雪人的影子。

圣诞夜，一家人在阴暗的地下室开心地打雪仗、堆雪人。Max是无比激动的，与此同时我也看到了Hans一家和Max内心的自由与希望，我想正是这种信念支撑着他们渡过了一个又一个难关。Hans一家用生命守护着Max，Max可以说是

Liesel精神上的一位导师。他们一起读书、生活，朝夕相处地感受文字的奥秘，体会生活的美好。尽管Max一直生活在地下室，但在我眼中他的形象越来越鲜活和顽强，有种蓬勃的生命力，而我相信这种生命力也会润物细无声地在Liesel的身上得到延续。

——王之光

“Just past the rubble of Cologne，a group of kids collected empty fuel containers，dropped by their enemies. As usual，I collected humans. I was tired.And the year wasn’t even halfway yet.”

这段话描写的是死神眼中的战争。可悲的是，无辜的孩子去收集空的燃料容器来当玩具，而死神去收集的是战争造成的尸体。死神为什么累了？因为战争造成了无尽的死亡。然而，这场战争并没有结束。

“Papa sat at the table，Rosa Prayed in the corner mouthing the words，Liesel was cooked：her knee，her chest，the muscles in her arms. I doubt any of them had the audacity to consider what they’d do if the basement was appointed as a shelter.They had to survive he inspection first.”

纳粹搜查了Liesel的家。家里的每一个人都很焦虑，但是他们不得不假装和往常一样，每个人都假装手上在做些什么好让他们自己冷静下来。爸爸在那儿静静地坐着，Rosa默默地祈祷着，Liesel痛苦的身体和焦虑的心灵在挣扎，最后他们平安无事。在我看来，他们已经把Max当作他们的家人了。

——董筱妍

“Death’s Diary”这一章，是死神对自己的独白及对人类的启示。他以局外人的角度对这个世界进行审视。书中是这样描写的：“除了天冷，他不带镰刀，也不穿黑袍，看起来像任何一个普通人。1942年对他来说非常忙碌，那么多的人类需要收集，有那么多的颜色需要观察，他需要一个假期。俗话说，战争不是死神最好的朋友，而是一个苛刻的老板。他也喜欢想起那一年的一点点美丽，所以他回忆起偷书贼的故事。”

作者再次反观战争的影响——死神一直以来的超时工作。死神提醒读者，他讲这个故事是为了让大家明白人生的美丽和价值，要人们远离战争。作者曾经说过，正是“战争与死亡是最好的朋友”这句话激发了他将死神作为小说叙述者的想法。

——郑剑湘

这部分就像坐过山车一样。

Rudy为了拿回Liesel的书，跳进冰冷的水里，这一情节既甜蜜又感人。尤其是当他极度渴望Liesel的吻，但又害怕被拒绝的时候，我情不自禁地想起了初恋的激情。通过死神的描述，我们可以看到战争的残酷，战争夺走了很多人的生命，让人们忍受饥饿和贫穷。“Forget the scythe，Goddamn it，I needed a broom or a mop. And I needed a vacation.” “... They increase the production of bodies and their escaping souls. A few bombs can do the trick. Or some gas chambers，or the chitchat of faraway guns. If none of that finishes proceedings，it at least strips people of their living arrangements，and I witness the homeless everywhere. They often come after me as I wander through the streets of molested cities. They beg me to take them with me，not realizing I'm too busy as it is. ... I complain internally as I go about my work，and some years，the souls and bodies don't add up；they multiply.”死神以一种轻松随意的语调告诉我们这些灾难。

后来，Liesel给地下室里的Max带了些雪，他们在那里打雪仗、堆雪人，玩得很开心。连Hans和Rosa也加入了他们。看起来他们真的是一个快乐的家庭。多么美好的时光啊！战争可以毁灭家庭，也可以团结人们。正当我快乐地享受书中所描述的美好时光时，故事情节突然陷入了两难境地。Max病了，而且病得很厉害。在那段艰难的日子里，我再一次看到Liesel、Rosa和Hans是那么的善良和坚强！这部分很有趣，但也很让人害怕。

——李秀文

“How did Max Vandenburg end up in Liesel's bed？”这个问题一开始就引起了我的好奇心。然后当我看到“He fell”时，我意识到他可能生病了。结果证明我是对的。Max病得很重，一直没醒。然而，在Max摔倒之前，他们一起堆雪人，在地下室扔雪球扔得很开心。对他们四个人来说，这是多么惬意的时刻啊！很高兴可以看到他们在逆境中享受生活，哪怕只有一次。还是那句话，好时光不会持续太久。在某种程度上，Max就是因为那个雪人而卧病在床、高烧不退的。全家人都很担心他。如果他病死了，从情感上他们都会很难过，但从另外一个角度看，会给他们一家带来危险，因为根本不知道要如何处理他的尸体。从访客评分表上，我能看出来Liesel最关心的是他。她甚至还给他准备了13件礼物，每一件礼物都有它的意义，可谓是用心良苦，从中可以看出他们之间的深厚情感。

——麦佩莹

这几章里关于Rudy和Liesel的片段描写真的很温馨，让我感受到Rudy对Liesel的感情真的很可贵。之前听过一首歌叫作“为爱勇敢”，感觉Rudy就是这样的，因为他之前已经受过太多挫折，一直想成功却一事无成。而这次Liesel的书被抢走并且被扔到河里之后，Rudy却立刻跳进水里救书并且拿到书了还不舍得上来，让人感觉到他对自己这次英雄救美的行动感到特别自豪，忍不住想沉浸在那一刻久一点。这份纯纯的爱在战争之下显得那么渺小，小到几乎可以忽略，又是那么强大，大到可以把灰色的生活点亮。

——莫 然

1. 死神的日记。死神在谈论他自己，因为他想让读者了解他是谁，战争对他做了什么。他说他和我们大家长得很像，但是和大众的看法相反，他讨厌战争。他有时必须留下一些想死的人，这给他带来了痛苦和不快，战争使他的工作超负荷。

2. 雪人。圣诞节前夕，Liesel决定把雪作为礼物送给Max。全家人聚在地下室打雪仗，堆了一个小雪人。这给了他们一个从未有过的最棒的圣诞节，一个充满乐趣的圣诞节。

然后，雪人融化了，Max开始生病。他的病情越来越严重，直到2月的一个晚上，他几乎崩溃了。他被放在了Liesel的床上，Liesel睡在她父母的房间里。他似乎无法暖和起来，反而变得更冷了。虚弱的Max没有醒来，死神来找他，但Max与死神搏斗，所以他又活了一段时间。与此同时，Rosa给他喂汤时，他确实醒了一会儿，一周后他又睁开了眼睛。Liesel认为是她把雪带到地下室才导致了Max的疾病，她是有罪的。我还记得“那天夜里，Max被看望了七次：Hans两次，Rosa两次，Liesel三次。他们陪着Max。许多次，Liesel忍不住默默地哭泣”。

因此，她决定给他带些她在往返学校路上找到的礼物。她一共给他带来了十三件礼物，最后一本是她偷来的书。Hans、Rosa和Liesel想通过这十三件礼物让Max醒来。

——宋碧燕

看完“Snowman”这个故事，我不禁有个疑惑，为什么Liesel要带雪到地下室和Max打雪仗、堆雪人呢？明明Max住在地下室，又冷又暗，吃不饱穿不暖，Liesel还特地装了几大袋雪。后来看到她给Max的13份礼物，都是破烂，但都是她喜欢而且珍惜的东西，我才反应过来，Liesel只是一个13岁的小姑娘。因为她有好东西要和好朋友分享，庆祝圣诞节，另外还要负起 weather reporter的责任，所以她才满心欢喜地送来了雪。孩子们的童真需要我们每一个人去珍惜和尊重。就像Rosa和Hans安慰Liesel的话一样，这不是她的错，反而是她给了Max希望和快乐。

——夏丽炎

在“Snowman”这个章节中，下面这些场景令我印象深刻。

“On Christmas Eve，Liesel brought down a double handful of snow as a present for Max. ‘Close your eyes，’ she’d said. ‘Hold out your hands.’ As soon as the snow was transferred，Max shivered and laughed，but he still didn’t open his eyes.

He only gave the snow a quick taste, allowing it to sink into his lips. 'Is this today's weather report? ' Liesel stood next to him. Gently, she touched his arm. He raised it again to his mouth. 'Thanks, Liesel.' It was the beginning of the greatest Christmas ever. Little food. No presents. But there was a snowman in their basement. After delivering the first handfuls of snow, Liesel checked that no one else was outside, then proceeded to take as many buckets and pots out as she could. She filled them with the mounds of snow and ice that blanketed the small strip of world that was Himmel Street. Once they were full, she brought them in and carried them down to the basement.

All things being fair, she first threw a snowball at Max and collected a reply in the stomach. Max even threw one at Hans Hubermann as he made his way down the basement step."

虽然身处暗无天日的地下室，此刻在地下室玩雪的画面，还是会让我感觉到丝丝温暖。再难过的日子，心若向阳，一切皆能美好。在这个地下室里，有画画，有游戏，有阅读，Liesel和Max渐渐温暖着彼此。与书结缘的Liesel因读书而与Max包括市长夫人Ilsa走得更近。他们都是战争直接或间接的受害者，既要忍受因战争带来的家破人亡的现实，又要在战争罪恶的笼罩下寻找庇护心灵的一席之地。读书便成了一种暂时的享受与解脱。两人同住一室，共同调侃元首的长相和话语，无不表达对战争的厌恶和对自由生活的希冀。他们在寒冷的地下室，一起学习读书，探讨生活，共同探寻文字背后的奇妙世界。莎士比亚曾经说："书籍是全世界的营养品。"书，寄托着人类热切的希望，蕴含着人类丰富的感悟。可是紧接着话锋一转，Max大概因为着凉，出现了生病、昏迷不醒的情况，让我们读者的心一下子悬起来，只愿一切安好。

——徐 燕

那天在Amber River上，其实就是一本很普通的书在那漂浮着，但对Rudy来说却非同一般。那是Liesel的书，如果他拿不到，该是多大的失败啊！所以他全然不顾冬天的水有多冷，他的伤口有多痛，都得下去帮Liesel把书找回来。Rudy在我心中就是一个可靠的人，他时而古灵精怪，时而淘气，非常有安全感。当他向Liesel索要一个吻却不敢时，我想他是真的太爱Liesel了，所以他害怕会受伤或被拒绝，可能付出比得到更能让他满足吧。

礼物对我们每个人来说都很重要，有时候它代表的是一份力量。圣诞节时堆雪人、收礼物的环节会让人们开心。但对一个躺在床上的病人Max来说，家人的陪伴尤其是Liesel的谈话对他来说更像是珍宝。Liesel给他送了云，因为她抬起头看天空时，她想到了Max；她不管去哪里，都会想到他。总是叫不醒Max的Liesel，无奈只好大哭。这种无力感被作者描写得太深刻了。

——袁泳施

In this part, we can sense the character's bitter and happiness during those hard times.

In Chapter Floating Book, Liesel sensed warmth from friendship in cold weather.

In Chapter The Snowman, Liesel and her family with Max enjoyed short happiness on Christmas Eve by throwing snow at each other, making a snowman.

But most of the time, they were suffering from deep bitter.

In Chapter Thirteen Presents, the whole family tried the best to keep Max alive. Liesel even came up with kinds of ideas to help him. She kept reading to wake him up, she searched around to get Max presents to wake him up. Even though all the presents were just litter, they all carried Liesel's care, love for Max.

What impressed me most is the war in Death's eye.

The war is like the new boss who expects the impossible. He stands over your shoulder. You get the job done. The boss, however, does not thank you. He asks for more.

——Ting Feng

Part Six of The Book Thief

Fresh Air, an Old Nightmare, and What to Do with a Jewish Corpse—The Schmunzeler

导读

今天我们一起来读*The Book Thief*的“Fresh Air，an Old Nightmare，and What to Do with a Jewish Corpse” “Death’s Diary：Cologne” “The Visitor” “The Schmunzeler”这几个章节。

讲到偷书这件事，条件已经完全符合了。“It was a gloomy afternoon early in March and only a few degrees above freezing—always more uncomfortable than ten degrees below. Very few people were out on the streets. Rain like gray pencil shavings. ‘Today it’s my turn，’ he said as their fingers froze to the bike handles.”灰蒙蒙的下午，寒冷的天气，很少人走在街上。环境描写一下子把读者拉进氛围里去了。两个孩子之间的对话也让人忍俊不禁。

“Are we going? ’

‘Today it’s my turn.’

Liesel thought fast. ‘Maybe you shouldn’t，Rudy. There’s stuff all over the place in there. And it’s dark. An idiot like you is bound to trip over or run into something.’

‘Thanks very much.’ In this mood，Rudy was hard to contain.

...

‘Just make sure you remember to take yours home.’

‘Very funny，Saumensch. It’s a bit bigger than your filthy shoes.’ ”

Rudy说今天轮到他去偷东西了，Liesel说他还是别去了，那里很多东西很暗，像他一样的蠢蛋肯定会被绊倒的！Rudy回了一句“我谢谢您！”，可是还屁颠地去帮Liesel偷书。

讲到偷书这事儿，Liesel可是有点驾轻就熟了，让我们先来回忆一下她前一次是怎么样偷书的。“They scouted the street and crossed the yard silently... The sound of their breathing amplified... The noise of it passed through overhead，like a low-flying plane."她的心跳声很急促，他们蹑手蹑脚地走到偷书处，他们几乎能听到自己的呼吸声，那声音大到穿过头顶，就像一部低飞的飞机。

但现在呢？"She placed the handlebars in the gutter，looked out for any neighbors，and walked to the window. There was good speed but no hurry. She took her shoes off using her feet，treading on the heels with her toes. Her fingers tightened on the wood and she made her way inside."这一次，她感觉更自在了，她慢慢地周围看下旁人，走到窗户边。速度是刚刚好的，用脚脱掉鞋子，再缓缓地踮起脚，手摸到窗框，人进去了。偷书不是一件光荣的事，但在这里，为了她的精神支柱，她已经能坦然面对风险了。

而在这一章里，我们能更清晰地了解到Liesel对书是很认真的，也很有原则。从何而知？第一，Rudy叫她出去，"Liesel didn't come. There was no decision to be made. She wasn't leaving without a book."。她一定要带着书本走。她本想着要不要多带点。"For now，only one book was necessary."她不想扰乱这个偷书的系统。关于阅读，她也有她的想法："Every day，Liesel read two chapters of the book. It became her mission."。她每天都要给Max读书，似乎书上的文字会给他滋养一样，如果是真的话，可能这是她美好的愿望了。她也坚信Max会醒过来，"'He's not dead yet.' Half hopes didn't dare rise any higher. He isn't dead yet. He isn't dead yet."。阅读对她来说是强大的、有原则的，以及必要的。

Liesel的梦境也让我印象深刻。她的梦是否预示了Max的死？Max替代了她弟弟在她心中的位置吗？

"Perhaps it was even a deep-seated（内心深处的） wish for Max to die. After all，it was good enough for this Jew.

'Is that what you think？' she whispered，standing above the bed.

'No.' She could not believe it. Her answer was sustained."

难道Liesel想让Max离开吗？毕竟这对一个犹太人来说已经足够仁慈了，Liesel说"No."，她坚决地说，一直说，当然她是不想的！这样的文字也让作为读者的我们心痛。

Max居然醒过来了！妈妈用她特别的方式来告诉Liesel，因为她是最想知道的人。"Her face was severe，but it was smiling.She looked left and right，her voice like needle and thread. 'He woke up，Liesel. He's awake.' From her pocket，she pulled out the toy soldier with the scratched exterior. 'He said to give you this. It was his favorite.' She handed it over，held her arms tightly，and smiled."这里用独特的方式来告诉Liesel也包括我们这个喜人的消息，但因为Max的特殊身份，这个消息不得声张，这里妈妈的演技着实让我惊讶了，也很暖心。得知消息后，"Liesel was on such a high that she felt indestructible（坚不可摧的）. She stood there and attempted to hold off the grin because Max was alive."。就像是突然又找到了人生的

目标和方向，Liesel全身都充满了力量，没什么可以打败她了。

回到家后，兄妹俩的对话也让人动容。

"'Thank you for the cloud. Your papa explained that one a little further.'

After an hour，Liesel also made an attempt on the truth. 'We didn't know what we'd do if you'd died，Max. We—'

It didn't take him long. 'You mean，how to get rid of me？'

'I'm sorry.'

'No.' He was not offended. 'You were right.' He played weakly with the ball. 'You were right to think that way. In your situation，a dead Jew is just as dangerous as a live one，if not worse.'"

让人动容的是，Liesel的担忧，担忧Max真的会离开他们；还有Max的善解人意和懂事，懂得自己的存在也是一个累赘。

"'I'm afraid，' he said，'of falling asleep again.'

Liesel was resolute. 'Then I'll read to you. And I'll slap your face if you start dozing off. I'll close the book and shake you till you wake up.'"

相信我们都对这段对话印象很深，的确，如果Max再次昏迷，Liesel也会义无反顾地继续去帮助他，去唤醒他，不会放弃。

接下来，死神再次把我们拉回到残酷的现实当中。结合战争中的环境描写和死神的自述，我们可以清晰地了解到，战争蔓延得有多快，对人民的影响有多大。"Five hundred souls. I carried them in my fingers，like suitcases. Or I'd throw them over my shoulder." 五百个灵魂，死神把他们扛在肩上，把他们握在手中，生命的脆弱，后面还会有多少次的500个灵魂呢，让人不忍往下想。

其中一段文字描写了战争中孩子们的生活：

"Kids being kids. 'Can we keep it，Papa？'

'No.' He was bombed and shocked，this papa，and clearly not in the mood. 'We cannot keep it.'

'Why not？'

'I'm going to ask my papa if I can have it，' said another of the girls.

'Me too.'

Just past the rubble of Cologne，a group of kids collected empty fuel containers，dropped by their enemies."

原本天真的孩子们，居然拿掉落的空气油瓶来玩，那是来自他们敌人的武器，讽刺却又真实。

下一章节，是让我们心惊胆战的一节。纳粹分子来到Liesel家里，欲搜索地下室。面对此情此景，"How could she get back inside without looking too suspicious？Panic generated in that awful way. Throat and mouth. Air became sand.

Think，she thought. Come on，Liesel，think，think." 。Liesel的心里一直想着Max，她也不闹了，成熟得像个大人一样帮着思考怎么解决问题，怎么才能帮助Max。

"Papa stopped. He fought off the urge to open the door and look up the street. He set her down. 'Smart girl，' he said，then called for Rosa.

Does he know? Liesel thought. Can he smell we're hiding a Jew? "

这里用smell就很妙，证明他们真的非常担心。

"Their heartbeats fought each other，a mess of rhythm. Liesel tried to eat hers down. The taste of heart was not too cheerful." 他们的心跳声此起彼伏，就像凌乱的合奏。

"Papa sat at the table. Rosa prayed in the corner，mouthing the words. Liesel was cooked（煎熬的）：her knee，her chest，the muscles in her arms." 爸爸妈妈和Liesel都是备受煎熬的，搜查的时间越长，他们的心就越焦灼。相信我们在等待的时候也会有同样的想法。

"...Rosa melted next to the stove the moment the party man was gone. They collected Liesel and made their way to the basement，removing the well-placed drop sheets and paint cans...

...

... 'You're alive，' she said. 'We all are.' ...

...

...For her，the Jew in her basement had not been revealed. Her foster parents were not taken away，and she herself had contributed greatly to both of these accomplishments. 'Everything's good，' she said.She was fine."

搜查队离开了，Max没有被发现，妈妈几乎"瘫软"了，焦灼的心终于可以放下，外面依然兵荒马乱，但对Liesel来说，Max在，爸爸妈妈也没有被带走，她就已经非常感恩了。她说，一切都好。她很好。或者越是慌乱，我们就越要努力去找寻内心的平静；而告诫自己要珍惜现在，或许就是我们内心平静的最大来源！

工作室人员分享

让我印象深刻的是"Fresh Air，an Old Nightmare，and What TO Do with a Jewish Corpse"章节里描述的两个场景。第一个场景是Max昏迷后数日不醒，Hans都准备给他料理身后事的场景描写：

" 'Look.' His voice was quiet but heavy. 'If it happens—if he dies—we'll simply need to find a way.' Liesel could have sworn she heard him swallow. A gulp like a blow to the windpipe. 'My paint cart，some drop sheets...'

Liesel entered the kitchen.

‘Not now，Liesel.’ It was Papa who spoke，though he did not look at her. He was watching his warped face in a turned-over spoon. His elbows were buried into the table. *The Book Thief* did not retreat. She took a few extra steps and sat down. Her cold hands felt for her sleeves and a sentence dropped from her mouth. ‘He's not dead yet.’ The words landed on the table and positioned themselves in the middle. All three people looked at them. Half hopes didn't dare rise any higher. He isn't dead yet. He isn't dead yet. It was Rosa who spoke next.

Possibly the only time that Max's illness didn't hurt was at dinner. There was no denying it as the three of them sat at the kitchen table with their extra bread and extra soup or potatoes. They all thought it，but no one spoke.”

我们可以感受到其实这一家人早已把Max当成了家里的一员，关心着他，希望他能快快康复。所幸我们后来看到了Max的逐渐苏醒和好转。接下来的这一幕就显得非常温馨了。

“‘Liesel.’ He made her look at him. ‘Don't ever apologize to me. It should be me who apologizes to you.’ He looked at everything she'd brought him. ‘Look at all this. These gifts.’ He held the button in his hand. ‘And Rosa said you read to me twice every day，sometimes three times.’ Now he looked at *The Curtain*s as if he could see out of them. He sat up a little higher and paused for a dozen silent sentences. Trepidation found its way onto his face and he made a confession to the girl. ‘Liesel？’ He moved slightly to the right. ‘I'm afraid，’ he said，‘of falling asleep again.’ Liesel was resolute. ‘Then I'll read to you. And I'll slap your face if you start dozing off. I'll close the book and shake you till you wake up.’

That afternoon，and well into the night，Liesel read to Max Vandenberg. He sat in bed and absorbed the words，awake this time，until just after ten o'clock. When Liesel took a quick rest from *The Dream Carrier*，she looked over the book and Max was asleep. Nervously，she nudged him with it. He awoke. Another three times，he fell asleep. Twice more，she woke him. For the next four days，he woke up every morning in Liesel's bed，then next to the fireplace，and eventually，by mid-April，in the basement. His health had improved，the beard was gone，and small scraps of weight had returned. In Liesel's inside world，there was great relief in that time. Outside，things were starting to look shaky.”

看到Max苏醒过来，全家人都很欢欣，也很珍惜这份美好，一切都显得那么的美好。

我们总是在失去或者快要失去的时候才会特别珍惜眼前的一切，说一些假如一切可以重来的话，但是从故事里、从书籍中，我们也能真切地感受到这份失而复得的喜悦，为主人公感到开心。

——徐 燕

"Liesel placed *The Dream Carrier* beneath her jacket and began reading it the minute she returned home. In the wooden chair next to her bed, she opened the book and whispered, 'It's a new one, Max. Just for you.' She started reading.

Every day, Liesel read two chapters of the book. One in the morning before school and one as soon as she came home.

It became her mission.

She began *The Dream Carrier* to Max as if the words alone could nourish him. On a Tuesday, she thought there was movement.She could have sworn his eyes had opened. If they had, it was only shortly, and it was more likely just her imagination and wishful thinking."

我想分享Liesel去市长家偷书的那段情节。天色不早了，但Liesel舍不得走，她舍不得就这么回家，因此她又费了很大的周折返了回去。她拿了一本红色的书，书脊上印着黑色的书名*The Dream Carrier*。

这一部分写道"Max，这是一本新书，只读给你听"。每一天，Liesel会朗读文章。早晨上学前读一章，放学回家后马上再读一章。在某些夜晚，当她睡不着的时候，还会给他读上半章。这成了她的使命。这让我非常感动，Liesel这个十几岁的小女孩竟然如此坚持和执着，丝毫没有放弃Max，即使有那么一点点希望，她都要不断去尝试、去努力。Max身边有这么个女孩陪伴，也是无比的幸福，希望Max早点醒过来。

——宋 蕾

Liesel从市长家里偷走了*The Dream Carrier*这本书，她开始每天读两次给Max听。她叮嘱她妈妈如果Max醒来，请一定要第一时间告诉她，不管她在哪里。三月中旬，Rosa来到Liesel的学校，告诉她Max醒了。Liesel很高兴，尽管她的妈妈因为怕外人起疑她匆忙来学校的真正原因而打了她一巴掌，留下了一只又大又红的五指印，但是Liesel很庆幸Max还活着。

那天下午，Liesel高兴地回到家，和Max聊天。他们的谈话让我伤心、心碎又感动。

"是妈妈强迫你吃的吗？"

"不过很不错。"

"妈妈的汤吗？真的吗？"

他给她的不是微笑。

"谢谢你的礼物。"更多的是嘴角的轻微撕裂。

"谢谢你的云。你爸爸解释得很详细了。"

Max感谢Liesel的礼物，并要求她不要向他道歉，应该是他向她道歉才是。他还告诉她，他怕睡着，所以她整晚给他念书。每次Max睡着，Liesel就把他叫醒。在那之后，他慢慢好转，到4月中旬，他再次睡回地下室。

——宋碧燕

在Liesel的梦里，Hans一家在讨论Max万一发生了意外怎么办。的确，在战争之下，作为犹太人，活着也好，死了也好，都不能解脱；而活着的人也是一样。虽然这只是一个梦，但我已经闻到了危险的气息，这也许真的是Hans一家以后要面对的情况……

而Liesel梦到Max的死亡之后，一直很担心他会真的离去，所以立刻去地下室确认他是不是还活着。Max的变化同样让人心疼，他已经从骄傲的拳击手变成了胆小鬼，可是我认为成为胆小鬼也是很需要勇气的，因为心中装着别人，担心别人因为自己受牵连而成为胆小鬼并不丢人，反而是一种更加难得的坚强。这一切都是为了保全那些关心他的人，特别是Liesel，那个每天都来为他读书的女孩，那个如果发现他睡着就会把他唤醒的女孩，那个让他感受到被关心，让他感觉自己还活着的女孩。

——莫 然

Max病危，可怜的Liesel又再次需要面对重要朋友的生离死别，战争实在是太残酷了！在一段时间的相处后，Liesel和Max惺惺相惜，成为彼此的精神支柱，从Max昏迷时Liesel的担忧和养母赶去学校告知她Max苏醒时的喜悦，可以看出Liesel对Max倾注了深厚的感情，而这份感情是成熟的、冷静的。当Liesel得知Max苏醒时，她第一时间考虑的依然是尽全力保护Max。她表现得很冷静，不让任何人察觉到异常。年纪轻轻的她能够做到这样，一方面是过往的经历使她变得成熟，另一方面是因为Max在她心中非常非常重要。相信此时的Liesel希望的并不多，只要爸爸妈妈、Max、Rudy没有被战争带走，就已经足够了。我们国家也是一个饱受战火的国家，看到这一幕幕，不禁感慨，感谢前辈们为我们的付出，我们今天才得以过上和平幸福的日子！

——莫洁文

在Max醒来之前，Liesel的感觉复杂而矛盾。一方面，她当然不希望Max死。但她担心Max会像他哥哥一样。另一方面，在那个时期死亡并不总是坏事。在某种程度上，这可能是一种解脱。对Hans、Rosa和Liesel来说，等Max醒来这么长时间是一种折磨。他们不得不考虑如何处理一具犹太人的尸体，尽管他们希望Max活着。幸运的是，他醒了。Rosa告诉Liesel关于Max醒来的消息那里很奇怪。为了避免被怀疑，她假装审问Liesel，问她愤怒地把梳子放在了哪里。作为回报，Liesel在背后骂她，以掩盖事实。我认为这是一个有趣的场景，他们都是很好的演员，包括Hans。当纳粹分子在地下室时，他们三个真的很难保持冷静，好像一切都很正常。多亏了放置良好的掉落纸和油漆罐，他们才逃过了检查。同时，我也感到如释重负。对Liesel来说，目前一切都很好。“It was June.It was Germany. Things were on the verge of decay.”这是六月。这是德国。一切都处于崩溃的边缘。从这三句话中，我有了一种不祥的预感。

——麦佩莹

这部分有两个特别的时刻，一个是奇迹般的搞笑，而另一个是扣人心弦般的令人窒息。

一个时刻是Max在Hans一家长时间的等待和担忧后终于醒了。Liesel给他读书，还给他带礼物。Rosa照顾着他。当Max很有可能成为一具犹太尸体的压力达到极限时，Max醒了。就像黑夜中的烟火，惊人的美丽，突然，这本书又复活了。Rosa告诉Liesel Max吵醒她的那部分很搞笑。Rosa在课堂上的出现引起了尴尬，和老师对Liesel的批评和掌掴。但不知怎的，Max醒来的兴奋感让Liesel把所有不好的事情都抛诸脑后了。Rosa的脸“was severe，but it was smiling.” “Instinct told her to run home immediately，but common sense did not allow it.” “Liesel was on such a high that she felt indestructible... she beamed... she didn’t have to wait a single moment for the teacher’s hand to slap her. ... but it had little effect. The girl merely stood there and attempted to hold off the grin. ... ”顺便提一下，作为一名教师，我真的不喜欢书中的教师形象，真的很粗鲁、很无能。

另一个时刻是一个纳粹分子来到Liesel家要检查地下室是否适合作为避难所。那一刻真的很折磨人和扣人心弦。事情突然发生了，他们不可能有时间准备或是想出解决办法，因为除了保持冷静，他们什么也做不了。书中的描述精准细致：“Their heartbeats fought each other，a mess of rhythm. Liesel tried to eat hers down. The taste of heart was not too cheerful... Everything slowed... ”。但幸运的是，他们很安全。他们都还活着。

读这本书就像坐秋千一样，从一个矛盾转向另一个矛盾，有时候是舒适的，有时候是揪心甚至扣人心弦的。看这本书也是对心灵和思想的一个很好的考验。

——李秀文

这几章的内容让我的心情跌宕起伏。“Fresh Air，an Old Nightmare，and What to Do With a Jewish Corpse”一章让人内心温暖，Liesel最好的伙伴——阳光而又热心肠的Rudy，再次陪伴Liesel去市长家偷书；市长夫人依旧不着痕迹地虚掩窗户，让Liesel尽情偷书；刀子嘴豆腐心的养母Rosa在昏迷数日的犹太人Max苏醒时第一时间来到Liesel的学校，偷偷告知Liesel这个喜讯，一系列的外貌描写、语言描写、动作描写将养母Rosa的可爱和内心的温柔、善良描写得淋漓尽致。“A small wardrobe of a woman with a lipstick sneer and chlorine eyes. This was the legend. She was wearing her best clothes，but her hair was a mess，and it was a towel of elastic gray strands.” “Her face was severe，but it was smiling.” “She looked left and right，her voice like needle and thread. ‘He woke up，Liesel. He's awake.’ ”此时的Liesel高兴得过了头，她觉得自己已经刀枪不入，就连脸上被扇了5个指头印也无关紧要。Liesel放学回到家见到苏醒的Max那一幕也倍感温馨。特别是在Max说害怕自己再次睡过去时，Liesel坚决的话语着实让人感动。“Then I'll read to you. And I'll slap your face if you start dozing off. I'll close the book and shake you till you wake up.”然而，“Death's Diary：Cologne”一章让人心痛，其中的一些语句将战争的残酷和无情描写到了极致。“My arms ached and I could not afford to burn my fingers. There was still so much work to be done. There were several more places to go，skies to meet and souls to collect. As usual，I collected humans. I was tired. And the year wasn't even halfway over yet.”接下来的“The Visitor”一章则让人心急如焚。纳粹分子挨家挨户搜查地下室看是否能做防空洞时，Liesel的智勇双全让在地下室的Max没有被发现，她的养父母没有被带走。Liesel的爱一直在传播……

——李 丹

如果你的朋友去世了，你会怎么办？常人很难从这种痛苦的深渊里走出来。Liesel在很小的时候就目睹了弟弟的死。她花了很长时间才恢复过来。然而，她又一次经历 Max 的垂死。Max 昏迷了好几个星期。整个家庭都忧心不已。Liesel每天都在床前为Max读书，希望故事能让他清醒过来。小小年纪的她，警惕性很高。她报告爸爸，纳粹分子正在挨家挨户搜查的消息。当妈妈专门去学校告诉她Max醒了的时候，她出奇的平静，没有让任何人知道她的内心感受。那天她是个好演员，没有让老师和同学们看出一点破绽。尽管老师扇了她一巴掌，她还是相当高兴。因为Max还活着。他还活着！没有什么比这更让人欣慰的了。

Liesel和她的养父母把Max视为家庭成员之一。他们冒着生命危险照顾他、保护他。Max很感激他们。当Liesel向他道歉时，他说：“No，You were right. You were right to think that way. In your situation，a dead Jew is just as dangerous as a live one，if not worse. Don't ever apologize to me. It should be me who apologizes to you.” 。一个刚刚跟死神擦肩而过的男人，竟然如此善解人意。

死神先生忙着接收灵魂。每天都有炸弹。战争除了给人们带来饥饿、死亡和分离之外，别无其他。对Liesel来说，地下室里的犹太人还没被发现，她的养父母没有被带走，就是她最大的幸福。

——关少娟

八天后，Rosa在学校找到Liesel，假装因为丢了梳子而生她的气。Rosa把她带到大厅，故意大声责骂，然后找准机会小心翼翼地告诉Liesel，Max醒了（这一段的描写栩栩如生，和读者印象中的Rosa形成鲜明对比）。Liesel回到座位坐了下来，欣喜若狂（喜欢这个用词）。她回到家后，Max感谢她给的礼物，以及她给他读书，诉说自己害怕再次入睡不醒。那天下午和晚上，Liesel大声给Max朗读The Dream Carrier 这本书，并在Max睡着的时候轻轻推醒他。Max在 Liesel的床上睡了好几天，才又回到地下室。Liesel很高兴，但死神知道轰炸马上就要开始了。Liesel继续通过大声朗读来安抚自己和Max，当然她的朗读水平也提高了不少。自从在学校的阅读考试失败后，Liesel已经进步了很多。Rosa再次用细节证明，在她那易怒的外表下，有一颗金子般的心，而这种易怒对于保守善意的秘密是有用的。死神也失去了对Liesel悲剧预知的兴趣。

——郑剑湘

书中第327页和第328页Liesel为Max读书的情节让我难忘：

“She thought of Max Vandenberg and his dreams. Of guilt，Surviving，Leaving his family，Fighting the Fubrer. She also thought of her own dream—her brother，dead on the train，and his appearance on the steps just around the corner from this room. *The Book Thief* watched his bloodied knee from the shove of her own hand.”（P327）

“Every day，Liesel read two chapters of the book. One in the morning before school and one as soon as she came home. On certain nights，when she was not able to sleep，she read half of a third chapter as well...It became her mission.”（P328）

地下室的雪人融化了，让地下室异常寒冷，本就身体虚弱的Max当天晚上就得了很严重的风寒，陷入了昏迷。为了唤醒他，Liesel每天都到地下室为他朗读。Max可以说是Liesel精神上的一位导师。他们一同读书、生活，在朝夕相处中体会文字的奥妙和生活的美好。虽然Max只能生活在地下室里，但是他对生活的热爱和朝气蓬勃的顽强生命力也在润物细无声中影响着Liesel。

纳粹分子走进地下室的那几分钟，是Hans一家有史以来最漫长的几分钟，Hans一家用生命在守护着Max。平凡普通的家庭在战争中面对两难，违背良知会终身内疚，不违背良知随时会遭受灭顶之灾，他们也会有胆怯无助的时刻，这些因爱而生的人性光芒散发出来的希望支撑着人们度过了最艰难的战争岁月。

——王之光

“Just past the rubble of Cologne，a group of kids collected empty fuel containers，dropped by their enemies. As usual，I collected humans. I was tired.And the year wasn’t even halfway yet.”

这段话描写的是死神眼中的战争。可悲的是，无辜的孩子去收集空的燃料容器用来当作玩具，而死神是去收集战争造成的尸体。死神为什么累了？因为战争造成了无尽的死亡。然而，这场战争并没有结束。

“Papa sat at the table，Rosa Prayed in the comer mouthing the words，Liesel was cooked：her knee，her chest，the muscles in her arms. I doubt any of them had the audacity to consider what they’d do if the basement was appointed as a shelter. They had to survive the inspection first.”

纳粹搜查了Liesel的家。爸爸在那儿静静地坐着，Rosa默默地祈祷着，Liesel痛苦的身体和焦虑的心灵在挣扎。最后他们都平安无事。

——董筱妍

“I carried them in my fingers，like suitcases. Or I’d throw them over my shoulder. It was only the children I carried in my arms. By the time I was finished，the sky was yellow，like burning newspaper. If I looked closely，I could see the words，reporting headlines，commentating on the progress of the war and so forth. How I’d have loved to pull it all down，to screw up the newspaper sky and toss it away. My arms ached and I couldn’t afford to burn my fingers. There was still so much work to be done.

As you might expect，many people died instantly. Others took a while longer. There were several more places to go，skies to meet and souls to collect，and when I came back to Cologne later on，not long after the final planes，I managed to notice a most unique thing.”

这周又读到死神的日记。“Death’s Diary：Cologne”这一章节再次从死神的工作——收集亡魂来侧面反映战争的残酷。我从文中的一些字眼中感受到的是死神更加厌倦、憎恨这场战争。“My arms ached and I couldn’t afford to burn my fingers. There was still so much work to be done.”此外，这一章节也写到死神对小孩的一种怜惜。在收集亡魂时，唯独小孩是被死神放在怀中的。“It was only the children I carried in my arms.”我们都明白，我们可以从死神的自述中了解到作者自己的观点。小孩是战争中最无辜、最可怜的一个群体，作者对于在战争中死去的小孩深感难过。我感觉我好像已经进入到死神的角色当中，心情也很沉重……

——陈雪芬

Of these three chapters，there are several scenes that interest me. The most thrilling is，of course，The Visitor. While I’d like to share another two scenes. Scene 1 is Rose’s talking to herself about worrying about Max. In this part，we can’t image How hard it is for the family to hide Max，a Jewish at home at that time.

Here are Rosa’s voice：

“What if he doesn’t wake up？What if he dies here，Han？Tell me. What in

God's name will we do with the body? We can't leave him here, the smell will kill us... and we can't carry him out the door and drag him up the street, either. We can't just say, 'You'll never guess what we found in our basement this morning...' They'll put us away for good."

Scene 2 is that Rosa brought Liesel the news of Max's coming alive.

How lovely Rosa is!

Hope is the only light that led people walk further in those hard times. When Rosa couldn't wait to tell Liesel the news that Max was still alive, how interesting her words were!

" 'Liesel? ' ... 'What, Mama? ' She turned. 'Don't you "what Mama" me, you little Saumensch! ' Liesel was gored by the speed of it. 'My hairbrush! ' A trickle of laughter rolled from under the door, but it was drawn instantly back. 'Mama? ' Her face was severe, but it was smiling. 'What the hell did you do with my hairbrush, you stupid Saumensch, you little thief? I've told you a hundred times to leave that thing alone, but do you listen? '

'Of course not! ' ... It ended abruptly, with Rosa pulling Liesel close, just for a few seconds. Her whisper was almost impossible to hear, even at such close proximity. 'You told me to yell at you. You said they'd all believe it.' She looked left and right, her voice like needle and thread. 'He woke up, Liesel. He's awake.' From her pocket, she pulled out the toy soldier with the scratched exterior. 'He said to give you this. It was his favorite.' "

——Ting Feng

Part Six—Seven of The Book Thief

Death's Diary：The Parisians—The Sound of Sirens

导 读

今天我们共读"Death's Diary：The Parisians""Champagne and Accordions""The Trilogy""The Sound of Sirens"这几个小节。

*The Book Thief*用朴实的语言向我们讲述了一个发生在战火纷飞年代的故事。书中有纳粹的专制和残暴，也有普通人建立的坚固的友谊和爱，最触动我心灵的还是女主人公Liesel对阅读的痴迷。

读"Death's Diary"，我忍不住搜索相关的背景知识；读"Champagne and Accordions"，我感受到了音乐的力量；读"The Trilogy"，我领略了文字的魅力；读"The Sound of Sirens"，我听到了死神的脚步声。

"Death's Diary"这章一开始就是死神写的一个悲伤的故事。

"For me，the sky was the color of Jews. When their bodies had finished scouring for gap in the door，their souls rose up. When their fingernails had scratched at the wood and in some cases were nailed into it by the sheer force of desperation，their spirits came toward me，into my arms，and we climbed out of those shower facilities onto the roof and up，into eternity's certain breadth. They just kept feeding me. Minute after minute. Shower after shower.

I will never forget the first day in Auschwitz，the first time in Mauthausen."（P349）

这里提到的Auschwitz和Mauthausen都是纳粹分子为杀害犹太人而建立的集中营。为了更好地理解这章的内容，我查阅了相关的历史知识。

Auschwitz占地40平方公里，里面设有实验室、煤气浴室和焚烧炉。被关押的人们，特别是犹太人，在这里遭受了残酷的迫害和杀戮。据报道，约有130万人死于Auschwitz。死者中有一百万是犹太人。1944年前后，每天大约有六千人被纳粹杀害。1945年，它被苏联军队解放时，140000条用人类毛发制成的毯子，在Auschwitz被发现！我被这些数字震惊了。不！它们不是数字，而是一条条鲜活的生命。

Mauthausen比Auschwitz小。然而，从1938年到1945年，纳粹分子在这里关押了超过20万人，并残忍地杀害了超过10万人。人们临死的时候是多么的绝望和恐惧啊！请看本书的描写——

The first person I took was close to the door，his mind racing，then reduced to pacing，then slowing down，slowing down...（P350）

我带走的第一个人离门很近，他的思绪飞快，然后开始踱步，然后慢下来，慢下来……我们可以感觉到那个人的无助和无望。最终在绝望中，一个生命就这样消失了。这是一个充满了眼泪和鲜血的历史时期。没有人，尤其是犹太人，愿意谈论这样惨无人道的杀戮。但这是历史上真实存在的，我们不应忽视这段历史。希望这个世上不再有法西斯主义！愿世界和平！

读“Champagne and Accordions”，我们能感受到音乐的力量。

战争期间，为了不成为空袭目标，人们不得不把房子漆成黑色。所以大家都找作为油漆工的Liesel的爸爸帮忙。

“Never did he tell them to cover their windows with spare blankets，for they knew they’d need them when winter came.”（P354）

“Who else would do some painting for the price of half a cigarette? That was Papa.”（P355）

爸爸真的很善良，无偿帮助每一个有需要的人，即使报酬只有半根香烟。爸爸的善良和勇敢，其实是深深影响着Liesel的。所以Liesel喜欢在旁边打下手，并且享受和爸爸在一起的时光。

“Whenever they had a break，to eat or drink，he would played the accordion，and it was that Liesel remembered best...Better that we leave the pain behind than ever forget the music... It was well and good to share bread and music... At times，in that basement，she woke up tasting the sound of accordion in her ears. She could feel the sweet burn of champagne on her tongue.”（P356-P358）

爸爸相当乐观。没有食物，没有报酬，空袭时有发生，但是，他还是会拉手风琴。在黑暗的战争时期，正是他的乐观给了Liesel一点阳光。音乐的力量其实就是爸爸的力量。

“The Trilogy”是非常鼓舞人心的一个章节，它突出了书的魅力。Liesel对书籍的渴望越来越强烈。她从市长家里偷了几本书。偷书的场景描写得很细致，很有画面感。

“It was a morning rich with both sun and frothy clouds. Liesel stood in the mayor’s library with greed in her fingers and books titles at her lips. She was comfortable enough on this occasion to run her fingers along the shelves—a short replay of her original visit to the room—and she whispered many of the titles as she made her way along.”（那

是一个蓝天白云的早晨。Liesel贪婪地站在市长的图书馆里，嘴里念着书名。在这种情况下，她非常舒服地用手指在书架上滑动——这是她最初来到这个房间时的简短回放——她边走边小声念着许多书名）（P365）

以上文字我重复读了几遍，无论是英文还是中文，都细腻到可以触碰心灵中最柔软的地方。充满阳光和白云，明媚的天气象征着Liesel愉悦的心情。贪婪，指尖在书架上滑动，小声念着书名——一个渴望阅读、爱书的小女孩形象跃然纸上。人都有欲望，有人渴望金钱，有人渴望权力，有人渴望地位。对于一个如此渴望读书的孩子来说，这是多么珍贵啊！她喜欢书就像蓝天喜欢白云一样！在战火纷飞的年代，能够感受文字的力量，有书本的滋养，从这点来看，Liesel是幸福的。

“She went about her work and read the book next to the Amper River... No one came，no one interrupted，and Liesel read four of the very short chapters of *A Song in the Dark*，and she was happy. It was the pleasure and satisfaction. Of good stealing.”（P366）

拿到书之后，Liesel找到了一个安静的所在，一个人静静享受阅读的乐趣。阅读的快乐属于那些热爱阅读的人，比如Liesel。她静静地坐着，不被打断地阅读，享受文字的魅力。正是这些书为Liesel打开了一个多彩的世界，给了她克服困难的力量。

这是Ilsa知道她的书被Liesel偷走后，写给Liesel的信。她写道：“It made me smile. I should have been angry，but I wasn’t. I hope you find this dictionary and thesaurus useful as you read your stolen books.”。Ilsa在某程度上是Liesel的引路灯塔。她给Liesel提供了各种各样的书，并且教会她阅读的方法。最重要的是，她小心翼翼地保护着Liesel阅读的热情，默默地支持着她。

读“The Sound of Sirens”，气氛陡变，我们似乎能听到死神的脚步声。战争来了，人们不得不跑进地下室躲避炸弹。

“Himmel Street was a procession of tangled people，all wrestling with their most precious possession. In some cases，it was a baby. In others，a stack of photo albums or a wooden box. Liesel carried her books，between her arm and her ribs.”（P372）

在你生命的最后一刻，你会选择带什么？你最珍贵的财产是什么？对Liesel来说，那就是书。你呢，我的朋友们？我对你们的回答很感兴趣。我想我会听到各种各样的答案。

“Did they deserve any better，these people? How many had actively persecuted other，high on the scent of Hitler’s repeating his sentences，his paragraphs，his opus? Was Rosa Huberman responsible? The hider of a Jew? Or Hans? Did they all deserve to die? The children? ”（P375-376）

作者提出了一系列问题。答案显而易见！他强烈谴责法西斯主义和纳粹分子。像Rosa这样的普通人，像Hans这样善良的人，还有所有的犹太人，他们都是无辜的。他们是战争的受害者。

最后，我想跟大家分享几句格言：

If we are peaceful，if we are happy，we can smile and blossom like a flower，and everyone in our family，our entire society，will benefit from our peace.

如果我们和平，如果我们快乐，我们可以微笑，像花朵一样绽放，我们家庭的每个人，我们的整个社会，都会从我们的和平中受益。

Books are the food for the hungry of great mind.

书籍是伟大思想饥饿者的食物。

Books are treasure banks storing wisdom passed down from generation to generation.

书籍是储藏世代相传的智慧的宝库。

工作室人员分享

"Whenever they had a break，to eat or drink，he would play the accordion，and it was this that Liesel remembered best. Each morning，while Papa pushed or dragged the paint cart，Liesel carried the instrument. 'Better that we leave the paint behind，' Hans told her，'than ever forget the music.'"（P355）

Liesel和她爸爸对待生活时总能保持一种乐观的态度，这让我深感触动。无论生活有多么艰难，无论他们遇到了怎么样的困难，Hans和Liesel总是能开怀大笑，因为Hans总有很多精彩的故事，这些故事来自Hans美好的记忆。再者，Hans和Liesel经常一起打闹玩耍，他们还一起喝着美味的香槟，更重要的是他们还有美妙的音乐。他们正一起度过人生中最美好的时光！

这本书讲述的是发生在战争时期的故事，有些事情也许对于我们这些生在和平年代的人来讲是很难理解的，例如Hans和Liesel，在生活如此艰难的情况下，他们还能做到笑对人生。他们的故事给了我很大的启迪，每个人的一生中总难免会有磕磕碰碰的时候，但是只要我们保持一颗乐观的心，用积极的态度去面对生活，不管这世界是怎样的，我们都能活出自己人生的精彩。

——陈雪芬

"The Parisians"这一章节，我看了以后深感郁闷。对于死神来说，天空就是犹太人的颜色。为什么呢？因为太多的死去的灵魂复活，他们笼罩在空中，使天空变得阴森灰暗。在Auschwitz和Mauthausen两处集中营的第一天，这里又冷又黑，谈及死亡，令人不寒而栗。精疲力竭的死神祈祷着上帝能帮助解决这个悲惨的处境。又一群犹太人被带走了。"The death watch the sky as it turned from silver to gray to the color of rain."死神注视着天空的颜色从银色变成灰色再变成雨的颜色。从生到死，从银色到灰色，这意味着生命正在一点一点耗尽，给人一种无力感。生命是多么渺小啊！“They were French，they were Jews and they were you.”到最后，他们是法国人，他们是犹太人，他们也会是你——简单的话语，但意味深长。可悲的是，在战争面前，所有的死亡都是平等的。

——董筱妍

小说借死神的视角来讲述人间的故事，发表对战争的看法。一场战争带走了四十多万的生命，死神奔波于其中，开始对死亡极其冷漠，但当我们读到第二篇死神日记时，他目睹了一千多架飞机轰炸科隆，收走了五百人的灵魂，见证了五万人无家可归。死神慢慢地呈现出一些小讽刺、小鄙夷，对这些灵魂或手提或肩扛，嘴里不住地发牢骚，抱怨工作沉重。这种叙事方式无疑缓解了血淋淋的战争对我们视觉的冲击感，但我们也感觉到了死神开始有了凡人的情绪。但是当读到今天的第三篇日记时，我觉得死神越发有温度，我想，面对这么多无辜的灵魂，最后连死神都会产生仁慈。到他读到Liesel描述在防空洞那晚的文字时，死神说他心中涌现出了对他们的怜悯之情。

同时，读到这几章的内容让我有了一种希望时间就停留在这一刻的感觉。尤其是当读到战争前短暂的平和与美好时，有父女间的陪伴，有分享面包和音乐快乐的美好。

“She wanted none of those days to end，and it was always with disappointment that she watched the darkness stride forward.”（P355）

看到黑暗降临时，她总是十分失望，她真希望这样的日子永远不要结束。

“In the basement，when she wrote about her life，Leisel vowed that she would never drink champagne again，for it would never taste as good as it did on that warm with accordions.”（P357）

日后她在地下室写自己的故事，她发誓自己永远不再喝香槟，因为香槟的滋味永远没办法像那个七月温暖的午后那般美好。她觉得这是她生命中最美好的时光。

防空洞地窖里的每个人都握着另一个人的手，这群德国人仿佛围成一个圆圈。冰冷的手在别人温暖的手中融化，有些时候，还能感觉到另一个人的脉搏在跳动，这跳动是通过一层苍白而僵硬的皮肤传来的。有人闭上眼睛，等待着最后时刻的到来，或者只是在盼望空袭结束的信号。这让我想到“人性的丰满和反复都在这黑暗中，最深的同情和最大的悲悯也都在这黑暗中”。越是苦难的日子，人越要好好生活，越过重重困难，便能成就自己的人生。

——王之光

对“The Sound of Sirens”这一章的分享：

Hans买了一台收音机，用来听空袭来临时的声音，但九月的一个晚上，直到空袭警报响起，他们才知道。他们不得不来到邻居Fiedler家的大地下室躲避，被迫把Max留在家里。Himmel Street的人们都聚集在那里，每个人都带着他们最珍贵的财产。Liesel观察着那些看起来最害怕的人。过了一会儿，大家便安静了下来，房间充斥着明显的恐惧感，很快每个人都开始互相牵着手（细节描写非常仔细）。

随着第一次袭击开始，战争实际上已经来到了Himmel Street。所有的人现在都聚集在一起，因为恐惧而团结起来。Max作为一个二等公民的地位再次被强调，因为他不能来到防空洞，只能在地下室独自面临死亡的危险。

死神审视着这些人的生命，想弄清楚他们是否值得同情还是应该死去。最后，死神决定同情防空洞里的人们，但没有同情集中营里的犹太人。Liesel很担心Max一个人在地下室里的安危。最后，警报又响了，这次意味着轰炸结束了，Hans一家马上回家找Max。Max坦言他在突袭期间上楼看了看窗外，因为他已经有将近两年没见过外面的世界了。他说星星很刺眼。那晚他们彻夜未眠，Liesel在黑暗中诵读了一首歌，Max边听边画画写字。

死神让我们看得更远：这些人正经历着困难的战争时期，但他们至少有自主权，不会像动物一样被赶到一起屠杀。在死神看来，犹太人遭受的苦难，比这些德国人更可怜，这些德国人至少是自由的。Max在地下室住了那么久，连星星的光芒对他来说都太亮了。

——郑剑湘

对于书中的这一部分，我对战争给人们尤其是犹太人带来的伤害深感痛心。死神说：“For me，the sky was the color of Jews.”很多人死得很惨。“There were broken bodies and dead，sweet hearts. Still it was better than the gas... All of them were light，like the cases of empty walnuts. Smoky sky in those places. The smell like a stove，but still so cold.”最让我害怕的是谋杀背后的冷血。死神说：“I blow warm air to keep them warm when the souls still shiver.”。犹太人在身体上和精神上都受到了折磨。死神甚至向上帝询问事件的意图，当然，没有答案。似乎只有死亡才能解除他们的恐惧。

第一部分一方面很可怕，另一面又很甜蜜。在黑暗笼罩Himnel street之前，Liesel和她的家人度过了一段美好的时光。Rudy和Max，在内心深处，他们知道最黑暗的日子即将来临，并做好了准备。Liesel忙着和她父亲一起工作。她有强烈的幸福感。“Happiness：Coming from happy—enjoying pleasure and contentment. Related words：joy，gladness，feeling fortunate or prosperous.”Liesel和她父亲之间的温馨互动，安慰了此前我因看到死亡而引起的沮丧感受。我也为Rudy高兴。

一个敏感但好胜的男孩，终于有机会了。

不过，我还是能感受到以下部分的悲伤和疯狂。一方面，我想知道更多关于他们的事，但另一方面我又害怕知道更多。希望作者不会对他们太苛刻，或者说不会对我们读者太苛刻。

——李秀文

第四章，警报声，给我印象最深。生活在战争时期，每个人都害怕听到警报声，因为没人知道他们这次能否活下来。一群乱糟糟的人，带着他们认为最珍贵的东西，以防再也回不去了。每次都像是最后一次，人们一无所有地聚集在地窖里，还有很多事要做，但必须等待警报结束。此外，这个章节生动地描述了人们在地窖里的一举一动，呈现出令人窒息的气氛。

尤其是下面的句子——

“The children hugged their parents，and it took many minutes for all of them tofully realize that they were alive，and that they were going to be alive.Only then did their feet climb the stairs.”

在读到这个句子的时候，我很伤心。如果我是他们，我真的不知道我该如何在那么可怕的环境下生存。而且我也无法想象像Max一样22个月没有看到外面的世界的心情。只在外面看几秒钟，这对他来说甚至是奢侈的。他们活该吗？当然不是，但这是战争。我很感激我们能活在一个和平的世界，我们不需要担心生计，更别说生存了。珍惜，活在当下！

——麦佩莹

这几章中有很多细节都让我感觉印象深刻，死神的日记让我们看到战争带走了很多人的生命，作为收割生命的死神都有点看不下去了，一边抱怨工作繁忙，一边也替死去的人们惋惜……毕竟还有很小的孩子。他们有什么错呢？只是运气不好罢了……而在战争面前，单独的个体是多么渺小！但是同样的，在残酷的战争面前，孩子依然是孩子，看到空的燃料瓶都觉得很好奇，都想收起来做玩具。我想，这就是生命的强韧吧，就好像夹缝中生存的小植物一样，战争中生存下来的这些孩子依然可以苦中作乐，坚强地活着，不被战争磨灭生命中的乐趣和美好。

——莫 然

死神说这个夏天被犹太人占据。当他们试图跳下悬崖逃跑时，他抓住了他们。他特别记得在波兰战俘营中的一群法国犹太人，他已经尽量温柔，甚至在把他们拿走的时候还亲吻了一下这些可怜的犹太人。在这一刻，我可以感觉到，即使是死神，他也感受到了他带走的灵魂是多么可怜。当死神谈到他的工作时，我可以想象犹太人的生活有多艰难，纳粹对他们有多冷酷和残忍。战争让无辜的犹太人和人们失去了生命和家人，有多少人一生都生活在深深的悲伤中，这就是战争带来的创伤。我们应该为我们有一个强大的祖国而感到高兴。

说回故事本身，为了防御空袭，爸爸的油漆生意开始好转，因为人们需要把窗户漆成黑色，这样轰炸机就看不见他们的家了。有时人们只能付他一块饼干或半根烟的价钱。爸爸对这个并不在意。他还总是随身带着手风琴，在休息时为Liesel演奏。在这里，Hans是一个善良的人，对他所拥有的一切都感到满足。他热爱生活，尽管他的生活很穷苦，甚至快要饿死了，他还愿意收留Max和Liesel。对Liesel来说，这是她一生中最美好的时光。糟糕的日子很快就来了，但现在她很享受和爸爸妈妈在一起的时光。

在Hitler青年狂欢节上，Rudy参加了四项比赛，赢得了其中三项。他向自己证明了——他是一个胜利者。我喜欢Rudy，他是如此的乐观和阳光。

Liesel又从市长的图书馆偷了一本书。那是一本字典和词典。书里有一封市长夫人写给Liesel的信，信中说，市长夫人早就知道Liesel偷书的事，希望她下次能以正确的方式来拜访。Liesel想回去和她道歉，但她做不到。看完这部分，我很感动，因为Liesel曾经对市长夫人说过那么多残酷无情的话。但市长夫人仍然欢迎Liesel在她的图书馆读书，Liesel对此感到不安和内疚。

——宋碧燕

“‘Frau Hallah，I’m sorry，I have no black paint left，’ he would say，but a little farther down the road，he would always break.There was tall man and long street.‘Tomorrow，’ he’d promise，‘first thing，’ and when the next morning dawned，there he was，painting those blinds for nothing，or for a cookie or a warm cup of tea.”

Hans家里虽然很贫穷，但是他却不计报酬地去给别人家刷油漆，人们甚至说，他会为了半支香烟帮人刷窗户。Hans善良、乐观、坚强，每到休息时，他都会拉手风琴，这也是Liesel记忆里最为鲜活的时刻。在战争年代，Hans这种积极面对生活的勇敢乐观的品格深深地感染了Liesel，就像Liesel所说的，即便是世界上最伟大的手风琴家也无法与他媲美。

——宋 蕾

在读完“The Trilogy”的故事之后，我也和Liesel有着同样的疑惑：为什么Rudy要故意输掉比赛呢？按照设定，面对最后一站，男主角身心疲惫，即便获胜的可能性极低，他还是会拼到最后；因为主角光环，他最后总是冠军。没有主角光环的Rudy告诉我们，原来放弃也是一种勇敢，即承认自己无法赢，满足并珍惜已取得的胜利，不在乎旁人的不理解。就像硬币有两面，勇敢也分两面。

——夏丽焱

这几章读下来，感觉到的是战争局势的日益紧张，气氛也有些压抑。越来越多的犹太人失去性命，在集中营里，或被炸死，或被毒气折磨死。令我印象深刻的有以下几点：

首先是死神带走生命时对人物和环境的刻画。在“the Death’s Diary：The Parisians”这一章节中，我可以感受到犹太人心中的那种绝望。描述性的词汇比如：weary、poisonedcheeks、last、gasping cries、vanishing words。“Sometimes I imagined how everything looked above those clouds，knowing without question that the sun was blond and the endless atmosphere was a giant blue eye. They were French，they were Jews and they were you.”能感觉到连死神都充满了无奈之感，战争只会带来两败俱伤的结果。

其次，故事的承接都是从一些关键词开始的，这里面包含太多的深意。

1. DUDEN DICTIONARY MEANING

Zufiedenheit—Happiness Coming from happy—enjoying pleasure and contentment. Related words：joy，gladness，feeling fortunate Or prosperous.

当中谈到的Rudy在跑步比赛中，为什么要在赢得三场比赛的情况下故意输掉最后一场比赛呢？是如原文提到的要“please his new Hitler Youth leaders”吗？

2. DUDEN DICTIONARY MEANING

Verzeihung—Forgiveness：To stop feeling anger animosity，or resentment. Related words：absolution，acquittal，mercy。

提到市长夫人发现 Liesel经常偷书时，不是揭穿，而是包容，能感觉到她的善良和大度。

3. DUDEN DICTIONARY MEANING

Angst—Fear An unpleasant，often strong emotion caused by anticipation or awareness of danger. Related words：terror，horror panic，fright alarm.

有一处描写大家第一次去防空洞躲藏安全出来以后回到家里的：

“With Mamas permission Liesel stayed with him till morning，reading *A Song in the Dark* as he（Max） sketched and wrote in his book. From a Himmel Street window，he wrote，the stars set fire to my eyes.”

连黑夜中的星星都能灼伤Max的眼睛，由此表现出22个月没有见过外面的世界的辛酸。

——徐 燕

标题是“死亡日记”吗？读到死神的自述，我被书中的描写重重地压着，战争中没有一个人是幸运的，“他们的灵魂向我走来，包围着我；他们一直跟着我，越来越多的牺牲者，一分钟接着另一分钟，一波接一波”。战争中的平民百姓无疑是最无辜的，死神给我们铺开了一个清晰的画面，悲伤而深沉。所幸在第二部分，当我读到爸爸的手风琴和香槟时，我是愉悦的。这让我想起我和我的爸爸相处的时光，我也确信Liesel会像我感激爸爸那样，去感激她的Papa。细节总是很打动人心的，“Who else would do some painting for the price of half a cigarette? That was Papa，that was typical and I loved him.”。跟爸爸一起工作让他们之间更亲近了，对Liesel来说，爸爸就像是一个超人，他很有魅力也很会照顾人。我想这是父母教育最好的呈现方式，就是在相处中教育孩子。每天Liesel都会坐在爸爸身旁，双手放在膝间，在日光中等待。她不希望这样的日子结束，夜幕降临时她总是很失望，失望陪爸爸上班的时间结束了，如果可以，她希望可以一直听着爸爸的琴声，去感受爱和温暖。

——袁泳施

Of the three chapters. I was still struggling in a nightmare while reading，even though there was bitter joy.

Chapter Champagne and Accordions pictured a warm-hearted man helping in the neighbor happily with a little girl following him. Hans was paid for a cookie，or a warm cup of tea，a half a cigarette，or even nothing for his work. However，he enjoyed it a little. Liesel regarded that period of time as the best time of life.

Chapter The Trilogy a thread of light during the hard time by holding a Hitler Youth carnival. Rudy was intend on winning four events，the 1500，400，200 and of the 100. He liked his new leaders and wanted to please them. And he wanted to show his old friend Franz a thing or two. So in the last event，he gave it up on purpose.

Liesel successfully stole another book from the mayor's library while she was enjoying her success. She was shocked to find the mayor's wife standing behind the glass. And Rudy got a letter in the stolen book. It was for Liesel from the mayor's wife. The mayor's wife expressed her absolution，acquittal，mercy and forgiveness.

Chapter The Sound of Sirens shows us what people's life was like in the World War II. Terror，horror，panic，fight and alarm filled people's hearts，eyes. People couldn't help thanking God for their lives. They hugged each other for just being alive.

——Ting Feng

Part Seven of The Book Thief

The Sky Stealer—Peace

导读

今天我们来读“The Sky Stealer”“Frau Holtzapfel's Offer”“The Long Walk to Dachau”和“Peace”这四个章节。我想先用以下关键词来总结每一个部分，分别是战争、交易、残酷、影响和悔恨。

在“The Sky Stealer”中有这样一段话：

“Again，Himmel Street was a trail of people，and again，Papa left his accordion. Rosa reminded him to take it，but he refused.‘I didn't take it last time，’he explained，‘and we lived.’War clearly blurred the distinction between logic and superstition.”

我觉得当我们绝望的时候，我们都需要一点信念，我们需要坚持一些事情，不管它看起来是多么迷信或不合逻辑。

“One of the younger boys contemplated crying again，but Liesel stopped at that moment and imitated her papa，or even Rudy for that matter. She winked at him and resumed. Only when the sirens leaked into the cellar again did someone interrupt her.‘We're safe，’said Mr. Jenson.‘Shhh！’said Frau Holtzapfel.”（P382）

从这段话中可以看出Liesel是一个暖心的人，她知道如何在不打断自己阅读的情况下安慰孩子。我很喜欢“leaked into”这个词，它生动地表现了当时的宁静和人们的专注，尤其是“Shhh”一词，说明没有人想要分心。

Frau Holtzapfel不是一个容易相处的女人。她为她的两个儿子感到骄傲，同时也担心他们的安全。她以前对Liesel没有礼貌，但知道Liesel尊重她的儿子们，她也希望以一些礼貌来回报Liesel。

读到“The Long Walk to Dachau”时，我特地去网上搜索了一些关于Dachau的背景材料，从下面的这些数据就可以知道Dachau简直就是一个地狱！

“Their eyes were enormous in their starving skulls. And the dirt. The dirt was molded to them. Their legs staggered as they were pushed by soldiers' hands—a few wayward steps of forced running before the slow return to a malnourished walk.”

（P391-P392）

这些描述性的词语很好地说明了囚犯们的悲惨处境。尤其是“molded”一词，意思是他们很长时间没有洗澡了。他们连吃的都没有，更不用说洗澡了。

“She could only hope they could read the depth of sorrow in her face，to recognize that it was true，and not fleeting. She understood that she was utterly worthless to these people.”（P393）

Liesel是如此的善良，以至于她无法忍受看着犹太人受苦。更重要的是，她的地下室里有个犹太人。对她来说，同样的情况有一天也会发生在Max身上。“They could not be saved，and in a few minutes，she would see what would happen to those who might try to help them.”这句话就像是预示着爸爸接下来的下场。对于大多数人来说，他们不敢冒生命危险去帮助犹太人，他们会坚持认为麻烦越少越好。不像其他人，Hans用行动同情囚犯。对囚犯们来说，这真是一个奇迹。然而，Hans因为他的所作所为被士兵打倒了。

“When he made it to Frau Diller’s，he looked back one last time to number thirty-three. He could not see the figure in the kitchen window，but she could see him. She waved and he did not wave back.”（P397）

从这里我们就知道，Max根本没有打算回来。

“The last words of Max Vandenburg：You’ve done enough.”（P398）

读到这里，我的鼻子就已经酸了。Max宁可自己处于危险中，也不愿让Liesel一家因为他而受到牵连。Hans因为自己“愚蠢的”善良，导致Max不得不离开，无尽的遗憾几乎吞噬了他。我想Hans不仅在等军队，也在等Max的出现。

如果Hans被抓了，他反而会好受得多，至少Max离开是有原因的。而且，他很担心Max的安全。

有其父必有其女。Hans和Liesel都很有同情心，虽然他们都对犹太人表示同情，但连Liesel都知道他们无能为力。可是爸爸做了什么呢？我知道善良并没有错。有些人可能会说，提供帮助是正义的，不能袖手旁观。但有时我们就是无能为力。做事要三思而后行！

工作室人员分享

我觉得“Frau Holtzapfel’s Offer”这一章节挺有趣的。Mrs. Holtzapfel来到Rosa家找Liesel约定读书的事。一开始她们见面时，Rosa以为她是来找麻烦的。“What do you want here？You want to spit on my kitchen floor now，too？”而Liesel就以为她是来抢夺她的书的。但令人感到意外的是，她想叫Liesel到她家读书给她听，还另外给了她咖啡。最后，双方都放下了原有的芥蒂，达成了约定。外表看似很难相处的Mrs. Holtzapfel，受到了书的感染。我想说书给予了她们力量，主要就是给了她们勇气。在乱世中，每个人最需要的就是勇气，而恰恰正是

Liesel读书的行为给予了大家“勇气”——活下去的“勇气”。读书真好，继续认真读书！

——陈雪芬

下一次突袭即将来临，Himmel镇上所有的人再次陷入恐慌。“战争明显模糊了逻辑和监督的界限。”只有一个想法就是活下去。孩子们的哭声和紧张的气氛都不能使他们平静下来。与此同时，Liesel大声朗读《口哨者》给他们听。听着她的朗读声，每个人都神奇地被安抚下来。这就是文字的魔力。书留下了很大的空间，让人们思考，把故事传递出去。现在，书籍似乎逐渐被多媒体所取代。人们花在读书上的时间变少了，但是书给你的惊喜和有用的反馈总是比你认为的要多。所以，让我们从现在开始阅读，感受书的魅力。

在前往达豪的路上，一群可怜的犹太人痛苦地缓慢移动着。他们的眼睛盯着Liesel，因为他们不想死。这是一个非常令人伤心的场景，活着对他们而言竟是一种奢望。

——董筱妍

对“The Sky Stealer”这一章的分享：前几天的空袭只是警报器意外的响了，然而，几天后的空袭才是真的。Himmel Street的人们又聚集起来了，这一次还是在Fiedler家的地下室里，气氛比上次更加紧张。Liesel开始大声朗读*The Whistler*安抚自己，但很快周围的人们也安静下来，开始听她读书。Liesel 感觉大声朗读就像演奏手风琴一样。即使在突袭结束的警报声响起之后，人们还是会留下来听完剩下的章节，离开的时候他们会感谢Liesel。庆幸的是Himmel 街并没有受到炸弹袭击。

这对Liesel来说是个非常重要的时刻，这表明她成熟了很多。那个没通过阅读测试的女孩，现在能为一群成年人朗读。她不再需要Hans来安慰她，她现在正逐渐成为别人的安慰者。这也再次显示了语言和艺术在困难时期表现出来的伟大，Liesel用她的朗读缓解了地下室里所有人的恐惧，就像Hans用他的音乐缓解了Liesel的恐惧一样。

——郑剑湘

这几章内容引发了我的深思。Liesel对阅读的热情影响了附近的居民，她通过讲故事成功地平息了庇护所的混乱。甚至经常在她家门上吐口水的Holtzapfel，也愿意用一杯咖啡来交换一个故事。因此，我们可以看到，阅读可以对人们产生积极的、深远的影响。在战火纷飞、生命都得不到保证的年代，文字抚慰了人们的心灵。

“The Long Walk To Dachau”这一章节向读者展示了犹太人遭受迫害的场

景。“When was the last time we took these rats for some fresh air？”士兵竟然把犹太人比作老鼠！犹太人受到了不人道的对待。我们来看看第392页的一些部分。“When they arrived in full，the noise of their feet throbbed on top of the road. Their eyes were enormous in their starving skull. And the dirt. The dirt was molded to them. Their legs staggered as they were pushed by soldiers' hands... Their feet could barely rise above the ground.”犹太人被绑着游街，衣衫褴褛，面黄肌瘦，已经没有力气走路。他们在身体上和精神上都受到了迫害，在死亡的边缘挣扎。事实上，他们中的大多数都会死，要么死于饥饿，要么直接被杀。Hans忍不住给了一个犹太人一片面包。我想那一刻他只是想帮助那个犹太人，没有考虑后果；结果他被打了。

Max不得不离开，因为地下室不再安全。那天晚上，Hans抱着头，沉思到天亮。他很后悔白天的行为，不是后悔给了游街的犹太人面包，而是后悔打草惊蛇了。“Peace”中的心理描写，表明了Hans是多么善良的人。他想帮助更多的犹太人，只是超出了他的能力范围。“I'm an idiot.”“No，Papa，You're just a man.”我们同意Liesel的观点，爸爸是个伟大而勇敢的人。

——关少娟

这几章的内容让人揪心而又暖心。残酷的战争带给人们的不安和恐惧是揪心的，而在这样的背景下，Liesel和养父Hans的行为是暖心的。地下室里，Liesel朗读的声音让邻居获得心灵的安宁而变得更加坚强，邻居们安静聆听一个陌生故事的曲折，借此遗忘轰炸、死亡以及更细节的恐惧。作者详细地描写了这一场景。“Liesel remained focused on the first page. When she turned page two，it was Rudy who noticed. By page three，everyone was silent but Liesel. She didn't dare to look up，but she could feel their frightened eyes hanging on to her as she hauled the words in and breathed them out. Liesel read on. For at least twenty minutes，she handed out the story. The younger kids were soothed by her voice. One of the younger boys contemplated crying again，but Liesel stopped at that moment and imitated her papa，or even Rudy for that matter. She winked at him and resumed.”

Liesel的朗读也促成了与冤家Frau Holtzapfel的握手言和，Liesel一共为她读了四次书。

“The Long Walk To Dachau”一章中描写犹太人被游街示众的一幕是令人揪心的。“Their gaunt faces were stretched with torture. Hunger ate them as they continued forward，some of them watching the ground to avoid the people in the side of the road. Some looked appealingly at those who had come to observe their humiliation，this prelude to their deaths. Others pleaded for someone，anyone，to step forward and catch them in their arms.”养父Hans因同情其中一位可怜的犹太老人给他递面包

的一幕是暖心的，Hans不怕遭受当众的鞭打，他的一举一动无不闪耀着人性的光辉。

——李 丹

这部分的前两页真的很有趣，当Mrs. Holtzapfel给Liesel一个很好的机会为她读书时，我觉得很有趣。Liesel想："This is my punishment for all that steeling. It's finally caught up with me."。一方面，作者以幽默的方式告诉我们，Liesel总是因为内心深处的坚强而感到内疚；另一方面，虽然作者没有直接告诉我们，但我们还是可以感觉到Liesel对Mrs. Holtzapfel的态度。

犹太人被游街示众的情节非常扣人心弦。他们很可怜，但是没有人敢上来帮助他们。而老犹太人糟糕的情况将这部分推向了高潮。Hans试图给他一块面包，这一行为向其他人表明他不仇视犹太人。他的所作所为给自己带来了极大的麻烦和危险，Max不得不离开他们的家。于是痛苦、折磨、绝望变成了遗憾的平静，既平静又不平静。似乎每个人都在等待，可怕事情的发生令人无法忍受。

突然，不知从哪里冒出两个穿大衣的人来，他们不是为了Hans，而是为了Rudy。它让我的心悬在那里，让我迫不及待地想往下阅读，很想知道为什么他们想要Rudy。这些情节确实写得太精彩了，它再一次成功地引起了读者的注意。

——李秀文

这几章内容让人读得很是揪心啊！士兵说"When was the last time we took these rats for some fresh air?"，犹太人被当作老鼠看待。"Their eyes were enormous in their starving skull. And the dirt. The dirt was molded to them. Their legs staggered as they were pushed by soldiers' hands... Their feet could barely rise above the ground."（他们的眼睛在饥饿的脑壳上显得非常大。污垢、泥土紧紧地黏在他们身上。士兵们用手推着他们，他们的腿摇摇晃晃的……他们的脚几乎不能离开地面）亲眼看着犹太人受到如此残忍的迫害，善良的Hans忍不住递上一个面包，并因此惹祸上身被惩罚了。唉！在战争中，就是因为某几个霸权主义者的私欲，千千万万的老百姓便遭受折磨甚至送上性命。现在世界上依然有国家在经历战火纷飞，真是为自己处在和平时代的中国而感到无比幸运！

——莫洁文

这几章中，让我印象深刻的片段就是大家都在地下室里躲着的时候，一开始很多人都很焦虑、很紧张，特别是孩子们，而这时候Liesel拿出了一本书开始朗读，用这种方式转移人们的注意力，让他们冷静下来……而孩子们也很快完全安静下来，在Liesel的朗读声中，他们享受着战争下的片刻安宁。

这让我感觉到有时候阅读的意义真的不在于学会多少知识，更多的时候是让人有一个心灵的避风港，一个温暖的小角落，在那里可以放松身心，然后满血复活，继续接受世事无常的敲打，并在一次一次倒下之后爬起来，继续前行。

——莫 然

第一次空袭只是虚惊一场，但在9月19日，这次是真的。那群人也聚集在费德的地下室。Liesel为了缓解大家的紧张情绪，大声朗读。

很快，每个人都在听她朗读，Liesel意识到这是她的天赋，就像爸爸会拉手风琴一样。在听到解除警报的信号后，大人们感谢她通过朗读让大家不再惊慌不安。家人回到家，发现Max正等着他们。

第二天，Mrs. Holtzapfel来到门口跟Rosa说话。由于她们彼此憎恨，这是一件令人惊讶的事情。她马上就说到了点子上，她想让Liesel读书给她听。Mrs. Holtzapfel喜欢那本书，想听听它的结局。约定是Liesel朗读，她不再往他们的门上吐痰，并给Rosa定量供应咖啡。Liesel每周给她读两次书，但是要马上开始。

两周后，犹太人游行。他们几乎不能走路，快要死了。一位老人走路特别吃力，Hans不忍心看着他一次又一次地跌倒在街上，所以他递给那个人一片面包。因为Hans的所作所为，他们俩都被一个士兵鞭打。直到有人把他从街上扶下来，Hans才想起Max，说道："天哪，Liesel，我做了什么？"

Max当晚就带着装满食物和衣服的行李箱离开了。他本打算四天后在远离莫尔钦的安珀河与Hans见面，然而他只留下了一张纸条。当Hans到达现场时，他发现了Max的纸条，上面写着："你已经做得够多了。"他再也没见过Max。

Max离开的那天晚上，爸爸坐在厨房里，等着有人来把他带走。Rosa和Liesel无法安慰他。他觉得自己像个白痴，竟然帮了那个老人，这就是Max不得不离开家的原因，但没有人来接Hans。帮助有困难的人不是一件错事，然而，由于这个原因Max不得不离开。这是最让人悲伤的。

——宋碧燕

"When she turned to page two，it was Rudy who noticed. He paid direct attention to what Liesel was reading，and he tapped his brother and his sisters，telling them to do the same. Hans Huberman came closer and called out，and soon，a quietness started bleeding through the crowded basement. By page three，everyone was silent but Liesel.

For at least twenty minutes，she handed out the story. The youngest kids were soothed by her voice，and everyone else saw visions of the whistler running from the crime scene. Liesel did not.

Only when the sirens leaked into the cellar again did someone interrupt her. ‘We’re safe，’ said Mr. Jenson.

“Shhh！” said Frau Holtzapfel.

Liesel looked up. ‘There are only two paragraphs till the end of the chapter，’ she said，and she continued reading with no fanfare or added speed. Just the words.”

让我印象如此深刻的是“The Sky Stealer”这一部分。在9月19日的晚上，人们遭受了严重的空袭，成群结队地进入了地下室。当时整个地下室开始摇晃，最年幼的几个孩子开始号啕大哭。即便身处地下室，他们依然能隐隐约约听见炸弹的声音。为了摆脱地下室的嘈杂，也为让自己好受一些，Liesel开始朗读*The Whistler*。她的读书声给人们以安慰，尤其是年幼的小孩，让他们变得越来越坚定，也帮人们减轻了在地下室里的恐惧。空袭过后，人们安全了。Liesel只剩下最后两段就读完这一章了，于是她不急不躁、不紧不慢地继续朗读。出于尊重，大人们让大家保持安静，直到Liesel读完第一章。大人们都感谢Liesel帮他们消除了恐惧。

作者详细地描写了这一场景，让我深受感动和鼓舞，也让我看到了Liesel不仅善良而且遇事坚定沉稳的个性。

——宋 蕾

读完“The Long Walk to Dachau”后，我的心情久久不能平静，心脏好像被紧紧攥住一样。作者没有直接描写战争场面，仅是通过犹太人赶路的场景，让每一位读者体会到战争的残酷以及人性的黑暗。

犹太人在纳粹的迫害下，他们忍受饥饿、尘土、鞭打、虐待。而德国民众，除了偶尔空袭，他们的生活则相对平静，但当他们要直面残酷的战争时，每个人都震惊到不敢说话。而德国纳粹是一切黑暗的源头。

我不敢相信，驱赶犹太人下车步行的原因，不是卡车出了故障，也不是犹太人需要新鲜空气，只是纳粹士兵要拿他们取乐。

希望世界和平，没有硝烟。

——夏丽焱

在“The Idion and the Coat Men”这一章节中，死神用“the idiot”来形容Hans，其实是带着一些戏谑意味的。Hans真的傻吗？他只不过是出于善良，出于对弱者的同情，想给游街的那个犹太人一点吃的，但是后来却让自己陷入麻烦。让Max离开也许对彼此都好，但是他也知道，Max一旦暴露在外，生死便是难料。Hans不禁自责让Max陷入了危险境地。此刻他的心情是多么的矛盾与惆怅啊。

“On the night of the parade，the idiot sat in the kitchen，drinking bitter gulps of Holtzapfel’s coffee and hankering for a cigarette. He waited for the Gestapo，the soldiers, the police—for anyone—to take him away, as he felt he deserved. Rosa ordered him to come to bed. The girl loitered in the doorway. He sent them both away and spent the hours until morning with his head in his hands, waiting.

Nothing came.

...

'What have I done? ' he whispered again.

'God, I'd love a cigarette, ' he answered. He was all out. Liesel heard the repeated sentences several times, and it took a lotto stay by the door. She'd have loved to comfort him, but she had never seen a man so devastated. There were no consolations that night. Max was gone, and Hans Hubermann was to blame."

在那样的年代，任何一个决定似乎都关乎生死，每一份帮助都显得沉重。但是也正因如此，我们感受到人性中最伟大的光辉，也更感叹即使是小人物也值得我们尊敬。

——徐 燕

读完这三章，我不由得停下来缓一下，总是忍不住回想书中的画面，仅仅作为一个读者去目睹这一切已经很让人沮丧了，更别说当时正在经历的人。"stealer"一词让我印象深刻。蓝天白云本来如此美丽，但现在的天空却是这一场灾难的目击者，也带走了很多无辜的灵魂。尽管如此，Max还是没有吝啬每一次可以仰望天空的机会。在去集中营的路上，人们的绝望和无助被无视，对于士兵来说，犹太人就如老鼠过街。但爸爸无法袖手旁观，他向他们伸出援手，送了些面包。这不就是Liesel心目中的超人吗？可惜犹太人需要的，不仅是一片面包，而是真的如魔法般的力量去帮助他们扭转命运。所幸，书本能治愈他们。Max离开了他们，他最后一句话"你们做的足够多了"也足够让这家人心碎了；虽然离开可能是他能为Liesel一家做的唯一的一件事了。

——袁泳施

I felt it hard to breathe while reading through these chapters. Bitter, sorrow, anger filled my heart.

Reading—Magical, powerful

... soon, a quietness started bleeding through the crowded basement. By page three, everyone was silent but Liesel. ... Liesel read on. For at least twenty minutes, she handed out the story. The youngest kids were soothed by her voice, and everyone else saw visions of the whistler running from the crime scene. Liesel did not. *The Book Thief* saw only the mechanics of the words—their bodies stranded on the paper, beaten down for her to walk on.

War—No humanity

In a small gap in the procession, there was a man, older than the others. He wore a beard and torn clothes. His eyes were the color of agony, and weightless as he was, he was too heavy for his legs to carry. Several times, he fell. The side of his face was flattened against the road. On each occasion, a soldier stood above him. "Steh' auf," he called down. "Stand up." ... They gave way one more time before he stood and took another group of steps. He was dead. The man was dead.

Kindness—Fearless

Papa reached into his paint cart and pulled something out. He made his way through the people, onto the road. The Jew stood before him, expecting another handful of derision, but he watched with everyone else as Hans Hubermann held his hand out and presented a piece of bread, like magic.

Thank—Soundless

Max left. Hans got a note from Max with only four words "You've done enough." Silence was not quiet or calm, and it was not peace.

Genius or Idiot—Indistinguishable

On the night of the parade, the idiot sat in the kitchen, drinking bitter gulps of Holtzapfel's coffee and hankering for a cigarette. He waited for the Gestapo, the soldiers, the police—for anyone—to take him away, ... waiting. Nothing came. Every unit of time carried with it the expected noise of knocking and threatening words. They did not come. The only sound was of himself. "What have I done? " he whispered again. "God, I'd love a cigarette," he answered. He was all out.

——Ting Feng

Part Seven—Eight of The Book Thief

The Idiot and the Coat Men—The Promise Keeper's Wife

导 读

今天我们一起来读“The Idiot and the Coat Men”“Dominoes and Darkness”“The Thought of Rudy Naked”“Punishment”和“The Promise Keeper's Wife”这几节。

当征兵工作人员到了Steiner家中，一位母亲为了她的孩子祈求的模样，让每一位读者都不禁心疼。

“Until one person，previously silent，came between them.

‘No，’ she said. It was repeated. ‘No.’ Even when the rest of them resumed their arguments，they were silenced again by the same voice，but now it gained momentum. ‘Please，’ Barbara Steiner begged them. ‘Not my boy.’

A mother's beg really break our hearts.”

征兵人员企图用利益和各种优越的条件，诱惑母亲支持儿子当兵，为战争献身。而她看不到这些物质条件，她心心念念的只有孩子的安全。在战争中，她的孩子只是一名士兵，一个符号，但是在她心中，Rudy独一无二。

“‘But I've heard what happens there.’ That was the unmistakable，oaky voice of his father.

‘Yes，but understand，Herr Steiner，this is all for a greater purpose. Think of the opportunities your son can have. This is really a privilege.’

‘Privileges? Like running barefoot through the snow? Like jumping from ten-meter platforms into three feet of water?’”

Rudy终于赢得了田径比赛，但是第一名的身份并没有让他获得好处，反而是让他脱颖而出，候选征兵。这真是一个黑色幽默！

“Between the doctor's coughing and wheezing，they were put through their paces.

‘Breathe in.’ Sniffle.

‘Breathe out.’ Second sniffle.

'Arms out now.' A cough. 'I said arms out.' A horrendous hail of coughing.

As humans do, the boys looked constantly at each other for some sign of mutual sympathy. None was there. All three pried their hands from their penises and held out their arms. Rudy did not feel like he was part of a master race."

我想主要介绍两个角色的转变。Rudy从一个小男孩，充满怒气的斗士，变成了一个满怀后悔、怨恨以及愤怒的小男人。这个角色的转变，注定他要保护家庭，放弃自己的快乐。

同时，Rosa也从之前章节中描写的强大女人，变成了一位伤心欲绝的妻子。她不再唠叨，反而沉默而忧伤，等待着丈夫从战场上回家。

This chapter serves not only to describe the changes that have come to Himmel Street, but also to provide a bit more examination of Rosa Hubermann's character. She tries to remain strong around those she loves, which she demonstrates by dumping cold water on Hans to get him up and ready for his train ride. But after he leaves, Liesel sees her in a softened state, holding Hans's accordion to her body. Liesel can see the great amount of love that she has for Hans, how worried she is about him. This chapter shows a rare look at Rosa's vulnerability.

It also shows the anger that's growing in Rudy, how he would like to take on the Führer in much the same way that Max used to take him on in his dreams.

工作室人员分享

Hans被应征入伍，加入到德国军队。离别时刻，站在火车站的月台上，Rosa什么也没有对Hans说，只是默默地拥抱了Hans。当天晚上，Rosa拿出Hans的手风琴，安安静静地坐在床边。过了不知多久，Rosa竟然抱着手风琴睡着了。我读到此处，一股强烈的心酸涌上心头。Rosa是多么思念她的丈夫Hans啊！Rosa其实是非常爱Hans的，虽然平时她总是对他唠唠叨叨的。睹物思人，Rosa只能用这种方法来寄托对丈夫的思念。除此之外，Rosa其实也是很担心Hans的，战争年代，丈夫会不会一去不复返呢？如果真是那样的话，Hans留下来的东西中，最能让人想起他的就是这把手风琴了。这把手风琴十分重要，它承载着太多美好的回忆了，对于Rosa而言是这样，对于Liesel是这样，对于整个家庭而言更是这样。手风琴给他们带来了美妙的音乐，手风琴能让大家想起一切关于Hans的事情。起初，我以为Hans会把手风琴带在身边，跟着他入伍，读到这里我明白了为什么Hans决定不带上他心爱的手风琴，因为Hans自己很清楚，手风琴对于Rosa、对于Liesel的意义。他也清楚自己不一定能安全回来，但在他离开的这些日子里，他希望手风琴能代替他本人，陪伴Rosa和Liesel。祈求Hans终有一天能平安归来！

——陈雪芬

Rudy的家让人印象深刻，作者用独特的写作方式描述了Rudy家人的相处方式。我想，Rudy就像是他们在玩的多米诺骨牌吗？他们会有同样的命运吗？但拥有私心的我不想Rudy那么快离开我们。

在“Punishment”那个长章节里，那种让人窒息的恐惧感支配着我。自那天Mr. Steiner和Hans被带走，我就开始陷入想象，标题是“惩罚”，会是很艰难的未来在等着他们吗？我不忍细想。但讽刺的是，这些惩罚居然是给这两个义无反顾去帮助群众的、不忍放弃自己孩子的爸爸的。可想而知，战争中的人类有多么悲惨的命运！

但我也被家人之间深深的牵绊所感动，家人的爱在战争中无疑是最珍贵也是最无价的。当papa要离开时，他跟Liesel说：“You're half woman now. Look after mama，will you? Could you look after my accordion？”。面对离别，他们都不忍心让对方伤心，但他们彼此的信任是最感人的。很难说再见，但生活还要继续，希望Liesel会保护好这一切。

——袁泳施

“There was no denying the fact that Rosa Hubermann was sitting on the edge of the bed with her husband's accordion tied to her chest. Her fingers hovered above the keys. She did not move. She didn't even appear to be breathing.

The keys were not stuck. The bellows didn't breathe. There was only the moonlight，like a long strand of hair in *The Curtain*，and there was Rosa.”

作者的叙述一直都是浅浅的、淡淡的，没有大喜大悲，只有一些平和的笔触。但是慢慢的一些小细节就会让我们感动。Rosa的形象一直都是粗鲁和有点小寒酸的，从最初用木勺打Liesel骂她小母猪，到在防空洞里太担心Liesel而把她的手都捏疼了的小细节，对于突然来到家里的流浪汉一样的Max，Rosa的善良和淳朴就一点一点地显现在我们眼前，那个平日里喜欢斤斤计较、粗鲁、没有多少教养的Rosa在面对生活的窘迫和整天担惊受怕的时候，丝毫没有怨言，让我们越来越能感受到她的那份坚强和勇敢。这个拥有能轻易惹到每个她遇到的人的特殊本领的女人，在黑暗中抱着奔赴战场的丈夫的手风琴，整夜保持这个姿势坐在床沿，没有碰过一下琴键，也没有拉开手风琴。陪伴她的只有淡淡的月光和默默注视她的养女。我们又看到了她的柔情。这一幕不止会在Liesel的脑海中挥之不去，也会让我们深深地感动。

——王之光

在“The Promise Keeper's Wife”这一章中，凌晨3点的火车站里，Hans Hubermann 被征入伍。虽不愿去，却也无力反抗。一家人清晨在火车站台道别。

父女相拥，但我们没看到哭哭啼啼、哭天抢地的场面。父亲只是轻声交代女儿，替他保管好风琴，继续为大家念书。

“No hours，no minutes till goodbye：He holds her. To say something，to say anything，he speaks over her shoulder. ‘Could you look after my accordion，Liesel? I decided not to take it.’ Now he finds something he truly means. ‘And if there are more raids，keep reading in the shelter.’ The girl feels the continued sign of her slightly growing chest. It hurts as it touches the bottom of his ribs. ‘Yes，Papa.’ A millimeter from her eyes，she stares at the fabric of his suit. She speaks into him. ‘Will you play us something when you come home？’”

女儿也只是轻轻地提了一个请求：“回家，继续拉琴给我们听。”“Hans Hubermann smiled at his daughter then and the train was ready to leave. He reached out and gently held her face in his hand. ‘I promise，’ he said，and he made his way into the carriage.They watched each other as the train pulled away. Liesel and Rosa waved. Hans Hubermann grew smaller and smaller，and his hand held nothing now but empty air.On the platform，people disappeared around them until no one else was left. There was only the wardrobe-shaped woman and the thirteen-year-old girl.”

Hans Hubermann 带着对女儿的承诺走向未知。但我们知道，这个承诺会是他克服一切困难、早日回家的力量。

——郑剑湘

这两个“怪物”来见Rudy的父母，说服他们允许Rudy上一所精英学校。Rudy的母亲不想让她的孩子和男人一起去。她和她的丈夫都听说过这样的学校里的学生所遭受的残酷待遇。最后，男人们离开了，Rudy不打算去学校了。这个决定会使Rudy后悔。

Rudy的学校在前一周就做出了录取他的决定。他和另外两个男孩被叫到学校办公室，被告知要去做体检。在场的护士向Rudy的老师解释说，他们正在创建一个“由身体和智力都很发达的德国人组成的新班级”。

考试结束后，孩子们听到大人们说他们会带走两个孩子。Rudy就是其中之一，这就是为什么“怪物”会来到他家。

11月的一天，Hans收到一封信，信上说他已被纳粹分子接纳。两天后，另一封信来了，告知他被征召加入德国军队。Hans、Rosa和Liesel听到这个消息都惊呆了。

几天后，Liesel发现Mr. Steiner也要去打仗。

就在Hans去参加训练的前一天晚上，Hans和朋友去当地的酒吧喝得酩酊大醉。尽管他的妻子对他并不满意，但第二天在火车站，一想到他要离开，她还是难过。Hans告诉Liesel要照顾好妈妈和他的手风琴。他答应等他从战场上回来后为她弹奏一曲。

一天晚上，Liesel发现Rosa坐在床上，紧紧地把手风琴拽在她的胸前。她没有演奏，她只是需要手风琴给她带来安慰。作为一个妻子，她深深地思念着自己的丈夫。

我的感觉就像书中第416页所说的：

"On the ration cards of Nazi Germany，there was no listing for punishment，but everyone had to take their turn. For some it was death in a foreign country during the war. For others it was poverty and guilt when the war was over，when six million discoveries were made throughout Europe."

——宋碧燕

这几章中有两个关于Rudy和Liesel的片段让我忍不住嘴角上扬。虽然现在是战时紧张的时候，可是不管是Rudy还是Liesel，他们都还是孩子。一个脱光了衣服参加身体检查，各种尴尬紧张，甚至都吓哭了；另一个听他说了这个事情忍不住脑子里幻想他的裸体。这两个细节让我忍不住幻想：如果不是在战争年代的话，如果不是在这场残酷的战争背景下，这也许可以从一个可怕的悲剧变成一个甜甜的青葱爱情故事。

不过反过来说，战争虽然很残酷，但是也很难磨灭人性，有些情感是战争也无法压抑的。

——莫 然

相比前几章的内容，这一部分看起来令人沮丧。前面的部分至少有一部分幽默或甜蜜。但这部分就像天空一样，是灰色的。每个人都感到沮丧和窒息。Rudy被裸体考试羞辱了。Rudy、Rudy的父亲和Liesel的养父Hans被派去参战。Liesel、Rosa和Rudy的母亲都非常担心，想念他们。他们无能为力，失去了对生活的控制。Hans生活在内疚之中，试图向Liesel道别，要她答应照顾Rosa。Rosa甚至在严寒的天气里给Hans浇水。我在想，也许在她的内心深处，她希望他生病，这样他就不会被派去参战。或者她生他的气，惩罚他制造麻烦。但有一点是肯定的，就是她对Hans的爱，是如此的温柔，深深地融化在日常生活的点滴中。

我欣赏其中的一些句子，它们用得很漂亮。在第417页，"Hans Hubermann was being rewarded..."——真是讽刺。在第419页，"When they come and ask you for one of your children，... you're supposed to say yes."——既讽刺又残酷。在第421页，"In the living room，Rosa was snoring with enthusiasm."——形象的对

比。在第423页，“But it was not the usual wink. It was heavier，clumsier. The post-Max version，the hangover version.”——美丽却带有一点忧伤。在第430页，“She waited for the suffocation of sleep.”——令人有筋疲力尽、窒息的感觉。这些美丽的文字都精准地描述了书中人物细腻的感情。虽然书中这部分内容太让人压抑了，但是这些精准的词汇却是这一部分里唯一令人愉悦的地方了。

——李秀文

最让我意外的是Hans被应征入伍了。Liesel在车站送别父亲、母亲抱着手风琴在月夜想念父亲、Rudy的愤怒疾走等情节，都深深地触动了我。然而今天，我不想再直面战争的残酷，我想分享一个有趣的章节，那就是Rudy被要求脱光检查身体的文字描写。

“When his underpants came down，it was with abject humiliation that he stood in the small，cool office. His self-respect around his ankles。”（P413）

当内衣都被脱掉之后，Rudy的尴尬跃然纸上。透过文字，我们仿佛看到处于青春期的Rudy，羞得面红耳赤，恨不得找一个地洞钻进去。没想到，他还把这件事告诉了Liesel。结果同样处于青春期的Liesel晚上睡不着觉了。

“She would lie in bed，missing Max，wondering where he was，praying that he was alive，but somewhere，standing among all of it，was Rudy. He glowed in the dark，completely naked. There was great dread in that vision，especially the moment when he was forced to remove his hands. It was disconcerting to say the least，but for some reason，she couldn’t stop thinking about it.”

这段描写把一个对异性充满好奇的少女刻画得很细腻。一个裸体的男性在黑暗中发光，Liesel忍不住想象Rudy把手拿开的画面。这里作者其实想表达Rudy和Liesel都由小孩长成少年了。对异性的好奇和朦胧的认识是成长的标志。

——关少娟

在“Punishment”这一章中，Hans先生受到了惩罚——他应征加入了德国军队。军队需要更多的人，Hans他们并没有权利拒绝，只因这是他们的责任和义务。得知这个消息，一家人都陷入了沉默。入伍就意味着分离。爸爸非常平静，而妈妈内心很悲伤。Liesel太小了，不会掩饰自己的感情，她呆呆地看着天空。爸爸要去打仗，Max也离开了。战争导致了家人和朋友的分离。

另一个场景，Hans收到入伍信后，他和亚历克斯去酒吧度过了疯狂的最后一夜。他过去内敛敏感，但在最后一天借着酒精，他释放了自己，那天晚上两人都喝得不省人事。

“‘I can’t lose you now，too.’In response，the hungover man digs his elbow into the table and covers his right eye：‘You’re half a woman now，Liesel.’He wants to break down but wards it off. He rides through it.‘Look after Mama，will you？’The girl can make only half a nod to agree.‘Yes，Papa.’”

爸爸的离开迫使Liesel一夜之间长大了，作为家中的半个女人，现在轮到她去学着照顾自己的妈妈了。真令人心碎，我希望Hans能够活着回家。

——董筱妍

Part Eight of The Book Thief

The Collector—The Anarchist's Suit Collection

导 读

今天我们来读“The Collector”“The Bread Eaters”“The Hidden Sketchbook”和“The Anarchist's Suit Collection”四个小节。

在“The Collector”这一章节中，我们了解到了Hans的工作——空袭特勤队the LSE。Hans的工作就是当空袭来临时，他要留守在地面上，负责扑灭大火，解救那些被困的人。然而Hans的战友在他来的第一天就告诉他，空袭特勤队，还有另一个名字，叫“收尸人”。这是为什么呢？

其实LSE的工作是非常危险的，正如Hans所说的那样，“Just remember that the enemy here is not in front of you.”“the enemy isn't over the hill or in any specific direction. It's all around.”。

其次，因为时常有倒塌的房屋，整个城市都被烟尘所覆盖，而Hans和他的队友们也是全身沾满了灰尘。正如文中所描述的那样，“His hands were packed tightly with splinters，and his teeth were caked with residue from the fallout. Both lips were set with moist dust that had hardened，and there wasn't a pocket，a thread，or a hidden crease in his uniform that wasn't covered in a film left by the loaded air.”。

然而，这份工作最糟糕之处不是漫天的灰尘，而是他们工作中所遇到的人。那Hans遇到什么人了？Hans遇到了在城市废墟中苦苦寻找自己家人的人，如那个寻找儿子的妇女，她的儿子正好也叫“Rudy”。Hans还遇到了那些在空袭中受伤的人，如那位受伤严重的老头。而Hans见到最多的还是在空袭中不幸死去的人的尸体，如那位已经死去许久的12岁男孩。Hans如何能去拯救这些人呢？他唯一能做到的就是学着忘记这一切，学着面对死亡并对死亡习以为常，又或者只能对别人说出善意的谎言。Hans和他的队友根本拯救不了任何人，所谓的“空袭特勤队”唯一能干的活就是“收尸”，因此LSE也被称为“收尸人”队伍。

以下这几句是我印象最为深刻的，它生动地描绘出空袭下城市里上映的一幕幕人间悲喜剧。“As the density subsided，the roll call of names limped through the ruptured streets, sometimes ending with an ash-filled embrace or a knelt-down howl of grief. They accumulated, hour by hour, like sweet and sour dreams, waiting to happen.”意思是：“随着灰尘逐渐散去，人们在只剩下残垣断壁的街道上一瘸一拐地走着，嘴里叫着这些名字。有时候这一幕会以两个人满身灰尘的拥抱结束，有时候是以双膝跪下的号啕大哭而剧终。这一幕一幕的戏剧，一小时又一小时地重复上演，就像一个个甜蜜而酸楚的梦。”德国人，在纳粹统治下的德国人，也正遭受着家破人亡的惨痛悲剧，而这一切都是由战争造成的。在这一章节里，作者通过Hans的工作——LSE，向读者展示了战争的残酷及战争对人世间造成的创伤。

在“The Bread Eaters”这个章节里，我们很高兴又能读到有关Rudy和Liesel的故事，这次他们俩做了一件很有意义的事。冒着被逮住和挨鞭子的风险，Rudy和Liesel骑车来到游街队伍的前头，把面包碎撒在犹太人经过的路上。最终他们被领队的士兵发现了，但幸运的是他们没有被抓到，而且队伍中的大多犹太人吃到了面包。

“Was this Germany? Was this Nazi Germany?”在书中第440页出现的这两个句子引起了我的注意。是谁提出了这两个问题？是Liesel吗？是死神吗？还是作者？这两个句子出现在这里是要表达什么意思呢？在我看来，作者是想告诉我们，即使在这个有那么多人憎恨犹太人的纳粹德国，也还是有一些人，他们心中美好的东西是战争带不走的，那就是“善良和仁爱”。

在“The Hidden Sketchbook”这个章节里，提到Max创作的一本简单的素描本*The Hidden Sketchbook*。我认为里面除了一些画和涂鸦外，还隐含着很多思想和故事。“The Word Shaker”就是其中之一。在这个奇怪的故事里，有4个主要人物，而这4个人物都与Max生活中出现的真实人物相对应，他们分别是：

1.The strange, small man. 这个奇奇怪怪的矮小的男人，他想通过他的文字去统治世界，他想在整个德国建造一座伟大的文字森林。他是一名独裁者。他指代的是Hitler。

2.The small, skinny girl. 这个瘦小的女孩，她是最佳的采字人，因为她有欲望，尤其是对学习文字有着极大的欲望。她指代的是Liesel。

3.The new axman. 这个新的斧头工，女孩的朋友。他努力地爬上树，最终和女孩一起从树上下来，然后他们走在树桩上。他指代的是Liesel的朋友，其实就是Max自己。

4. The word shakers.其他采字者，是已经被迷惑或催眠的人们，他们努力去采摘一些丑陋的文字。他们试图用斧头砍倒女孩在做的树木。他们其实就是生活在纳粹统治下的德国人。

Max画这些画、写这些故事，是想告诉Liesel什么呢？我认为，Max想告诉Liesel文字的力量是巨大的，文字不仅能摧毁人类世界，而且能拯救人们、拯救世界。

我们再来仔细观察一下Max所画的那些树木。在属于元首的树上，我们看到了纳粹标志。除此之外，我们还看到了树上有一些贬义词，如“hate，hatred，fear”。这些词语都是被元首用来思想统治国家和人民的。而女孩的树比其他树木都要高大、强壮，而且怎么砍都砍不倒，正如文中所说：“The world shook，and when everything finally settled，the tree was laid out among the rest of the forest. It could never destroy all of it，but if nothing else，a different-colored path was carved through it.”。

在这本素描本上，Max还写道：“I hope you can find some good in it.”。我想Max想以此鼓励Liesel继续勇敢地向前走，通过阅读尽可能地多学习文字，从而认识到文字的伟大意义。

最后，“The Anarchist’s Suit Collection”这一章节给大家呈现了十分甜蜜又有趣的一幕。让我们来看看书中第455页的这几段文字：

“Rudy placed the lantern on the counter and came toward her in mock-anger，and Liesel had to admit that a nervousness started gripping her. It was with both relief and disappointment that she watched him trip and fall on the disgraced mannequin.

On the floor，Rudy laughed.

Then he closed his eyes，clenching them hard.

Liesel rushed over.

She crouched above him.

Kiss him，Liesel，kiss him.

‘Are you all right，Rudy？Rudy？’

‘I miss him，’said the boy，sideways，across the floor.”

哇！Rudy和Liesel他们俩太紧张又害羞了。让人感到遗憾的是，他们俩最终也没有亲吻对方。前面几个章节的内容都与战争息息相关，给读者的感觉是比较压抑的，但到了这一章，我们读到的是发生在两位小青年身上有趣的事，让我们感受到一丝喜悦。尽管我们都知道最后Rudy死了，他再也没有机会亲吻到Liesel了。战争是残酷的，但是人间还有爱，还有值得去追寻的美好事物。读完这几章，我最大的感受是：Time waits for no man. Cherish our life and our time with the family，with the one you love. Express our love bravely. 时光不等人，珍惜我们的生活，珍惜我们与家人和所爱的人相处的时光，并且勇敢地向他们表达自己的爱意。

工作室人员分享

我之所以想分享“The Anarchist’s Suit Collection”这一部分，因为这是我读到现在感觉比较轻松愉快的一个场面，之前的描述都是战争给人类带来的残酷和痛苦，灰色调太浓厚，让人感到压抑和焦虑。但是在读到这一部分时，感受Rudy

和Liesel偷偷进The Steiner那一幕，既让人感到不太道德，但是又充满了童趣。在平安夜那个夜晚，Liesel想出个鬼主意，她说想送给Rudy一个礼物，当然她是没钱买的，所以她想到了裁缝铺。Liesel和Rudy的对话也被描写得很风趣。他们之间好像真的很有默契。当Rudy问："那份礼物到底在哪儿？"Liesel说："先别急。"Rudy马上就明白了，他嗅到了Liesel贼溜溜的眼神和跃跃欲试的手指，她浑身散发着小偷的气息。当Liesel问道："你有钥匙吗？"Rudy马上就明白过来了，他回到屋子里，很快又出来，模仿着Viktor的口吻说："该出门买东西了。"在那个物资匮乏的年代，他们偷偷进店试穿西服给他们带来了很多快乐。Rudy穿好精致的西服，映照在灯笼下面，反衬他西装底下肮脏的衬衫和Rudy那双破烂的鞋子时，他们更加兴奋不已。Rudy突然被躺在地上的假人模特绊倒了，Liesel冲上前去，Rudy心里想："亲我亲我。"但是Liesel却说："你没事吧，Rudy？Rudy？""圣诞快乐！"他们之间的感情描写也是风趣幽默、生动形象的。

——宋 蕾

战争的废墟下，一个小男孩的尸体满是灰尘与污垢。这个年龄的他，本应在父母的庇护下，无忧无虑地玩耍。可是，他已经离开了这个充满杀戮的世界。如果此刻，他的父母看到他离开时的样子，该是怎样一种撕心裂肺的疼痛。于是，Hans和他的同伴说了一个善意的谎言。这是我看过的最简短又最震撼人心的对话。

"They found a woman calling the name Rudolf. She was drawn to the four men and met them in the mist. Her body was frail and bent with worry.

'Have you seen my boy？'

'How old is he？' the sergeant asked.

'Twelve.'

... but the sergeant could not bring himself to tell her or point the way...'You won't find him down there.'

The bent woman still clung to hope. She called over her shoulder as she half walked，half ran."（P436）

男孩的妈妈虽然没有得到答案，却仍是满怀希望。尽管知道凶多吉少，但是至少她没有看到尸体，说明孩子还有活着的可能。作者用了clung这个词，虽然希望渺茫，但妈妈还是紧紧抓住，也许孩子突然就站在她的面前了呢。虽然不是正面描写士兵在战场上厮杀，但是这个情节从侧面给读者展现了一个最残酷的画面。亲人的生离死别，幼童的去世，无不让读者动容。

另一方面，战争也让一个小孩瞬间成长了，从一个偷水果的调皮小男孩成长为一个善良、勇敢、有担当的男子汉。

“How things had changed，from fruit stealer to bread giver. His blond hair，although darkening，was like a candle. She heard his stomach growl—and he was giving people bread.”（P440）

两个小孩冒着被打的危险，给犹太人撒面包。最感人的是他们的肚子也饿得咕咕叫。战争摧毁城市、掠夺生命，但是善良与正义从来不会缺席。

——关少娟

这本书的这一部分写得相当人性化。在最困难的时候，Hans仍然努力照顾别人、帮助别人。一开始，我担心Hans的安全。幸运的是，这是个假警报。后来，善于处理危机的妻子Rosa给了Liesel一本Max的素描本，里面有一个美丽的故事，可能暗示了他在哪里。Liesel和Rudy之间的甜蜜互动，让我们看到他们度过了一个心满意足的圣诞节。人们互相关心、互相牵挂，与战争形成了强烈的对比，从甜到苦，从热到冷，从暖心肠到无情。

在读这本书的时候，一个问题经常出现在我的脑海里。那就是：我们应该活在当下还是继续等待？

我们常说，真爱经得起时间的考验，如果是真爱它就可以等待，或者只是没有什么可以失去，只是忘记它。但是当我读到这本书，读到战争年代生活的时候，我对拖延理论就不是很肯定了。人们是不是应该因为不知道自己还能活多久而活在当下？但他们能接受感性决定带来的后果吗？就像Hans那样？也许有些东西太有价值了，我们只是太看重它了，导致我们对此再谨慎也不为过。但是我们会后悔太迟才遇见真爱吗？人生苦短，不应活着留有遗憾，因此我深感困惑。

——李秀文

Hans的信件里说的全部是自己很安全，一切安好。这个小细节让我感觉很触动，因为我发现好多出门在外的人都有这个习惯——报喜不报忧。明明自己在外面很苦，但还是为了不让家里人担心而说谎，这可能就是white lies吧。

后面又继续描绘了一个普通人在战争面前的无力。除了get used to it之外，并没有什么能做的事情了。这样的无力感会对人的心态产生很大的影响，可能慢慢就对生命没有那么在意了，反正这个世界每分钟都有人在走向死亡，但是不管怎么目睹别人的死亡，自己在乎的家人的生命是最宝贵的。正是因为生命无常，活着才显得那么不易、那么珍贵，我们更要好好珍惜自己、守护家人。

可是这也让我看到了一个悖论：我们国家现在处在和平年代，没有什么战争，可是现在青少年的心理压力却非常大，心理有问题的也不在少数，甚至不少有自杀倾向的……所以真的不存在什么绝对的好或坏的年代，每个年代都有它的问题，都有很多在挣扎着活着的人，他们都在经历着不一样的事情，也都在克服不一样的困难，最终能好好活着而不被无常的世事压垮的人都是拥有强大灵魂的人。

——莫 然

在“The Collector”一章里面感受到的是 sadness。有很多悲伤的画面让我印象深刻，如爆炸过后一个老人拿着自己的一条腿的画面，他对Hans说：“你能帮我支起来吗？”当Hans带他走出迷雾时，还没等到走出来，他就已经死了。

“Midway through the shift，there was an old man who staggered defenselessly through the streets. As Hans finished stabilizing a building，he turned to find him at his back，waiting calmly for his turn. A bloodstain was signed across his face. It trailed off down his throat and neck. He was wearing a white shirt with a dark red collar and he held his leg as if it was next to him. ‘Could you prop me up now，young man？’

Hans picked him up and carried him out of the haze.

A SMALL，SAD NOTE

I visited that small city street with the man still in Hans Hubermann’s arms. The sky was white-horse gray.

It wasn’t until he placed him down on a patch of concrete-coated grass that Hans noticed.

‘What is it？’ one of the other men asked.

Hans could only point.

‘Oh.’ A hand pulled him away. ‘Get used to it，Hubermann.’”

还有一具12岁孩子的尸体，以及他的妈妈找他的身影。

“The corpse was facedown.

It lay in a blanket of powder and dust，and it was holding its ears.

It was a boy.

Perhaps eleven or twelve years old.”

在“Bread Eaters”一章里面感受到的是暖。温暖于Liesel和Rudy对犹太人的帮助。另外感动于当两个孩子被纳粹士兵发现后，意外发现有一个士兵放过Liesel的画面。很暖，很感动。

“They ran，and after a hundred meters，the hunched breath of the soldier drew closer. It sidled up next to her and she waited for the accompanying hand.

She was lucky.

All she received was a boot up the ass and a fistful of words. ‘Keep running，little girl，you don’t belong here！’ She ran and she did not stop for at least another mile. Branches sliced her arms，pinecones rolled at her feet，and the taste of Christmas needles chimed inside her lungs.”

在“the Anarchist’s Suit Collection”一章里感受到了小男生和小女生之间的快乐，甚至嗅到了一丝爱情萌芽的味道。Liesel会失落于Rudy的没有亲下去。

“Rudy placed the lantern on the counter and came toward her in mock-anger（假装生气），and Liesel had to admit that a nervousness started gripping her. It was with both relief and disappointment that she watched him trip and fall on the disgraced mannequin.

On the floor，Rudy laughed.

Then he closed his eyes，clenching them hard.”

这几章给我的感受就是有悲伤也有快乐，情绪跟随着情节起起伏伏。这就是那时的生活，一边是成年人直面现实的悲伤，一边是孩子们不谙世事的童真，让人感慨不已。

——徐 燕

在“The Hidden Sketchbook”这一章中，圣诞节前的一次突袭，让避难所里的每个人都安静地听Liesel 朗读*The Whistler*。空袭后，Liesel和Rosa回到家，Rosa剪开被套，拿出了Max的素描本。Rosa告诉Liesel，Max说过等Liesel准备好了就给她，其实Liesel早已经准备好了。书的封面上写着*The Word Shaker*：*A Small Collection of Thoughts for Liesel Meminger*. Liesel在厨房里看着。第一部分内容，大都是配有标题的涂鸦、想法、梦想，或者是Vandenburg家族的回忆。

Rosa再次表达了她对Liesel的骄傲——她觉得Liesel已经足够成熟，能够理解Max内心深处的想法了。这是Liesel一生中又一本重要的书，引导她将语言作为有力的手段去克服、消除仇恨和虐待。

这本书的第二部分是一个带插图的寓言，叫“The Word Shaker”，死神再现了这些页面。故事开始于Hitler发现了语言的力量，然后决定用语言来统治世界。在这个故事里，文字像种子一样生长，很快Hitler就种出了巨大的森林，当文字经过传送带时，它们就会进入人们的大脑。有些人爬上树，向下面的人传递信息，这些人被称为“word shakers”。

Max的故事基本上是小说主题的浓缩——语言对善和恶的影响力量。Hitler决定用语言来统治世界，暗示语言比武器、金钱等的影响力更强大。他种植的文字森林，实际上是对纳粹的宣传。

——郑剑湘

战争中没有人能逃得过悲哀和伤痛。前面章节里讲述了Liesel经历过的生离死别，故事发展到这里，借助养父Hans入伍，把读者的视角转向了更多老百姓的生离死别和悲哀场面上。Hans入伍后被安排负责收集尸体。这是一个多么残忍、非人道的任务啊！Hans目睹了战争中太多的悲哀故事了，其中令我印象最深刻的是一位母亲在战火中寻找自己12岁孩子的情景。

“They found a woman calling the name Rudolf. She was drawn to the four men and met them in the mist. Her body was frail and bent with worry. ‘Have you seen my boy? ’

‘How old is he? ’ the sergeant asked.

‘Twelve.’

... but the sergeant could not bring himself to tell her or point the way... ‘You won’t find him down there.’

The bent woman still clung to hope. She called over her shoulder as she half walked，half ran.”

看到这样的画面，作为妈妈的我也会有窒息的感觉。妈妈该如何面对自己孩子以这么痛苦的方式离开这个世界呢？Hans那善意的谎言也许给妈妈留下了找回孩子的一点希望。

——莫洁文

在这几章中，我们可以看到三种工作——the collector、the bread eater 和the word shaker。它们有不同的含义。

The collector是Hans，他在军队里当过尸体收集者。工作内容是营救在突袭中被困的人。事实上，那些人受了重伤，甚至已经死亡。这份工作最糟糕的部分就是要面对活着的人。他们固执地四处游荡，呼喊着她或他亲戚的名字。有时以一个满是灰烬的拥抱或一声悲伤的嚎叫结束。Hans不得不面对那些不幸。

接下来，我们来谈谈 the bread eaters。他们是一群被游街示众的犹太人，被带到达豪。Rudy在路上分发面包。虽然Rudy很饿，但他还是把这些面包分给了他们。Rudy从一个偷水果的人变成了送面包的人。

最后一个人是the word shaker，来自Max的素描本。Liesel就是书中的主角。爬上文字之树的人被称为“鲨鱼”。最好的文字撼动者是那些懂得文字真正力量的人。Liesel爬到树上去保护他们。Max来了，他们成了朋友。他们齐心协力修剪他们的友谊之树。这本书是送给Liesel最好的礼物。

——董筱妍

如往常一样，这些章节依然让人心痛、引人落泪。两个爸爸被带走了，战争更严峻了，人们的生活更糟糕了。作者也开始不留余地地用大量篇幅告诉我们战争有多残酷。Hans被任命去LSE，他是一名尸体收集者。他原本是一个多么善良；多么温暖的人啊，这份工作对他来说是残酷而无奈的，也是非常不人道的，更别说他还得去躲避炸弹，那是多么危险啊。收集尸体时，不知道他心里作何感想。“In late November，he had his first smoky taste of an actual raid. The truck was mobbed by rubble and there was much running and shouting. Fires were burning and the ruined cases of buildings were piled up in mounds. Framework leaned. The smoke bombs stood like matchsticks in the ground，filling the city's lungs."战火蔓延，人们乱作一团，关于战争的片段即如电影般的画面掠过我的脑海，战争当前，人类真的很无力，看着人们死去更是让人难以忍受的。

——袁泳施

Hans和Mr. Steiner没有被驱逐出德国。Mr. Steiner被派到一家军队医院补衣服。当Hans在伦敦政治经济学院的空袭特别部队时，他是负责在空袭后进入城镇捡碎石、灭火和转移死者的。

这项工作并不容易，因为他们经常被烟雾和污垢覆盖，而且必须处理死者。他们还经常被幸存者询问是否见过失踪的亲人。Hans是一个心地善良的人，他能做的只是忘记死亡的痛苦和悲伤。有时候，善意的谎言对别人来说也是一种希望，因为他们能借此继续活下去。

在圣诞节前，Rosa把Max留给Liesel的速写本拿了出来，里面的故事是一个关于Hitler如何用文字掌权的。他写了Hitler如何种植文字，这些文字长成了树，他用文字养活人民。然后，一个女孩为了一个在自己国家里被放逐的病人哭泣，她的眼泪干涸后变成一颗种子，这颗种子长成了一棵不可砍伐的大树。这本写生本所描述的正是当时德国残酷的现实。但Max从未失去希望，也从未放弃生活。我认为无论我们面临多么困难的情况，我们都不应该放弃希望。

1942年的平安夜，宵禁后，Liesel去看望Rudy。她知道她不应该出去，但她想给他一个圣诞礼物。首先她得说服Rudy帮她。他们用Rudy父亲西服店的钥匙闯进了店里。她四处看了看，找到了一套蓝色的西装，那正是Rudy的尺码。这是她送给Rudy的礼物。他穿那套衣服很好看，但却让他意识到父亲已经离开的现实。

剩下的人只能勇敢地生活下去，深深地思念着他们的家人。我们可以失去一切，但不能失去希望。

——宋碧燕

我最喜欢的是"The Hidden Sketchbook"一章中Max送给Liesel的*The Word Shaker*，这本像寓言又像童话故事的书。在书里，Max告诉Liesel，那个"把头发朝与大家相反的方向分、留着一撮小胡子的狂热德国人"是如何撷取文字，并通过文字来控制德国人思想的，从而把那些被催眠了的人们放到传输带上，去为他统治世界的狂妄梦想献出生命。他还告诉她，最优秀的撷取文字的人是那些懂得文字真正力量的人。Max觉得Liesel就是那个小小的、瘦弱的、爬上那棵树爬得最高的人。她的内心充满了热切的求知欲，对文字充满渴求，她终将长成参天大树，不惧元首，从而获得自由。这些书和文字，帮助Liesel在未来的岁月里，一点点摆脱纳粹舆论机器的控制，在思想上自由健康地成长。

可能也正因如此，当Max在Liesel的生活中消失以后，在犹太人被游街示众遭受惩罚的时候，偷书贼冒着被处罚的危险给犹太人面包、给他们同情，以减轻自己作为旁观者的痛苦。她同时还在思考：那他们的痛苦呢？那些脚步蹒跚、饱受折磨的人的痛苦呢？那些在集中营大门后的痛苦呢？

在战争年代里，死亡虽然如影随形，但是文字就像是种子，一点点地深埋在每个人的心中，庇护苦难中的人。

——王之光

important, but she enjoyed the fact that the roomful of books belonged to the woman. It was she who introduced her to the library in the first place and gave her the initial, even literal, window of opportunity. This way was better. It all seemed to fit."（P349）

读完这几个章节，我的感悟是：与书中的战火纷飞不同，我们身处和平安宁的时代，这是一件多么幸福的事啊！然而生活中不如意之事十之八九，每个人都会有沮丧、悲伤的时候，让心灵获得平静最好的方法，大概就是阅读了。因为文字能够滋养人的心灵。都说知识就是力量，文字也是力量。愿每一个人都能健康快乐地生活。

工作室人员分享

在大雪中，Michael把他哥哥的死告诉了Rosa。他所说的话和沾满鲜血的手让Rosa大吃一惊。简单的文字、生动的画面在她的脑海中浮现。然后死神分享了一个关于Robert的小故事。在一个寒冷的日子里，他的腿被炸吹断了。他弟弟保证Robert很快就会回家。Robert挣扎了三天。最后，他被死神带到了临时医院。每个人都想活着。然而，Robert的生命正在消逝。我能感觉到他的无力感。

Liesel的爸爸还没回来，Liesel只能做一些轻松的事情来消磨时间。在她14岁的前几个星期，Liesel梦到了她身边的人——她的弟弟、母亲、Hans和赤裸的Rudy。她非常想念他们，但只有Rosa在家陪她。每天晚上，Rosa坐在那里，拉着手风琴，祈祷她的丈夫能活着回来。战争让战士们奔赴战场，而他们的家人则在家中祈祷着、煎熬着。

——董筱妍

"The Bitter Taste of Questions"这一章深深地触动了我。因伤退役的Hans终于平安归来。在他回来的那一天，一家人聚在一起，享受着战火纷飞中短暂的喜悦。然而，从战场上回来的Hans并没有多少幸存后的狂喜，而是为他们身边发生的一切感到黯然心痛。书中的"A broken leg was certainly something to celebrate."这句话让人觉得心酸和苦涩。Liesel和Rosa在厨房抱在一起，跳起来，断了一条腿，这可真是一件值得庆祝的事。还有Rudy努力挤出来的笑容。这个苦涩的笑容也让我深深体会到了战争的苦涩，在战争和生死面前，断了一条腿是值得庆祝的，看到小伙伴的爸爸回来了，勉强的欢笑背后是对自己爸爸的担忧和挂念。作者避开了正面描写战场上的残酷与血腥，但是侧面描写遭受着战争折磨的普通民众，会使故事和人变得更加鲜活，也能让人体会到战争给人带来的伤痛。

——王之光

Liesel和Rudy回到市长家偷书，但这次市长夫人把饼干放在了桌子上。Liesel

带走了饼干，还有一本叫作*The Last Human Stranger*的书，但是当她爬出窗户的时候，看到市长夫人正站在窗户旁边，穿着一件印有纳粹十字的浴袍。Liesel突然意识到图书室一定是市长夫人的，而不是市长的。夫人告诉Liesel，以前她经常和她儿子在那里读书。她说Liesel是最近经常出入这个房间的人，Liesel不好意思地离开了。

——郑剑湘

这几章作者继续讲述着战争的残酷、人们所遭受的苦难以及在这种水深火热的情形下邻里之间彼此温暖的举动，其中一些场景给我留下了深刻的印象。在“the Snows of Stalingrad”一章，作者详细地描写了Frau Holtzapfel小儿子的逝去，通过大儿子Michael和Liesel的对话、Michael和Rosa的对话、一个名叫Pieter的士兵和小儿子的对话以及作者的自述，将战争的残酷活生生地表现了出来。加上雪天这一景象描写更能勾起读者内心的伤痛。

“In Frau Holtzapfel's kitchen，Liesel read. The pages waded by unheard，and for me，when the Russian scenery fades in my eyes，the snow refuses to stop falling from the ceiling. The kettle is covered，as is the table. The humans，too，are wearing patches of snow on their heads and shoulders. The brother shivers. The woman weeps. And the girl goes on reading...”（P470）

“The Ageless Brother”一章写到了Liesel对逝去的母亲和弟弟的怀念、Rosa对Hans的想念和祈祷。其中提到了*The Last Human Stranger*中的一个句子：“There were people everywhere on the city street，but the stranger could not have been more alone if it were empty.”。在我看来，这句话足以表达出人们对战争的无奈，将因为战争而痛失亲人的痛苦、孤独描写得淋漓尽致。

——李 丹

书中的这一部分再次讲述了战争的残酷，许多家庭因此支离破碎。有时候死亡并不是最难的，往往亲人死后的生活是最难应付的。Liesel走进市长夫人的生活之前，她没有灵魂。Liesel就像她的儿子一样，也对阅读很感兴趣。不幸的是，像市长夫人那样的人还有很多，战争让人们生活在恐惧的黑暗中。

然而，这部分也是苦乐参半的。Liesel和Rudy从市长夫人那里拿了些不新鲜的饼干。他们之间的对话很有趣。我很欣赏第459页上的“feast”这个词，“His eyes feasted on the cookies ...”，非常有画面感，我们可以在脑海中想象到Rudy有趣滑稽的表情。最令人惊讶的是Hans，Hans要回家了。但在此之前，我们好像目睹了其中的原因，那一起造成一些人死亡和受伤的卡车事故。不管怎样，这对Liesel和Rosa来说都是个好消息。第479页上有一句讽刺味道很浓的句子：“A broken leg was certainly something to celebrate.”。看来Hans不得不牺牲他的腿才得以摆脱战争。听起来多么荒谬啊！这场战争又何尝不是？

——李秀文

"The Snows of Stalingrad"给我留下了特别深刻的印象。根据对应门者的描述，一开始我还以为不是他们的儿子。但事实证明，他真的是他们的儿子之一。他们看起来不像兄弟俩，因为他看起来太老了，连Rosa都认不出他了。作者对Michael的外表轻描淡写，但它仍然可以显示出战争对士兵身心的摧残。我注意到了"血樱桃"这个词，意思是"新伤"，他刚从战场上回来。他呼出一口气——回答"stalingrad"。读到这里，我倒抽一口凉气，能深深感受到战争给他带来的创伤以及不可磨灭的噩梦。从死亡的角度来描述发生在Robert身上的事情，使其更加生动和痛苦。我忍不住在脑海里想象俄罗斯的风景。那是多么可怕的一幕。战场就像炼狱。在这一章结束时，两句短短的话让我沉默了好一会儿。"The brother shivers.The woman weeps."这些句子只是简单的文字，却能完全反映出战争给Robert家人带来的后果。

——麦佩莹

在这几章里，令我印象深刻的是，Liesel问市长夫人这是不是她的图书室，而市长夫人提到了自己的儿子和他的逝去，这时Liesel仿佛看到了一个母亲带着儿子在看书的画面，可见Liesel是很有想象力并富有同理心的孩子。通过这次的对话，她和市长夫人心与心之间的距离也拉近了。

一袋曲奇饼就可以让他们开心，而且那些语言也特别生动："你还骗我？明明嘴巴边上还有糖呢！"这个片段又让我感觉到少年不知愁滋味的意味。

看到这里，就忍不住感慨，多么希望后面的悲剧没有发生，让他们一直停留在这样无忧无虑的小确幸中。

——莫 然

在这几章里，我印象最深的是希望和好运。

希望：

1943年1月，Liesel去Mrs. Holtzapfel家给她读书。一个男人在门口迎接她，并对她说，等Mrs. Holtzapfel准备好了，他就来接她。几个小时后，他来接她，他是Michael，刚从战场回来，要告诉母亲他的兄弟Robert死了。

战争期间，有时没有消息就是好消息。我们渴望得到一些关于我们所爱的人的信息，但是当我们得到它的时候，我们也不知道自己是否会因此而崩溃。如果是坏消息，我们还有勇气活下去吗？我们怎么能经受住这股邪恶的暗涌？所以没有消息就是好消息，至少我们还心存希望。

幸运星Hans：

至于家人，Liesel发现Rosa午夜坐在手风琴旁祈祷，她在祈祷爸爸能平安归来。至于Hans，当时Hans和其他一些人在打牌。获胜者将得到香烟，因为他们不是玩现金，而是玩香烟。Hans连赢了三局，每输一局，Zucker就更生气。正是因为这种愤怒，几周后，他坚持要和Hans在卡车上交换座位。

当卡车在路上行驶时，它的左前轮被刺破，导致司机失去对车辆的控制。卡车翻了，Zucker的脖子断了，他死了。Hans的一条腿摔断了，因此军士把他送到Munich，要么在办公室工作，要么做清洁工作。正是Hans的慷慨救了他，正如中士在第478页所说："听起来不错，中士。"

二月，Liesel生日后的一个星期，Rosa和Liesel收到了Hans的来信。信上告诉了她们事故经过和Hans断腿的消息，但更重要的是，信中告诉她们Hans要回家了。Hans还告诉Rosa，他听说小Hans还活着，在苏联。Liesel把这个消息告诉了Rudy的家人，他们都欣喜若狂，但是Rudy想知道为什么回家的是Hans而不是他的父亲。这一刻，我们可以看到人类的自私，虽然我们会为别人的好消息而高兴，但是当我们遇到同样的情况时，我们总是希望幸运的人是我们自己。自私虽然是人类的天性，但我们可以改变我们的想法，希望所有人都是幸运和健康的。

——宋碧燕

读完这一章，我特别想和大家分享"The Snows Of Stalingrad"这节。虽然没有经历过战争，但文章再一次让我身临其境，感受战争带给人类的无尽痛苦，带给老百姓的巨大伤痛以及妻离子散、家破人亡的悲惨。故事讲述了1943年1月中旬，Himmel依然阴暗而充满痛苦。Liesel准备到Mrs. Holtzapfel家去给她读书。正当她敲门的时候，出来开门的人让她大吃一惊。这个男人看起来很老，不像是Mrs. Holtzapfel的儿子。他脸上点缀着稀疏的胡须，眼神中透着强烈的痛苦，外衣袖子下的胳膊绑着绷带，绷带上渗出血迹。Liesel通过和他交谈，才知道他确实是Mrs. Holtzapfel的大儿子。他的外貌让Rosa都认不出他本人来了，因为确实显得太老。Michael主动说起："我弟弟死了。"Rosa听后受到了巨大的震撼。他又说："我听说你儿子也在苏联。"Rosa马上显得很激动，抓住他的衣袖，不停地和他说着她儿子的事情。

接着，书中又以死神的口吻来详细地描写了Mrs. Holtzapfel的小儿子在战场上是怎么死的。最后，当Liesel在Mrs. Holtzapfel家里大声朗读时，哥哥在颤抖，Mrs. Holtzapfel在哭泣，苏联的雪景浮现在眼前，那里飘的都是雪花，他们在想念他们的家人。读完这一部分之后感到揪心和难受，战争年代，人们的神经时刻都处于紧绷状态，每一根神经都极其敏感和脆弱，战争就意味着死亡，死亡就意味着家人的离世，家人的离世就意味着无限痛苦和无尽悲哀。

——宋 蕾

Liesel快14岁了，可她意识到自己的弟弟将永远停留在6岁。但是弟弟再也不会出现在自己的梦中了，而是在床头陪着自己，还有她的妈妈、Max、Hans，伴随她入眠的还有Rosa的哭泣。小主人公为什么不再做有关弟弟的噩梦了呢？弟弟的灵魂不再萦绕梦中，而是出现在她的床边。大概是她有了更多人的陪伴吧？Max的友情、Hans的父爱，还有Rosa的母爱，让她不再感到孤单恐惧。越来越多的爱，让她更有勇气战胜噩梦。

——夏丽焱

These parts show us how the war was cruel. The writer didn't use very large words to describe the war.And he didn't show the readers terrible pictures. Instead，he depicted how the war was miserable by some details.In fact，nothing is more sorrowful than watching a loved one dying in front of you while you could do nothing except sorrow. Sorrow fills in the eyes，nose，ears，mouth and every cell. It rises from the bottom of heart and rushes all over the body. It makes you could breathe. No words can express the feeling of losing a loved one. How did the writer describe Michael's sadness?

"'My brother's dead，'....

'I was in one of the buildings we used for a hospital when they brought him in. it was a week before I was coming home. I spent three days of that week sitting with him before he died...'Please，don't say anything...

... A SMALL WAR STORY...

His legs were blown off at the shins and he died with his brother watching in a cold，stench-filled hospital."

All through the lines，we can't find any words to describe how Michael felt sad. The writer pictured the whole thing as an very very old man tells a far away story. While you are reading，the brother died once more in front of us. And we can sense the Michael experience. Silence speaks louder than words. I think maybe this is why the story touches the readers，why it is a classic.

——Ting Feng

Part Nine of The Book Thief

One Toolbox, One Bleeder, One Bear—The War Maker

导 读

今天我们要读的是*A Book Thief*第九章和第十章中的“One Toolbox，One Bleeder，One Bear”“Homecoming”“The End Of The World（Part I）”“The Ninety-eighth Day”和“The War Maker”这几个小节。

“One Toolbox，One Bleeder，One Bear”一节主要讲述了四个内容：3月9日发生的空袭，Liesel读书给街坊邻居帮助他们保持冷静，被袭击摧毁的飞机以及死神的感叹。3月9日的空袭这一部分主要描述的人物是Frau Holtzapfel。她陷在丧子的极大悲痛中，对即将到来的空袭无动于衷，尽管Rosa、Liesel和小儿子Michael极力劝说也无济于事，但庆幸的是最终她自己来到了防空洞。在这里，坚强而勇敢的Liesel读书给大家听，让大家镇静而不恐慌。

在被袭击摧毁的飞机这一部分，作者主要描述了Rudy和Liesel。其中对Rudy的一处细节描写给我留下了深刻印象：“Rudy placed the smiling teddy bear cautiously onto the pilot's shoulder. The tip of its ear touched his throat.”。这一描写让我们感受到Rudy的体贴及其思想日趋成熟的一面。

让我内心难以平静的是有关死神的感叹：

“It is probably fair to say that in all the years of Hitler's reign，no person was able to serve the Fubrer as loyally as me. A human doesn't have a heart like mine. The human heart is a line，whereas my own is a circle，and I have the endless ability to be in the right place at the right time. The consequence of this is that I'm always finding humans at their best and worst. I see their ugly and their beauty，and I wonder how the same thing can be both. Still，they have one thing I envy. Humans，if nothing else，have the good sense to die.”

这样的一番感叹充分表达了死神对战争带给人们伤痛的同情和无助；在他看来，是人们自己掀起战争而自相残杀的。

“Homecoming”一节主要讲述的是养父Hans从战场返回家中。父女相见的一幕足够暖心而给我留下了深刻的印象：“‘Papa，Papa.’ She must have said it a hundred times as she hugged him in the kitchen and wouldn’t let go. At 1 am，Liesel went to bed and Papa came in to sit with her，like he used to. She woke up several times to check that he was there and he did not fail her. The night was calm. Her bed was warm and soft with contentment.”。一系列的动作描写将这一温馨场景描写得淋漓尽致。

“The End Of The World（Part I）”这一小节向读者提前告知了故事的结局，可谓是伤痛而震惊。睡梦中的Himmel街刹那间被摧毁，大家都失去性命，只有待在地下室的Liesel存活了下来。她看到失去性命的养父Hans的场景描写催人泪下。

“The rescuing hands pulled Liesel out and brushed the crumbs of rubble from her clothes.‘Young girl，’ they said，‘the sirens were too late. What were you doing in the basement？How did you know？’What they didn’t notice was that the girl was still holding the book. She screamed her reply.A stunning scream of the living.‘Papa！’

A second time. Her face creased as she reached a higher，more panic-stricken pitch.‘Papa，Papa！’They passed her up as she shouted，wailed，and cried.If she was injured，she did not yet know it，for she struggled free and searched and called and wailed some more.She was still clutching the book.She was holding desperately on to the words who had saved her life。”

其中，a stunning scream、face creased加上一些动词的连用，如shouted、wailed、cried等，充分展现了Liesel失去养父的悲痛之情。

“The Ninety-eighth Day”一节主要讲述了犹太人被游街示众、Frau Holtzapfel小儿子Michael的自杀以及死神的再次感慨。犹太人被游街示众这一部分，主要描写了Liesel的内心感受和渴望见到Max的心情。而在八月的一个温暖午后，Max也在试图寻找Liesel，渴望与她相见。让我印象深刻、内心难以平静的还是死神的这段感慨：

“So many people chased after me in that time，calling my name，asking me to take them with me. Then there was the small percentage who called me casually over and whispered with their tightened voices.‘Have me，’ they said，and there was no stopping them. They were frightened，no question，but they were not afraid of me. It was a fear of messing up and having to face themselves again，and facing the world，and the likes of you.

There was nothing I could do.They had too many ways，they were too resourceful—and when they did it too well，whatever their chosen method，I was in no position to refuse.”

这段感慨一方面反映出残酷战争带给人们的痛苦和绝望，另一方面也流露出死神的同情和无助。

"The War Maker"再次描写了战争的残酷。从死神的一段自述中就能深刻体会到。

"... JULY 27，1943...

Michael Holtzapfel was buried and *The Book Thief* read to the bereaved. The Allies bombed Hamburg—and on that subject，it's lucky I'm somewhat miraculous. No one else could carry close to forty-five thousand people in such a short amount of time. Not in a million human years.

Still，I'll give him something，that Fuhrer. He certainly had an iron will. There was no slackening off in terms of war-making，nor was there any scaling back on the extermination and punishment of a Jewish plague. While most of the camps were spread throughout Europe，there were some still in existence in Germany itself."

作者的这段自述流露着讽刺的味道，将战争的残酷描写到极致。在他看来，战争满足了一些人的野心，却无情地夺去了无数无辜人的性命。读完这几章，内心很压抑。但有一点我们要明白，那就是：纵使有时我们无力面对一个看似扭曲不堪的世界，但我们也不要失去对求生的渴望，对光明与美好的追寻。

工作室人员分享

Liesel 的爸爸终于回来了，这一幕终于被我们等来了。家人的团圆重聚是多么的珍贵，他们可以坐在桌旁一直聊到深夜，就算到了睡觉的时间，Hans也不愿离开Liesel。这个夜晚宁静如水，我认为这里的"宁静"更多的是心灵的平静，没有了担忧、焦虑、恐惧……但是很遗憾，这样的宁静只能维持三个月。另外一章让我深感触动的是描述Michael的自杀。文章以死神的口吻来叙述当时的德国人是如何面对死亡的："那段日子里，许多人追赶着我，呼唤着我的名字，哀求着我把他们带走……他们有多种寻死的方法，各种各样的方法……"这样的描述，更加突显了战争对人类的摧毁，不仅仅是对生命的，而且是对精神的。这让身处和平年代的我们是无法想象的。生命不是最宝贵的吗？如果这些宁愿选择死亡也不愿继续活下去的人，也像Liesel那样有书的滋养的话，相信他们会继续活下去的。

——陈雪芬

Rudy was very angry because of his father's recruitment to army，so he prepared something for showing his anger to the government. He decided to steal from the rich Nazis in the street with a toolbox. Surprisingly, a teddy bear was in it. It was friendly looking nonetheless. It was a very cute reason that he used the bear to calm them down. The teddy bear is a tool for stealing.UGLY.However，Rudy cancelled this action. The next threat was coming，fires were burning and over two hundred murdered souls were picked up by the death. A pilot was dying by the river. Rudy climbed to him. He placed the smiling teddy bear cautiously onto the pilots shoulder. The tip of its ear touched his throat. The nonetheless teddy bear is like a comfort to the dying man.He said thank you to Rudy. Then his soul was taken with a teddy bear on the shoulder. At this time，the bear was for BEAUTY. The same bear had different meanings in this chapter. As the death put，he was always finding humans at their best and worst. One is an angel and the other is a demon right time. The consequence of this is that I'm always finding humans at their best and worst I see their ugly and their beauty，and I wonder how the same thing can be both. Still，they have one thing I envy. Humans，if nothing else，have the good sense to die.

——董筱妍

What shocked me most was the death of Michael.

"Tell me Rosa，how she can sit there ready to die while I still want to live? I shouldn't want to. But I do."（P487）

"Michael knew what he was doing. He killed himself for wanting to live...Michael was worn down not by his damaged hand or any other injury，but by the quilt of living."（P503）

Reading these words，I felt unutterably depressed.War not only took away people's lives，but also psychological health. On the battlefield，Michael experienced the cruelty that not a normal person could stand. Blood，broken bodies... living lives disappeared in a second in front of him. Worst of all，his brother died. The pain was almost too great to endure. In deed，he was suffering from a mental disease called the aftermath of the war. "So many people passed away，why am I alive? I should have been together with them，with my brother. However，I want to live！I feel guilty about this." These probably were Michael's inner thoughts. If there were professional doctors comforting and curing him. He wouldn't commit suicide. Unluckily. Everyone was in the fear of being bombed. Everyone was in the pain of losing family. Everyone was in need of help.

I think this is the most brutal part of a war.It devastated people's will and took away all the beauties in life. People felt hopeless. Thus，they wanted to die. Because there was nothing else in the world that could keep them living.

"So many people chased after me in that time，call my name，asking me to take them with me."（P503）

We have been reading the book for nearly a term. And the characters in this book were so vivid that they seemed like our friends in real life. Rudy，Mama and Papa，Frau Holtzapfel，Frau Diller，Tommy Muller. They were all nice and kind. But all sleeping. All died. It was miserable to read this chapter.

——关少娟

If the former parts of the book are bittersweet and humorous，this part of the book is just painful，period.

The war leaves great influence to the people physically and mentally. They worried and missed their family so much that they didn't want to live. They even felt guilty for living. It seemed that they should not be allowed to live. Life was torment. Michael and his mom were the ones.

I was struck by the words，"Tell me，Rosa，how she can sit there ready to die while I still want to live... why do I want to live? I shouldn't want to，but I do."

"The young man wept uncontrollably." Michael was worn down not by his damaged hand or any other injury but by the guilt of living. "What surprised me most is that Death offered a glimpse of the end，which was surprisingly cruel." In short，Himmel Street was flattened. "Only one person survived，Liesel was sitting in a basement reading while others were sleeping. I'm not sure whether it was lucky for Liesel to be the only one to live. Sometimes death may set us free from pain and torment. But it leaves others around in the dark. The people alive have to be brave to face the cruel world." So I'm deeply concerned about Liesel afterwards. What will she do? Will she become someone like Michael? Struggle to live? Or will she be like her foster father Hans Hubermann? Be forgiving and nice to people around?

——李秀文

It is oppressive for me to finish reading the five chapters. I am glad that Liesel and Rosa had papa back. Though good time didn't last long，at least they had a chance to feel happy again before they died.I still can't accept the fact that Himmel Street was bombed and only Liesel survived. What a tragedy! It was heartbreaking and desperate pain to her，When I read about her scream for papa，I kind of feel the same for Liesel. She was just too young to suffer. What kind of believe on earth did she have to stay strong for the rest of her life? I couldn't imagine and I really admire Liesel deep in my heart.

And I feel awful to know that Michael killed himself because of the guilt of wanting to live. Frau Holtzapfel lost her two sons in six months. Poor mother.

After reading these chapters，I feel even more fortunate to live such a harmonious and happy life.

——麦佩莹

“Four years earlier，Liesel Meminger was coaxed through that doorway when she showed up for the first time. Max Vandenburg had stood there with a key biting into his hand. Now it was Hans Hubermann’s turn. He knocked four times and *The Book Thief* answered——

‘Papa，Papa.’

She must have said it a hundred times as she hugged him in the kitchen and wouldn’t let go. At 1 a.m，Liesel went to bed and Papa came in to sit with her，like he used to. She woke up several times to check that he was there，and he did not fail her.

The night was calm.

Her bed was warm and soft with contentment.

Yes，it was a great night to be Liesel Meminger. And the calm，the warm，and the soft would remain for approximately three more months.”

这两个细节描写真的太生动了，Liesel和Hans的亲情跃然纸上，a hundred times呼唤爸爸，把Liesel对爸爸的想念表现得淋漓尽致。Liesel一个晚上醒来好多次，就怕爸爸突然消失不见了，也是把她的不放心完全表现出来了。

“In short，Himmel Street was flattered.

Houses were splashed from one side of the street to the other. A framed photo of a very serious-looking Fubrer was bashed and beaten on the shattered. Yet he smiled，in that serious way of his. He knew something we all didn’t know. But I knew something he didn’t know. All while people slept.

Rudy Steiner slept.Mama and Papa slept. Frau Holtzapfel，Frau Diller，Tommy Miller. All sleeping. All dying.

Only one person survived.”

没想到悲剧来得这么快。看到这里真的很难受，我曾经看过一个杂文是这么写的：“这个世界上没有幸存者，因为幸存者的内心都是千疮百孔的后悔和悲伤。”谁会愿意带着对所有失去生命的人们的思念继续活下去呢？到处都是回忆，走到哪里都会触景伤情。

——莫 然

In April of 1943，Hans Hubermann was sent home to rest，after his broken leg had healed enough for him to travel. He told Liesel and Rosa all about his war experiences. Liesel was very glad her Papa was home and Hans would sit just as he used to be when Liesel was asleep. Liesel woke up several times to check if papa was there.

After making sure that papa really came back, Liesel's heart was full of happiness. However, her calmness she had not felt for a long time. Unfortunately, it would only last for three more months, then the turmoil would start again.

Death talks of what happened on October 7, 1943. The bombers dropped their load on Himmel Street. The only survivor was Liesel, because she had been in the basement checking to see if she had made any errors, in the story she had written about her life.The rescuers were happy to see that someone had lived, but Mama and Papa lost their lives that night and Liesel was devastated. In this part, Death was quite different from he used to be.In the past, I think Death was cruel and he didn't care who died, he just did his everyday job to take people's souls away. But this time, Death behaved just like a human, he would envy, though he had the endless ability to be the right place at the right time, humans had the good sense to die. In this moment, I could feel Death also had something he couldn't control. On July 24, 1943, Michael Holtzapfel hung himself, because he could not bear to live. Because he thought as a son, he didn't do a good job with his mom. He left his mom alone in the kitchen when the air raid came, he just run to the shelter to hide. He was living in the guilt in the later days. Finally, he was devastated, he hung himself one day. From P504:

"Can you ever forget me? I just couldn't stand it any longer.

I'm meeting Robert. I don't care what the damn Catholics say about it. There must be a place in heaven for those who have been where I have been. You might think I don't love you because of what I have done, but I do. Yours Michael."

I could feel he was desperate. Hans told Michael's mother and he sat with her in the middle of the street while she mourned.I also felt sad that Michael's mother lost two son in six months.

——宋碧燕

What impressed me most is the Chapter Homecoming.

Liesel missed her papa very much. Though he was her stepfather. The love between the Liesel and her papa was getting stronger and stronger during the time of war. When Liesel hugged her papa, she wanted to call him papa one hundred times, because she didn't want her papa go away. Later, after they ate dinner, they talked with each other for several hours until midnight. Finally, Liesel felt warm, soft and calm for only three more months. Families should have a common and happy life in a peaceful time, however in wartime, the people have to suffer from the misery away from the families.

It was dark when he arrived home. It was a day later than expected, as the train was delayed due to an air-raid scare. He stood at the door of 33 Himmel Street and made a fist. For years earlier，Liesel Meminger was coaxed through that doorway when she showed up for the first time.Max Vandenberg had stood there with a key biting into his hand. Now it was Hans Hubermann' turn. He knocked four times and *The Book Thief* answered. At 1 a. m.，Liesel went to bed and Papa came in to sit with her，like he used to. She woke up several times to check that he was there，and he did not fail her. The night was calm. Her bed was warm and soft with contentment.

Yes，it was a great night to be Liesel Meminger and the calm，the warm，and the soft would remain for approximately three more months.

——宋 蕾

Liesel and Rosa receive a letter from Hans telling them about his broken leg and also stating that he'll be coming home. They celebrate his broken leg and take the news over to the Steiners，who celebrate with them. Despite Rudy's happiness，Liesel can sense his question—why Hans and not his father?

Analysis

With Rudy's question，Death admits that Rudy has a point，illustrating how so much of life is left up to luck and chance. Why one and not the other? Why lightness and not darkness? Or why darkness and not lightness? While Rudy can be happy for Liesel，he can，simultaneously，be upset for his family and jealous of the good fortune that has come to Liesel and Rosa.

——夏丽焱

I always like bears. Because they are likely to be connected with innocent and naive children. To me，Liesel and Rudy are like one of them. As the pages move on，I kind of witness how they've grown. They would risk stealing something from others and gave it to someone in need. They had little tricks to crawl into the mayor's house for food and ran for miles for being afraid to be caught. In my eyes，they are not real thieves. To quote Rudy "Stealing is what the army does. Taking your father and mine." It's heartbroken to hear such words from a little boy，however angry and disappointed he was，he had no choice but to steal something back to relief himself. "He gripped the handle with much force as he could，and his movements were stiff with rage." How clever he was to go with a teddy bear，and considerate. "The commitment had disappeared，and although he still watched the imagined glory of stealing，she could see that now he was not believing it. He was trying to believe it." Which proved that he was still that kind and innocent boy. Moreover，it reminds me of a sentence from him：I guess I am better at leaving things behind than stealing things. I guess so. But it just didn't occur to me how touching it was to see the last scene of the chapter. "Carefully, he climbed to the dying man.He placed the smiling teddy bear cautiously onto the pilot's shoulder. The tip of its ear touched his throat." It's like a movie clip pictured in my mind. Two beautiful souls meet each other. Despite the chaos outside, we can still sense the power of human nature.

——袁泳施

Rudy's anger at the world keeps growing and he gathers a toolbox of things to help him in stealing. Liesel sees him leaving and catches up with him. She asks him about the teddy bear (which is in his toolbox) and Rudy says it is to comfort a child if one finds him stealing. They keep walking and Liesel realizes Rudy had intended to rob the mayor's house, but he has already lost his conviction. When they get to Gelb Strasse, Rudy sits down and decides he is "better at leaving things behind than stealing them." Rudy tries to cheer himself up by stealing again, hoping for another "win", but most of his attempted crimes fail because of his own natural compassion. Rudy doesn't want to hurt anyone except Hitler and the Nazis—he just wants to take some kind of control over the mad world he finds himself in. He now accepts his own giving nature and stops trying to make himself into a criminal.

——郑剑湘

The writer described what miserable life people led in World War II.I could hardly breathe while reading these parts. To the people in World War II, they lived in the end of the world, in a living hell. It was a shame for them to live, and they were so fearful to face endless sorrow that they had no choice but to die. I think there would not be a worse disaster than it.

"So many people chased after in that time, calling my name, asking me to take them with me. Then there was a small percentage who called me casually over and whispered with their tightened voices. "Have me," they said, and there was no stopping them. They were frightened, no question, but they were not afraid of me. It was a tear of messing up and having to face themselves again, and facing the world and likes of you.

There was nothing that I could do. They had too many ways.They were too resourceful—and when they did it too well, whatever their chosen method, I was in no position to refuse. Michael Holtzpfel killed himself for wanting to live. Of course, I did not see Liesel at all that day. As is usually the case, I advised myself that I was far too busy to remain on Himmel Street to listen to the creams. It is bad enough when people catch me red-handed, so I made the usual decision to make my exit, into the breakfast-colored sun."

It was such a mess! Even such a great writer as Markus Zusak could describe such a scene even with hundreds of hands, so the writer let "I" exited and the readers imagine.

While looking back the war, I just wonder how the war maker should end up himself for the huge disaster he had brought to those people.

——Ting Feng

Part Ten of The Book Thief

Way of the Words—The Rib-Cage Planes

导读

本周我们将一起分享*A Book Thief*的“Way of the Words”“Confessions”“Ilsa Hermann's Little Black Book”和“The Rib-Cage Planes”四个小节的内容。这四个小节的主题可以概括为：成长、友情、爱和救赎。我们看到了无情的战争，看到了冷血的杀戮，体会到了生离死别。但是我们也能看到，夹杂在无尽伤痛和恐惧中的那些温暖和人性的光辉。而读到此时，书中的人物也被刻画得越发饱满和充实。这四章的故事主要围绕着如下几个主要人物展开：

Liesel：她知道语言有巨大的力量，她渴望它们。在看到Max被送进集中营后，Liesel将自己的绝望转化为书写自己生命故事的力量。

最终，当Liesel体验到人性的美好与残忍时，她学会了运用语言的力量，影响人类的善恶行为。

Max：Max在游街示众时和Liesel相遇的那一幕让人难忘。我认为他们之间的爱超越了男女之间的爱。即使被纳粹分子鞭打，Max仍然有勇气面对自己的生活。

Rudy：Rudy是Liesel一个真正的朋友。我们不仅可以看到他眼中的生命之火，还可以看到他对Liesel深深的爱。在我眼中，他是一个拥有一头柠檬色头发，纯洁、勇敢、体贴、忠诚的男孩。

Ilsa：Ilsa是一个鼓舞人心的人物，她渴望帮助Liesel继续阅读；她拜访Liesel，给了她一本日记，并告诉她不要为自己无法控制的行为和环境惩罚自己。

除了作者成功塑造的这些鲜活动人的主角外，还有不少值得我们回味的场景，可能本周让我们触动最大的就是今天要分享的“文字之路”。

“Liesel shrugged away entirely from the crowd and entered the tide of Jews, weaving through them till she grabbed hold of his arm with her left hand...

‘I'm here, Max,’ she said again. ‘I'm here.’ ‘I can't believe...’ The words dripped from Max's mouth. ‘Look how much you've grown.’ There was an intense sadness in his eyes. They swelled. ‘Liesel... they got me a few months ago.’ The voice was crippled but it dragged itself toward her. ‘Halfway to Struttgart.’

As he stood, Max looked first at the girl and then stared directly into the sky who was wide, blue, and magnificent. There were heavy beams—planks of sun—falling randomly, wonderfully to the road. Clouds arched their backs to look behind as they started again to move on. ‘It's such a beautiful day’, he said, and his voice was in many pieces. A great day to die. A great day to die, like this.

Liesel walked at him. She was courageous enough to reach out and hold his bearded face. ‘Is it really you, Max?’ Such a brilliant German day and its attentive crowd. He let his mouth kiss her palm. ‘Yes, Liesel, it's me,’ and he held the girl's hand in his face and cried onto her fingers. He cried as the soldiers came and a small collection of insolent Jews stood and watched. Standing, he was whipped. ‘Max,’ the girl wept.”（P510-511）

当Liesel看到游街队伍中被逮捕的Max时，她勇敢地上去拥抱他，即使遭到毒打也在所不惜。他们不顾一切地希望待在彼此身边，那种爱是超出男女之爱的关心与忠诚。身体的疼痛掩盖不了见到亲人的喜悦，所以即使被纳粹鞭打，Max仍然说：“真是美好的一天！”我们看到了无情的战争，看到了冷血的杀戮，体会到了生离死别。但是我们也能看到，夹杂在无尽伤痛和恐惧中的那些温暖和人性的光辉。

在接下来的一节“Confessions”中，与Max相遇后，Liesel默默地去火车站等Hans下班回来。Rudy把Rosa叫来，他们一起等。Hans回来了，那天晚上他拉起了手风琴，但是音符听起来怎么都不对。在那之后，Liesel卧床三天。当她终于起来的时候，Liesel找到Rudy，并告诉了他关于Max的事情，并让他多次承诺保守秘密。Liesel想让Rudy吻她，她意识到她一直都爱着他，但还是什么都没发生。死神说Rudy只能活一个月了。从不掩饰对Liesel喜爱之情的Rudy总是愿意在Liesel身边默默地支持和陪伴她。他们之间懵懵懂懂的感情，更多的应该是一种友情。两个孩子一路相携相助的友谊永远都让我们感到温馨和甜蜜。

在下一节“Ilsa Hermann's Little Black Book”中，Liesel朝市长家走去，希望偷点东西让自己振作起来。此时的Liesel心情是低落的，她觉得这个世界是一锅丑陋的浓汤，她看着美丽的Amper River，想着人性的丑陋，甚至觉得这个世界不配拥有这样一条河。书房是理性、安宁和尊严的象征，在一片狂乱的战争氛围中，如同暴风眼般安静。Liesel数次冒险去那里，每一次抵达，都是对心灵的慰藉。Liesel被她的悲伤和愤怒所淹没，她称这些书是“可爱的混蛋”，并开始撕下书页，把它们撕成碎片。她思考着这些文字，它们是如何赋予Hitler权力的，并想知道它们有什么价值。此时此刻，市长夫人Hermann太太是Liesel的精神守护者，她渴望帮助Liesel继续阅读。Ilsa拜访Liesel，给了她一本日记，并告诉她不要为自己无法控制的行为和环境惩罚自己。从她第一次见到Liesel在焚书中偷书时起，她就选择了善良，选择了满足一个小女孩在颠沛流离的艰难时期对文字的渴望。

" 'I thought if you're not going to read any more of my books, you might like to write one instead. Your letter, it was...' She handed the book to Liesel with both hands. 'You can certainly write. You write well.' 'And please,' Ilsa Hermann advised her, 'don't punish yourself, like you said you would. Don't be like me, Liesel.'

Ilsa Hermann not only gave Liesel Meminger a book that day. She also gave her a reason to spend time in the basement—her favorite place, first with Papa, then Max. She gave her a reason to write her own words, to see that words had also brought her to life.

'Don't punish yourself,' she heard her say again, but there would be punishment and pain, and there would be punishment and pain, and there would be happiness, too. That was writing."

最后一章，"敞开肚皮的飞机"。第一个晚上，Liesel写了11页，从她弟弟的死开始写起，到在雪地里找到*A Grave Digger's Handbook*。她在地下室睡着了，Rosa找到了她。从那以后，Liesel每天晚上都在写。有时她会在故事中插入当前的动作，比如描述Hans演奏手风琴。

当死神来到Himmel的时候，Liesel已经写完了她的书，但她还在地下室里。她反反复复地读自己的最后一行文字：

"I have hated the words and I have loved them, and I hope I have made them right."

这四章诠释了文字的伟大力量。战争是残酷的，但人性是美丽的。洗脑、独裁、恐怖、暴力虽然能控制非常时期民众的思想，带来血雨腥风与人类灾难，但文字的正义力量是强大无比、无法操控的，它必将拯救绝望。

这四章让我想起普希金的一句话："所有的痛苦都会过去，而过去了的痛苦会成为美好的回忆。"

工作室人员分享

正如中国的一句老话所说，"言之所至，心之所向"。Liesel和Max分开了几个月，终于Liesel在拥挤的人群中找到了Max。这是一个浪漫的场景，就像是电视剧中的场景。他们相望着：" 'I'm here, Max!' Louder. 'Max, I'm here!' He heard her."。他听到了她的呼喊。简单的文字，浓烈而复杂的感情。Max变得比以前虚弱多了。他用尽全身力气把Liesel扶起来。他想把Liesel从游街的队伍中拉出来。虽然Liesel被士兵发现了，但她还是留在了这里，找到了Max。

"There was once a strange, small man, she said. Her arms were loose but her hands were fists at her side. But there was a word shaker，too.”这就像是他们之间的密码。这让我想起了他们在地下室的日子。当时，他们以文字的形式互相取暖，阅读让他们的距离越来越近。然而，Max还是被带走了。Liesel遭到毒打，Rudy把她保护起来。她最终选择与Rudy分享这个秘密。她找到了她爱的Rudy，她在等那个吻。也许她想要一些安慰，安慰她空虚的灵魂。

——董筱妍

Munich街上又有一群犹太人在游街示众，Liesel再次在队伍中寻找Max。这次她看到了他，Max也在人群中找到了Liesel。Liesel感觉心都要碎了，她走到路上，大声呼喊着Max的名字，他们终于找到了彼此。Max 告诉她，他在去Stuttgart的路上被抓了。一方面，知道Max还活着的消息让人安心，但悲剧的是纳粹抓住了他，他现在成了被押往集中营受苦的囚犯之一（那里很少有人幸存）。

一个士兵看到Liesel，把她从Max的身边拖走，并将她推倒在地上。Liesel站起来后，又从另一个方向走回来重新找到了Max，并对他说起曾经说过的话“The Word Shaker”。世界似乎停止了，Max 吻了吻Liesel的手，抬头看着明亮的蓝天。但是他再次被士兵们鞭打到倒在地上，士兵也鞭打了Liesel好几次。Rudy 找到Liesel，在其他人都惊呆了的时候，把她扶走了。这是这本小说中最美妙的时刻之一——Liesel引用Max自己的话给予他最大的力量和安慰，描述了两个朋友共同拥有的安全港；Max也在这一刻享受到了天空的颜色，再一次在痛苦的脸上拥有了欣慰的表情。

Max和其他囚犯一起被拖走了，Liesel 试图再次跟上去，Rudy 拦住她。她哭着打了Rudy，其他人散开时，他们一起瘫倒在地上。这也说明Liesel认为世界不公平的愤怒又回来了，她仍然试图用身体攻击以表示反抗，就像Rudy想要杀死Hitler，Max想要揍死神一样。

——郑剑湘

“Perhaps it was the sudden bumpiness of love she felt for him. Or had she always loved him? It’s likely. Restricted as she was from speaking，she wanted him to kiss her. She wanted him to drag her hand across and pull her over. It didn’t matter where. Her mouth，her neck，her cheek. Her skin was empty for it，waiting.”

我被这段细腻的描写深深吸引了。Rudy是Liesel生命中重要的人之一。他们一起踢球，一起挨饿，一起偷水果吃，一起偷书，一起给游街示众的犹太人撒面包片，一起感受生命中的酸甜苦辣。这种青梅竹马、患难与共的关系，在战火纷飞的年代，弥足珍贵。长到了对爱情懵懵懂懂的年纪，Liesel从孩童时期拒绝Rudy的吻，到如今少女时代热烈的渴望。文章没有直接描写Rudy的心理活动，但他冒险从士兵的皮鞭下去拉回Liesel，说明他是可以用生命去保护她的。很遗憾，这刚刚萌芽的爱情却没法发展，只能存活于Liesel的美好记忆中。因为一个月后，Rudy将离开这个世界。文字先暖后冷，给读者营造了巨大的落差，刚好反映了战争的残酷。

——关少娟

阅读了这几章，内心久久不能平静。每一章都有足以震撼人心的场面。“Way of the Words”一章详细地描绘了Liesel和Max的久别重逢。是Max专心致志观察人群努力寻找Liesel的那副神情让Liesel认出了Max。Liesel不顾Max的劝阻，士兵的推搡、鞭打，Rudy的相劝，直到重重摔倒在地。尽管如此，Liesel苏醒时还会固执地迈开步子奔跑起来，试图追赶Max最后的脚步……最终还是Rudy拦住了她，任凭她的拳打脚踢、纷飞的唾沫和眼泪。在“Confessions”一章，Liesel将隐藏在心中的秘密对Rudy和盘托出，将*The Word Shaker*里描写Rudy的一页翻开给Rudy看，隐约地表达着对Rudy的爱意。然而作者话锋一转，末尾的一句“He was a month from his death. She was saying goodbye and she didn't even know it.”着实让人心痛。“Ilsa Hermann's Little Black Book”一章描写了Liesel对文字又爱又恨的表现，因为毁书心生愧疚而写给Ilsa最后一封信。然而Ilsa没有怪罪Liesel，反而主动上门安抚Liesel并送给她一本小黑书，鼓励她动笔写书。Liesel从中再次深深地体会到了文字的力量——是文字挽救了她的生命。Ilsa温暖如初的关爱让人感动，一句“不要惩罚自己”给我留下了很深的印象，回味无穷。

——李 丹

到来了，但是一点也不愉快。在读这部分的时候，我真诚地希望Max能听到Liesel所说的话，鼓励他不要放弃他的生活，而是继续他的梦想。那是一段感人的友谊。

幸运的是，每当Liesel遇到麻烦时，Rudy总是在那里。Liesel告诉了他关于Max的事和感受到对他的“sudden bumpiness of love ”。那是青少年爱情的甜蜜时刻，尽管我们知道Rudy再过一个月就要死了。

回顾她生命中发生的那么多不幸，Liesel认为丑陋的世界来自语言，罪恶感的源头是文字操纵。所以这个世界不值得拥有任何好东西。没有好男人应该活着，也没有好事会发生在她身上。换句话说，Liesel不会再读书，也不会再快乐地生活，而是像市长夫人那样生活，在痛苦和仇恨中自暴自弃。幸亏市长夫人来了，激发了Liesel利用文字进行创作的灵感。“As it turned out，Ilsa Hermann not only gave Liesel a book that day. She also gave her a reason to spend time in the basement—her favorite place，first with Papa，then Max. She gave her a reason to write her own words，to see that words had also brought her to life.”那是Liesel生命中值得纪念的重要时刻。

语言本身是中性的，既可以是好的也可以是坏的。世界和生命也是如此。阅读能让我们真我地生活。也许这也就是教育的重要性。So live truly and wisely，让我们真性情地、明智地生活。

——李秀文

Liesel在犹太人群中发现Max的场景让我印象深刻。“Never had movement been such a burden.Never had a heart been so definite and big in her adolescent chest.”作者用倒装句更好地表现了当时Liesel内心的困惑。当Max看到Liesel的成长时，他的眼中有一种强烈的悲伤。他离开已经很长时间了。为了Liesel的安全，Max试图把她推开。他不能，因为他饿到没有力气了。饥饿通常用来形容一个人，这里作者用它来形容胳膊，更能表达饥饿和痛苦。此外，Liesel还能感觉到Max的手指和每个指关节的骨头。他就像非洲难民，甚至更糟。Liesel从来没有见过Max这样害怕过，这说明他受到了难以想象的折磨。然而，她却无能为力。当她重复有关shaker的一些句子时，我被那个场景感动了，久久无法平静下来。

我觉得Rudy就是Liesel的泰迪熊，他一直都是。当她需要帮助时，他出现了；当Liesel需要一个人来忏悔时，他就在她身边。我希望Liesel能告诉他，她爱他，想在他死前吻他。我们都应该珍惜身边的人。

——麦佩莹

在战争中，没有人能逃得过痛苦和悲哀。尽管Liesel得以幸存，但是也许幸存者要承受更多的痛苦和悲哀！有亲生母亲和弟弟陪伴的日子，有养父养母爱护的日子，和养父共读的时光，和Rudy争吵的画面，和Max互相支持日子……这些温暖的画面只能在回忆中搜索了，他们再也回不来了。面对生命中这么多重要人物的离开，要活下去是需要极大的勇气的！令人鼓舞的是，Liesel就有这股勇气。上天也奖赏了她这股勇气，居然让她在前往集中营的路途中，与Max重逢。这种幸福太突然了，Liesel难以置信地问“Is it really you? Is it from your cheek that I took the seed? ”战争对人的伤害大到人们根本不敢对任何开心抱有希望。这些残酷的画面在当今世界中依然每天都在发生。但愿尽快实现世界和平，还给人类过上美好生活的权利！

——莫洁文

一开始，Liesel在人群中看到的都是些死气沉沉的人，他们已经和行尸走肉差不多了……可是突然，在人群中出现了一个那么特别的人，那个曾经和她一起生活的人，那一刻，她还以为自己在做梦，眼睛都直了，于是她大声地告诉他：“我在这儿！我在这儿！”

这个重逢的描写太有画面感了，我的脑海中甚至响起了电影背景音乐一样温情又沉重的旋律。这里的“His face fell on her.”真的太生动了，那种久别重逢的激动好像从书里蹦了出来。这时Liesel再次说了一句“I'm here.”。这次不是告诉他自己在哪里，而是告诉他：“有我在！”Max看到Liesel之后心就好像有了归属一样，这段时间的委屈就这样轻飘飘地从他嘴里冒了出来。如果对方不是Liesel，他是不可能这么轻易说出来的。

有时候，生命的长短已经不重要了，能在有生之年遇到那个让自己全身心信任和依赖的人，是多么幸运和值得感恩的事！

——莫 然

一天，当一些犹太人被押着游街穿过街道时，Liesel和Max发现了对方。Liesel跑过去抓住他的手，告诉他她是来找他的。他们被士兵发现，并被士兵鞭打。他们努力不向疼痛屈服。Rudy看到了她，在Tommy的帮助下把她从马路上拖了下来，但当Max被押送到街上时，她仍然追赶着他。

之后的三天里，Liesel一直躺在床上，但第四天她去见了Rudy，她把他带到森林里，在他答应不告诉任何人后，她告诉了他关于Max的事。Rudy明白了她的行为，她把他的事告诉了Max，这让他非常感动。就在那一刻，Liesel知道她爱上了Rudy。她不知道的是Rudy只能活一个月了。

Liesel决定是时候去市长夫人的图书室偷一本书了，这会让她感觉好些，但当她回想起她所看到的和感受到的恐惧时，她开始把她的愤怒转向那些文字。她在焦虑中撕碎了一本书，并为破坏了Ilsa的财产而感到内疚。她给她写了一封道歉信，并承诺再也不去图书室了。几天后，Ilsa带着一本日记出现在Liesel家。她希望Liesel能写作，而不是像她那样惩罚自己。这就是为什么空袭那晚Liesel会在地下室，因为地下室是她写故事的地方，她正在写一个关于偷书贼的故事。Liesel每天晚上都在地下室写作，试图以正确的方式讲述她的生命故事。她于1943年10月2日完成了这本书。与此同时，盟军的飞机轰炸了Himmel Street，让死神进入每一个家庭，夺走他想要的无数灵魂，包括Rudy、Hans和Rosa。

“*The Book Thief*—last line，I have hated the words and I have loved them，and I hope I have made them right.Outside，the world whistled. The rain was stained.”

通过这些简短的句子，我可以看出Liesel对这本书的态度——爱与恨。她恨的是世界变得如此残酷，使人变得冷血。然而，因为文字和书拯救了她的生命，使她有勇气面对她的未来，使她干涸的生命变得丰富多彩。这也使她变得更加坚强，能够更勇敢地活下去。

——宋碧燕

“Liesel searched them and it was not so much a recognition of facial features that gave Max away. It was how the face was acting—also studying the crowd. Fixed in concentration. Liesel felt herself pausing as she found the only face looking directly into the German spectators. It examined them with such purpose that people on either side of *The Book Thief* noticed and pointed him out. 'I'm here, Max!' Louder. 'Max, I'm here!' He heard her. 'I'm here, Max,' she said again. 'I'm here.' 'I can't believe...' The words dripped from Max's mouth. 'Look how much you've grown.' There was an intense sadness in his eyes.

No soldier has seen her yet, and Max gave her a warning. 'You have to let go of me, Liesel.' He even tried to push her away, but the girl was too strong. Max's starving arms could not sway her.

The soldier took her.His hands manhandled her clothes. The girl had landed sprawling with pain, but now she stood again.She recovered and waited.She reentered."

在战争年代，命运悲苦的微小人物无处不在，读这章故事让我泪流满面。犹太人被迫游街示众，Liesel想找寻Max的踪迹，她想起了Max那像羽毛一样的头发，但如今他很久没有洗头了，头发应该像一些枝丫才对，Liesel认出Max的原因不是他的面部特征而是他的表情，因为此时Max也在极力地寻找Liesel，唯一一个犹太人直视德国看客的脸，连Liesel两旁的人都注意到了Max的表情。Liesel从人群中挤出来，冲进如浪潮般涌来的犹太人中，在他们中间穿梭，直到用左手抓住他的胳膊。Max想和Liesel说说他的境况，但是Liesel处于犹太人的洪流之中，Max又怕她被士兵发现，告诫她说："你现在必须离我远点，Liesel。"Max甚至要把她推开，但是他有气无力的双臂没法推开她。她三番五次地被士兵拽出犹太人的队伍，痛苦地摔倒在地，又三番五次地挤进队伍中去。士兵手上的皮鞭不断落下，一下下落在Max脸上，削着他的下巴，割着他的喉咙。

Liesel向他走去。她勇敢地伸出手，捧住他长满胡须的脸庞，"真的是你吗，Max？"他吻了吻女孩的手掌，"是啊，Liesel，是我。"他捧起女孩的手，贴在脸上，在她的指间哭泣。"Max。"女孩的眼泪夺眶而出，然后她说不出话了，因为她也被士兵拖走了。

在这种情境中，Liesel本应该老老实实地站在一群德国看客的队伍中，但是她却不顾危险，一次次地冲进犹太人的队伍，又一次次被士兵拖出队伍，摔倒在地，她就是想好好再看看Max并和他说说话。但是在当时的纳粹德国，正是因为对Hitler的极端崇拜，人们对他盲目地服从，因种族歧视，犹太人没有平等的权利和德国人交往。

读到这里我在想，在纳粹德国，难道真的所有人都如此痛恨犹太人吗？还是他们只是麻木地跟从，为了让别人觉得自己不是一个异类，而对无辜的陌生人施以迫害？

——宋 蕾

The chapter Ilsa Hermann's Little Black Book 让我印象深刻。Hermann夫人不仅给了Liesel一本书看，她其实也给了孩子一个理由让她在她喜欢的地下室里阅读。这个地方一开始是和“爸爸”，然后是和Max共同阅读的场所。同时她也给了Liesel一个理由去书写心情，用语言来感知生活、表达想法，而正是这些文字滋养了她的生活。

“*The Book Thief*—Last Line：I have hated the words and I have loved them，and I hoped have made them right.

These words makes me feel very happy for Liesel. Liesel used to read only. But now Ilsa Hermann gives her an idea to write，then she becomes interested in writing the words because of words she reads sentences he writes. She has a fully-filled mind to face the difficult moment in her life. She was so lucky to escape from the accident.”

其实这也是伏笔，死神之所以知道故事的细节，也源自“偷书贼”所写的内容。由此也可见作者构思的巧妙。感受故事魅力的同时，对于作者的构思以及语言的运用，也让我为之惊叹与拜服。

——徐 燕

原来阅读的力量真的很强大，当我读到Liesel在前往集中营的路途中，与Max重逢时，我不禁鼻子一酸、心头一震。“Is it really you? Is it from your cheek that I took the seed？”“真的是你吗？”Liesel问。每一个字都击中了我的心，这些看似奇怪又不相关的字眼一直在我眼前漂浮着。“Yes，Liesel，it's me.”还记得那片云吗？我想Max的回答肯定是“记得”。过去的章节，一些遥远的、模糊的碎片，一瞬间自己拼凑起来了，呈现在我的眼前。

时光缓缓过去，他们之间的感情依然真挚。回首战时的故事，作者通过一些生活碎片让我们看到了生活的本质，或者让我们回忆起一些熟悉又陌生的人和事。我们读到了一夜之间失去至亲的痛苦，感受到了战争把周围熟悉的人都带走的悲惨，也让我们学会了要在生活中忆苦思甜。

——袁泳施

After a long deep，dark，heavy travel with the writer，we see a slight of brightness. Meeting Max，beginning writing. Bitter happiness colored Liesel's life. Even it was pleasant to meet Max，still we can't avoid sorrow.

Let's enjoy the scene they met：

There were twigs of hair，just like Liesel thought，and the swampy eyes stepped across，shoulder to shoulder over the other Jews. When they reached her，they pleaded. His beard stroked down his face and his mouth shivered as he said the word，the name，the girl. Liesel.

He stood absolutely still as the others swerved morosely around him, leaving him completely alone. His eyes staggered, and it was so simple. The words were given across from the girl to the Jew. They climbed on to him.

The next time she spoke, the questions stumbled from her mouth. Hot tears fought for room in her eyes as she would not let them out. Better to stand resolute and proud. Let the words do all of it. "Is it really you? the young man asked," she said. "Is it from your cheek that I took the seed?"

How much she missed him!

Max Vandenburg remained standing. He did not drop to his knees.

…

His face fell on her. It reached down as she tripped, and the Jew, the nasty Jew, helped her up. It took all of his strength.

"I'm here, Max," she said again. "I'm here."

"I can't believe. The words dripped from Max Vandenburg's mouth. "Look how much you've grown." There was an intense sadness in his eyes. They swelled. "Liesel ... they got me a few months ago." The voice was crippled but it dragged itself toward her. "Halfway to Stuttgart."

How the words warm the readers!

Max Vandenburg remained standing...

As he stood, Max looked first at the girl and then stared directly into the sky who was wide and blue and magnificent... "It's such a beautiful day," he said, and his voice was in many pieces. A great day to die. A great day to die, like this.

How gratified Max was!

From the inside, the stream of Jews was a murky disaster of arms and legs...

When she ignored him completely, the soldier used his arm to separate the stickiness of people. He shoved them aside and made his way through. He loomed above her as Liesel struggled on and noticed the strangled expression on Max Vandenburg's face. She had seen him afraid, but never like this.

How much terror he had suffered!

…

The whip. The whip. The whip continued from the soldier's hand. It landed on Max's face.

It clipped his chin and carved his throat.

How cruel and inhuman!

——Ting Teng

Part Ten—Epilogue of The Book Thief

The End of the World（Part Ⅱ）—The Handover Man

导读

今天我们共读*The Book Thief*的结尾部分"The End of the World（Part Ⅱ）""Death and Liesel""Wood in the Afternoon""Max"和"The Handover Man"。

这本书终于结束了。在这一部分，我们可以从叙述者死神的角度看到结局。一切都充满着矛盾。名叫"天堂"的街道被炸了。除了Liesel还活着，其他人都死了。一些人意外死亡，而一些人却在抱怨，到底是什么让死神这么久才来带走他们。我们被要求以一种精确而充满矛盾的方式来回顾书中重要的人物：Rudy、Hans、Rosa、Max和Liesel。

Rudy，在漆黑的晚上，我们能看到"His candlelit hair ignited the bed."。他用泰迪熊安慰飞机上一个死去的男孩，但在此时却没有人安慰他。一个充满激情和同情心的男孩，成功地在死神的心里留下痕迹。幸运的是，Liesel吻了他，我相信这成功地安慰了他。书里多次提到他的头发 candlelit 和lemon，这颜色是Rudy的象征，是Liesel生命中一道清新的阳光。

Hans，经历了两次世界大战。当死亡来临时，他已经准备好离开，却不想离开。他对生活充满渴望。书里的语言很美，对Liesel来说，他坚强、富有同情心，是一个慈爱的父亲。

Rosa，"make no mistake，the woman had a heart. She had a bigger one than people would think. There was a lot in it，stored up，high in miles of hidden shelving."这话是对Rosa的点睛描绘。她是"an instrument strapper，a Jew feeder and an arm reacher"。她可能脾气不好，但她绝对勤奋，擅长冒险，拥有温暖的心。她也是Liesel慈爱的好妈妈。

书里提到了两样比较重要的物品，分别是手风琴和*A Book Thief*这本书。手风琴是Liesel和家人在一起共度快乐时光的标志。*A Book Thief*这本书把死神和Liesel紧密联系在一起，从而让死神给我们带来了这么一个感人的故事。现在故事已经结束，但这不是一个为死亡哭泣的时刻，而是一个回忆Liesel是如何在残暴的环境中活出精彩的时刻，以及苏萨克的诗意写作风格是如何美化Liesel故事的时刻。这是一个纪念生命和人类伟大的时刻。就像我们的叙述者死神告诉我们的那样，"I am haunted by humans."。我想和你们分享一段文字，很美，希望你们也会喜欢。

"Life is full of beauty and brutality. Humans can't be simply estimated. Humans can be ugly and so glorious，and words and stories so damning and brilliant."（事物都有多面性，结果都取决于我们自己的态度和选择）

不管生活多残酷，对于每一个为生存而奋斗的人来说都是会有回报的。活着，永远不要放弃。

工作室人员分享

在"The End of the World"章节中，在我看来，这意味着Liesel的整个世界都崩塌了。身边的人都被带走了。Rudy，她最好的男朋友，死的时候搂着他的妹妹。他曾经充满能量地去战斗。现在他还没有来得及给Liesel一个吻就静静地死了。当Liesel看到他的身体，她在他柔软真实的嘴唇上吻了下去。那一刻，Rudy对她来说就像珍宝。

Rosa比人们想象的要强大得多。她独自拿着乐器，勇敢地给犹太人送饭，还把一本速写本交给一个女孩。Liesel回忆起和妈妈在一起的每一刻。在她眼里，她是她的世界里最漂亮的妈妈。Liesel不愿意也不能接受爸爸的死。爸爸是她生活中的安慰和光明。他在Liesel的一生中培养了她对阅读的热爱。他们在手风琴声中度过了一个个美好的夜晚。爸爸的手风琴和Himmel就是Liesel的家。

——董筱妍

Liesel 四处游荡，迷迷糊糊，所到之处一片凌乱，什么都看不到。她随身带着她的书，继续寻找Hans、Rosa、Max。最后她看到了那个坏掉的手风琴，开始接受现实。之后，她看到了Rudy的尸体，扔下书跑过去，大声地哭喊着告诉Rudy她爱他，并亲吻着他的嘴唇，但Rudy已经死了。手风琴的破裂成了Liesel失去一切的象征，同时也是战争悲剧的象征。Liesel把书扔掉走向Rudy，意味深长，但这一切来得太晚了，他们的初吻竟成了最后的吻别，这一场景让人动容，令人心碎。

接着Liesel相继找到了Rosa和Hans，她头脑中不停地重复着和他们一起时最美好的回忆，但是在见到爸爸的那一刹那，Liesel还是彻底崩溃了。她把手风琴放在爸爸的身旁，想象着爸爸还在站着弹琴，她感谢爸爸教她读书，救了她，并保证她再也不会喝香槟了。从LSE来的人把Liesel带走了，死神在废墟中看到了*The Book Thief* 这本书，在被扔进垃圾车之前，他捡起了这本书。Liesel现在孤身一人，特别是没有了Hans，她必须接受爸爸教给她的东西，从小事中创造美好和幸福，即使面对苦难也要善良，为自己构建新的生活。面对这样的毁灭，倒下的书显得如此渺小，但死神意识到*The Book Thief*是值得被拯救的，它的文字是对纳粹和战争造成的毁灭的最好回应。

——郑剑湘

当读到"The End Of The World"这一章的时候，我感觉到一种失去生命的强烈悲伤。对Liesel来说，这真的是世界末日。当她去地下室读书写字时，一切都很好。然而，当她回到地面上时，一切都消失了，包括她爱的Rudy、爸爸和妈妈。书中有很多关于Liesel的细节描述和心理描述。"'Wake up，I love you. Come on，Rudy，come on，Jesse Owens，don't you know I love you，wake up，wake up...，In disbelief，Liesel buried her head into Rudy's chest... She looked up his lifeless face and kissed her best friend."Liesel非常痛苦，她无法接受Rudy死去的事实，最后又不得不接受。她几乎不能忍受离开Rudy的身体。她终于情不自禁地吻了他的嘴唇，第一次也是最后一次，吻得又长又温柔。我被他们的爱情深深感动了。"爸爸。她不愿意，也不能看爸爸。还没有。不是现在。""Papa. She would not，and could not，look at Papa. Not yet. Not now."爸爸是对Liesel影响最大的人。他救了她，教她认字读书。他们一起喝香槟。他最了解Liesel。对Liesel来说，他是朋友、导师和父亲。所以Liesel很伤心。爸爸的死让她痛不欲生。她在妈妈面前表现得完全不同。她握住妈妈的手，摸了摸她的手腕。她仍然清楚地记得来到新家的第一天。妈妈很漂亮，尽管她经常说粗话，但是她很热心。最重要的是，她把Liesel当成自己的女儿。当然，Liesel也爱她。

看到亲人的离开是最难过的。自2020年1月以来，全球有数亿人感染了COVID-19。有些人失去了母亲，有些人失去了父亲，有些人失去了孩子和好朋友。这是自第二次世界大战以来人类所面临的最大的挑战。我真希望人类能战胜病毒，世界恢复正常，不再有生离死别。

——关少娟

故事的结局是令人心痛的。战争夺走了无数条人命，摧毁了无数个家庭，断垣残壁、天崩地裂，留下来的却是Liesel孤单茫然的脆弱心灵。小镇没有明亮的颜色，只有黑、红、灰交织融合。死神细致地描写了捡起每个人灵魂时的场景，带着读者再次回忆他们善良的人性，加上对自己内心感受的一些描写，着实让人心酸。死神在捡起Rudy的灵魂时说："I carried him softly through the broken street，with one salty eye and a heavy，deathly heart. He does something to me，that boy. Every time. It's his only detriment. He steps on my heart. He makes me cry."。死神在捡起养父Hans的灵魂时说："This one was sent out by the breath of an accordion，the odd taste of champagne in summer，and the art of promise-keeping."。死神在捡起养母Rosa的灵魂时说："Make no mistake，the woman had a heart. She had a bigger one than people would think. There was a lot in it，stored up，high in miles of hidden shelving."。然而让人更加红了眼眶的是作者描写Liesel面对至亲尸体时的一幕。悲伤的同时让人更加感受到的是战争下的德国还闪烁着的人性光辉。文章最后一句"I am haunted by humans."，连死神也不得不承认他在不断低估人类。这是因为，无论死神如何威胁人类，人类善良的人性永远不会泯灭。

——李 丹

之前总是分享细节对我的触动，这次我想分享一下最后几个小节整体给我的感觉。

首先，虽然根据前面的章节铺垫，我早就知道Rudy要死，可是没想到他是这样一种死法，而且也没想到他不是唯一一个死去的人。

一切都那么出乎意料，又在情理之中。

我想，在这样的轰炸中幸存下来的Liesel肯定能像泰坦尼克号的女主Rose一样，在幸存之后没有寻死觅活，反而平安又精彩地度过她漫长的一生，最后在子孙后代的簇拥下离开世界，要感谢她遇到的那些温暖的人，爸爸、妈妈、Max、Rudy，还有市长夫人。特别是市长夫人，是她让Liesel在想要放弃文字的时候告诉她文字是最好的倾诉方式，甚至给了她一本书让她开始自己写作，而正是因为有了写作这个发泄情绪的出口，Liesel才没有在那样绝望的境地崩溃，文字成了她的救赎。

看完这本书，我的想法是：不管命运如何捉弄人，我都要像Liesel一样活得内心丰盈并充满能量。

——莫 然

小伙伴们读这本书也有大概一年的时间了，对于这本书我感触良多。在最后的几个章节里，我印象最深的是来自死神独白的一句话："I am haunted by humans."。

温柔死神，他会拥抱死者，他会合上死者的眼睛，他在带走Liesel的亲人时，想要对她说对不起……该是怎样的惨烈，会让原本冷酷的死神，都如此不忍？撼动死神的，到底是人性的邪恶还是人性的光辉？

我也不知道，只知道，死神也迷茫了。他喃喃地说，人性，如此光辉，如此邪恶。也许最后并不是人类困扰着死神，而是人性困扰着我们每一个人。当Liesel获救后，她发现所有最重要的人都离她远去了，她当时是崩溃而绝望的。

当她看到死去的Rudy时：

"He lay with yellow hair and closed eyes，and *The Book Thief* ran toward him and fell down. She dropped the black book.‘Rudy，’ she sobbed，‘wake up.’ She grabbed him by his shirt and gave him just the slightest disbelieving shake.‘Wake up，Rudy，’ and now，as the sky went on heating and showering ash，Liesel was holding Rudy Steiner's shirt by the front.‘Rudy，please.’ The tears grappled with her face.‘Rudy，please，wake up，Goddamn it，wake up，I love you. Come on，Rudy，come on，Jesse Owens，don't you know I love you，wake up，wake up，wake up ...’

She kissed him long and soft. ”

当她看到死去的爸爸和妈妈时：

“When she noticed the tall man and the short，wardrobe woman. That's my mama. That's my papa. The words were‘They're not moving’，she said quietly.‘They're not moving.’

Perhaps if she stood still long enough，it would be they who moved，but they remained motionless for as long as Liesel did. I realized at that moment that she was not wearing any shoes. What an odd thing to notice right then. Perhaps I was trying to avoid her face，for *The Book Thief* was truly an irretrievable mess. ”

在Himmel，只有Liesel活了下来。小小的Liesel，要靠什么去支撑她什么都没有了的、一片蛮荒的人生？她13岁那年的那些人和事，在发生的时候并不知道，它会滋养一个被遗弃的女孩一生的回忆吧？总有一些柔软的生命之花，只绽放过一次，却温暖了人一生。

比如Hans爸爸：

那个个子高大、眼睛里闪着柔和的银光的男人；

那个在斜阳下拉手风琴的男人；

那个陪着女儿在地下室读书的男人；

那个把家门的钥匙巧妙地藏在书里帮助逃亡的犹太人的男人；

那个会为了半支烟替人刷房子的男人；

那个因给犹太人面包被当众鞭打的男人；

那个告诉女儿体会夏天里的香槟酒味道的男人；

那个身上有着天使般光辉的男人。

比如隔壁男孩Rudy：

那个把自己涂成小黑炭在操场上奔跑的男孩；

那个憎恨法西斯却差点被法西斯当作高标准的下一代培养的男孩；

那个站在齐腰深的冰水里追赶一本书的男孩；

那个把微笑的泰迪熊放在死去的飞行员怀中的男孩；

那个在睡梦中、在裁缝店、在偷苹果的郊外，一次次期待并且永生错过他最爱的女孩子的吻的男孩；

那个青春绽放、生命怒放的可爱的男孩。

比如Rosa妈妈：

那个抡起木勺就打人，动不动就咆哮怒吼的女人；

那个总是叫人家猪猡的女人；

那个在漆黑的夜里，抱着手风琴怀想丈夫的女人；

那个毫不迟疑地接纳犹太人的女人；

那个替女儿藏好精神之书的女人。

"He does something to me，that boy. Every time. It's his only detriment. He steps on my heart. He makes me cry."温柔的死神这样说Rudy。

文字的力量是无穷的，Liesel在地下室写作，沉浸在文字带给她的乐趣中，才得以逃脱轰炸成为唯一幸存者。文字，拯救了Liesel的生命，Liesel又用文字来救赎饱受战争摧残的人民。

——宋碧燕

结尾这几章的一大亮点便是叙述方式的与众不同：Liesel的故事由收割生命的死神口中道出。你听过死神讲故事吗？他一开口就显出理智、冷静与幽默来，甚至还带着一丝温暖，死神用一种包容的情感讲述一段破碎的故事。

"The End of the World（Part Ⅱ）"以死神为第一人称向我们诉说了炸弹轰炸Himmel街时他自己的心情，街道的景象和人们死去时的场景，还有Liesel见到死去的挚友Rudy和爸爸、妈妈时那撕心裂肺的表情。死神带走了Liesel的一切，然而她却幸存了下来，因为文字让她躲过了这次死亡。然而，文字带给他们的又是什么？战争？摧毁？对于犹太人而言呢？死亡吗？他们又有什么过错，需要承受如此沉重的代价？

A Book Thief 这本书让我得到了很多，并引发了我更多思考。"I am haunted by humans."（我对人类百思不得其解）关于生命，关于人性，还有战争。对于生命，我们应该热爱，不应该有种族歧视，不应该有仇恨妒忌，要有希望，有信心，去追求光明。对于人性，要充分发挥人性的美而不是恶。我想如果这个世界上不再有人想着战争，想着独权主义，那么，人性也就没有那么复杂了。

——宋 蕾

读完这四节，我只能想到莎士比亚说过的一句话："悲剧就是把美好的东西毁灭给人看。"炎热的八月，Max与 Liesel的痛苦重逢，已经预示着阴霾的未来。十月的Himmel Street被空袭炸成一片火海，只留下 Liesel一人，绝望无助。

我想她是不幸的，失去了爱她的养父养母、朋友和熟悉的一切。但她又是幸运的，逃过空袭，活着就有可能。就像文字，能治愈人，也能伤害人。文字或好或坏，都取决于使用者。

这也是死神为什么对人类充满感情。即便身处战争，绝望中也心怀希望，这就是爱的滋养了。

——夏丽焱

在“The Handover Man”这一章节中，以下文字深深打动着我。

“When I traveled to Sydney and took Liesel away，I was finally able to do something I’d been waiting on for a long time. I put her down and we walked along Anzac Avenue，near the soccer field，and I pulled a dusty black book from my pocket.

The old woman was astonished. She took it in her hand and said，‘Is this really it？’ I nodded.

With great trepidation，she opened *The Book Thief* and turned the pages. ‘I can’t believe...’ Even though the text had faded，she was able to read her words. The fingers of her soul touched the story that was written so long ago in her Himmel Street basement. She sat down on the curb，and I joined her.

‘Did you read it？’she asked，but she did not look at me. Her eyes were fixed to the words.

I nodded，‘many times.’

‘Could you understand it？’

And at that point，there was a great pause. A few cars drove by each way. Their drivers were Hitlers and Hubermann，and Maxes，killers，Dillers，and Steiners ...”

对于Liesel来说，也许她要用尽一生去治愈失去至亲朋友的痛苦，她是不幸的。但是她能够努力生活、热爱生活，苦难让她成长与成熟，她又是着实幸运的。当我读到这部分的时候，整个小说的故事画面一幅幅又在脑海中重现。那些栩栩如生的人物，那些琐碎的日常生活，仿佛历历在目，平凡又打动人心，也许有一天我们终将同归大地，世界还是原来的模样，活着便是一种幸运，我们应该好好过每一天。

——徐 燕